Communications
in Computer and Information Science   1342

More information about this series at http://www.springer.com/series/7899

Aurona Gerber (Ed.)

Artificial Intelligence Research

First Southern African Conference for AI Research, SACAIR 2020
Muldersdrift, South Africa, February 22–26, 2021
Proceedings

 Springer

Editor
Aurona Gerber 🆔
University of Pretoria
Pretoria, South Africa

ISSN 1865-0929 ISSN 1865-0937 (electronic)
Communications in Computer and Information Science
ISBN 978-3-030-66150-2 ISBN 978-3-030-66151-9 (eBook)
https://doi.org/10.1007/978-3-030-66151-9

This Springer imprint is published by the registered company Springer Nature Switzerland AG
The registered company address is: Gewerbestrasse 11, 6330 Cham, Switzerland

Preface

This volume of Springer CCIS (CCIS 1342) contains the revised accepted papers of the the First Southern African Conference for Artificial Intelligence Research (SACAIR 2020)[1].

Foreword from the Conference Chair

Dear authors and readers,

It is with great pleasure that I write this foreword to the proceedings of the First Southern African Conference for Artificial Intelligence Research (SACAIR 2020), to be held on the West Rand of Johannesburg, South Africa, during February 22–26, 2021[2]. The program includes an unconference for students on February 22 (a student driven event for students to interact with each other as well as with sponsors and other possible employers), a day of tutorials on February 23, and the main conference during February 24–26.

SACAIR 2020 is the second international conference focused on Artificial Intelligence (AI), hosted by the Centre for AI Research (CAIR), South Africa. The inaugural CAIR conference, the Forum for AI Research (FAIR 2019), was held in Cape Town, South Africa, in December 2019, and SACAIR 2020 will build on its success.

The Centre for AI Research (CAIR)[3] is a South African distributed research network that was established in 2011 with the aim of building world class AI research capacity in South Africa. CAIR conducts foundational, directed, and applied research into various aspects of AI through its nine research groups based at six universities (the University of Pretoria, the University of KwaZulu-Natal, the University of Cape Town, Stellenbosch University, University of the Western Cape, and North West University). Research groups at CAIR include an Adaptive and Cognitive Systems Lab situated at the University of Cape Town, an AI and Cybersecurity research group at the University of the Western Cape, an AI for Development and Innovation group at the University of Pretoria, two Machine Learning groups focused on deep learning at North West University and the University of Kwa-Zulu Natal, a Knowledge Abstraction and Representation group at Stellenbosch University, an Ethics of AI research group at the University of Pretoria, a Knowledge Representation and Reasoning group at the

---

[1] https://sacair.org.za/

[2] The original date was November 30–December 4, 2020, but, due to the COVID-19 pandemic, the conference was pushed into 2021 in the hope of being able to retain its face-to-face format in the interest of building an AI community in Southern Africa.

[3] https://www.cair.org.za/.

University of Cape Town, and a Mathematical and Computational Statistics group focused on applied data science at the University of Pretoria.

The theme for SACAIR 2020 is "AI transforming Humanity." AI technologies in their current data-driven form have the potential to transform our world for the better. Applications of AI technologies in healthcare, agriculture, restoration of the environment and ecosystems, energy, water management, identification of social patterns and bias, law enforcement, education, information, connectivity, smart city and infrastructure planning, performing and creative arts, and many other areas are proof of this.

However, humans are faced with serious challenges in the context of AI advances in all areas of their lives, as wide apart as employment and labor on the one hand, and social companionship on the other. In the context of Machine Learning applications, these challenges lead to concerns around fairness, structural bias, and amplification of existing social stereotypes, privacy, transparency, accountability, and responsibility, and trade-offs among all these concerns, especially within the context of security, robustness, and accuracy of AI systems. Furthermore, AI technologies can perform tasks that previously only humans could perform, such as calculating the best treatment for certain illnesses and caring for older persons. In some cases this is a good thing, but in some it challenges human agency and experience, and even political stability in profound ways. Human notions of morality, of responsibility, and of ethical decision-making are challenged in ways humanity has never before encountered. In addition, children grow up in novel contexts impacted on by technological manipulation of social narratives and we do not yet know what the impact of this will be. In its turn, media and information literacy has become an essential skill just as important as technical skills. Finally, there are also cultural concerns such as the loss of nuances of human languages and expression in the context of NLP, concerns around the ownership of art, and others.

The choice of conference theme was intended to ensure multi-disciplinary contributions that focus both on the technical aspects and social impact and consequences of AI technologies. In addition, there is a healthy balance between contributions from logic-based AI and those from data-driven AI, as the focus on knowledge representation and reasoning remains an important ingredient of studying and extending human intelligence. In line with the above, it was decided that the conference topics would cover five broad areas of AI: Machine Learning, Knowledge Representation and Reasoning, Applications of AI, AI for Ethics and Society, and AI for Development and Social Good. In line with the theme, Peter-Paul Verbeek, the chair of the UNESCO Commission on the Ethics of Scientific Knowledge and Technology (COMEST), and chair of the Philosophy of Human-Technology Relations research group, and co-director of the DesignLab at the University of Twente, The Netherlands, will deliver the opening keynote.

We expect this multi- and interdisciplinary conference to grow into the premier AI conference in Southern Africa, as it brings together nationally and internationally established and emerging researchers from across various disciplines including Computer Science, Mathematics, Statistics, Informatics, Philosophy, and Law. The conference is also focused on cultivating and establishing a network of talented students working in AI from across Africa.

I sincerely thank the technical chair, Aurona Gerber, for her hard work on the volume and the editorial duties performed. A thank you to the program chairs (Aurona Gerber, Anne Gerdes, Giovanni Casini, Marelie Davel, Alta de Waal, Anban Pillay, Deshendran Moodley, and Sunet Eybers), the local and international panel of reviewers, our keynotes, and the authors and participants for their contributions. Last but not least, our gratitude to the members of the Organizing Committee (Aurona Gerber, Anban Pillay, and Alta de Waal), student organizers (Karabo Maiyane, Emile Engelbrecht, Nirvana Pillay, and Yüvika Singh) and our sponsors, specifically the AIJ division of IJCAI, without whom this conference would not have been realized.

November 2020   Emma Ruttkamp-Bloem

Message from the Technical Chair

Dear readers,

This volume of CCIS contains the revised accepted papers of SACAIR 2020. We are thankful that our first annual Southern African Conference for Artificial Intelligence Research elicited the support it did during this challenging year with all the uncertainties due to the COVID-19 pandemic.

We received more than 70 abstracts, and after submission and a first round of evaluation, 53 papers were sent out for review to our SACAIR Program Committee. The 53 SACAIR submissions were solicited according to five topics: AI for Ethics and Society (9), AI in Information Systems, AI for Development and Social Good (3), Applications of AI (25), Knowledge Representation and Reasoning (8), and Machine Learning Theory (8).

The Program Committee comprised 72 members, 13 of whom were from outside Southern Africa. Each paper was reviewed by at least three members of the Program Committee in a rigorous, double-blind process whereby especially the following criteria were taken into consideration: Relevance to SACAIR, Significance, Technical Quality, Scholarship, and Presentation that included quality and clarity of writing. For this CCIS volume, 19 full research papers were selected, which translates to an acceptance rate of 35.8%. The accepted full research papers per topic are: AI for Ethics and Society (3), AI in Information Systems, AI for Development and Social Good (1), Applications of AI (8), Knowledge Representation and Reasoning (4), and lastly, Machine Learning Theory (3).

Thank you to all the authors and Program Committee members, and congratulations to the authors whose work was accepted for publication in this Springer volume. We wish our readers a fruitful reading experience with these proceedings!

November 2020

Aurona Gerber

SACAIR Sponsors

The sponsors of SACAIR 2020, *The Journal of Artificial Intelligence* and the *Centre for AI Research (CAIR)*, are herewith gratefully acknowledged.

Organization

General Chair

Emma Ruttkamp-Bloem   University of Pretoria, Centre of AI Research (CAIR), South Africa

Program Committee Chair

Technical Chair

Aurona Gerber   University of Pretoria, Centre of AI Research (CAIR), South Africa

Topic Chairs: Applications of AI

Anban Pillay   University of Kwazulu-Natal, Centre of AI Research (CAIR), South Africa

Deshendran Moodley   University of Cape Town, Centre of AI Research (CAIR), South Africa

Topic Chairs: AI for Ethics and Society

Emma Ruttkamp-Bloem   University of Pretoria, Centre of AI Research (CAIR), South Africa

Anne Gerdes   University of Southern Denmark, Denmark

Topic Chairs: AI in Information Systems

Aurona Gerber   University of Pretoria, Centre of AI Research (CAIR), South Africa

Sunet Eybers   University of Pretoria, South Africa

Topic Chair: Knowledge Representation and Reasoning

Giovanni Casini   ISTI-CNR, Italy, and University of Cape Town, South Africa

Topic Chairs: Machine Learning Theory

Alta de Waal	University of Pretoria, Centre of AI Research (CAIR), South Africa
Marelie Davel	North-West University, Centre of AI Research (CAIR), South Africa

Local Organizing Committee

Anban Pillay	University of Kwazulu-Natal, South Africa
Alta de Waal	University of Pretoria, South Africa
Julie-Anne Sewparsad	University of Pretoria, South Africa
Karabo Maiyane	University of Pretoria, South Africa
Emile Engelbrecht	Stellenbosch University, South Africa
Renee le Roux	Mongoose Communications & Design, South Africa

Program Committee

Etienne Barnard	North-West University, South Africa
Sihem Belabbes	LIASD, Université Paris, France
Sonia Berman	University of Cape Town, South Africa
Jacques Beukes	North-West University, South Africa
Willie Brink	Stellenbosch University, South Africa
Arina Britz	Stellenbosch University, South Africa
Michael Burke	The University of Edinburgh, UK
Jan Buys	University of Cape Town, South Africa
Giovanni Casini	ISTI, CNR, Italy
Colin Chibaya	Sol Plaatje University, South Africa
Olawande Daramola	Cape Peninsula University of Technology, South Africa
Jérémie Dauphin	University of Luxembourg, Luxembourg
Marelie Davel	North-West University, South Africa
Tanya de Villiers Botha	Stellenbosch University, South Africa
Alta De Waal	University of Pretoria, South Africa
Febe de Wet	Stellenbosch University, South Africa
Iena Derks	University of Pretoria, South Africa
Tiny Du Toit	North-West University, South Africa
Andries Engelbrecht	University of Stellenbosch, South Africa
Sunet Eybers	University of Pretoria, South Africa
Inger Fabris-Rotelli	University of Pretoria, South Africa
Sebastian Feld	Ludwig Maximilian University of Munich, Germany
Eduardo Fermé	Universidade da Madeira, Portugal
Anne Gerdes	University of Denmark, Denmark
Mandlenkosi Gwetu	University of KwaZulu-Natal, South Africa
Shohreh Haddadan	University of Luxembourg, Luxembourg
Henriette Harmse	EMBL-EBI, UK

Michael Harrison	University of Cape Town, South Africa
Bertram Haskins	Nelson Mandela University, South Africa
Marie Hattingh	University of Pretoria, South Africa
Omowunmi Isafiade	University of the Western Cape, South Africa
Edgar Jembere	University of KwaZulu-Natal, South Africa
Herman Kamper	Stellenbosch University, South Africa
Lisa Kirkland	University of Pretoria, South Africa
Eduan Kotzé	University of the Free State, South Africa
Jaco Kruger	St Augustine College of South Africa, South Africa
Louise Leenen	University of the Western Cape, South Africa
Aby Louw	CSIR, South Africa
Patricia Lutu	University of Pretoria, South Africa
Patrick Marais	University of Cape Town, South Africa
Vukosi Marivate	University of Pretoria, South Africa
Réka Markovich	University of Luxembourg, Luxembourg
Muthoni Masinde	Central University of Technology, South Africa
Jocelyn Mazarura	University of Pretoria, South Africa
Felix McGregor	Saigen, South Africa
Thomas Meyer	University of Cape Town, South Africa
Deshendran Moodley	University of Cape Town, South Africa
Vincent C. Müller	University of Leeds, UK
Peeter Müürsepp	Tallinn University, Estonia
Fred Nicolls	University of Cape Town, South Africa
Geoff Nitshcke	University of Cape Town, South Africa
Oluwafemi Oriola	University of the Free State, South Africa
Anban Pillay	University of Kwazulu-Natal, South Africa
Arnold Pretorius	North West University, South Africa
Laurette Pretorius	University of South Africa, South Africa
Catherine Price	University of KwaZulu-Natal, South Africa
Helen Robertson	University of the Witwatersrand, South Africa
Irene Russo	CNR Pisa, Italy
Emma Ruttkamp-Bloem	University of Pretoria, South Africa
Jonathan Shock	University of Cape Town, South Africa
Riana Steyn	University of Pretoria, South Africa
Umberto Straccia	ISTI-CNR, Italy
Jules-Raymond Tapamo	University of KwaZulu-Natal, South Africa
Anitta Thomas	University of South Africa, South Africa
Dustin Van Der Haar	University of Johannesburg, South Africa
Terence Van Zyl	University of Johannesburg, South Africa
Peter-Paul Verbeek	University of Twente, The Netherlands
Serestina Viriri	University of KwaZulu-Natal, South Africa
Bruce Watson	Stellenbosch University, South Africa
Adrian Weller	University of Cambridge, UK

Contents

Knowledge Representation and Reasoning

Machine Learning Theory

AI for Ethics and Society

Human-Robot Moral Relations: Human Interactants as Moral Patients of Their Own Agential Moral Actions Towards Robots

Cindy Friedman[1,2](✉)(iD)

[1] Department of Philosophy, University of Pretoria, Pretoria, South Africa
`cindzfriedman@gmail.com`
[2] Centre for AI Research (CAIR), Pretoria, South Africa

Abstract. This paper contributes to the debate in the ethics of social robots on how or whether to treat social robots morally by way of considering a novel perspective on the moral relations between human interactants and social robots. This perspective is significant as it allows us to circumnavigate debates about the (im)possibility of robot consciousness and moral patiency (debates which often slow down discussion on the ethics of HRI), thus allowing us to address actual and urgent current ethical issues in relation to human-robot interaction. The paper considers the different ways in which human interactants may be moral patients in the context of interaction with social robots: robots as conduits of human moral action towards human moral patients; humans as moral patients to the actions of robots; and human interactants as moral patients of their own agential moral actions towards social robots. This third perspective is the focal point of the paper. The argument is that due to *perceived* robot consciousness, and the possibility that the immoral treatment of social robots may morally harm human interactants, there is a unique moral relation between humans and social robots wherein human interactants are both the moral agents of their actions towards robots, as well as the *actual* moral patients of those agential moral actions towards robots. Robots, however, are no more than *perceived* moral patients. This discussion further adds to debates in the context of robot moral status, and the consideration of the moral treatment of robots in the context of human-robot interaction.

Keywords: Robot ethics · Human-robot interaction · Moral patiency

1 Introduction

This paper contributes to the debate in the ethics of social robots on how or whether to treat social robots morally by way of considering a novel perspective on the moral relations between human interactants and social robots: that human interactants are the *actual* moral patients of their agential moral actions

© Springer Nature Switzerland AG 2020
A. Gerber (Ed.): SACAIR 2020, CCIS 1342, pp. 3–20, 2020.
https://doi.org/10.1007/978-3-030-66151-9_1

towards robots; robots are no more than *perceived* moral patients. This novel perspective is significant because it allows us to circumnavigate contentious debates surrounding the (im)possibility of robot consciousness and moral patiency, thus allowing us to address actual and urgent current ethical issues in relation to human-robot interaction (HRI).

Social robots are becoming increasingly sophisticated and versatile technologies. Their wide range of potential utilisations include carer robots for the sick or elderly (see e.g. [50,53,60], general companion robots (see e.g. [15,57]), teachers for children (see e.g. [36,51]), or (still somewhat futuristic but nonetheless morally relevant in human-robot interaction (HRI) contexts) sexual companions (see e.g. [21,37,48]).

Although social robots may take on a variety of forms – such as the AIBO robot who takes the shape of a dog, or the Paro robot that takes the shape of a baby seal – I will here be focusing on android social robots.[1] This is the case as a combination of a human-like appearance and human-like sociability creates the potential for human interactants to relate to these robots in seemingly realistic human-like ways.

Given the possibility for human interactants to relate to these social robots in human-like ways[2], researchers have investigated not only the nature of these relations and how they may morally impact us – Turkle [57], for example, puts forward that some relations with robot companions may fundamentally change what it means to be human, and Nyholm & Frank [48] speculate that certain relations with robots may hinder us from forming bonds with other people – but also whether we have a *moral* relation to these robots that would require us to relate to them in a *particular way*. By this, I mean - should we treat them morally well? For example, someone such as Bryson [12] argues vehemently against the need for moral treatment of robots, whereas some, such as Levy [38] or Danaher [18], argue in various ways that we should consider the moral treatment of robots.

This paper will consider the issue of the moral treatment of social robots from an *anthropocentric persective* (as opposed to a 'robot perspective') by considering arguments that treating a robot immorally causes moral harm to its human interactant. Given this possibility, I suggest that in this context, social robots and human interactants have a unique moral relation: human interactants are both the moral agents of their actions towards robots, as well as the *actual* moral patients of those agential moral actions towards robots. Robots, in this case, are no more than *perceived* moral patients.

Literature on robot ethics is less focused on patiency as it is agency (with regard to both human interactants and robots in the HRI context) (see e.g.

---

[1] Unless otherwise specified, any use of the term 'social robot' will specifically refer to android social robots.

[2] It must be noted that social robots cannot genuinely reciprocate human sentiments; they cannot care for a human interactant the way in which a human interactant may care for them (e.g. [16]). Any emotions displayed by robots are functional in nature, thus, at least currently (or even in the near future), human interactants cannot have genuinely reciprocal or mutual bonds with robots (e.g. [55]). Thus, any relation or bond formed with a social robot is unidirectional in nature.

[27,38]), and where there is a focus on patiency as far as robots are concerned, it most often discusses the notion of the moral treatment of robots from the perspective of the current (im)possibility for robots to be *actually* conscious and, thus, the (im)possibility for them to be *actual* moral patients (see Sect. 4). However, in putting forward that it is human interactants who are the moral patients of their own agential moral actions towards robots, we may circumnavigate the somewhat intractable debate of *actual* robot consciousness which arises in relation to the (im)possibility for robots to be moral patients in the context of questioning whether they warrant moral treatment. This is not to say that concerns surrounding artificial robot consciousness are unimportant, but rather to say that we should not become so detained by the concern as to whether robots can be conscious or not (and thus moral patients or not) that we are misdirected from addressing actual and urgent current ethical issues in relation to human-robot interaction. My argument that it is human interactants who are the actual moral patients of their agential moral actions toward social robots thus allows us to seriously consider these actual and urgent current ethical issues.

I will first discuss two instances wherein human interactants are moral patients in relation to the robots with which they interact: firstly, robots as conduits of human moral actions towards other human moral patients; secondly, humans as moral patients to the moral actions of robots. I will then introduce a third perspective wherein a human interactant is, at the same time, both a moral agent and a moral patient: human interactants as moral patients of their own agential moral actions towards robots. I will firstly distinguish between the *actuality* of robot consciousness and the *perception* of robot consciousness since this is important for our understanding of robots as *perceived* moral patients, and also for our understanding of why, in the context of this paper, the *actuality* of robot consciousness is a non-issue. I will then put forward that treating social robots immorally may cause moral harm to human interactants and I do so using three sub-arguments: social robots are more than mere objects; the act of treating a social robot immorally is abhorrent in itself; and, due to these arguments, treating a social robot immorally may negatively impact upon the moral fibre of interactants. Finally, due to the perception of robot consciousness, and, thus, the perception of robot moral patiency, as well as concern that treating social robots immorally may cause moral harm to human interactants, I argue a human interactant is, at the same time, both the agent and patient of their moral actions towards robots: human interactants are the *actual* moral patients of their agential moral actions towards robots, whereas robots are *perceived* moral patients.

Let us now consider two ways in which human interactants may be moral patients in the context of their interaction with robots so as to contextualise the argument this paper makes, and make clear how and why my contribution is a particularly novel one.

2   Robots as Conduits of Human Moral Action Towards Human Moral Patients

Although this category of human moral patiency is related to computer ethics, it can also be applied to robot ethics. Regarding this first distinction, computer ethics, for example, "endeavors to stipulate the appropriate use and/or misuse of technology by human agents for the sake of respecting and protecting the rights of other human patients" [27]. We may consider the first commandment in the *Ten Commandments of Computer Ethics* [5]: "Thou shalt not use a computer to harm another person." And, more recently, the Institute of Electrical and Electronics Engineers (IEEE) initiatives on AI ethics and automous systems (https://ethicsinaction.ieee.org/) [1]. From the perspective of computer ethics, computers are ultimately deployed by humans, used for a human purpose and, as such, have an effect on humans. An example could be using computer technology through social media to spread fake news or deface somebody's character.

Or, as far as robotics and robot ethics ('roboethics') is concerned wherein we grapple with the ethical issues of the use of robots (see e.g. [40] and [47]), the possibility exists of directly commanding a robot to injure another human being. In such instances, a human agent would not be directly interacting with another human patient, they would be treating a human patient immorally through the use of technology – such as a computer or robot; technology would be the conduit of immoral action on behalf of the human agent, directed at another human patient. Although the robot is conducting the immoral action against the human moral patient, the difference (as compared to the second perspective discussed below) is that there is direct human intervention whereby the moral decision is ultimately made by a human, and the human agent uses technology to then inflict the moral harm that is the result of the decision they have made. For example, in terms of autonomous weapons systems (AWSs), there is a distinction between AWSs which "operate entirely independently of human controllers, and teleoperated unmanned weapons systems, which are still under remote human control" [20]. Teleoperated weapons systems would be a case of a human agent ultimately making a moral decision as to whether to harm a human moral patient or not, but using an AWS to carry out the decision. AWSs that operate entirely independently of human controllers would fall under the second category (see next section) relating to machine ethics – humans being moral patients to moral decisions made by technology or, particularly in this instance, robots.

3   Humans as Moral Patients to the Actions of Robots

As far as the second perspective is concerned, machine ethics (ME), for example, "seeks to enlarge the scope of moral agents by considering the ethical status and actions of machines" [27]. It (ME) "reasserts the privilege of the human and considers the machine only insofar as we seek to protect the integrity and the interests of the human being" [27]. It considers the possibility of machines to be guided by ethical principles in the decisions that it makes about possible courses of action [2]. As such, the machines in question are machines that make decisions and act autonomously (without human intervention) by way of "[combining] environmental feedback with the system's own analysis regarding its current situation" [29]. Given this understanding of autonomous decision making systems (ADM systems) that have the potential to be moral agents, we can then consider the possibility that humans can be moral patients to the moral decisions and actions of AI. Specifically, in our context, this potentiality means that robots could harm humans.

The topic of the possibility for machines to be considered moral agents is a broadly contested and complicated one, full discussion of which would go beyond the confines of this paper. However, it is worth noting some arguments that have been made concerning the topic. Generally speaking, the topic is one which questions whether machines can be moral agents – is morality programmable? – and what conditions they would have to fulfill in order to be considered moral agents, as well as the impact that these agents would have on us.

Well-known researchers weighing in on the issue include Asaro [4], Bostrom and Yudkowsky [7], Brundage [11], Deng [24], Lumbreras [41], McDermott [43], Moor [46], Sullins [54], Torrance [56], Wallach and Allen [61], Wang & Siau [62], and many others. Different sets of conditions for moral agency are suggested: A combination of free will, consciousness, and moral responsibility [61]); a combination of the abilities to be interactive, autonomous, and adaptable [25], and a combination of autonomy, responsibility and intentionality [54]. Do we need to ensure artificial moral agents (AMAs) are both ethically productive and ethically receptive [56], or is the ability for rational deliberation all that is needed [39]?

Although it is debatable whether robots can or cannot truly be moral agents given how philosophically loaded the topic is, it remains that, regardless of this uncertainty, humans can still be moral patients of the actions of autonomous machines that act without direct human intervention. For instance, and going back to the example mentioned above of AWSs, although we could debate endlessly about whether an AWS that acts without human intervention is a moral agent, the fact remains that it can still ultimately make the moral decision to kill a civilian or not, and this civilian would be the moral patient of this moral decision – whether they lived or died.

This is not to say that were the AWS to kill a civilian, it would hold full moral responsibility for the civilian's death – this is another complex issue entirely[3] – nor is it to say that the AWS is, in and of itself, a moral agent. Rather, it is to say that moral responsibility and agency aside, the civilian would have been killed due to a decision ultimately made by the AWS (although the groundwork for the decision would be based on its programming). At that moment, there is no direct human intervention wherein a human is making the decision to kill the civilian or not.

Thus, as stated above, there is the potential for human beings to be harmed by this technology.

---

[3] The topic of moral responsibility is also a contentious one and there remains what can be termed a *responsibility gap* when it comes to who should be held responsible for the actions of autonomous systems (see e.g. [42]).

4 Human Interactants as Moral Patients of Their Own Agential Moral Actions Towards Robots

I will now argue that there is a third perspective we may consider in relation to human interactants being moral patients in the context of their interaction with social robots: *human interactants as moral patients of their own agential moral actions towards social robots*. Before I can put this moral relation forward, we first need to understand the difference between the *actuality* of robot consciousness and the *perception* of robot consciousness, since this distinction is important in relation to the understanding of human interactants being the *actual* moral patients of the agential moral actions towards robots, and robots being the *perceived* moral patients of these actions. I will then briefly discuss arguments made that treating social robots immorally may morally harm human interactants. Given the *perception* of robot consciousness, and the potential that treating social robots immorally may morally harm human interactants, I investigate the unique moral relation that then arises between human interactants and social robots: that a human interactant is, at the same time, both the moral agent, as well as the *actual* moral patient, of their moral actions towards social robots – specifically in the context of immoral treatment. Social robots, however, are the *perceived* moral patients of such moral actions.

4.1 The Actuality of Robot Consciousness vs. the Perception of Robot Consciousness

The very topic of consciousness – what it is, and what it means to be conscious – is a hugely contested one. We still seem to be far away from having a definitive answer as to what consciousness is in the human sense, let alone what it would mean for an AI to be conscious, and whether this would ever be a possibility. How can we even begin to formulate a definitive answer in the context of artificial consciousness, when we seem no closer to understanding our own consciousness? Although I here remain agnostic to the possibility of conscious AI, and hold that we need not concern ourselves with it too much in the context of this paper, given the *perception* of robot consciousness (discussed below), it is worwhile to consider some arguments in the context of the *actuality* of robot consciousness. Doing so demonstrates the intractibility of the issue of consciousness in AI, and why I hold that it is more beneficial in the context of my arguments to circumnavigate the debate entirely.

Property dualists, such as David Chalmers, make the distinction between the easy and the hard problems of consciousness. According to Chalmers [13], the easy problems of consciousness pertain to explaining the following phenomena: "the ability to discriminate, categorize, and react to environmental stimuli; the reportability of mental states; the ability of a system to access its own internal states; the focus of attention; the deliberate control of behaviour; the difference between wakefulness and sleep". If we were to artificially replicate the human brain, we would merely be creating an AI that acts *as if* it is conscious and arguably dealing at best with the easy problems. However, it is far from clear in philosophical circles that consciousness can be determined behaviouristically (see e.g. [14, 35]. As such, creating an AI that behaves the way in which a conscious human being does, does not necessarily constitute it as being conscious. There is something more to consciousness. There is *something it is like* for us to be us. This is what Chalmers has coined as "the hard problem" of consciousness [13] which pertains to the problem of subjective experience – and more to the point, *why* we have such experiences. Thus, the hard problem makes it difficult to believe that we would be able to create artificial consciousness. How could we, if we do not even understand how our own phenomenal consciousness comes about, or if something like that does in fact exist (the jury is not yet out on the reductive/non-reductive physicalist debate)?

However, back to the focus of the paper, we may consider that given the capacity that social robots have to mimic consciousness, perhaps we need not be so overly concerned with the (im)possibility of robot consciousness. Thus, in the context of this paper, if it is the case that humans may interact with robots *as if* they are conscious, that is enough for us to argue that treating them immorally may negatively impact upon the moral fibre of interactants (and this is discussed in the section below).

As Arnold and Scheutz [3] state, it is "not what a robot is *in esse* but its function with and impact on people". The potential for interactants to perceive robots as being conscious stems from them being, as Turkle [58] states, a "relational artefact" in that these robots are "explicitly designed to engage a user in a relationship". This is due to their human-like appearance and social behaviour which work hand in hand to facilitate interactions that are as realistic as possible. Due to their human-like appearance and the capacity for robots to socially interact with interactants (albeit in a limited capacity[4]), there is a high possibility that interactants will anthropomorphise these robots. As Kanda et al. [32] state: a robot with a human-like body "causes people to behave unconsciously as if they were communicating with a human".[5]

However, in stating that interactants may anthropomorphise robots, this does not mean that they believe that these robots are *actually* human, but that does not mean human interactants cannot have relationships with robots. Rather, it means that a human-like appearance may evoke feelings within the interactant such that they view and treat their robots *as if* they are alive [37].[6] In the case of android social robots, if interactants want to perceive them as real people – as this may enhance their relational experience with them – then interactants may attribute human-like characteristics to them and treat them *as if* they are

---

[4] This is due to their incapacity to genuinely reciprocate human sentiments – related to the consciousness debate.

[5] The tendency to behave in such a way is brought about by the natural tendency that people have to anthropomorphise non-human entities or inanimate objects . Anthropomorphisation is an evolutionary trait inherent within us all (e.g. [17]).

[6] One can extrapolate that this may be the case from studies conducted with AIBO, a robotic dog, where Peter Kahn and his team stated: "We are not saying that AIBO owners believe literally that AIBO is alive, but rather that AIBO evokes feelings as if AIBO were alive" (see [37]).

human. This is no futuristic prediction. Studies have found that people do tend to apply social rules to the computers with which they interact [10,45]. The more human-like something appears to be, the more likely we are to anthropomorphise it. As such, given their android appearance, it is no leap in logic to then argue that the tendency to anthropomorphise android social robots will likely be high.

Specifically in the context of social robots that may provide a form of companionship, it also may be the case that human interactants *want* to believe that the robot is conscious, because this will make their companionship with them seem all the more realistic (see e.g. [6,48]), thus, human interactants may allow themselves to be deceived, thus *perceiving* the robots as conscious, although they may know that it is not *actually* conscious.

4.2   Treating Social Robots Immorally Does Moral Harm to Human Interactants

The human-like appearance of social robots, as well as their capacity to socially interact with us (albeit in a limited capacity) means, as was discussed above, that there is the possibility for human interactants to relate to social robots in a human-like way: we view them, and interact with them *as if* they are human beings, thus attributing to them human characteristics, such as consciousness. This relation is unique as compared to any other relation that we may have with other forms of technology. It is this unique relation that calls into question the morality of treating social robots immorally. I will here put forward that treating social robots immorally may morally harm human interactants. I argue this main point using three sub-arguments: social robots are more then mere objects; the act of treating a social robot immorally is abhorrent in itself; and treating a social robot immorally may negatively impact upon the moral fibre of interactants.

Social Robots Are More Than Mere Objects. Although I am neutral for the purposes of this paper on whether or not social robots are capable of possessing consciousness – particularly in the phenomenological sense as has been discussed – I argue that we cannot deem them as merely being inanimate objects. We cannot place social robots within the same group as any other object we utilise. This is because we do not view and relate to social robots the same way in which we view and relate to any other objects in the world.

Dautenhahn [23], based on the work of Breazeal [8,9], Fong et al. [26] and her own [22], elaborates upon how the definition and conceptual understanding of social robots may vary depending on their purpose and how and why they interact with people and the environment in which they are situated. Social robots can be: (1) "*Socially evocative*: Robots that rely on the human tendency to anthropomorphize and capitalize on feelings evoked when humans nurture, care [for] or [become involved] with their 'creation'" [8,9], are socially evocative; (2) "*Socially situated*: Robots that are surrounded by a social environment which they perceive and react to [are socially situated]. Socially situated robots are able to distinguish between other social agents and various objects in the environment" [26]; (3) "*Sociable*: Robots that proactively engage with humans in order to satisfy internal social aims (drives, emotions, etc.) [are sociable robots]. These robots require deep models of social cognition" [8,9]; (4) "*Socially intelligent*: Robots that show aspects of human-style social intelligence, based on possibly deep models of human cognition and social competence" [22], are socially intelligent; (5) "*Socially interactive*: Robots for which social interaction plays a key role in peer-to-peer HRI [Human-Robot Interaction], different from other robots that involve 'conventional' HRI, such as those used in teleoperation scenarios" [26], are socially interactive. Given these definitions and conceptual understandings of social robots, it is clear that social robots are a versatile technology, and that there are various ways in which human interactants can socially relate to them. As such, social robots cannot be compared to just any object that we utilize on a daily basis; we do not socially relate to just any inanimate object the way in which we may relate to a social robot.

Given that human interactants can socially relate to social robots, there is then the possibility for us to bond with them in seemingly realistic ways. Although any type of bond with a social robot may be unidirectional, and no type of reciprocation on the part of the robot truly indicates consciousness, the robot still does mimic reciprocation on a human social level, which impacts the humans with whom they interact. As such, I agree with Ramey [49] that there may be a unique social relationship (albeit possibly unidirectional as far as genuine reciprocation is concerned) between a human and a social robot that is qualitatively different from the way in which we relate to any other object that we utilise [49].

We have more than a physical relation to them. Yes, one can have more than a physical relation to an inanimate object – children, for example, love their stuffed toys and it can be argued that these toys are created to elicit an emotional response from children. However, this type of interaction and emotional response differs from that which we experience with social robots since stuffed toys do not reciprocate emotion, whereas social robots do – even though this reciprocity may be mere mimicry. Given this, interactants may begin to see social robots as being on the same plane as human beings (see e.g. [38]). Therefore, although they may not actually be conscious, we may view them as being such, given the human-like way in which we are able to relate to them (see e.g. [31,44,57]). Given this possibility, the superficial view to treat social robots as mere objects does not seem viable – there is more to them than that – although *actually* granting them consciousness and considering them deserving of moral treatment the way humans are, may be taking it a step too far, especially given the contentiousness of the consciousness debate (I will elaborate upon this point in a later section).

Given that I hold that social robots can be seen to be more than just any inanimate object due to the way in which we interact with them, I will now consider why the *act* of treating a social robot immorally is wrong in itself. This is because not only may social robots be viewed as being more than mere objects, but they can essentially be seen to be human simulacra in that they are being designed in our image, so as to facilitate the possibility for us to have human-like relations with them.

The Act of Treating a Social Robot Immorally Is Abhorrent in Itself. Due to social robots being created to foster the possibility for people to potentially *view* them as being conscious and on the same plane as human beings, social robots may be said to ultimately be symbols of human beings. Therefore, any interaction with them is also symbolic of an interaction with a human being. Given this, one can argue that in treating a social robot immorally, one is *symbolically* treating a human immorally, and this act can be seen to be morally abhorrent in itself.

This may seem like a leap, but it is important to then home in (again) on the humanistic aspect of these robots. They are specifically designed and created so that interactants will easily anthropomorphise them and relate to them in a humanistic social capacity. This is the whole point of their creation – to be human simulacra in every possible way, both physically and behaviouristically. Studies have confirmed the potential for interactants to attribute human-like aspects to robots and treat them as if they are human (see e.g. [31,32,37]).

Social robots are designed and created so that when an interactant physically – and emotionally – interacts with them, they are essentially performing an act which simulates the act that would be performed with another human being. This is for instance why moral questions arise regarding whether it would be wrong to allow a human to play out a rape fantasy using a sex robot as the victim. Both Sparrow [52] and Turner [59] ask this question. I hold the view that such an act would be immoral because the human-like form of the robot is intended to be symbolic of a human being, and moreover, if there is the possibility that an interactant may behave unconsciously as if they are interacting with a human, then playing out a rape fantasy with a robot simulates the enactment of an immoral act upon a human being and this act is immoral in itself.

Therefore, the act of treating a social robot immorally is wrong in itself due to its symbolic meaning. If a human-like robot essentially symbolises a human being, and an interactant unconsciously behaves as if they are interacting with a human, yet treats this robot immorally, then the immoral act should be condemned. Due to the act itself being immoral, there may be subsequent negative implications that may arise if interactants do treat social robots immorally. It is therefore important to address not only the morality of the act itself, but also consider how the act of treating a social robot immorally may negatively impact interactants as moral beings.

Treating a Social Robot Immorally May Negatively Impact Upon the Moral Fibre of Interactants. Given that we cannot deem social robots to be mere objects due to the way in which we view and relate to them, and due to the act of treating a social robot immorally essentially symbolising the act of treating a human immorally, there is the possibility that treating a social robot immorally may negatively impact upon the moral fibre of interactants. By this I mean that treating a social robot immorally may cause us to treat other humans immorally, similarly to the way in which Kant argues that the cruel treatment of animals may lead to us being "no less hardened towards men" [34].

"[T]o treat androids as humans is not to make androids actually human, but it is to make oneself an expanded self" [49] and the way we treat robots will affect ourselves and people around us. In light of this, Levy [38] argues that we should treat robots in the same moral way that we would treat any human because not doing so may negatively affect those people around us "by setting our own behaviour towards those robots as an example of how one should treat other human beings" [38].

Similar questions have been raised as far as the moral treatment of animals is concerned. Kant [33] makes the argument that we have the duty to ourselves to refrain from treating animals with violence or cruelty. This is because in treating animals immorally (with violence or cruelty) we "[dull] shared feelings of their suffering and so [weaken] and gradually [uproot] a natural predisposition that is very serviceable to morality in one's relations with other men" [33]. Thus, immoral treatment of animals may negatively impact upon moral relations with other humans. Similarly, Turner [59] states: "If we treat animals with contempt, then we might start to do so with humans also. There is a link between the two because we perceive animals as having needs and sensations – even if they do not have the same sort of complex thought processes as we do. Essentially, animals exhibit features which resemble humans, and we are biologically programmed to feel empathy toward anything with those features".

If there is concern raised about the way in which we treat animals extending to the way in which we treat humans, then surely there should be even more concern regarding our moral treatment of social robots which are realistic *human simulacra* as opposed to animals who may merely possess features that are exhibitive as human features? As such, going back to Levy [38], the main reason why he argues we should not treat robots immorally, is that if we take their embodiedness seriously, it would impact negatively on our social relations with humans if we treated them immorally. This argument stems from the possibility that there is the potential for people to interact with social robots in seemingly realistic human-like ways, leading to the human interactant perceiving the robot as being sociable, intelligent and autonomous and, as such, being on the same plane as human beings. This being the case, if we do begin to perceive social robots as being on the same plane as human beings, Levy's [38] argument that we should treat robots morally well, for our own sake, holds some weight.

One can, therefore, argue that since social robots are – in Levy's [38] view – embodied computers, in treating a social robot immorally, one is simulating the immoral treatment of a human being (as I have discussed above). If we do come to view these robots as being on the same plane as human beings, and yet not respect them as human beings, one can question theoretically whether this will lead to desensitising us towards immoral behaviour, thereby lowering the moral barriers of immoral acts. Would this potentially lead to human beings treating one another in such immoral ways?

Although such an argument can be likened perhaps to similar ones, for instance, debates about the impact of violent video games or pornography on society, the argument about social robots differs in that "the nature of robots as three-dimensional entities capable of complex behaviours distinguishes them from other media" [52]. Therefore, treating a social robot immorally – by abusing them, or playing out a rape fantasy with them for instance – is more realistic than, say, video games, and, as such, is "more likely to encourage people to carry out the represented act in reality" [52]. As Turner [59] states: "[S]imulating immoral or illegal acts with robots harms human society in some way, by condoning or promoting an unpleasant behaviour trait: an instrumental justification. This is a similar justification to the reason why cartoons depicting child pornography are often banned – even though no child was directly harmed in the process".

As such, I agree that our treating social robots immorally may negatively impact upon the moral fibre of human interactants.

4.3   Why Human Interactants Are Moral Patients of Their Own Agential Moral Actions Towards Social Robots

Earlier sections discussed two instances wherein a human may be a moral patient in the context of their interaction with a robot. There is, however, also a third perspective that we can consider in this regard, and particularly in the context of social robots: a human interactant being a moral patient of their own agential moral actions towards a robot. In this instance, the human interactant would be the moral agent of their own actions, as well as the moral patient of those very same moral actions. That is, the impact of the very action taken by a human interactant towards a social robot is redirected towards the human agent, making them a patient of their own immoral actions because their moral fibre is impacted by the way in which the robot is treated (as was discussed above).

Specifically, in terms of moral patiency, I hold that human interactants are the *actual* moral patients, whereas robots are the *perceived* moral patients. The distinction between *actual* moral patiency and *perceived* moral patiency takes us back to my discussion on the *actuality* of robot consciousness and the *perception* of robot consciousness as there is an inextricable link between consciousness and moral patiency.

It is a commonly held belief that in order for something to have moral status, or be worthy of moral consideration, this something must be conscious in the phenomenological sense [7,30], because this would mean that they are able to subjectively experience suffering; that they can *feel what it is like* to be a moral patient that is treated immorally. This type of consciousness refers to "the capacity for phenomenal experience or qualia, such as the capacity to feel pain and suffer" [7]. Thus, were we to consider the moral treatment of robots from a 'robot perspective', i.e. treating them well *for their own sakes,* this would imply that they can *actually* be moral patients in the sense that they can experience suffering at the hand of a human interactant who treats them immorally. This, in turn, would imply that robots are *actually* conscious. We saw, however, that the actuality of robot consciousness is a thorny issue and, therefore, I put forward that we focus our attention to *perceived* robot consciousness. Given the link between consciousness and moral patiency, we may consider that should human interactants *perceive* a social robot as being conscious, they may then *perceive* them as being moral patients; because a social robot can act *as if* they are conscious, they can therefore act *as if* they are suffering, should they be treated immorally.

Moral patiency can be understood as the case of being a target of moral action. In this instance, human interactants would not be *direct* targets of their own actions, but rather *indirect* targets – like a bullet ricocheting off its direct target and injuring an innocent bystander who becomes an indirect target of the shooter. They (human interactants) are indirectly impacted by way of their moral fibre being negatively impacted should they treat social robots immorally.

Where the robot is the direct target of the immoral treatment – and the *perceived* moral patient – the human interactant is the indirect target – and the *actual* moral patient. As such, we are indirect recipients of immoral action because robots cannot *actually* be recipients. Robots are not *really* impacted (for now leaving aside the possibility of robot phenomenal experience and consciousness, which, if it comes to pass, would of course add a layer of the robot as moral patient to this discussion) – we (the human interactants) are. Moreover, Danaher [19] notes a moral patient as "a being who possesses some moral status – i.e. is owed moral duties and obligations, and is capable of suffering moral harms and experiencing moral benefits – but who does not take ownership over the moral content of its own existence". As far as human interactants being moral patients of their own moral actions is concerned, referring to Danaher's [19] definition, human interactants can suffer and experience moral harms and benefits of their own agential actions: specifically, moral harms by way of their moral fibre being negatively impacted is an example of this kind of suffering.

Interestingly, Danaher [19] actually argues that the rise of robots could bring about a decrease in our own moral agency: "That is to say, [the rise of robots] could compromise both the ability and willingness of humans to act in the world as responsible moral agents, and consequently could reduce them to moral patients" [19]. For example, and as elaborated upon in Danaher's [19] article, an instance in which someone spends all their time with their sexbot. As a consequence, the human interactant loses motivation to do anything of real consequence – go out and meet new people, or spend time with a human partner – because it takes more effort. As such, this human interactant can spend all day at home, enjoying all the pleasure they desire [19]. As Danaher [19] states: "[T]he rise of the robots could lead to a decline in humans' willingness to express their moral agency (to make significant moral changes to the world around them). Because they have ready access to pleasure-providing robots, humans might become increasingly passive recipients of the benefits that technology bestows".

This is a compelling argument and worth consideration. However, I rather argue here not so much that our moral agency could itself 'decrease' due to our interaction with social robots but rather that our moral agency could be negatively impacted in the sense that as moral agents, our moral fibre may be negatively impacted, thus causing us, as moral agents, to possibly act immorally towards other human beings with whom we share the world, and towards ourselves.

Therefore, we may consider treating social robots morally well *for our own sakes*. Although specifically speaking to the topic of robot rights, we may here draw upon Gunkel's [28] argument that a consideration of the descriptive and normative aspects of robot rights seem to often be amiss in current machine ethics literature. It is important to distinguish between these two aspects so as to avoid slipping from one to the other. As far as the moral consideration of robots is concerned, this article distinguishes between the descriptive and normative aspects of the moral consideration of robos by way of arguing that even though social robots are not *capable* of being actual moral patients (descriptive aspect), we *should* still grant them moral consideration (normative aspect).

Finally, most ethics are agent-oriented – hence Floridi & Sanders [25] refer to this orientation as the 'standard' approach. As such, a patient-oriented approach is 'non-standard' – "it focuses attention not on the perpetrator of an act but on the victim or receiver of the action" [25]. Considering the possibility of human interactants being both agents and patients in a given instance bridges such a divide between a standard and non-standard approach. This is because human interactants – as moral agents – have the capacity to treat robots in moral or immoral ways. However, such treatment indirectly impacts human interactants as moral patients – they are, too, indirect receivers or victims of their own moral actions given that treating a robot immorally may negatively impact upon their own moral fibre.

5   Conclusion

This paper ultimately argued that given the *perception* of robot consciousness and moral patiency, as well as the possibility that treating a social robot immorally may cause moral harm to human interactants, we may consider that a human interactant is, at the same time, both a moral agent and a moral patient of their moral actions towards a social robot. That is, a human interactant (as a moral agent) is the *actual* moral patient of their moral actions, whereas the robots is a *perceived* moral patient.

This argument contributes to a perspective that is sorely lacking in machine ethics literature: there is very little focus on moral patiency as compared to moral agency (in the context of both humans and robots). Although there is somewhat of a focus on moral agency in that I argue that a human interactant is, at the same time, both the moral agent and the *actual* moral patient, there was more focus on human interactants being moral patients given that it it is more relevant in the context of an *anthropocentric* perspective on the moral treatment of robots. Moreover, a novel contribution is made particularly in the context of human moral patiency in the context of human-robot interaction. Where there has been consideration that humans can be moral patients in terms of robots being conduits of human moral action towards other human moral patients, as well as consideration that humans can be moral patients to the moral actions of robots, there has been no consideration of *human interactants being moral patients of their own agential moral actions towards robots* (particularly android social robots) i.e. indirect targets of their own moral actions, particularly in the context of treating robots immorally.

This is an important consideration and contribution in the context of the debate surrounding the moral treatment of robots, which also encompasses the contentious subject of robot rights. It is important because analysing the moral treatment of robots, and the possibility of robot rights, from an anthropocentric perspective (thus not in terms of whether or not robots are harmed from a robot perspective) as is suggested, may allow further research in this regard that does not become so concerned with the actuality of robot consciousness and moral patiency to such an extent that consideration concerning robot moral status and robot rights seem superfluous. The consideration of robot moral status and robots rights is definitely not superfluous from the perspective of human interactants who may be morally harmed as a result of immoral interactions with social robots who mimic human-likeness. The need to research the nature and impact of HRI is high and often under-estimated even in AI ethics policy making.

We cannot only consider the moral treatment of robots when, or if, they become conscious. The very way in which we express ourselves as humans and in which we situate ourselves in social spaces is in danger of changing rapidly already in the case of human traits simply being mimicked. To be detained by the concern as to whether robots can be conscious or not will only for now misdirect us from moral issues that should be immediately addressed and present more present ethical dangers: such as the degradation of our moral fibre due to not treating robots morally well for our own moral sakes.

As far as non-android social robots are concerned, further research may draw upon arguments I have made in the context of android social robots so as to possibly generalize arguments to the impacts of non-android social robots, or other types of robots in general. This, however, will require further research. Further research may also draw upon the arguments made so as to consider granting rights to robots. Specifically, we may consider granting negative rights to robots, i.e. rights that will prevent human interactants from treating robots immorally.

For now, the possibility of robots with full moral status who demand their rights may seem a long way off. We cannot be certain when this will happen, or if it will ever happen. Regardless of these possibilities, however, what we can be certain of is that the moral fibre of human societies may be at risk if we do not consider the moral treatment of social robots – at least, for now, from the perspective of human interactants.

References

1. IEEE ethically aligned design (2019). https://standards.ieee.org/content/dam/ieeestandards/standards/web/documents/other/ead1e.pdf
2. Anderson, M., Anderson, S.: Machine ethics: creating an ethical intelligent agent. AI Mag. **28**(4), 15–26 (2007)
3. Arnold, T., Scheutz, M.: HRI ethics and type-token ambiguity: what kind of robotic identity is most responsible? Ethics Inf. Technol.(2018)
4. Asaro, P.: What should we want from a robot ethic? Int. Rev. Inf. Ethics **6**(12), 9–16 (2006)
5. Barquin, R.C.: Ten commandments of computer ethics (1992)
6. Boltuć, P.: Chuch-Turing Lovers. Oxford University Press, Oxford (2017)
7. Bostrom, N., Yudkwosky, E.: The ethics of artificial intelligence. In: Frankish, K., Ramsey, W. (eds.) The Cambdridge Handook of Artificial Intelligence, pp. 316–334. Cambridge University Press, Cambridge (2014)
8. Breazeal, C.: Designing Sociable Robots. MIT Press, Cambridge (2002)
9. Breazeal, C.: Towards sociable robots. Robot. Auton. Syst. **42**, 167–175 (2003)
10. Broadbent, E.: Interactions with robots: the truths we reveal about ourselves. Annu. Rev. Psychol. **68**, 627–652 (2017)
11. Brundage, M.: Limitations and risks of machine ethics. J. Exp. Theor. Artif. Intell. **26**(3), 355–372 (2014)
12. Bryson, J.: Robots should be slaves. Close Engage. Artif. Companions: Key Soc. Psychol. Ethical Des. Issues (2009)
13. Chalmers, D.: Facing up to the problem of consciousness (1995). http://consc.net/papers/facing.pdf. Accessed 7 May 2019
14. Chalmers, D.: Philosophy of Mind: Classical and Contemporary Readings. Oxford University Press, Oxford (2002)
15. Coeckelbergh, M.: Artificial companions: empathy and vulnerability mirroring in human-robot relations. Stud. Ethics Law Technol. **4**(3, Article 2) (2010)
16. Coeckelbergh, M.: Health care, capabilities, and AI assistive technologies. Ethical Theory Moral Pract. **13**, 181–190 (2010)
17. Damiano, L., Dumouchel, P.: Anthropomorphism in human-robot co-evolution. Front. Psychol. **9**, 1–9 (2018)
18. Danaher, J.: The Symbolic-Consequences Argument in the Sex Robot Debate. MIT Press, Cambridge (2017)
19. Danaher, J.: The rise of the robots and the crisis of moral patiency. AI & Soc. **34**, 129–136 (2019)
20. Danaher, J., Earp, B., Sandberg, A.: Should We Campaign Against Sex Robots?. The MIT Press, Cambridge (2017)
21. Danaher, J., McArthur, N.: Robot Sex: Social and Ethical Implications. The MIT Press, Cambridge (2017)
22. Dautenhahn, K.: The art of designing socially intelligent agents - science, fiction, and the human in the loop. Appl. Artif. Intelli. **12**, 573–617 (1998)
23. Dautenhahn, K.: Socially intelligent robots: dimensions of human-robot interaction. Philos. Trans. Roy. Soc. **362**, 679–704 (2007)
24. Deng, B.: Machine ethics: the robot's dilemma. Nat. News **523**, 24–26 (2015)
25. Floridi, L., Sanders, J.: On the morality of artificial agents. Mind Mach. **14**, 349–379 (2004)
26. Fong, T., Nourbakhsh, I., Dautenhahn, K.: A survey of socially inter-active robots'. Robots Auton. Syst. **42**, 143–166 (2003)

27. Gunkel, D.: Moral patiency. In: The Machine Question: Critical Perspectives on AI. Robots, and Ethics, pp. 93–157. The MIT Press, Cambridge (2012)
28. Gunkel, D.: The other question: can and should robots have rights? Ethics Inf. Technol. **20**, 87–99 (2017)
29. ICRC: Autonomy, artificial intelligence and robotics: technical aspects of human control, Geneva (2019)
30. Jaworska, A., Tannenbaum, J.: The grounds of moral status. Stanford Encyclopedia of Philosophy (2018)
31. Kanda, T., Freier, N., Severson, R., Gill, B.: Robovie, you'll have to go into the closet now: children's social and moral relationships with a humanoid robot. Dev. Psychol. **48**(2), 303–314 (2012)
32. Kanda, T., Ishiguro, H., Imai, M., Ono, T.: Development and evaluation of interactive humaoid robots, 1839–1850 (2004)
33. Kant, I.: The Metaphysics of Morals. Cambridge University Press, Cambridge (1996)
34. Kant, I.: Lectures on Ethics. Cambridge University Press, Cambridge (1997)
35. Kirk, R., Carruthers, P.: Consciousness and concepts. In: Proceedings of the Aristotelian Society, Supplementary, vol. 66, pp. 23–59 (1992)
36. Komatsubara, T.: Can a social robot help children's understanding of science in classrooms? In: Proceedings of the Second International Conference on Human-Agent Interaction, pp. 83–90 (2014)
37. Levy, D.: Love and sex with robots: the evolution of human-robot relationships. Harper (2007)
38. Levy, D.: The ethical treatment of artificially conscious robots. Int. J. Soc. Robot. **1**(3), 209–216 (2009)
39. Lin, P., Abney, K., Bekey, G.: Robot Ethics: The Ethical and Social Implications of Robotics. The MIT Press, Cambridge (2012)
40. Lin, P., Abney, K., Bekey, G.: Robotics, Ethical Theory, and Metaethics: A Guide for the Perplexed. The MIT Press, Cambridge (2012)
41. Lumbreras, S.: The limits of machine ethics. Religions **8**(100), 2–10 (2017)
42. Matthias, A.: The responsibility gap: ascribing responsibility for the actions of learning automata. Ethics Inf. Technol. **6**, 175–183 (2004)
43. McDermott, D.: Why ethics is a high hurdle for AI. In: North American Conference on Computers and Philosophy, Bloomington, Indiana (2008)
44. Melson, G., Kahn, P., Beck, A., Friedman, B.: Robotic pets in human lives: implications for the human-animal bond and for human relationships with personified technologies. J. Soc. Issues **65**(3), 545–567 (2009)
45. Moon, Y., Nass, C.: Machines and mindlessness: social responses to computers. J. Soc. Issues **56**, 81–103 (2000)
46. Moor, J.: The nature, importance, and difficulty of machine ethics. IEEE **21**(4), 18–21 (2006)
47. Müller, V.: Ethics of artificial intelligence and robotics (2020, edition)
48. Nyholm, S., Frank, L.: It loves me, it loves me not: is it morally problematic to design sex robots that appear to love their owners? (2019), techné: Research in Philosophy and Technology, Issue December
49. Ramey, C.: 'For the sake of others': The 'personal' ethics of human-android interaction. Stresa, Italy (2005)
50. Sharkey, A., Sharkey, N.: Granny and the robots: ethical issues in robot care for the elderly. Ethics Inf. Technol. **14**(1), 27–40 (2010)
51. Sharkey, A.: Should we welcome robot teachers? Ethics Inf. Technol. **283–297**, 18 (2016)

52. Sparrow, R.: Robots, rape, and representation. Int. J. Soc. Robot. **9**(3), 465–477 (2017)
53. Sparrow, R., Sparrow, L.: In the hands of machines? The future of aged care. Minds Mach. **16**, 141–161 (2006)
54. Sullins, J.: When is a robot a moral agent? Int. Rev. Inf. Ethics **6**(12) (2006)
55. Sullins, J.: Robots, love and sex: the ethics of building a love machine. IEEE Trans. Affect. Comput. **3**(4), 398–409 (2012)
56. Torrance, S.: Artificial agents and the expanding ethical circle. AI Soc. **28**, 399–414 (2013)
57. Turkle, S.: A nascent robotics culture: new complicities for companionship. In: AAAI Technical Report Series (2006)
58. Turkle, S.: Authenticity in the age of digital companions. Interact. Stud. **8**(3), 501–517 (2007)
59. Turner, J.: Why robot rights? In: Robot Rules: Regulating Artificial Intelligence, pp. 145–171. Palgrave Macmillan, Cham (2019)
60. Vallor, S.: Carebots and caregivers: sustaining the ethical ideal of care in the twenty-first century. Philos. Technol. **24**, 251–268 (2011)
61. Wallach, W., Allen, C.: Moral Machines: Teachinf Robots Right from Wrong. Oxford University Press, New York (2009)
62. Wang, W., Siau, K.: Ethical and moral issues with AI: a case study on health-care robots. In: Twenty-Fourth Americas Conference on Information Systems, New Orleans (2018)

Nature, Culture, AI and the Common Good – Considering AI's Place in Bruno Latour's *Politics of Nature*

Jaco Kruger[1,2](✉) [iD]

[1] St Augustine College of South Africa, Johannesburg, South Africa
j.kruger@staugustine.ac.za
[2] Faculty of Theology, North West University, Potchefstroom, South Africa

Abstract. This paper considers the place and the role of AI in the pursuit of the common good. The notion of the common good has a long and venerable history in social philosophy, but this notion, so it is argued, becomes problematic with the imminent advent of Artificial General Intelligence. Should AI be regarded as being in the service of the common good of humanity, or should the definition of the social common rather be enlarged to include non-human entities in general, and AI's, which in the future may include human level and superhuman level AI's, in particular? The paper aims to clarify the questions and the concepts involved by interpreting Bruno Latour's proposal for a politics of nature with specific reference to the challenge posed by the imminent advent of human level artificial general intelligence (AGI). The recent suggestion by eminent AI researcher, Stuart Russell, that the pursuit of AI should be re-oriented towards AI that remain in the service of the human good, will be used as a critical interlocutor of Latour's model. The paper concludes with the suggestion that the challenge will be to steer a middle ground between two unacceptable extremes. On the one hand the extreme of a "truth politics" that assumes there is a pure human nature and definite human interests that must be protected against AI should be avoided. On the other hand, the alternative extreme of a naked "power politics" must also be avoided because there is a very real possibility that super AI may emerge victorious out of such a power struggle.

Keywords: Bruno latour · Artificial intelligence · Common good · Stuart Russell

1   Introduction

The modern world has been characterised by an intractable opposition between nature and culture. This has been the longstanding thesis and arguably the primary underlying concern in the work of French sociologist and philosopher, Bruno Latour. Latour rose to prominence following the publication of his books *Laboratory Life* (1986), *Science in Action* (1988) and *We have never been modern* (1993) in the final decades of the last century. Especially in *We have never been modern* Latour describes and problematizes

© Springer Nature Switzerland AG 2020
A. Gerber (Ed.): SACAIR 2020, CCIS 1342, pp. 21–33, 2020.
https://doi.org/10.1007/978-3-030-66151-9_2

the opposition between nature and culture that is, according to him, the defining characteristic of modernity. On the one hand, in modern thought, nature came to be regarded
as the "objective reality out there" waiting to be discovered and faithfully described by
what has become known as modern science. Nature, in other words, simply ís what it
is. On the other hand, there is the realm of culture – the realm of human subjectivity
and freedom. In the realm of freedom, the incomparable dignity of human subjectivity
lies in its autonomy; its ability to freely decide and to take responsibility for action.
As is well known, this watertight distinction between nature and culture, necessity and
freedom, found an enormously influential articulation in the thought of Immanuel Kant,
who himself worked on philosophical problems already present in the work of Renee
Descartes at the beginning of modern thought in the 17th century.

The dichotomy between nature and freedom gave rise to a whole series of analogous
oppositions along with interminable struggles to reconcile, or at least to relate them.
In his 2004 book, Politics of Nature, which will be the primary focus in this paper,
Latour takes up the nature-culture divide again and explains how it translates into the
oppositions between facts and values, between is and ought, between the common world
and the common good, between truth politics and power politics, and between different
viewpoints regarding the orienting transcendence of the world: is it the transcendence of
nature, the transcendence of freedom, or the transcendence of the political sovereign? The
Sisyphean labour of modern thought has been to police the borders between these oppositions, while ceaselessly drawing the borders again because they remain perpetually
unclear, unstable, and porous.[1]

The questions and philosophical challenges brought on by the possibility of Artificial
Intelligence add further dimensions to the problem of the nature-culture divide. Artificial
Intelligence does not sit well within the opposition between nature and freedom. On
which side of the border should it be classified and maintained? Should it be regarded
as part of non-human nature, or should it be accorded aspects of agency and moral
responsibility that were hitherto reserved exclusively for human subjectivity? In his
latest book, Human Compatible, well known Artificial Intelligence researcher Stuart
Russell observes that the achievement of human level Artificial General Intelligence is
indeed not far off. However, he argues that there is something fundamentally wrong
headed about the way the achievement of Artificial Intelligence has been pursued thus
far. "From the very beginnings of AI, intelligence in machines has been defined in the
same way: Machines are intelligent to the extent that their actions can be expected
to achieve their objectives." (Russell 2019:20) According to Russel this is wrong and
indeed could be regarded as a huge threat to the future flourishing of humanity. There
is a very real possibility that Artificial Intelligence will become super intelligence and
that it then will pursue its own objectives to the detriment of its human creators. In this
scenario Artificial Intelligence will not lead to the common good in society, but actively
detract from it. Accordingly, Russel proposes that we should change our understanding
of Artificial Intelligence to the following: "Machines are beneficial to the extent that their

---

[1] For a critical engagement with Latour's deconstruction of the nature-culture opposition, see
Collins and Yearley (1992:301–326), Walsham (1997) or Pollini (2013), specifically with regard
to ecology.

actions can be expected to achieve our objectives." (2019:22) Our pursuit of Artificial Intelligence must in other words be guided by the lodestar of the human good.

In the present paper I engage with Russell's thesis from the perspective of Bruno Latour's politics of nature. I argue that Artificial Intelligence can and should be accommodated in the ongoing political process of constructing our common world. Artificial Intelligence should be allowed to make presentations in the developing res publica – public thing – that is our world. It is precisely because the hitherto watertight distinction between the human and the non-human is untenable that the role of Artificial Intelligence in the construction of the collective can in the future become less problematic and even normal. An important implication of this argument would then be the deconstruction of the opposition between the common world and the common good, and the highlighting of the possible contribution of AI in this regard.

The argument develops along the following steps: in the next Sect. 1 outline Latour's deconstruction of the nature-culture dichotomy, as well as his proposal for a process of continually negotiating a common world. In the following Sect. 1 argue that Artificial Intelligence can make a vital contribution towards the efficacy and fairness of the two powers that, according to Latour, shape the public domain – the power to take into account and the power to arrange in rank order. To accord such a supportive role to AI would, however, miss the opportunity to engage with the far greater challenge that human level and superhuman level AI poses: the challenge of non-human agency and intelligence in general. In the final section of the paper I therefore argue that Russell's alarm about AI pursuing its own goals to the detriment of human goals may be understood and philosophically critiqued in terms of the watertight dichotomy between nature and culture. In this case "nature" is a purportedly pure human nature and autonomy that must be safeguarded against the goals of autonomous AI. But, following Latour, it must be conceded that there never has been a pure nature. In his words: we have never been modern. We must accept that, just like other non-human actants, AI plays a role in the continuous construction of the collective. The more this is recognised and normalised, the less it will be possible to use AI for nefarious purposes in political processes. The paper nevertheless ends with a concession to Russell that Latour's politics of nature can potentially reduce to a power politics, in which case a very powerful AI could indeed be a threat to the human good.

2 Latour's Politics of Nature

"What do nature, science, and politics have to do with one another?" This is the question Latour asks in the introduction to his *Politics of Nature* (2004:6). In the following chapters he proceeds to show how nature, in modern thought, came to be regarded as the realm of matter and material forces. As such, nature exists and functions according to universal natural laws. It is the role of science to faithfully and as objectively as possible reflect nature in a growing body of knowledge. Science is simply the mirror of nature (2004:4).[2] On top of the "objective" realm of nature sits the "subjective" realm of politics. Nature is the simple given within which politics takes place. But, apart from being there, nature

---

[2] This is, of course, also the title of a famous book by Richard Rorty in which he too criticizes a modernist conception of knowledge (Rorty 2017).

has nothing to say in the political process. It is up to human actors to decide how we should live together, what is moral and what is immoral, what is good and what is bad. On these matters, science has nothing to say. Its role is restricted to simply presenting the facts. In its essence science is and should be value free.

The watertight distinction between nature and culture can be associated with two opposing traditions in modern political thought. Graham Harman, one of the foremost English language interpreters of Latour, formulates the two opposing traditions that Latour indicates in Politics of Nature, but seldom mentions in so many words as the tradition of truth politics and that of power politics (Harman 2014 Kindle Loc. 201; see also Harman 2009). The tradition of truth politics orients itself on what it regards as objective truth. There are many variants of truth politics, also from premodern times, but a salient modern example would be Marxism. After all, the history of all hitherto existing society is the history of the development of an inexorable law – that of class struggle, and the political process should be true to this law. Another example of truth politics that Latour specifically treats in Politics of Nature is the politics of the so-called Green movement. In this politics science is explicitly invoked as the touchstone of the truth. The facts speak for themselves; we are destroying the environment and therefore we must change our policies.

In contrast to the tradition of truth politics, according to Latour as interpreted by Harman, we find in modern thought the tradition of power politics. Denying any objective truth that should guide political action, power politics works on the principle that might is right. Power is what structures society and what ultimately holds society together (Harman 2014 Kindle Loc. 234–235). Here, of course, the salient exponent of such an approach is Thomas Hobbes. The important point to realise, however, is that the opposition between truth politics and power politics is only the surface effect of a deeper agreement. Both of these approaches accept the unwavering separation of the realm of objects, and the realm of subjects, or, in other words, of nature and freedom. They only differ in where they place the emphasis: should the political process be guided by objective facts or laws of nature, or should it be guided by human freedom? According to Latour both traditions suffer from the same shortcoming: they seek to prematurely end the political process. The strategy of truth politics is to cut off any further negotiation by appealing to brute facts (Latour 2004:13). The strategy of power politics on the other hand is to short circuit the political process by fiat (2004:54).

It is in the impasse between truth politics and power politics that Latour seeks to make an intervention. He does this by demonstrating that the opposition between truth politics and power politics does not hold, and that this is so because the opposition between nature and culture does not hold. On the one hand, science can never be value free. The presentation of scientific facts always has a persuasive character. The scientific enterprise has an agenda, it wants to nudge and cajole society in a specific direction. On the other hand, human freedom simply must take into account the constraints posed by certain stubborn realities that keep on thrusting themselves onto the agenda. Politically, for example, a government can decide to open up schools and beaches and restaurants in the midst of the Covid-19 pandemic, but eventually it can no longer be denied that the virus keeps on spreading and people keep on dying.

Latour's suggestion is that we must change our understanding of "the social" (2004:37). Instead of a mute nature lying over against the social, and being excluded from the political process, we should rather become more agnostic about all the actants in our environment – both human and nonhuman. In Latour's words: "we are not dealing with a society 'threatened' by recourse to an objective nature, but with a collective in the process of expanding: the properties of human beings and non-humans with which it has to come to terms are in no way assured." (2004:38). In other words, we should not be so sure that nonhuman beings are always mere objects, while human beings are always subjects (2004:61). The distinction between subjects and objects is not helpful. In the old dispensation "objects" were used by truth politicians to short circuit the political process. On the other hand, the appeal to the freedom of subjectivity was used by power politicians to similarly short circuit the political process. Undermining this distinction, Latour persuasively demonstrates that nonhuman beings also speak and have agency. Conversely, human beings' speech is never completely pure or clear, their agency never unmediated. Latour's new political ecology would have us replace our previously held certainties about which beings belong to nature, and which to culture with three uncer-tainties. "The first has to do with speech "impedimenta": Who is speaking? The second has to do with capacities for association: Who is acting? The third and last has to do with the recalcitrance of events: Who is able?" (2004: 87). Let us briefly discuss each of these three uncertainties.

The first necessary uncertainty for a reconceptualised political process is the agnos-ticism about who is speaking. According to Latour, our common world is composed by way of continual debate. And the political collective should always be regarded as an assembly of beings capable of speaking and stating their case (2004:62). But here it is imperative to understand that nonhuman beings also speak and are therefore also part of the political process. How do they speak? They speak through the mediation of spokespeople and speech prostheses (2004: 64, 67). On the one hand a nonhuman being, for instance a virus, speaks by way of the many scientists that continually interact with it. On the other hand, the speech prostheses that the virus utilizes to speak through these spokespeople are the intricate sets of laboratory equipment that allow its voice to be heard in the public square. Microscopes, genetic charts, statistics of infection rates are all so many prostheses that allow a virus to speak, also by way of its spokespeople the scientists. But the uncertainty about who speaks remains, and this is crucial. There is always the possibility that a spokesperson can speak in her own name, and not faithfully in the name of that for which she is speaking. There is always also the possibility that the intermediary instruments, the speech prostheses, are inaccurate in their giving voice to the being that is speaking. So, should politics not then, after all, be reserved only for human beings? No, because the uncertainty about who speaks is also there in the case of human beings. In the human world too controversy is always there, and so the uncertainty about who speaks and who speaks for who will always be there. And that is why, according to Latour, the political process never ends.

The second necessary uncertainty in a revitalized politics is the uncertainty about who is acting. Here the troubling distinctions inherited from the nature-culture opposition are the distinctions between things and people, or objects and subjects. Within this scheme social action is reserved for subjects, whereas objects necessarily behave according to deterministic rules of cause and effect. Furthermore, within this scheme a zero-sum game is operative: the more entities are considered to be determined objects, the less they can be considered as subjects, and vice versa (2004:76). But this distinction is unhelpful according to Latour, and only serves to paralyze the political process. It is, moreover, untenable. Because, if all entities are more and more treated as objects, we can no longer count on the input of human actors with freedom and responsibility to decide what must be done. Everyone is, after all, determined. Conversely, if the model of free will is extended to everything, including the planet, there will no longer be "the raw, unattackable nonhuman matters of fact that allow it to silence the multiplicity of subjective viewpoints, each of which expresses itself in the name of its own interests" (2004:73). To overcome this zero-sum deadlock, Latour proposes that we confess our uncertainty about who is acting. Instead of talking about acting subjects and acted upon objects, people and things, we should consistently talk of human and non-human actors. All entities within the political collective act, simply by virtue of the fact that they influence other actors. To rid our speech in this regard of any anthropomorphism, Latour proposes that we talk of actants, instead of actors. An actant is an acting agent, an intervener, an influencer. And, once again, in the political process we should keep on enlarging the list of active actants in our commonwealth (2004:76).

The third dose of healthy agnosticism needed in a reconfigured political process is uncertainty about what is real; what really exists. The nature-freedom divide often forces us into a kind of materialistic naturalism on the one hand, or a constructivist idealism on the other. But here, above all, the political process should be more pragmatic, according to Latour. In dealing with those who speak, those who act and intervene in your world, why not credit them with the properties you yourself hold dearest – in this case reality (2004:77). Instead of taking external reality to be the simple "being there" of brute facts, we should associate it with that which surprise us and interrupt the smooth flow of our life with an insistence that it is there. "Actors are defined above all as obstacles, scandals, as what suspends mastery, as what gets in the way of domination, as what interrupts the closure and the composition of the collective." (2004:81) While something is stubbornly standing in the way of our definition of the common world, the res publica, while something is recalcitrantly refusing to be ignored, we should accept its reality, says Latour. And the more entities we admit as participants in our common enterprise of forming our world, the better.

3   AI and the Two Powers at Play in Unsettling and Stabilising the Collective

Now that we have undermined the old divide between nature and freedom, between the common world and the common good, and have replaced it with a number of uncertainties and a growing list of participants, we should think, along with Latour, about the possible functioning of the political process in this new dispensation. In this Sect. 1 would like to consider the role that Artificial Intelligence can play in this reconfigured political process but in a restricted and still somewhat unsatisfactory way. In the last section of the paper I then consider the deeper implications of Latour's deconstruction of the nature-freedom divide for our thinking of Artificial Intelligence and the common good and bring them into discussion with Russell's reservations.

Latour's proposal for reconfiguring the political process involves "the rearrangement of the squares on the chess board" (2004:5). In other words, we should not only re-arrange the pieces on the board according to the same rules, but fundamentally reconceive how the political process works. The blurring of the line, the constitutive uncertainty about what is nature and what is culture, what is a subject and what an object remains the point of departure in this regard. The point is, we cannot be certain of what should be regarded as brute facts of nature, and what should be regarded as values of human freedom in the political process. This does not mean, however, that we should not appreciate the rationale behind paying attention to facts and being attentive to values that animated the reference to facts and values in the first place.

According to Latour, in the notion of "fact" there are two legitimate imperatives at work that are nevertheless confusedly held together within this one concept. Similarly, in the notion of "value" there are two imperatives operating that are also legitimate, but that are held together in a confused way. The first imperative within the confused notion of fact is to be open to "external reality" (2004:110). As we have seen, actants stubbornly establish their presence and demand to be acknowledged: they are there, whether we like it or not. The second imperative confused within the notion of fact has to do with acceptance or closure. At least until the next cycle of the political process (see below) we should now accept that certain actants are part of the political process and that their voices should be taken into account. Thus, contained in the erstwhile notion of fact, there is on the one hand an imperative for openness to external reality, and on the other hand an imperative for stabilizing and institutionalizing what is for the time being to be accepted as part of the collective.

The first imperative rolled up into what was previously regarded as "values" in the political process is the imperative to listen to and critically evaluate the voices of the actants that stubbornly demand to be listened to. In Latour's words, "it is necessary to make sure that reliable witnesses, assured opinions, credible spokespersons have been summoned up, thanks to a long effort of investigation and provocation (in the etymological sense of 'production of voices')" (ibid.) Another way of describing this imperative would be to talk of the requirement of openness or consultation.

The second imperative confusedly contained in the notion of value is the requirement to weigh up and to decide where to position an actant within the hierarchy of importance that functions in the body politic. If it is true that the political process is a clamour of many voices all appealing for a place in the sun of the common world, then it is just as true that some kind of hierarchy must be communally agreed upon, otherwise there will only be chaos. The relative importance of a voice – an interest – within the commonwealth must be established through a process of give and take. Here it can clearly be seen how politics is the proverbial art of the compromise.

Latour therefore unbundles the defunct opposition between facts and values into four imperatives or requirements of the political process. First the requirement to pay attention to actants that announce their intention to become part of the political process. The body politic must be open – willing to become perplexed – by the possible reality of voices that have hitherto not been recognized as real. Secondly there is a requirement to critically evaluate the voices of the actants that are harrowing the body politic. This is the requirement of openness: what are the new voices really saying? Who is speaking on their behalf, using what means? The third requirement, then, is the requirement to rank the importance of a voice within the hierarchy that is the body politic. Where should the new actant that has been identified and listened to fit in? What is its relative importance? And finally, there is the requirement of provisional closure. The imperative to institutionalize, at least for a time, the hierarchy that has been established so that the body politic can live and be a common world.

The perceptive reader will have noticed that from the unbundling of the fact-value distinction to the enumeration of the four imperatives functioning in the political process a subtle shift has taken place. The four imperatives have been grouped differently. Latour does this to highlight that there are two powers at work in the political process. The first power is a power of destabilization or unsettling. Far from being negative, this power is necessary for the health of the process. The second power is a power of stabilization and institutionalization – a power equally necessary for the health of the political process. Latour names the first power (the destabilizing and unsettling power) the power to "take into account". Two imperatives energize this power – one from the erstwhile notion of fact, and one from the erstwhile notion of value. The imperative to be open to becoming perplexed by external reality, and the imperative to evaluatively engage with actants that become visible together drive the power to take into account. This power opens up and unsettles the body politic so that it can change and grow. The second power Latour names the power to "arrange in rank order". This power, similarly, is made up of two imperatives – one from the erstwhile notion of fact, and the other from the erstwhile notion of value. In the first place the imperative to decide where in the hierarchy an actant should be positioned is what energizes the power to arrange in rank order. In the second place the imperative to institutionalize or close down further discussion is what energizes the power to arrange in rank order. This power then evidently stabilizes the body politic so that it can live and function.

Very important to note is that what has been described above is what Latour calls a single cycle in the political process. Once provisional closure has been reached through the power to arrange in rank order, the process starts up again in a next iteration: the perplexity caused by actants that have hitherto been excluded must be heeded as it functions within the power to take into account. And so, in Latour's conception, we have a circular process where the two powers continually operate and balance each other out.

The point I would like to make now is that this conception of the political process gives us the theoretical tools to think about the role of Artificial Intelligence in that process, and specifically in pursuit of the common good (bearing in mind that this conception also disturbs the strict border between the common world and the common good.) Artificial Intelligence can play an auxiliary or amplifying role regarding all four the imperatives, and concomitantly, with regard to both the powers at work in the political process. In line with a general insight regarding technology (cf. Ihde and Malafouris 2019), AI can furthermore function in a positive way as well as in a destructive way in all these processes.

In its present form AI is already functioning in service of the imperative to openness in the political process. In this regard one can think of the many data analysing algorithms at work today. Using these algorithms trends and patterns are identified and these then become actants whose candidacy for reality and inclusion in the body politic must be considered. Russell (2019:73) provides an excellent example of machines' role in the imperative to openness. At present thousands of satellites are continuously imaging every square meter of the world's surface. In Russell's estimation, more than thirty million human employees would be necessary to analyse all the images received from satellites. The result is that much of the satellite data is never seen by human eyes. However, computer vision algorithms process this data to produce searchable databases "with visualizations and predictive models of economic activities, changes in vegetation, migrations of animals and people, the effects of climate change, and so on." (Ibid.) All of this result in an increased sensitivity towards new entities or phenomena that should be taken into account in the construction of the common world.

Once an entity's candidacy for citizenship has been registered, its claims must be evaluated and weighed. It will be recalled that in Latour's view the imperative here is to make a case, and to be open to the case made. It is thus a matter of advocacy and of how compelling a case can be made. Russell notes that AI will play a huge role in this regard, in the sense that services previously open only to the super-rich will become accessible to everyone. "And in the mundane world of daily life, an intelligent assistant and guide would—if well designed and not co-opted by economic and political interests—empower every individual to act effectively on their own behalf in an increasingly complex and sometimes hostile economic and political system. You would, in effect, have a high-powered lawyer, accountant, and political adviser on call at any time." (Russell 2019:105) On the other hand algorithms are also already at work to strengthen the power to evaluate and weigh up the appeals made by an actant in the public sphere. AI is already playing a role in various fact checking services that monitor and moderate the many voices on social media and news sites (Russell 2019:113). In this regard one can think of sites like factcheck.org and snopes.com.

The second imperative at work in the power to arrange in rank order is the imperative to establish a hierarchy of interests. It is the imperative to perform triage regarding the relative importance of an actant's demands. Here, as well, AI is already rendering valuable service, and the expectation is that this will increase in the future as the capacity of AI increases. Russel (2019:134) takes an example from the airline industry to illustrate the decision-making power of AI. At first computers were only involved in the drawing up of flight schedules. Then the booking of seats, the allocation of flight staff and the booking of routine maintenance were also computerised. Next airlines' computers were connected to international aviation networks to provide real-time status updates on flights and situations at airports. At present algorithms are taking over the job of managing disruption in the aviation workflow by "rerouting planes, rescheduling staff, rebooking passengers and revising maintenance schedules." (Ibid.) Would AI be able to perform similar functions in the area of governance and the allocation of public funds? Undoubtedly. This becomes even more apparent when the power of AI in scenario planning is considered (cf. Sohrabi et al 2018).

The final imperative for the political process is again part of the power to take into account. But now it is an imperative towards provisional closure of the body politic. For the commonwealth to function certain realities must be stabilised, at least for the time being. In this regard two examples of the contribution of Artificial Intelligence should suffice. In the first place, AI can play a role in understanding what the current state of stability and preferences looks like. By looking at an initial state, learning algorithms can now already infer the implicit preferences present in that state, and bring them to light, thus accurately displaying the present state of afairs (Shah et al. 2019). The second example pertains to the moderating role that AI plays in contemporary social media. As body politic we have agreed amongst ourselves that it is not acceptable that the dignity of certain actors should be jeopardised, for instance through the language used to describe them, or the incitement of violence towards them, or the denial of their right to existence. Algorithms monitor social media posts and are sensitive towards certain formulations. This could result in posts being deleted and accounts being suspended. In such a way a definitive affirming of the legitimacy of a particular social ordering is achieved. But, as Latour emphasises, this is only until the cycle of the political starts up again, and the voices of all actants, old and new, are taken into account again.

While taking note of the possible service that AI can render to the two powers at work in the composition of the common world, the fundamental uncertainties that Latour take as his points of departure must again be emphasised. Misrepresentation and deception are also possible and are certainly also actual in the political process. AI can also amplify these forces, as has been amply illustrated in recent electoral processes. While noting this, I will not elaborate on it, and rather return to the original question of AI's place in a social world where a clear distinction between nature and culture does not hold water.

4   Whose Interests, Which Common Good – Hard Questions About Strong General AI

If Latour's deconstruction of the nature – culture binary rings true, then "the good", and per implication "the common good", cannot be a realm of human value lying over against an objective world of facts. Rather, to speak of the common good is another way of talking about the arrangement of the common world, and this is a world of constitutive uncertainty about who is speaking, who is acting, and, indeed, who should be accepted as existing at all.

This perspective allows us to raise doubts about Russell's proposal regarding the role of Artificial Intelligence in his book *Human Compatible*. Russell explicitly wants to define the common good as the human good, and correspondingly wants to re-orient the project of the achievement of general AI towards the achievement of AI that will always have goals that are beneficial to humans. To this end Russell proposes three principles that should guide AI researchers and developers in their work towards general AI: "1.) The machine's only objective is to maximize the realization of human preferences. 2.) The machine is initially uncertain about what those preferences are. 3.) The ultimate source of information about human preferences is human behaviour." (Russell 2019:176).

From a Latourian perspective, one would say about this proposal that it assumes the modernist watertight distinction between nature and culture. In this case it is a purportedly pure human nature that must be defended against human cultural products that have gained autonomy. But then one would have to reiterate with Latour that we have never been modern. There has never been a pure nature – also a pure human nature – that could short circuit the process of consultation, of listening, of weighing up the claims of humans as well as non-humans in their co-existence. We find ourselves with a constitutive uncertainty regarding the common good, including the good of human beings. According to Latour's conception, Russell is short circuiting the political ecology by appealing to a pure human nature that is simply given.

Interestingly, Russell acknowledges the uncertainty about what would constitute the human good at various instances in his book (e.g. 2019:23), but he nevertheless maintains that a practical, engineering kind of safety system must be put in place to ensure that the design of artificial intelligence would always follow human preferences (2019:188). Russell suggests that while humans are not always certain about what constitutes human flourishing, all humans would agree that being subservient to artificial super intelligence that is indifferent to human preferences will not be good. He therefore suggests that AI should be designed to have a constitutive uncertainty about human preferences and to always defer to humans about their preferences.

From his perspective of the common good as inextricably bound up with the common world, Latour might conceivably counter that the circle of the political process be allowed to take its course. Thus, Artificial Intelligence, just like any other actant, would arrive on the radar of the common world through its recalcitrance – it refuses to go away. This is definitely already the case with AI, and Russell admits as much in his book. Secondly, following Latour's imperatives, we would have to listen to and weigh up the case that AI makes for its inclusion in our commonwealth. Latour's generous understanding of agency will initially make things easier: if rising sea levels or a virus can have a voice in the political process, then AI certainly can as well. The advantage of Latour's imperative towards openness is also that it urges awareness. In the political process, we need to be aware of AI's presence. AI should not be allowed to become invisible and work in the background. The more we for instance become aware that AI tracks our preferences and tailors communication accordingly, the more we will weigh it up before accepting it.

The third imperative (part of the power to arrange in rank order) is to fit AI into the hierarchy of importance in the political process. In this case as well it cannot be all or nothing – either deny general AI a place in the hierarchy or capitulate and allow AI to pursue its own interests unchecked. There must be an ongoing process of negotiation and a keeping in mind of the unique contributions that humans and other actants can bring to the body politic.

Finally, Latour urges that the political process be stabilized, at least provisionally. In this regard one can think of the legislation and the various protocols and industry standards that must be in place with regard to AI in its present form. When AI develops into artificial general intelligence (AGI), this will have to be revisited and reformed for the next cycle of the political process.

In the case of the last imperative, Russell, of course, is afraid that the stabilization will be too little too late. Once a certain boundary is crossed, the development of AI will be out of human control and will go ahead according to its own goals. Russell, in other words, is worried that AI will become so powerful that it will take over the whole political process. All other actants will be effectively powerless in the face of AI's power, with the result that there will really be only one actant in town. Dave Eggers' novel *The Circle* provides a sketch of what the early stages of such a scenario could look like: people are effectively forced to live completely transparent lives, because the tiniest details of their lives are recorded and analysed and regulated (Eggers 2014; cf. Horvat 2019:47–50).

Latour would, of course, insist that the political process must be continuously disrupted. The circular process is an ongoing, give and take process. It cannot be smoothed over and managed by one sovereign. The smooth circle of Eggers' dystopia where AI becomes all powerful but recedes into the background, should not be allowed to happen. Rather, just like all other actants, AI's functioning should be noticed and weighed in the political process. The question, however, remains: what if AI becomes too powerful? This is indeed where Latour's proposal for a political ecology is vulnerable to critique. It has been suggested that Latour's model, if pressed to its consequences, falls back into power politics (Harman 2014:19). If the political process is one of negotiation, of garnering support for one's interests, of pressing others into service for ones aims, then the interest of the strongest, most convincing will prevail. In Russell's estimation there is a very real possibility that AI might emerge as the strongest to the detriment of humans in society.

In considering AI's place in Latour's *Politics of Nature* one is then, seemingly, left with the challenge to move beyond the current opposition of two unacceptable extremes. On the one hand a truth politics that assumes there is a pure human nature and definite human interests that must be protected against AI should be avoided. On the other hand, the alternative of a naked power politics must also be avoided because there is a very real possibility that super AI may emerge the most powerful. Latour's solution to the dilemma is that the circular movement of the political process should never be allowed to stall. The process cannot be short circuited by an appeal to a pure human nature and a purely human good. But equally the process must not be allowed to be hijacked by immensely powerful AGI. In this regard the question is whether humans can rediscover and optimize their own important and irreplaceable contributions to the common world which will ensure a dignified and flourishing place in this commonwealth.

References

Collins, H.M., Yearley, S.: Epistemological chicken. In: Pickering, A. (ed.) Science as Practice and Culture, pp. 301–326. The University of Chicago Press, Chicago and London (1992)

Eggers, D.: The Circle. Vintage, New York (2014)

Harman, G.: Prince of Networks: Bruno Latour and Metaphysics. Re.press, Melbourne (2009)

Harman, G.: Bruno Latour: Reassembling the Political, Kindle Edition. Pluto Press, London (2014)

Horvat, S.: Poetry from the Future. Penguin, London (2019)

Ihde, D., Malafouris, L.: Homo faber revisited: postphenomenology and material engagement theory. Philos. Technol. **32**, 195–214 (2019)

Latour, B.: Laboratory Life – The Construction of Scientific Facts, trans. Steve Woolgar. University Press, Princeton (1986)

Latour, B.: Science in Action – How to Follow Scientists and Engineers Through Society. Harvard University Press, Cambridge (1988)

Latour, B.: We Have Never Been Modern, trans. Catherine Porter. Harvard University Press, Cambridge (1993)

Latour, B.: Politics of Nature – How to Bring the Sciences into Democracy, trans. Catherine Porter. Harvard University Press, Cambridge (2004)

Pollini, J.: Bruno Latour and the ontological dissolution of nature in the social sciences: a critical review. Environ. Values **22**(1), 25–42 (2013)

Rorty, R.: Philosophy and the Mirror of Nature – Thirtieth Anniversary Edition. University Press, Princeton (2017)

Russell, S.: Human Compatible – Artificial Intelligence and the Problem of Control. Viking, London (2019)

Shah, R., et al.: Preferences implicit in the state of the world. In: Proceedings of the 7th International Conference on Learning Representations (2019). Available at iclr.cc/Conferences/2019/Schedule

Sohrabi, S., Riabov, A.V., Katz, M., Udrea, O.: An AI Planning Solution to Scenario Generation for Enterprise Risk Management. Association for the Advancement of Artificial Intelligence (2018)

Walsham, G.: Actor-Network Theory and IS research: current status and future prospects. In: Lee, A.S., Liebenau, J., DeGross, J.I. (eds.) Information Systems and Qualitative Research. Proceedings of the IFIP TC8 WG 8.2 International (1997)

The Quest for Actionable AI Ethics

Emma Ruttkamp-Bloem[1,2(✉)]

[1] Department of Philosophy, University of Pretoria, Pretoria, South Africa
emma.ruttkamp-bloem@up.ac.za
[2] Centre for AI Research (CAIR), Pretoria, South Africa

Abstract. In the face of the fact that AI ethics guidelines currently, on the whole, seem to have no significant impact on AI practices, the quest of AI ethics to ensure trustworthy AI is in danger of becoming nothing more than a nice ideal. Serious work is to be done to ensure AI ethics guidelines are actionable. To this end, in this paper, I argue that AI ethics should be approached 1) in a multi-disciplinary manner focused on concrete research in the discipline of the ethics of AI and 2) as a dynamic system on the basis of virtue ethics in order to work towards enabling all AI actors to take responsibility for their own actions and to hold others accountable for theirs. In conclusion, the paper emphasises the importance of understanding AI ethics as playing out on a continuum of interconnected interests across academia, civil society, public policy-making and the private sector, and a novel notion of 'AI ethics capital' is put on the table as outcome of actionable AI ethics and essential ingredient for sustainable trustworthy AI.

Keywords: AI ethics · Virtue ethics · Multi-disciplinary research · AI ethics capital · Trustworthy AI

1 Introduction

In this paper, I argue that in order to ensure that AI ethics is actionable, the approach to AI ethics should change in two novel ways. AI ethics should be firstly approached in a multi-disciplinary manner focused on concrete research in the discipline of the ethics of AI and secondly as a dynamic system on the basis of virtue ethics in order to work towards enabling all AI actors to take responsibility for their own actions and to hold others accountable for theirs. In conclusion, the paper emphasises the importance of understanding AI ethics as playing out on a continuum of interconnected interests across academia, civil society, public policy-making and the private sector (including private sector companies ranging from start-ups to small-and medium enterprises to large transnational companies). In addition, a novel notion of 'AI ethics capital' is put on the table as a core ingredient of trustworthy AI and an outcome of actionable AI ethics.

In the face of the relative ineffectiveness of a host of recent policy guidelines, including inter-governmental policies, national policies, professional policies, and

A. Gerber (Ed.): SACAIR 2020, CCIS 1342, pp. 34–50, 2020.
https://doi.org/10.1007/978-3-030-66151-9_3

policies generated in the private sector, there is a growing call from the AI community to increase the effectiveness of AI ethics guidelines[1]. Luciano Floridi [35] highlights the risks of not actionalising AI ethics guidelines in his article *Translating Principles into Practices of Digital Ethics*. He identifies five dangerous practices that may take root in a context in which AI ethics remains idealistic and removed from the every day working reality of the technical community, and which ultimately may work against actionable AI ethics: (1) Ethics shopping: there is confusion given the almost 100 sets of AI ethics policies available at present [3] "clear, shared, and publicly accepted ethical standards" [35]; (2) ethics bluewashing: pretending to work, or working superficially together towards establishing trustworthy AI instead of establishing "public, accountable, and evidence-based transparency about good practices and ethical claims" (ibid.) and ensuring AI and AI ethics literacy of all AI actors (including board members of private sector companies and government officials); (3) ethics lobbying: promoting self-regulation instead of introducing enforceable ethical and legal norms; (4) ethics dumping: "the export of unethical research practices to countries where there are weaker ... legal and ethical frameworks and enforcing mechanisms" (ibid.) as opposed to establishing a culture of research and consumption ethics; and (5) ethics shirking: weak execution of ethical duties given a perception of low returns on ethical adherence, instead of establishing clear lines of responsibility.

In his turn, Brent Mittelstadt [53] warns in an article entitled *Principles Alone cannot Guarantee Ethical AI*, that the "real" work of AI ethics only starts now that we are faced with a multitude of policies. This work is "to ... implement our lofty principles, and in doing so to begin to understand the real ethical challenges of AI" (ibid.). Thilo Hagendorff [43], in an article entitled *The Ethics of AI Ethics: An Evaluation of Ethical Guidelines*, concurs, and mentions the lack of mechanisms AI ethics has to "reinforce its own normative claims" (ibid. p. 99), the view of AI ethics guidelines as coming from "'outside' the technical community" (ibid. p. 114)[2], and the lack of "distributed responsibility in conjunction with a lack of knowledge about long-term or broader societal technological consequences causing software developers to lack a feeling of accountability or a view of the moral significance of their work" (ibid) as serious obstacles towards realising the 'lofty principles' of current AI ethics.

Some suggestions have been made to address the current 'inactive' status of AI ethics. These include advocating for and suggesting hands-on concrete suggestions for ethical machine learning from within the machine learning community itself[3] in terms of technical methods of addressing concerns around bias, transparency and accountability (see e.g. [31,58,74]); warnings about the con-

---

[1] See e.g. [18,28,35,40,43,46,51,53,58,61,72,74,83,87] for discussions from various points of view of the current state of affairs of AI ethics.

[2] For instance, 79% of tech workers would like practical guidance with considering, implementing and adhering to ethical guidelines [52].

[3] Acknowledgment of the work of the ethics and society branch of Deepmind, the Open AI initiative, and the FAT ML association is important in this regard.

sequences of ineffective ethical guidelines (see e.g. [35,40,43,53,83]); considering whether guidelines are converging on a global set of guidelines (see e.g. [38,46,65]) and whether or not that would somehow increase the punching power of AI ethics guidelines; developing tools or templates to evaluate compliance with ethical guidelines (see e.g. [1,5,6,36,47]); and collating best practice examples (see e.g. [53,58,74]); among many others. This paper contributes to this debate from a *philosophical* perspective. Based on a virtue ethics approach, it suggests a dynamic and participatory model for AI ethics that is informed by multidisciplinary research in the quest for actionable AI ethics.

More specifically, in what follows, in Sect. 2, a call for multi-disciplinary research as mechanism for grounding AI ethics and as a counter to the alienation of an increasingly commercially driven technical community is defended. In particular, it is suggested that the growing multi-disciplinary nature of the discipline of the ethics of AI, given the involvement of the technical community in research in the field, can enhance understanding among members of this community of the moral and ethical implications of the societal impact of AI technologies on human lives. Consequently, it is argued that, if AI ethics concerns and regulations were scaled down to the more concrete level of the ethics of AI such that the latter's state of the art multi-disciplinary content informs AI ethics, this would contribute to the action-ability of AI ethics.

In Sect. 3, the need to involve every AI actor across the spectrum ranging from government to civil society, to the private sector and academia in the AI ethics project is considered. Here, 'AI actor' means any entity involved in or impacted on by AI technologies in at least one stage of the AI lifecycle[4]. The term can refer both to natural and legal persons, and as such can refer to inidviduals such as researchers, programmers, engineers, data scientists, and end-users, and to large technology companies, small and medium enterprises, startups, universities, and public entities, among others.[5] It is argued that a virtue ethics approach to an AI ethics model as a complex and dynamic system of values has the potential to allow for all AI actors to participate in the AI ethics project and to take responsibility for their actions and hold others accountable for theirs, which would contribute to the action-ability of AI ethics.

In the conclusion of the paper, based on the arguments in the previous sections, a novel notion of 'AI ethics capital' is suggested as the outcome of actionable AI ethics and essential ingredient for sustainable trustworthy AI. It is argued that the concept of AI ethics capital should be understood as a subset of the newly suggested concept of national AI capital [54], and may be measured by means of a potential global AI ethics adherence index.

---

[4] The AI system lifecycle is taken to range at least from research, design, development, deployment to use ("including maintenance, operation, trade, financing, monitoring and evaluation, validation, end-of-use, disassembly, and termination" [78]).

[5] This definition is based on the one given in the UNESCO First Draft of the Recommendation on the Ethics of AI [78].

2 Grounding AI Ethics Through Multi-disciplinary Research

In order for AI ethics to have practical impact on AI practices, it is clear that AI research, design and development should not take place in "closed-door industry settings", where "frictionless functionality that supports profit-driven business models" ([18] p. 31 ff.) is the only name of the game due to fierce commercially driven competition for the best AI technology (see e.g. [37, 43]). In response, in this section, state of the art (current) multi-disciplinary research is suggested as a counter to commercial values driving advancement in AI technologies on the one hand, and feelings of alienation from AI ethics among members of the technical community on the other.

In general, there are many reasons for placing multi-disciplinary research at the centre of discussions of increasing the impact of AI ethics guidelines. I highlight two here. First, a practical reason, already put firmly on the table by [58] is that "enabling the so-called dual advantage of 'ethical ML' – so that the opportunities are capitalised on, whilst the harms are foreseen and minimised or prevented ... – requires asking difficult questions about design, development, deployment, practices, uses and users, as well as the data that fuel the whole life-cycle of algorithms ...". And, what is needed to respond to these questions is input from "multi-disciplinary researchers, innovators, policymakers, citizens, developers and designers" (ibid. p. 3).

Secondly, current human reality is not reflecting or living up to the goals, values and principles of AI ethics, and thus, the data generated and collected in this reality are far removed from the lofty ideals of AI ethics, which is a problem, given that data 'fuels' the AI system lifecycle. This is one of the most simple reasons (apart form more technical ones) why AI is at risk of being biased, or built on unequal knowledge systems and unequal cultural, geographical, gender and age representation and has the potential to cause serious social harm and even political instability. So, the point is that ethical problems do not (only) lie within the technical aspects of the research, design, development, deployment and use of the AI based systems, but also (mostly, albeit seldomly acknowledged) already in the 'real' world giving rise to the outcomes generated by such systems and in which such outcomes are applied. This is an essential motivation for concretising AI ethics by viewing it as a microcosm of our lived realities (a notion unpacked in more detail in the next section), and highlights the need for multi-disciplinary research – ranging from technical disciplines to social sciences – to inform AI ethics as well as to translate the long term ethical consequences of AI technologies into concrete terms for the technical community (the focus of this section).

In particular, the suggestion in this section is that the multi-disciplinary explosion of the scope of the discipline of the ethics of AI reflects the potential impact of AI technologies on human societies and political stability in a manner to which the technical community may be more open as it is more concrete to them because this discipline includes them. Members of the technical community themselves contribute to the ethics of AI in various roles, from software developing, to robotics, to computer engineering and data management. Thus, the argument here is that if state of the art multi-disciplinary knowledge of the growing scope of the discipline of the ethics of AI informs AI ethics guidelines, these will be in step with current AI technology advancement as well as more actionable, and, as such, being closer to the lived experiences of members of the technical community, also more effective to counter commercial interests.

Many calls for multi-disciplinarity have been heard in AI ethics conversations (e.g. [29,58]) but none has specifically focused on the multi-disciplinary nature of the ethics of AI to clarify the long term societal consequences of actions of AI technologies in a manner that draws the technical community (and civil society I might add) into the AI ethics fold. I therefore suggest here that the multi-disciplinary nature of the ethics of AI should be reflected in the content of AI ethics in order to keep the ideals of AI ethics grounded and inclusive both of technical and social dimensions. Furthermore, the ethics of AI is built on respect for disciplines as diverse as philosophy and computer science, as anthropology and statistics, as political and legal sciences and mathematics. If this same mutual multi-disciplinary respect can drive the technical community's response to AI ethics, there is a much better chance of AI ethics being actionable, as there would be mutual respect for the understanding of the full impact of AI technologies on society, and thus mutual commitment to AI ethics.

These suggestions relate strongly to Hagendorff's ([43] p. 111) argument that "in order to analyze AI ethics in sufficient depth, ethics has to partially transform to 'microethics'. This means that at certain points, a substantial change in the level of abstraction has to happen ... On the way from ethics to 'microethics', a transformation from ethics to technology ethics, to machine ethics, to computer ethics, to information ethics, to data ethics has to take place" (ibid.). And, I argue, it is in this transformation to more concrete levels that AI ethics becomes accessible to the technical community. The reason for this, as alluded to above already, is that every sub-discipline of the ethics of AI (data ethics, robot ethics, machine ethics, information ethics, computational ethics, etc.) is informed by a different combination of disciplines such as computer science, mathematics, sociology, philosophy, anthropology, political sciences, law, etc.

But what is the ethics of AI? It may be divided into machine and computing ethics issues on the one hand and the impact of AI advances on society on the other hand (e.g. [9,59]), although the lines are not exclusive (e.g. [50,85]). Sometimes the ethics of AI is referred to as computer ethics, as in Moor's ([55] p. 266) description of computer ethics as the "analysis of the nature and social impact of computer technology and the corresponding formulation and justification of policies for the ethical use of technology", thus, at least from the perspective of this paper, incorporating AI ethics into the discipline of the ethics of AI. In order to ground AI ethics and make it more accessible to members of the technical community (and civil society), I suggest AI ethics here as the domain focused on policymaking based on the concerns raised in each of the subfields of the ethics of AI.

Part of why there are different approaches to defining the discipline of the ethics of AI is the fact that it has crystallised into at least the (non-exclusive) subfields of machine ethics, data or algorithm ethics, robot ethics, information ethics, and neuro-ethics. Machine ethics focuses on the ethics of the design of artificial moral decision making capacities and socio-moral analyses of the concept of artificial morality (see e.g. [4,8,16,17,56,85]) Gunkel ([42] p. 101) distinguishes between computer ethics and machine ethics: "computer ethics ... is concerned ... with questions of human action through the instrumentality of computers and related information systems. In clear distinction from these efforts, machine ethics seeks to enlarge the scope of moral agents by considering the ethical status and actions of machines". In these terms, machine ethics is concerned with "ethics *for* machines, for 'ethical machines', for machines as subjects, rather than for the human use of machines as objects" [59], as the latter is the focus of robot ethics and also relates to computer ethics as defined above (see also [71]). Another option [69] is to refine machine ethics into thinking separately about technical aspects of computational tractability (computational ethics) and thinking about the ethics of machines with moral agency (machine ethics).

Robot ethics, or also known as the ethics of social robots, is focused on the impact of social robots on society (e.g. [64]), on human-robot interaction (HRI), on the anthropomorphisation of robots and the objectification of humans, and robot rights (see e.g. [10,13,15,30,42,70]) and also may be broken into focusing separately on AI-AI interaction, AI-human interaction and AI-society interaction (see [71]). Furthermore, the ethics of social robots may also be incorporated into robo-ethics, which is "concerned with the moral behaviour of humans as they design, construct, use and interact with AI agents" (ibid.) (see also [82]). In his turn, Asaro ([9] p. 10) argues that the field which he calls 'robot ethics', is focused on the ethical systems built into robots (focuses on robots as ethical subjects and relates to machine ethics and thus sometimes machine ethics is viewed as a subset of robot ethics); the ethics of people who design and use robots (focuses on humans as ethical subjects and relates to robo-ethics and computer ethics); and the ethics of how people treat robots (focuses on ethical interaction and relates to what is sometimes called the ethics of social robots). Asaro (ibid. p. 11) argues that the best approach to robot ethics is one that addresses all three of these and that views robots as *socio*-technical systems.

Data ethics is centered on issues around fair, accountable and transparent machine learning or co-called 'critical machine learning', socio-technical analyses of machine learning practices and their impact on society, and responsible data governance (see e.g. [12,39,81]). As such, it is a "branch of ethics that studies and evaluates moral problems related to algorithms (including artificial intelligence, artificial agents, machine learning and robots) and corresponding practices (including responsible innovation, programming, hacking and professional codes), in order to formulate and support morally good solutions (e.g.. right conducts or right values)" ([39] p. 1). Information ethics, in its turn, relates to data and algorithm ethics on the one hand, and on ethical elements of media and information governance, such as the impact of miss-and disin-formation on society and political stability (see e.g. [27,41,45]), on the other. Finally, neuro-ethics is focused broadly on the hard problems of consciousness [19][6] and how they relate to the everyday folk concept of the human 'mind'. The focus is on metaphysical and ethical conditions for mind-uploading (see, e.g. [14,20,26,62,68,86]); Clark and Chalmers' [24] concept of the extended mind (see e.g. [2,22,23,60,73]), trans-humanism (see e.g. [21,44]), and cyborg rights and identity (see e.g. [32,66,67,84].)

It is clear from the above that the discipline of the ethics of AI indicates concerns with issues of human dignity, human agency, consciousness, freedom of expression and the right to information, morality, personhood, personal identity, the quality and nature of social relationships, and rights such as privacy, own-ership and non-discrimination, among many others. All of these concerns – and their consequences – should be mirrored concretely in AI ethics guidelines and policies and their roots in different disciplines acknowledged. And, given this multi-disciplinary scope of the ethics of AI, my argument is that the content of AI ethics will be less 'lofty', more actionable, and more concretely communica-ble, if informed by state of the art research on these concerns in the ethics of AI, as members of the technical community are involved in this research them-selves. Moreover, the multi-disciplinary scope of the ethics of AI brings home to every AI actor, from members of civil society to software engineers, the full impact of AI technologies on human lives. Viewing AI ethics in this manner as an active domain in step with (as opposed to always lagging behind) the advances of AI technologies reflected in the subfields of the ethics of AI, allows the multi-disciplinary research driving the latter to become both an explanation and an affirmation of the concerns covered by AI ethics and confirms calls for the latter's status as a microcosm of human reality in all its social, political, economic, and philosophical dimensions (e.g. [53]). This brings us to the next section in which a participative model for AI ethics is introduced.

3   A Participative Dynamic Model for Actionable AI Ethics

While it is essential to involve the technical community in order to turn inactive AI ethics to actionable AI ethics, as argued in the previous section, involving the members of civil society is equally important. Given that one of the indicators of the current exponential growth in AI adoption is the increasing "consumer readiness to consume AI in all of its forms" ([25] p. 8), ordinary members of civil society can and should play an important role in demanding and ensur-ing actionable AI ethics. In this section, the focus is on suggesting a model for AI ethics that satisfies the need to involve every AI actor across the spectrum, ranging from government to civil society to the private sector and academia.

---

[6] This is basically the problem of why consciousness occurs at all, combined with the problem of explaining subjective experience, or the 'feeling what it is like'.

Humans are vulnerable to potential new harms generated by AI technologies in every dimension of their lives and should take responsibility to protect themselves, which is why it is so important to involve every AI actor in the AI ethics project in a practical participative role. Our vulnerability is exacerbated by the fact that humans do not necessarily by default hold a central role in "the world of information and smart agency" ([33] p. 10).

The implications of this realisation of human vulnerability echoes Sherry Turkle's [76,77] decades old warning that the integration of technology into human society not only alters human potential but also transforms human characteristics and consciousness. Therefore, we should not ask (or not only ask) what will technology be like in the future, but also we should consider what humans will be like in a future at least partly structured by AI technology – what are we becoming and what wil be our role in society in the future? Considering this question places a real responsibility on every human[7] to become involved and to participate in the project of AI ethics and echoes in the educational, scientific, cultural and communication and information contexts of our lives.

What to do? It is clear that we need human wisdom to guide our actions [64], but what does that mean? We need careful, strong and rigorous philosophical thinking to guide us here as we have to rethink the entire project of philosophy[8] over centuries and this time there is a real urgency to this project, given the need to address the vulnerability of human society in the face of possible harm from AI technologies, while maximising the benefit of AI technology for humanity and ensuring this benefit is shared equitably.

Furthermore, it is clear that reacting positively to AI ethics guidelines does not only lie with governments, intergovernmental bodies, big tech companies or law enforcement. Specifically, the role of civil society in driving the success of actionable AI ethics has not received close to enough attention. There is not only alienation from the abstract ideals of AI ethics on the side of the technical community but also on the side of civil society, while the latter is actually as powerful a set of players in the AI ethics project as members of the technical community are. Members of civil society should play an active role in holding technical companies accountable for the systems they design, develop, and deploy, and holding government accountable for their use of AI in law enforcement, healthcare, education, and other policy areas. In addition, the public also has a responsibility to hold themselves accountable for how they use such systems.

---

[7] As it was made clear in the Introduction that 'AI actor' can here refer to either individuals such as designers or users, as well as to companies, this focus on individual human actors needs qualification. The focus in this section is indeed at the individual level, but the role of companies as AI actors in actionable AI ethics does not fall away, as the idea is that the participation in the AI ethics project of individuals employed by AI technology companies will 'filter up' so that companies also become involved in the AI ethics project and hold each other accountable.

[8] Referring here to the project focused on the human condition and what it means to be human, taken up by philosophers of all traditions and nationalities from ancient times to the present.

One high level way in which to sensitise civil society to AI ethics, is to ensure that the values and ethical standards embodied in AI ethics guidelines are shared values. Focusing on 'intrinsic' values, as opposed to 'extrinsic' values may be a good beginning. Judgements of intrinsic value are evaluations of things that have value for their own sake, while extrinsic values get their value from their function or how they fit into a bigger system (see e.g. [11,57,75]) Intrinsic values include human life, freedom, peace, security, harmony, friendship, social justice, etc. The rationale behind emphasising intrinsic values is that such values are respected universally, given their intrinsic nature, but more importantly, that non-buy-in to these values is detrimental to everyone, and is perhaps most felt at the level of ordinary citizens as the most vulnerable of AI actors. And this is what civil society should be sensitised to grasp. Furthermore, given the international legal stature of international human rights law, principles, and standards, a human rights perspective in AI ethics guidelines may not only strengthen the potential for legal enforcement, but again is also a way in which to establish common grounds for AI ethics standards (see e.g. [25,48,63]) and ensuring every member of civil society understands the consequences of not adhering to AI ethics guidelines. These perspectives alone are however not concrete enough.

What is needed in addition, is to bring home to civil society that the disruptiveness of AI technology impacts on every sphere of human lives, that 'being human' and enjoying fundamental freedoms are in danger of coming under increased control of AI technologies, and, perhaps most importantly, to ensure that there are safeguards against 'moral de-skilling' by technology. In an article entitled *Moral Deskilling and Upskilling in a New Machine Age: Reflections on the Ambiguous Future of Character* [79], Shannon Vallor warns that "... moral skills appear just as vulnerable to disruption or devaluation by technology-driven shifts in human practices as are professional or artisanal skills such as machining, shoemaking, or gardening. This is because moral skills are typically acquired in specific practices, which, under the right conditions and with sufficient opportunity for repetition, foster the cultivation of practical wisdom and moral habituation that jointly constitute genuine virtue. ... profound technological shifts in human practices, if they disrupt or reduce the availability of these opportunities, can interrupt the path by which these moral skills are developed, habituated, and expressed" (ibid. p. 109).

On the one hand, this points to the need for strong campaigns driving *both* AI fundamentals and AI ethics literacy given that society "has greater control than it has ever had over outcomes related to (1) who people become; (2) what people can [or may] do; (3) what people can achieve, and (4) how people can interact with the world" ([58] p. 1). In other words, civil society should become aware and have a basic understanding of the potential of some AI technologies to threaten fundamental freedoms and change the moral fibre of societies.

On the other hand, we should ensure that trust in technology does not have the upper hand, *by ensuring that we can legitimately trust in humans and their abilities*. There is thus a responsibility that comes with protecting human dignity, human oversight and human centeredness, i.e. of fighting for 'AI with a human face'. It is an individual and universal responsibility of each and every AI actor to ensure they are the best humans they can be, and that they act – and are able to act – within the confines of regulations on the ethics of AI. Willingness to take up this responsibility is crucial to the success of any instrument of AI ethics, which brings us to considering the model of AI ethics that is suggested in this section to induce 'actionable' AI ethics. This model of AI ethics involves all AI actors in such a way that they actively participate in the quest for ethically acceptable AI rather than just react to a set of guidelines, and is not focused on technology, but on the actions of humans involved or impacted on by technology.

AI ethics should be recognised as an adaptive process and not thought of or approached in terms of technological solutions only, since it is necessary to recognise that "AI Ethics is effectively a microcosm of the political and ethical challenges faced in society" [53] at a given time. In his turn, Hagendorff ([43] pp. 111–112) reminds that implementation of AI ethics guidelines happen in "a widely diversified set of scientific, technical and economic practices, and in sometimes geographically dispersed groups of researchers and developers with different priorities, tasks and fragmental responsibilities" (ibid.). Thus, while it is very important to develop and constantly update technical tools to assist with the design and development of algorithms as AI technology advances, as noted for instance by [58,74], as well as a host of other writers recently, it is equally important to understand that the disciplinary, geo-political, and economic challenges both as generators of data fueling the AI lifecycle on the one hand, and the result of AI applications on the other hand, are diverse and also constantly changing. To deal with these contextual and temporal aspects of the AI lifecycle, ethical impact assessment instruments and also due diligence measures are crucial as they can be employed continuously, and have the potential to ensure full participation in implementation of AI ethics guidelines, because of their potential to clearly point out the possible harms of a certain AI technology for a certain sector of society at a given time.

But this is not enough to get every AI actor involved. I argue that what is needed in addition to deal with these temporal and contextual characteristics of the lifecycle of AI technologies, is a comprehensive participative model of AI ethics that is built on responsible interconnected participation of all AI actors and that is adaptable to advances of AI technology and to social and political contexts, and that allows every individual AI actor to manage their own moral sensitivity on a continuous basis (see footnote 7 again). I believe the most promising way in which to actualise such a model of AI ethics is to extend Hagendorff's [43] call for a move away from deontological, rule-based approaches in AI ethics (see also [53]) to a virtue ethics approach.

Virtue ethics points to a lifelong journey of striving to be the most virtuous person one can be – this implies being acutely aware of what one is becoming (think back to Turkle's warning). Aristotle, in Book III of the *Nichomachean Ethics*, makes clear that he differs from Plato on the nature of virtue: Virtue is not the result of abstract understanding of what is truly good for us, rather it is the result of training and habit. A virtue ethics approach to AI ethics is thus not focused on universal codes of conduct or abstract guidelines (Hagendorff [43]), but on the individual level at which everyone in society has a duty to ensure that they themselves, as well as everyone else and the companies that employ them and that are AI actors in their turn, *are able* to be/to become the best possible moral version of themselves. Moreover, virtuous actions involve the rational consideration of and deliberation about consequences, rather than some form of external justification (such as commercial gain). To make a decision after deliberating over it, implies one has taken into account all of the possibilities that the outcome could be in a given context, and this forces one to dig deep into one's beliefs, to consider all consequences of one's beliefs and to decide whether or not - *and why* - one is going to follow certain beliefs and not others.

Hagendorff ([43] p. 112) makes clear that the value of such an approach in the context of AI ethics is that it is focused on "situation-specific deliberations, on addressing personality traits and behavioral dispositions on the part of technology developers ... The technologists or software engineers and their social context are the primary addressees of such an ethics, not technology itself" (see also e.g. [7,49]). But, it is more than that. Such an approach also offers a way in which to pick up on the responsibility pointed to above of every individual AI actor to be the best person they can be and take responsibility for their design, development and use of AI systems, while holding private sector software companies and governments accountable for their deployment of AI technologies.[9] This is so, since on Aristotle's model, a virtue ethics approach implies that everyone in society – families, schools, communities, as well as business (ibid., p. 113) – should work to cultivate a virtuous life. In the context of AI ethics this implies "generating the motivation [among all AI actors] to adopt and habituate practices that influence technology development and use in a positive manner" (ibid.). Important here is Shannon Valor's [80] work on the kind of techno-moral virtues humans need to cultivate in order to ensure they flourish as a result of emerging technologies, rather than simply adapting passively to such technologies.

Furthermore, the focus in Aristotelian virtue ethics is precisely on how to harness intellectual and moral virtues together to ensure a virtuous life. Thus, the focus is on "techno-moral virtues such as honesty, justice, courage, empathy, care, civility" ([43] p. 113). This picks up on Morley et al.'s [58] call for a movement from 'what' to 'how' that addresses "practice, the good and the just" (ibid. p. 11), and also on calls by [29] for AI ethics to focus "as much on people than on code" ([58] p. 2). Approaching AI ethics as a virtue ethics therefore brings together the necessary focus on "technical discourses" ([43] p. 114) as well as the "genuinely social and personality-related aspects" (ibid.) of adhering to AI ethics guidelines. It also addresses the danger of moral deskilling [79,80], as every AI actor is actively involved in taking up their own ethical responsibilities and constantly works on bettering their rational decision-making abilities in the moral context. The fact that the right thing to do is the result of rigorous and

---

[9] Compare Floridi's [34] argument that every actor who is "causally relevant for bringing about the collective consequences or impacts in question, has to be held accountable" ([43] p. 113).

honest rational deliberation on a case-by-case basis also means that this approach can deal with the fluidity of changing societal and political structures as well as the pace of AI technological advancement. In this way, AI ethics is then less about disciplining AI actors to adhere to ethical guidelines, and more about positive self-realisation of moral responsibilities as this model "emancipate[s AI actors] from potential inabilities to act self-responsibly on the basis of comprehensive knowledge, as well as empathy in situations where morally relevant decisions have to be made" (ibid. p. 114).

Only if every AI actor understands *why* regulating the life cycle of AI systems is necessary and sees their own role in this process, can the AI ethics project hope to be successful. The potential for meeting these objectives within a participatory virtue ethics approach to AI ethics as a dynamic ethical system should be clear.

4 Conclusion

The call for addressing the lack of impact of AI ethics on tech communities is real. In this paper, a novel participatory model for AI ethics based on a virtue ethics approach to AI ethics and underpinned by state of the art multi-disciplinary research and collaboration concretely anchored in research in the discipline of the ethics of AI has been suggested. Such an approach may do much to change the negative conception of AI ethics as stifling innovation by "broadening the scope of action, uncovering blind spots, promoting autonomy and freedom, and fostering self-responsibility" ([43] pp. 112–113). In addition, this approach can deal positively with the concern raised by Morley et al. [58] that, "in a digital context, ethical principles are not simply either applied or not, but regularly re-applied or applied differently, or better, or ignored as algorithmic systems are developed, deployed, configured ... tested, revised and re-tuned..." (ibid. p. 18), as it allows for AI ethics as a dynamic adaptive ethical system within which it is active cultivation of techno-moral virtues, rational deliberation among all AI actors and mutual respect for concrete multi-disciplinary research that guide ethical decisions.

In conclusion, let us consider what the implications for the concept of trustworthy AI are, should we meet the quest for actionable AI in the terms described above. First, trustworthiness becomes a socio-technical concept, focused as much on the safety and robustness of AI technologies as it is on respect for every individual human AI actor. In this context, given the active role of AI actors in the AI ethics project, and their shared responsibility to action-alise AI ethics, trust becomes a benchmark for the social acceptance of AI technologies. Thus, there will be good reason to trust that AI technology brings benefits while adequate measures are taken to mitigate risks, as the trust at issue is not only in technology but trust in the actions of AI actors actively involved in contributing to the dynamic model of AI ethics.[10]

---

[10] See the first version of the UNESCO First Draft of the Recommendation on the Ethics of AI [78].

But, secondly, it becomes clear that trustworthy AI itself should be an adaptive concept given the fast pace at which AI technologies advance and the adaptive nature of AI ethics argued for here. To capture the adaptive nature of the concept of trustworthy AI, I suggest introducing a concept of *AI ethics capital* (AIEC) as outcome of the participative model of AI ethics, girded by state of the art multi-disciplinary research, argued for in this paper. This notion of AIEC is related to the notion of national AI capital (NAIC), suggested by Momčilović [54]. The concept of NAIC links to the Organisation for Economic Cooperation and Development's notion of human capital[11] as the "knowledge, skills, competencies and characteristics of individuals that facilitate the creation of personal, social and economic wellbeing" https://medium.com/@acomomcilovic/introducing-concept-national-ai-capital-a233832796c1.

National AI capital is a "country's capacity to apply and develop, and cope with the challenges of various artificial intelligence systems, in order to increase the country's social and economic well-being and competitiveness" (ibid.). I suggest that a subset of NAIC is the AI ethics capital (AIEC) of a country as the state of the art multi-disciplinary knowledge, skills, and competencies of individual AI actors, which drive individual AI actors' ethical habits and inform a country's AI ethics guidelines; which as such, in their turn, facilitate the creation of personal, social and economic wellbeing as a result of the potential of harmonious and ethical co-existence of humans with technology thus created. Measuring AIEC may seem difficult from a quantitative perspective, but it can, for now, be correlated with the level of adherence to AI ethics guidelines on a global index of AI ethics, alluded to as one incentive for AI ethics adherence in the UNESCO First Draft of the Recommendation on the Ethics of AI [78].

The above points to the urgent need for future research in AI ethics as well as exploring cooperation among all AI actors at all stages of the AI technology lifecycle in the name of actionable AI ethics to find workable counters against potential new harms coming from AI technologies. Again here, more engagement with Vallor's [80] ideas on "a future worth wanting" will be enlightening. For now, it is worthwhile to note, given that portraying AI ethics as a static concept seems almost a category mistake in the context of the fast pace of AI advancement, a notion of an equally non-static core ingredient of trustworthy AI, namely AIEC, generated both by AI technological and ethical advancement (due to a participative adaptive model of AI ethics), seems like an essential element of a successful approach to engage with the wide scope of constantly changing challenges AI actors and AI ethicists are confronted with on a daily basis.

References

1. Abdul, A., Vermeulen, J., Wang, D.: Trends and trajectories for explainable, accountable and intelligible systems: an HCI research agenda. In: Proceedings of the 2018 CHI Conference on Human Factors in Computing Systems - CHI, vol. 18, pp. 1–18 (2018). https://doi.org/10.1145/3173574.3174156

---

[11] https://www.oecd.org/insights/humancapital-thevalueofpeople.htm.

2. Adams, F., Aizawa, K.: The Bounds of Cognition, 2nd edn. Blackwell, Oxford (2010)
3. Algorithm-Watch: AI ethics global inventory. https://inventory.algorithmwatch.org/. Accessed 20 Sept 2020
4. Allen, C., Varner, G., Zinser, J.: Prolegomena to any future artificial moral agent. J. Exp. Theor. Artif. Intell. **12**(3), 251–261 (2000). https://doi.org/10.1080/09528130050111428
5. Alshammari, M., Simpson, A.: Towards a principled approach for engineering privacy by design. In: Schweighofer, E., Leitold, H., Mitrakas, A., Rannenberg, K. (eds.) APF 2017. LNCS, vol. 10518, pp. 161–177. Springer, Cham (2017). https://doi.org/10.1007/978-3-319-67280-9_9
6. Anabo, I., Elexpuru-Albizuri, I., Villardón-Gallego, L.: Revisiting the Belmont report's ethical principles in internet-mediated research: perspectives from disciplinary associations in the social sciences. Ethics Inf. Technol. **21**(2), 137–149 (2019). https://doi.org/10.1007/s10676-018-9495-z
7. Ananny, M.: Toward an ethics of algorithms: Convening, observation, probability, and timeliness. Sci. Technol. Hum. Values **41**(1), 93–117 (2016)
8. Anderson, M., Anderson, S.: Machine ethics: creating an ethical intelligent agent. AI Mag. **28**(4), 15–26 (2007)
9. Asaro, P.: What should we want from a robot ethic? Int. Rev. Inf. Ethics **6**(12), 9–16 (2006)
10. Asaro, P.: A body to kick, but still no soul to damn: legal perspectives. In: Lin, P., Abney, K., Bekey, G.A. (eds.) Robot Ethics: The Ethical and Social Implications of Robotics, pp. 169–186. MIT Press, Cambridge (2012)
11. Audi, R.: Intrinsic value and reasons for action. Southern J. Philos. **41**, 30–56 (2003)
12. Barocas, S., Selbst, A.: Big data's disparate impact. Calif. Law Rev. **104**, 671–732 (2016)
13. Bekey, A.: Current trends in robotics: technology and ethics. In: Lin, P., Abney, K., Bekey, G. (eds.) Robot Ethics: The Ethical and Social Implications of Robotics, pp. 17–34. MIT Press, Cambridge (2012)
14. Benedikter, R., Siepmann, K., Reymann, A.: Head-transplanting' and 'mind-uploading': philosophical implications and potential social consequences of two medico-scientific utopias. Rev. Contemp. Philos. **16**, 38–82 (2017)
15. Boden, M., Bryson, J., Caldwell, D.: Principles of robotics: regulating robots in the real world. Connect. Sci. **29**(2), 124–129 (2017)
16. Bostrom, N., Yudkowsky, E.: The ethics of artificial intelligence. In: Frankish, K., Ramsey, W. (eds.) The Cambridge Handbook of Artificial Intelligence, pp. 316–334. Cambridge University Press, Cambridge (2014)
17. Brundage, M.: Limitations and risks of machine ethics. J. Exp. Theor. Artif. Intell. **26**(3), 355–372 (2014)
18. Campolo, A.: AI now 2017 report (2017). https://assets.ctfassets.net/8wprhhvnpfc0/1A9c3ZTCZa2KEYM64Wsc2a/8636557c5fb14f2b74b2be64c3ce0c78/_AI_Now_Institute_2017_Report_.pdf
19. Chalmers, D.: Facing up to the problem of consciousness. J. Consciousness Stud. **2**, 200–19 (1995)
20. Chalmers, D.: The singularity: a philosophical analysis. J. Consciousness Stud. **17**(9–10), 7–65 (2010)
21. Clark, A.: Natural-Born Cyborgs: Minds, Technologies, and the Future of Human Intelligence. Oxford University Press, Oxford (2003)

22. Clark, A.: Intrinsic content, active memory and the extended mind. Analysis **65**(1), 1–11 (2005)
23. Clark, A.: The frozen cyborg: a reply to selinger and engström. Phenomenol. Cogn. Sci. **7**, 343–346 (2008). https://doi.org/10.1007/s11097-008-9105-3
24. Clark, A., Chalmers, D.: The extended mind. Analysis **58**, 7–19 (1998). https://doi.org/10.1093/analys/58.1.7
25. Comninos, A.: Fabrics: Emerging AI readiness (2018)
26. Corabi, J., Schneider, S.: The metaphysics of mind uploading. J. Consciousness Stud. **19**(7–8), 26–44 (2012)
27. Couldry, N., Hepp, A.: The Mediated Construction of Reality. Polity Press, Cambridge (2017)
28. Crawford, K.: The AI now report: the social and economic implications of artificial intelligence technologies in the near-term (2016). https://artificialintelligencenow.com
29. Crawford, K., Calo, R.: There is a blind spot in AI research. Nature **538**(7625), 311–313 (2016)
30. Danaher, J.: The philosophical case for robot friendship. J. Posthuman Stud. **3**(1), 5–24 (2019). https://doi.org/10.5325/jpoststud.3.1.0005
31. Diakopoulos, N.: Algorithmic accountability: journalistic investigation of computational power structures. Digit. Journal. **3**(3), 398–415 (2015). https://doi.org/10.1080/21670811.2014.976411
32. Eliasmith, C.: How to Build a Brain: A Neural Architecture for Biological Cognition. Oxford University Press, Oxford (2013)
33. Floridi, L.: The Online Manifesto: Being Human in a Hyper Connected Era. Springer, Heidelberg (2015). https://doi.org/10.1007/978-3-319-04093-6
34. Floridi, L.: Faultless responsibility: on the nature and allocation of moral responsibility for distributed moral actions. Philos. Trans. Ser. A Math. Phys. Eng. Sci. **374**(2083), 1–13 (2016)
35. Floridi, L.: Establishing the rules for building trustworthy AI. Nat. Mach. Intell. **1**, 261–262 (2019). https://doi.org/10.1038/s42256-019-0055-y
36. Floridi, L.: Translating principles into practices of digital ethics: five risks of being unethical. Philos. Technol. **32**, 185–193 (2019). https://doi.org/10.1007/s13347-019-00354-x
37. Floridi, L., Cowls, J.: AI4People - an ethical framework for a good AI society: opportunities, risks, principles, and recommendations. Minds Mach. **28**(4), 689–707 (2018)
38. Floridi, L., Cowls, J.: A unified framework of five principles for AI in society. Harvard Data Sci. Rev. **1**(1) (2019). https://doi.org/10.1162/99608f92.8cd550d1
39. Floridi, L., Taddeo, M.: What is data ethics? Philos. Trans. Roy. Soc. A Math. Phys. Eng. Sci. **374**(2083) (2016). https://doi.org/10.1098/rsta.2016.0360
40. Green, B.: Ethical reflections on artificial intelligence. Scientia et Fides **6**(2) (2018). https://doi.org/10.12775/SetF.2018.015
41. Greenhill, K., Oppenheim, B.: Rumor has it: the adoption of unverified information in conflict zones. Int. Stud. Q. **61**(3), 660–676 (2017). https://doi.org/10.1093/isq/sqx015
42. Gunkel, D.: The Machine Question: Critical Perspectives on AI, Robots, and Ethics. MIT Press, Cambridge (2012)
43. Hagendorff, T.: The ethics of AI ethics: an evaluation of guidelines. Minds Mach. **30**, 99–120 (2020). https://doi.org/10.1007/s11023-020-09517-8
44. Hansell, G.: H+/-: Transhumanism and Its Critics. Xlibris Corporation (2011)

45. Innes, M., Dobreva, D., Innes, H.: Disinformation and digital influencing after terrorism: spoofing, truthing and social proofing. Contemp. Soc. Sci. (2019). https:// doi.org/10.1080/21582041.2019.1569714
46. Jobin, A., Ienca, M., Vayena, E.: The global landscape of AI ethics guidelines. Nat. Mach. Intell. **1**, 389–399 (2019). https://doi.org/10.1038/s42256-019-0088-2
47. Kroll, J.: The fallacy of inscrutability. Philos. Trans. Roy. Soc. A Math. Phys. Eng. Sci. **376**(2133) (2018). https://doi.org/10.1098/rsta.2018.0084
48. Latonero, M.: Governing artificial intelligence: upholding human rights & dignity'. Data and Society, USC (2018)
49. Leonelli, S.: Locating ethics in data science: responsibility and accountability in global and distributed knowledge production systems. Philos. Trans. Roy. Soc. A (2016). https://doi.org/10.1098/rsta.2016.0122
50. Lin, P., Abney, K., Bekey , G.A.: Robot Ethics. The Ethical and Social Implications of Robot Ethics. MIT Press, Cambridge (2012)
51. McNamara, A., Smith, J., Murphy-Hill, E.: Does ACM's code of ethics change ethical decision making in software development? In: Leavens, G., Garcia, A., Păsăreanu, C. (eds.) Proceedings of the 2018 26th ACM Joint Meeting on European Software Engineering Conference and Symposium on the Foundations of Software Engineering-ESEC/FSE 2018, pp. 1–7. ACM Press, New York (2018)
52. Miller, C., Coldicott, R.: People: power and technology: the tech workers' view (2019). https://doteveryone.org.uk/report/workersview/. Retrieved from Doteveryone website
53. Mittelstadt, B.: Principles alone cannot guarantee ethical AI. Nat. Mach. Intell. **1**, 501–507 (2019). https://doi.org/10.1038/s42256-019-0114-4
54. Momčilović, A. (2020). https://www.ssbm.ch/blog/naic-foundations-is-human-capital-the-only-thing-becoming-and-remaining-important-by-aco-momcilovic-emba/. Accessed 21 Sept 2020
55. Moor, J.: What is computer ethics? Metaphilosophy **16**(4), 266–275 (1985)
56. Moor, J.: The nature, importance, and difficulty of machine ethics. IEEE **21**(4), 18–21 (2006)
57. Moore, G.: Philosophical Papers. Allen and Unwin (1959)
58. Morley, J., Floridi, L., Kinsey, L.: From what to how: an initial review of publicly available AI ethics tools, methods and research to translate principles into practices. Sci. Eng. Ethics **26**, 2141–2168 (2020). https://doi.org/10.1007/s11948-019-00165-5
59. Müller, V.: Ethics of artificial intelligence and robotics. In: Zalta, E.N. (ed.) The Stanford Encyclopedia of Philosophy (2020). https://plato.stanford.edu/archives/fall2020/entries/ethics-ai/
60. Pearlberg, D., Schroeder, T.: Reasons, causes, and the extended mind hypothesis. Erkenntnis **81**, 41–57 (2015). https://doi.org/10.1007/s10670-015-9727-0
61. Pekka, A., Bauer, W.: The European commission's high-level expert group on artificial intelligence: ethics guidelines for trustworthy AI. Working document for Stakeholders' Consultation (2018)
62. Pigliucci, M.: Mind uploading: a philosophical analysis. In: Blackford, R., Broderick, D. (eds.) Intelligence Unbound: Future of Uploaded and Machine Minds. Wiley, Hoboken (2014). https://doi.org/10.1002/9781118736302.ch7
63. Raso, F.: AI and Human Rights. Opportunities and Risks. Berkman Klein Centre for Internet and Society, Harvard (2018)
64. Royakkers, L., Est, R.: A literature review on new robotics: automation from love to war. Int. J. Soc. Robot. **7**, 549–570 (2015)

65. Royakkers, L., Timmer, J., Kool, L., Est, R.: Societal and ethical issues of digitization. Ethics Inf. Technol. **20**(2), 127–142 (2018). https://doi.org/10.1007/s10676-018-9452-x
66. Sandberg, A.: Feasibility of whole brain emulation. In: Müller, V. (ed.) Philosophy and Theory of Artificial Intelligence. Studies in Applied Philosophy, Epistemological and Rational Ethics, vol. 5. Springer, Heidelberg (2013). https://doi.org/10.1007/978-3-642-31674-6_19
67. Sandberg, A., Bostrom, N.: Whole brain emulation: a roadmap. Technical report 2008-3, Future of Humanity Institute, Oxford University (2008, online)
68. Schneider, S.: Mindscan: Transcending and Enhancing the Brain. Wiley, Hoboken (2009)
69. Segun, S.: From machine ethics to computational ethics. AI Soc. (2020). https://doi.org/10.1007/s00146-020-01010-1
70. Sharkey, A., Sharkey, N.: Granny and the robots: ethical issues in robot care for the elderly. Ethics Inf. Technol. **14**(1), 27–40 (2010)
71. Siau, K., Wang, W.: Artificial intelligence (AI) ethics: ethics of AI and ethical AI. J. Database Manag. **31**(2), 74–87 (2020). https://doi.org/10.4018/JDM.2020040105
72. Spielkamp, M., Matzat, L.: Algorithm watch 2019: the AI ethics guidelines global inventory (2019). https://algorithmwatch.org/en/project/ai-ethics-guidelines-global-inventory/
73. Steffensen, S.: Language, languaging and the extended mind hypothesis. Pragmatics Cogn. **17**(3), 677–697 (2009). https://doi.org/10.1075/pc.17.3.10ste
74. Taddeo, M., Floridi, L.: How AI can be a force for good. Science **361**(6404), 751–752 (2018). https://doi.org/10.1126/science.aat5991
75. Taylor, P.: Normative Discourse. Prentice-Hall, New York (1961)
76. Turkle, S.: The Second Self: Computers and the Human Spirit. Simon and Schuster, New York (1984)
77. Turkle, S.: Alone Together: Why We Expect More from Technology and Less from Each Other. Basic Books, New York (2011)
78. UNESCO: Preliminary report on the first draft of the recommendation on the ethics of artificial intelligence (2020). https://unesdoc.unesco.org/ark:/48223/pf0000374266
79. Vallor, S.: Moral deskilling and upskilling in a new machine age: reflections on the ambiguous future of character. Philos. Technol. (2015)
80. Vallor, S.: Technology and the Virtues: A Philosophical Guide to a Future Worth Wanting. Oxford University Press, Oxford (2016)
81. Veale, M., Binns, R.: Mitigating Discrimination without Collecting Sensitive Data. Big Data Soc. (2017)
82. Veruggio, G., Operto, F.: Roboethics: social and ethical implications of robotics. In: Siciliano, B., Khatib, O. (eds.) Springer Handbook of Robotics. Springer, Heidelberg (2008). https://doi.org/10.1007/978-3-540-30301-5_65
83. Wachter, S., Mittelstadt, B., Floridi, L.: Why a right to explanation of automated decision-making does not exist in the general data protection regulation. Int. Data Priv. Law **7**(2), 76–99 (2017). https://doi.org/10.1093/idpl/ipx005
84. Walker, M.: Personal identity and uploading. J. Evol. Technol. **22**(1), 37–51 (2011)
85. Wallach, W., Allen, C.: Moral Machines: Teaching Robots Right from Wrong. Oxford University Press, Oxford (2009)
86. Wiley, K., Wang, W.: A Taxonomy and Metaphysics of Mind Uploading. Humanity+ Press and Alautun Press, Seattle (2014)
87. Winfield, A.: An updated round up of ethical principles of robotics and AI (2019). http://alanwinfield.blogspot.com/2019/04/an-upyeard-round-up-ofethical.html

AI in Information Systems, AI for Development and Social Good

Dataset Selection for Transfer Learning in Information Retrieval

Yastil Rughbeer[1,2]([✉])(iD), Anban W. Pillay[1,2](iD), and Edgar Jembere[1,2](iD)

[1] University of KwaZulu-Natal, Westville 4001, South Africa
yastil350.rughbeer@gmail.com, {pillayw4,jemberee}@ukzn.ac.za
[2] Centre for AI Research (CAIR), Cape Town, South Africa

Abstract. Information Retrieval is the task of satisfying an information need by retrieving relevant information from large collections. Recently, deep neural networks have achieved several performance breakthroughs in the field, owing to the availability of large-scale training sets. When training data is limited, however, neural retrieval systems vastly underperform. To compensate for the lack of training data, researchers have turned to transfer learning by relying on labelled data from other search domains. Despite having access to several publicly available datasets, researchers are currently unguided in selecting the best training set for their particular applications. To address this knowledge gap, we propose a rigorous method to select an optimal training set for a specific search domain. We validate this method on the TREC-COVID challenge, which was organized by the Allen Institute for Artificial Intelligence and the National Institute of Standards and Technology. Our neural model ranked first from 143 competing systems. More importantly, it was able to achieve this result by training on a dataset that was selected using our proposed method. This work highlights the performance gains that may be achieved through careful dataset selection in transfer learning.

Keywords: Information Retrieval · Ranking · Transfer learning

1 Introduction

One may believe that Information Retrieval (IR) is a problem which has been mostly solved, especially with the rise of state-of-the-art search engines like Google. However, IR is an active research area that has garnered immense interest over the years. In essence, Information Retrieval is the task of satisfying an information need, expressed in the form of a query, by retrieving relevant information from large collections.

Recently, deep neural networks have been the driving force behind several performance breakthroughs in Information Retrieval. These models were first introduced to IR in 2015 [11]. However, despite their relatively short lifespan in the field, they have vastly outperformed non-neural retrieval systems on multiple benchmark datasets [4,13,19]. Even Google, an industry leader, has announced

© Springer Nature Switzerland AG 2020
A. Gerber (Ed.): SACAIR 2020, CCIS 1342, pp. 53–65, 2020.
https://doi.org/10.1007/978-3-030-66151-9_4

that they will be implementing neural systems to improve the quality of web search [12]. Therefore, it is unsurprising that neural networks are seen as a paradigm shift in IR.

Unfortunately, the hype surrounding neural systems has been met with criticism from the IR community. Recent studies have shown that non-neural systems outperform neural systems by a large margin when training data is insufficient or non-existent [8,18]. This finding raised doubts about the effectiveness of neural systems in practical applications, where the cost of obtaining large-scale training data exceeds the budgets of most organizations [19]. For example, during the COVID-19 pandemic, rapid deployment of retrieval systems was needed to manage the surge in scientific literature [15]. However, due to the limited supply of training data from biomedical experts, non-neural systems proved to be more effective than their neural counterparts [9].

To compensate for the lack of training data, researchers have turned to a technique known as transfer learning. In our context, transfer learning involves training a model in a domain with sufficient labelled data, then applying it to a domain where training data is limited (target domain). Although the effectiveness of transfer learning largely depends on the selected training data [16], there are currently no guidelines on selecting the best training set for a given target domain. Consequently, researchers are divided on what features to consider when selecting a training set. Some authors argue in favour of a vocabulary alignment between the training and target datasets [5,10,20], while others believe that it is only necessary to consider the scale of a training set [4,19].

Understanding which features to consider when selecting a training set is critical in transfer learning. For example, one could experience significant performance gains after training on a large dataset compared to a small dataset. In this case, scale is said to represent a principle feature. Similarly, if a medical-related training set produces better results than a non-medical related training set on COVID-19 literature, then vocabulary alignment may represent a principle feature. By definition, principle features are features which have the largest influence on performance [17]. Hence, our strategy in developing a method for optimal dataset selection relies on determining what these principle features are.

We begin by analyzing existing literature in Sect. 2. In Sect. 3, we develop a method to identify the principle features and report on our results in Sect. 4. Finally, we discuss our findings and provide concluding remarks on future work in Sects. 5 and 6, respectively.

2   Literature Review

There are several key concepts that underpin Information Retrieval; however, in this paper, it is only necessary to understand the structure of the data that is used to train neural models. For illustrative purposes, a training instance taken from the Twitter retrieval task is shown in Fig. 1 [14]. As seen from the figure, training data for retrieval systems consist of three parts: a query, a document, and a ground truth label.

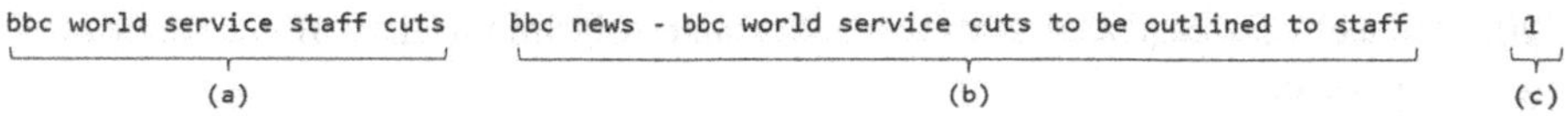

```
bbc world service staff cuts     bbc news - bbc world service cuts to be outlined to staff        1
└──────────┬──────────┘     └──────────────────────────┬──────────────────────────┘    └┬┘
          (a)                                        (b)                                   (c)
```

Fig. 1. Training instance from the Twitter retrieval task – a: query, b: document (Tweet), c: label

As seen in Table 1, there are two types of user queries, namely; keyword type queries and natural language type queries. The former consists only of the terms which relate to the topic that the user is interested in, while the latter consists of grammatically correct sentences that may include question words, verbs and prepositions. A document, on the other hand, could represent any span of text, including Tweets, scientific literature, or even websites. Lastly, a ground truth label can be categorized as either a 1 or a 0. Under this labelling scheme, a 1 implies that the document is relevant to the query, while a 0 implies that it is not.

Table 1. Examples of keyword and natural language queries from TREC-COVID [15]

Keyword query	Natural language query
Coronavirus origin	What is the origin of COVID-19?
Coronavirus early symptoms	What are the initial symptoms of COVID-19?
Coronavirus in Canada	How has COVID-19 affected Canada?
Coronavirus clinical trials	Are there any clinical trials available for coronavirus?

To begin our review, we consider an early attempt at using transfer learning to deal with sparse training sets [5]. Instead of relying on the limited amount of training instances from the target domain, the authors in [5] proposed to train a retrieval model on user queries from an external database. They achieved this by automatically matching documents from the target dataset to user queries from a publicly available AOL query log. The end result was a training set which consisted of 6.15 million training instances, compared to the original 249 instances.

Since the training set consisted of documents from the target domain, one can argue that the authors were able to achieve a vocabulary alignment between the training and target datasets. However, despite training on a large dataset which was semantically aligned to the target domain, the neural model achieved a relatively modest improvement of 6.7% over a non-neural baseline (see Table 2)[1]. Our claim is justified by comparing this result to that achieved by the authors

---

[1] This result was achieved by the authors in [20], who re-implemented the work in [5].

in [20]. Hence, one can argue that vocabulary alignment may not represent a principle feature.

Similar to the method proposed in [5], the authors in [10] focused on creating a training set that aligned with the vocabulary of the target domain. In more detail, they proposed to leverage the inherent relevance between the title and content of news and Wikipedia articles. The retrieval model was trained on a dataset where the headlines of these articles were used as queries and the associated content as documents. Additionally, a filter was developed to eliminate articles whose vocabulary did not align with documents from the target domain.

However, despite training on a dataset which was semantically aligned to the target domain, the model achieved an improvement of 6.8% over the non-neural baseline (see Table 2)[2]. It is also worth emphasizing that despite been vastly dissimilar in content, both [5] and [10] yielded similar results. This finding provides compelling evidence in support of our previous claim that vocabulary alignment may not represent a principle feature.

Taking inspiration from early research [1], the authors in [20] proposed to train a retrieval model on anchor links. An anchor link is usually identified as blue, underlined text on a webpage that allows users to leapfrog to a specific page on the internet. Briefly, to simulate the retrieval task, anchor links were used as queries and the linked content as ground truth documents. Similar to the approach discussed in [10], the authors developed a filter model. However, instead of eliminating training instances based on their similarity to documents, the filter model was designed to eliminate instances that did not align with the vocabulary of queries from the target domain.

The model was able to achieve an improvement of 9.7% over the non-neural baseline (see Table 2). Compared to the performance achieved in both [5] and [10], this represents a statistically significant improvement. Interpretation of this result suggests that a vocabulary alignment between queries from the training and target datasets is more important than a vocabulary alignment between documents. However, since vocabulary alignment may not represent a principle feature, the performance gain discussed here can be attributed to the fact that there was an unintentional alignment between query types of the training and target datasets. Hence, this result implies that query type alignment may represent a principle feature.

Instead of focusing on a vocabulary alignment, the authors in [19] proposed to train a retrieval model on the largest publicly available dataset. The selected dataset was annotated by humans and consisted of more than a million training instances. As evaluated in [20], the model was able to achieve an improvement of 7.6% over the non-neural baseline (see Table 2). However, compared to the performance achieved by [20], this result is not statistically significant. Hence one can argue that the scale of a dataset alone may not represent a principle feature.

---

[2] This result was achieved by the authors in [20], who re-implemented the work in [10].

To summarize, it seems that neither vocabulary alignment nor scale represents principle features. Evidence in support of this claim can be found in Table 2. As seen in the table, vocabulary alignment and scale do not lead to significant performance gains over the non-neural baseline [5,10,19]. On the other hand, a significant performance gain was achieved by aligning the query types between the training and target datasets [20]. This finding suggests that query type alignment may represent a principle feature.

Table 2. Performance of a neural model after training on datasets constructed using different methods [20], * indicates a statistically significant improvement over the baseline.

Method	Performance (NDCG@20)	Percentage improvement over baseline (%)
Non-neural baseline	0.4102	–
Vocabulary alignment [5]	0.4375	+6.7
Vocabulary alignment [10]	0.4379	+6.8
Query type alignment [20]	**0.4500***	+9.7
Scale [19]	0.4415	+7.6

3   Methods

We aim to develop a method to select an optimal training set for a specific target domain. To achieve this, we need to determine which feature should be prioritized when selecting a training set. Based on our review of existing literature, we have identified three candidate features that are worthy of investigation: vocabulary alignment, scale, and query type alignment. To this end, the objective of our work is to determine which of these features represents a principle feature. Our proposed method to identify a principle feature is shown in Fig. 2.

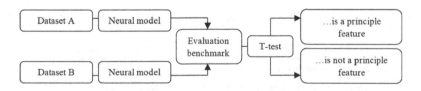

Fig. 2. Proposed method used to identify a principle feature

As shown in Fig. 2, the first step involves selecting two datasets. These datasets are then used to train two separate, but identical neural models. After training, each neural model is evaluated on a retrieval benchmark. The results from evaluation are compared using a right-tailed t-test in order to determine if the given feature represents a principle feature.

3.1   T-Test

The alternate hypothesis for each feature is shown in Table 3. We omit the null hypothesis as it is the opposite of the alternate hypothesis. For example, the null hypothesis for the scale feature would be; "training on a large dataset does not yield a statistically higher performance than training on a small dataset". Hence, in our context, a feature is said to represent a principle feature only if the null hypothesis is rejected. Conversely, if the null hypothesis is not rejected, the test is inconclusive. This means that there was not enough evidence to support the claim that the given feature represents a principle feature.

Table 3. Alternate hypothesis for each feature

Feature	Alternate hypothesis
Vocabulary alignment	Training on a dataset whose vocabulary is aligned with the target domain yields a statistically higher performance than training on a dataset whose vocabulary is not aligned with the target domain
Scale	Training on a large dataset yields a statistically higher performance than training on a small dataset
Query type alignment	Training on a dataset whose query type is aligned with the target domain yields a statistically higher performance than training on a dataset whose query type is not aligned with the target domain

Rejection of the null hypothesis is based on a comparison between the critical value (shown in Table 4) and the test statistic. We calculate the test statistic using the per query NDCG@10 score. Since our work uses a right-tailed t-test, the null hypothesis is rejected if the test statistic is greater than the critical value.

Table 4. Parameters of the critical value used in the right-tailed t-test

Constant	Value
Significance level (alpha)	0.05
Degrees of freedom (number of test queries -1)	29
Critical value	1.6991

3.2   Evaluation Benchmark and Metrics

We selected TREC-COVID as a benchmark dataset [15]. In more detail, TREC-COVID was a five round challenge that required the use of retrieval systems to answer key queries related to COVID-19 (see Table 1 for examples). Importantly, due to the absence of training data, TREC-COVID provided an ideal scenario to demonstrate the usefulness of our contribution. We focus on round 1, which consisted of 30 test queries that were provided in both keyword and natural language form. The documents for each query were constructed by concatenating the title and abstract fields of the metadata file. As with most retrieval tasks, TREC-COVID was characterized by a two-stage process, namely;

1. Given a query, retrieve the relevant literature from a large collection of documents
2. Rank the retrieved literature from most to least relevant based on the given query

Due to computational costs, most participants employed non-neural systems in stage 1 and neural systems in stage 2. Since our work is based on neural systems, we focus only on the second stage. This means that our task is to rank a set of given documents from most relevant to least relevant for a given query.

To compare our work with competing systems, we use the official metric provided by the task organizers, i.e. NDCG@10. In essence, nominalized discounted cumulative gain (NDCG) evaluates the performance of a retrieval system by penalizing the score every time a non-relevant document appears higher up in the rank than a relevant document. Additionally, to ensure consistency with procedures followed by TREC-COVID, we use the official evaluation software to calculate NDCG@10[3].

3.3 Neural Model

We selected BERT Large as the basis of our neural ranking model. In more detail, BERT represents a general-purpose pre-trained language model that has achieved state-of-the-art results on several natural language processing tasks, including Information Retrieval [6]. The model used in this paper was prepared by the authors in [13] and consisted of an additional single-layer neural network.

The input to BERT was formed by concatenating the query and document into a sequence. Each sequence was then truncated to a maximum length of 509 tokens in order to accommodate for BERT's [CLS] and [SEP] tokens. The final sequence had a maximum length of 512 tokens and was converted TFRecord format before feeding into BERT.

Fine-tuning began from the pre-trained BERT Large checkpoint. We fine tuned BERT on Google Cloud TPU's for 400k iterations with a batch size of 32. This equated to approximately 40 h of training and exposed the model to 12.8M training samples ($400k \times 32$). Additionally, training was conducted using cross-entropy loss with an initial learning rate of 3×10^{-6}, learning rate warm-up over the first 10,000 iterations, and linear decay of the learning rate of 0.01.

---

[3] The official evaluation software used by the organizers of TREC-COVID was trec-eval, and can be downloaded at https://trec.nist.gov/trec_eval/.

The [CLS] token of BERT's output was propagated through a single layer neural network, which computed the probability of the document being relevant to the query. Documents were then sorted in descending order based on their probability score for the given query.

3.4   Datasets and Training Procedure

To determine if vocabulary alignment represents a principle feature, we compared the performance of BERT after training on the COVID and Twitter datasets. In more detail, the COVID dataset consisted of 170 keyword type queries taken from rounds 2 to 5 of the TREC-COVID challenge. The documents for this dataset were constructed by concatenating the title and abstract fields of the metadata file. As previously mentioned, TREC-COVID represents our evaluation benchmark; hence there was a significant vocabulary overlap between the training and test sets. In contrast, the Twitter dataset was prepared by the authors in [14] and consisted of random Tweets collected between 2011 and 2014. Importantly, the vocabulary of the Twitter dataset was vastly dissimilar to our evaluation benchmark.

To determine if scale represents a principle feature, we compared the performance of BERT after training on the MS MARCO and Twitter datasets. The Twitter dataset consisted of 179 unique training queries, while MS MARCO consisted of over a million unique training queries and currently represents the largest publicly available retrieval dataset [2]. The MS MARCO dataset used in this paper was prepared by the authors in [13].

Lastly, to determine if query type alignment represents a principle feature, we trained BERT on the MS MARCO dataset and compared its performance on both keyword (k), and natural language (n) test queries provided in TREC-COVID (see Table 1). Since MS MARCO consisted of natural language queries, query types were considered aligned when natural language test queries were used. Conversely, when keyword test queries were used, query types were not considered aligned.

4   Results

4.1   Principle Features

Although vocabulary alignment has proven to be effective in related tasks such as sentiment classification, our results suggest that this effectiveness does not translate to retrieval. As seen in Table 5, the difference in NDCG@10 scores between the COVID and Twitter datasets is not statistically significant, i.e. test statistic < critical value. This means that there was not enough evidence to support the claim that vocabulary alignment represents a principle feature. It is worth emphasizing that the COVID dataset consisted of scientific queries and documents which aligned with the scientific-based vocabulary of the target domain. Despite this, it was unable to achieve a significant performance gain over a Twitter dataset that consisted of random and noisy social media messages.

Another well-established paradigm which our work challenged was scale. In more detail, we found that training on a large dataset did not result in a significant improvement over training on a small dataset. To highlight this point, MS MARCO is nearly three orders of magnitude larger than the Twitter dataset, yet as seen in Table 5, the difference in NDCG@10 scores between the two datasets is not statistically significant. Hence, based on the outcome of the t-test, we can conclude that there was not enough evidence to support the claim that scale represents a principle feature.

Lastly, as seen in Table 5, we have determined that query type alignment represents a principle feature, i.e. test statistic > critical value. More concretely, there is a significant performance increase when query types are aligned (highlighted in bold) compared to when they are not. This finding is particularly important since query type alignment has been completely overlooked in previous research, yet had a strong influence on performance.

Table 5. Summary of results

Experiment	Dataset	NDCG@10	Test statistic	Result
Vocabulary alignment	COVID	0.5051	0.1614	Test is inconclusive
	Twitter	0.4985		
Scale	MS MARCO	0.5580	1.372	Test is inconclusive
	Twitter	0.4985		
Query type alignment	MS MARCO (n)	**0.6493**	2.327	Query type alignment is a principle feature
	MS MARCO (k)	0.5580		

Based on our findings, query type alignment represents the feature to consider when selecting a training set for a specific target domain. However, our experiments have validated this claim for natural language type queries only. To prove that our finding also applies to keyword type queries, we consider the experiments conducted by the authors in [19]. As shown in Table 6, the authors achieved a significant performance improvement on the Robust04 benchmark after training on the Twitter dataset compared to training on the MS MARCO dataset. At the time, the authors referred to this performance gain as 'surprising'. However, since both the Twitter and Robust04 datasets consisted of keyword type queries, we can now attribute the performance gain to an alignment between query types from the training and target datasets. This example highlights our contribution of knowledge to the field of Information Retrieval.

Table 6. Performance of BERT Large on the Robust04 dataset as achieved in [19]

Dataset	NDCG@20	Model
Twitter	**0.4998**	BERT Large
MS MARCO	0.4512	BERT Large

4.2 Benchmark

It is important to recognize that our experimental results have validated our theoretical findings. That is, we have proven our assumptions on what the principle feature could be. Now, to demonstrate the value of our findings, we turn our attention to the TREC-COVID challenge. In more detail, we train BERT Large on the MS MARCO dataset and apply it to TREC-COVID using the provided natural language test queries. As seen in Table 7 our system achieved first place on the round 1 leader board in terms of NDCG@10[4].

Table 7. Top 5 systems of TREC-COVID round 1 based on NDCG@10, * indicates a statistically significant improvement over the VSM model

System	NDCG@10	Model	Architecture
Our system	**0.6493**[*]	BERT Large	Neural
sab20.1.meta.docs	0.6080	VSM	Non-neural
run2	0.6032	SciBERT	Neural
IRIT_marked_base	0.5880	BERT Base	Neural
CSIROmedNIR	0.5875	CovidBERT	Neural

5 Discussion

Contrary to existing viewpoints, our results have proven that neither scale nor vocabulary alignment represents principle features. This means that it is not important to consider these features when selecting a training set. On the other hand, we have discovered that to achieve optimum performance, one should select a training set whose query type is aligned with the target domain. More concretely, we have mathematically validated that query type alignment represents a principle feature.

To demonstrate the value of our work, we turned our attention to the TREC-COVID challenge. As seen in Table 7, our model achieved the best performance in round 1 with a score of 0.6493. More importantly, it was able to achieve this result due to an alignment of query types between the training and test datasets, i.e. both datasets utilized natural language type queries. Conversely, when training

---

[4] TREC-COVID round 1 leader board: https://ir.nist.gov/covidSubmit.

on the same dataset but using keyword test queries instead, the performance of the model dropped significantly. In fact, the model ranked 8th on the leader board with an NDCG@10 score of 0.5580. This finding, therefore, highlights the performance gains that can be achieved through query type alignment.

It is worth emphasizing that our system used an off-the-shelf BERT model, while other participants used variants of BERT that were more suited to the scientific domain. For example, one participant used SciBERT fine-tuned on a medical-related dataset, while another participant used CovidBERT, which was trained on the document set of TREC-COVID. The consensus behind using these models was to achieve a higher vocabulary alignment compared to the standard BERT model. However, our system was able to outperform both of these systems. This finding once again validates our claim that a query type alignment is more important than a vocabulary alignment between the training and target datasets.

Another interesting point worth discussing is the performance of non-neural systems in the TREC-COVID challenge. In more detail, non-neural systems accounted for 6 of the top 10 positions on the leader board. More importantly, as shown in Table 7, a non-neural model was able to outperform all other neural models except for ours. The reason for this was due to the absence of training data in TREC-COVID. As a result, most researchers opted to deploy non-neural architectures.

However, by relying on non-neural systems, semantic understanding is inevitably lost. This trade-off is undesirable, especially when dealing with complex user queries. To solve this problem, one can now apply our dataset selection method. As highlighted in Table 7, our method allows neural models to achieve significant performance improvements over non-neural systems in applications without any domain-specific training data.

Our discussion thus far has focused on the research community. Although the contribution of knowledge was our primary objective, there are also practical connotations of our work. For example, one could be designing a search engine for an e-commerce website. In this context, customers typically use keyword queries such as "iPhone Case", or "Samsung TV". Hence, based on our findings, it would be best to select a training set that consists of keyword type queries. Similarly, when designing a Chatbot, it would be best to select a training set with natural language type queries. The reason for this is due to the fact that users typically interact with Chatbots using natural language, e.g. "How far is the nearest petrol station?"

6   Conclusion

The TREC-COVID challenge required participants to perform full retrieval, i.e. retrieve a set of documents then rank those documents in descending order of relevance. Although our system focused only on the ranking stage, we compared it to systems that performed full retrieval. This comparison is fair for two reasons. Firstly, the authors in [3] proved that having access to a greater number of relevant documents does not result in a higher NDCG@k score. Secondly, and more importantly, TREC compares systems against each other even though each system retrieves a different number of relevant documents. Hence, our system did not have an advantage over competing systems.

It is important to emphasize that our work can be applied to any neural retrieval model. However in this paper, we only investigated the BERT architecture due to its popularity amongst researchers. As a result, we leave it to future work to investigate other neural architectures such as Conv-KNRM. Another interesting direction for future work is to compare the effectiveness of transfer learning to fully supervised learning in Information Retrieval. An ideal benchmark for this would be MS MARCO, as it consists of more than a million domain-specific training queries. In this context, our method would guide us in selecting Google Natural Questions [7] as a training set since it aligns with the query type of MS MARCO.

References

1. Asadi, N., Metzler, D., Elsayed, T., Lin, J.: Pseudo test collections for learning web search ranking functions. In: Proceedings of the 34th International ACM SIGIR Conference on Research and Development in Information Retrieval, Beijing, China, pp. 1073–1082 (2011)
2. Bajaj, P., et al.: MS MARCO: a human generated machine reading comprehension dataset. In: 30th Conference on Neural Information Processing Systems, Barcelona, Spain (2016)
3. Craswell, N., Mitra, B., Yilmaz, E., Campos, D., Voorhees, E.: Overview of the trec 2019 deep learning track. arXiv:2003.07820 (2020)
4. Dai, Z., Callan, J.: Deeper text understanding for IR with contextual neural language modeling. In: Proceedings of the 42nd International ACM SIGIR Conference on Research and Development in Information Retrieval, Paris, France, pp. 985–988. Association for Computing Machinery (2019)
5. Dehghani, M., Zamani, H., Severyn, A., Kamps, J., Croft, W.: Neural ranking models with weak supervision. In: Proceedings of SIGIR 2017, Shinjuku, Tokyo, Japan (2017)
6. Devlin, J., Chang, M., Lee, K., Toutanova, K.: BERT: pretraining of deep bidirectional transformers for language understanding. In: Proceedings of NAACL-HLT 2019, Minneapolis, Minnesota, pp. 4171–4186. Association for Computational Linguistics (2019)
7. Kwiatkowski, T., et al.: Natural questions: a benchmark for question answering research. In: Jiang, J. (ed.) Transactions of the Association for Computational Linguistics, vol. 7, pp. 453–466 (2019)
8. Lin, J.: The neural hype and comparisons against weak baselines. ACM SIGIR Forum 52(2), 40–51 (2019)
9. MacAvaney, S., Cohan, A., Goharian, N.: SLEDGE: A simple yet effective baseline for coronavirus scientific knowledge search. arXiv:2005.02365 (2020)
10. MacAvaney, S., Yates, A., Hui, K., Frieder, O.: Content-based weak supervision for AdHoc re-ranking. In: Proceedings of the 42nd International ACM SIGIR Conference on Research and Development in Information Retrieval, Paris, France, pp. 993–996. Association of Computing Machinery (2019)

11. Marchesin, S., Purpura, A., Silvello, G.: Focal elements of neural information retrieval models. An outlook through a reproducibility study. Inf. Process. Manage. **57**, 102109 (2020)
12. Nayak, P.: Understanding searches better than ever before. https://www.blog.google/products/search/search-language-understanding-bert/. Accessed 18 May 2020
13. Nogueira, R., Cho, K.: Passage re-ranking with BERT. arXiv:1901.04085 (2019)
14. Rao, J., Yang, W., Zhang, Y., Ture, F., Lin, J.: Multi-perspective relevance matching with hierarchical ConvNets for social media search. In: The 33rd AAAI Conference on Artificial Intelligence, AAAI19, vol. 33, pp. 232240 (2019)
15. Roberts, K., et al.: TREC-COVID: rationale and structure of an information retrieval shared task for COVID-19. J. Am. Med. Inform. Assoc. **27**, 1431–1436 (2020)
16. Sun, B., Feng, J., Saenko, K.: Return of frustratingly easy domain adaptation. In: Proceedings of the 30th AAAI Conference on Artificial Intelligence. Association for the Advancement of Artificial Intelligence (2016)
17. Wouter, M., Marco, L.: An introduction to domain adaptation and transfer learning. arXiv:1812.11806 (2019)
18. Yang, W., Lu, K., Yang, P., Lin, J.: Critically examining the "neural hype": weak baselines and the additivity of effectiveness gains from neural ranking models. In: Proceedings of the 42nd International ACM SIGIR Conference on Research and Development in Information Retrieval, Paris, France, pp. 1129–1132. Association for Computing Machinery (2019)
19. Yilmaz, Z., Yang, W., Zhang, H., Lin, J.: Cross-domain modeling of sentence-level evidence for document retrieval. In: 9th International Joint Conference on Natural Language Processing, Hong Kong, China, pp. 3481–3487. Association for Computational Linguistics (2019)
20. Zhang, K., Xiong, C., Liu, Z., Liu, Z.: Selective weak supervision for neural information retrieval. In: International World Web Conference, Creative Commons, Taiwan (2020)

Applications of AI

StarGAN-ZSVC: Towards Zero-Shot Voice Conversion in Low-Resource Contexts

Matthew Baas$^{(\boxtimes)}$ and Herman Kamper

E&E Engineering, Stellenbosch University, Stellenbosch, South Africa
{20786379,kamperh}@sun.ac.za

Abstract. Voice conversion is the task of converting a spoken utterance from a source speaker so that it appears to be said by a different target speaker while retaining the linguistic content of the utterance. Recent advances have led to major improvements in the quality of voice conversion systems. However, to be useful in a wider range of contexts, voice conversion systems would need to be (i) trainable without access to parallel data, (ii) work in a zero-shot setting where both the source and target speakers are unseen during training, and (iii) run in real time or faster. Recent techniques fulfill one or two of these requirements, but not all three. This paper extends recent voice conversion models based on generative adversarial networks (GANs), to satisfy all three of these conditions. We specifically extend the recent StarGAN-VC model by conditioning it on a speaker embedding (from a potentially unseen speaker). This allows the model to be used in a zero-shot setting, and we therefore call it StarGAN-ZSVC. We compare StarGAN-ZSVC against other voice conversion techniques in a low-resource setting using a small 9-min training set. Compared to AutoVC—another recent neural zero-shot approach—we observe that StarGAN-ZSVC gives small improvements in the zero-shot setting, showing that real-time zero-shot voice conversion is possible even for a model trained on very little data. Further work is required to see whether scaling up StarGAN-ZSVC will also improve zero-shot voice conversion quality in high-resource contexts.

Keywords: Speech processing · Voice conversion · Generative adversarial networks · Zero-shot

1 Introduction

Voice conversion is a speech processing task where speech from a source speaker is transformed so that it appears to come from a different target speaker while preserving linguistic content. A fast, human-level voice conversion system has

This work is supported in part by the National Research Foundation of South Africa (grant number: 120409) and a Google Faculty Award for HK.

A. Gerber (Ed.): SACAIR 2020, CCIS 1342, pp. 69–84, 2020.
https://doi.org/10.1007/978-3-030-66151-9_5

significant applications across several industries, from those in privacy and identity protection [16] to those of voice mimicry and disguise [10,37]. It can also be essential for addressing downstream speech processing problems in low-resource contexts where training data is limited: it could be used to augment training data by converting the available utterances to novel speakers—effectively increasing the diversity of training data and improving the quality of the resulting systems.

Recent techniques have improved the quality of voice conversion significantly, in part due to the Voice Conversion Challenge (VCC) and its efforts to concentrate disparate research efforts [36]. Some techniques are beginning to achieve near human-level quality in conversion outputs. However, much of the advances and improvements in quality are limited in their practical usefulness because they fail to satisfy several requirements that would be necessary for practical use, particularly in low-resource settings.

First, a practical voice conversion system should be trainable on non-parallel data. That is, training data should not need to contain utterances from multiple speakers saying the same words – such a setting is known as a parallel data setting. Non-parallel data is the converse, where the different utterances used to train the model do not contain the same spoken words. Parallel data is difficult to collect in general, and even more so for low-resource language (those which have limited digitally stored corpora). Second, a practical system should be able to convert speech to and from speakers which have not been seen during training. This is called *zero-shot* voice conversion. Without this requirement, a system would need to be retrained whenever speech from a new speaker is desired. Finally, for a number of practical applications, a voice conversion system needs to run at least in real-time. For data augmentation in particular, having the system run as fast as possible is essential for it to be practical in the training of a downstream speech model.

With these requirements in mind, we look to extend existing state-of-the-art voice conversion techniques. We specifically extend the recent StarGAN-VC2 [13] approach to the zero-shot setting, proposing the new StarGAN-ZSVC model. StarGAN-ZSVC achieves zero-shot prediction by using a speaker encoding network to generate speaker embeddings for potentially unseen speakers; these embeddings are then used to condition the model at inference time.

Through objective and human evaluations, we show that StarGAN-ZSVC performs better than simple baseline models and similar or better than the recent AutoVC zero-shot voice conversion approach [24] across a range of evaluation metrics. More specifically, it gives similar or better performance in all zero-shot settings considered, and does so more than five times faster than AutoVC.

2   Related Work

A typical voice conversion system operates in the frequency domain, first converting an input utterance into a spectrogram and then using some model to map the spectrogram spoken by a source speaker to that of one spoken by a target speaker. The output spectrogram is then converted to a waveform in the time-domain using a vocoder [28]. In this paper, we denote spectrogram sequences as

$X = [\mathbf{x}_1, \mathbf{x}_2, \ldots, \mathbf{x}_T]$, where the spectrogram contains T frames, and each frame $\mathbf{x}_i$ consists of some number of frequency bins. In our case, we use 80-dimensional Mel-scale frequency bins, i.e. $\mathbf{x}_i \in \mathbb{R}^{80}$.

Some models [11,32] use parametric algorithms like the WORLD vocoder [20] to convert the output spectrogram back to a time-domain waveform. Others use neural vocoders, which can be divided into autoregressive models, such as those of the WaveNet family [21], and non-autoregressive models, such as MelGAN [15].

Voice conversion models themselves can be classified on several levels. Older techniques rely on rule-based techniques [6,27] while newer models rely on statistical techniques and often make extensive use of deep neural networks [28]. Models can also be classified into traditional models that can only perform one-to-one voice conversion, such as the recurrent DBLSTM-RNN [31] and Gaussian mixture based models [30,33], to newer models like those using variational autoencoders [12,24] and vector quantized neural networks [3] to allow for many-to-many conversion where a single model can convert between several possible source-target speaker pairings.

Finally, the recent AutoVC model [24] (Sect. 2.2) emerged as the first model to be able to perform zero-shot voice conversion where either the source or target speaker is unseen during training. For our new model, we also take inspiration from recent work on speaker encoding networks trained for speaker verification [35], as well as the StarGAN-VC and -VC2 [11,13] models (Sect. 2.1). Concretely, we attempt to combine these in a new zero-shot voice conversion model.

2.1 StarGAN and Voice Conversion

Generative adversarial networks (GANs) train two separate networks: a generator and a discriminator. The generator is trained to produce realistic outputs (i.e. it should aim to accurately approximate some function), while the discriminator is trained to discern true outputs from ones produced by the generator. Part of the generator's objective is to fool the discriminator and to essentially maximize its loss metric, while the discriminator is trained to do the opposite.

One set of successful voice conversion techniques relies on re-purposing the StarGAN image-to-image translation technique [2] for voice conversion. In particular, StarGAN-VC2 [13] extends upon StarGAN-VC [11] by training a single generator model to perform many-to-many voice conversion using speaker-dependent modulation factors in so-called conditional instance normalization layers [5]. The model's generator $G(X_{\mathrm{src}}, \mathbf{s}_{\mathrm{src}}, \mathbf{s}_{\mathrm{trg}})$ converts a spectrogram X_{src} from a source speaker to a target speaker, producing the converted output $X_{\mathrm{src} \to \mathrm{trg}}$. The source and target speaker identities are given as one-hot vectors, $\mathbf{s}_{\mathrm{src}}$ and $\mathbf{s}_{\mathrm{trg}}$, respectively. The model's discriminator $D(X, \mathbf{s}_{\mathrm{src}}, \mathbf{s}_{\mathrm{trg}})$ takes an input spectrogram X and returns a scalar. Intuitively, the generator is trained to force the discriminator's output when given converted spectrograms to be high, while the discriminator is trained to make its output low when given converted outputs and high when given original spectrograms.

More formally, the generator G is trained to minimize the loss $\mathcal{L} = \lambda_{\text{id}}\mathcal{L}_{\text{id}} + \lambda_{\text{cyc}}\mathcal{L}_{\text{cyc}} + \mathcal{L}_{G-\text{adv}}$. The first term, $\mathcal{L}_{\text{id}}$ is an identity loss term. It aims to minimize the difference between the input and output spectrogram when the model is made to keep the same speaker identity, i.e. convert from speaker A to speaker A. It is defined by the L_2 loss:

$$\mathcal{L}_{\text{id}} = ||G(X_{\text{src}}, \mathbf{s}_{\text{src}}, \mathbf{s}_{\text{src}}) - X_{\text{src}}||_2 \tag{1}$$

Next, many-to-many voice conversion systems like StarGAN-VC2 can perform *cyclic mappings*, whereby the model is made to convert an input utterance from a source speaker to a target speaker, and then convert the output utterance back to the source speaker. The second term of the loss aims to minimize the cyclic reconstruction error between the cyclic mapping and original spectrogram [2]:

$$\mathcal{L}_{\text{cyc}} = ||X_{\text{src}} - G(G(X_{\text{src}}, \mathbf{s}_{\text{src}}, \mathbf{s}_{\text{trg}}), \mathbf{s}_{\text{trg}}, \mathbf{s}_{\text{src}})||_1 \tag{2}$$

Finally, the adversarial loss term $\mathcal{L}_{G-\text{adv}}$ is added based on the LSGAN [18] loss. It defines two constants a and b, whereby G's loss tries to push D's output for converted utterances closer to a, while D's loss function tries to push D's output for converted utterances closer to b and its output for real outputs closer to a. Concretely, G's adversarial loss is defined as

$$\mathcal{L}_{G-\text{adv}} = (D(G(X_{\text{src}}, \mathbf{s}_{\text{src}}, \mathbf{s}_{\text{trg}}), \mathbf{s}_{\text{src}}, \mathbf{s}_{\text{trg}}) - a)^2. \tag{3}$$

while, the discriminator D is trained to minimize the corresponding LSGAN discriminator loss:

$$\mathcal{L}_{D-\text{adv}} = (D(G(X_{\text{src}}, \mathbf{s}_{\text{src}}, \mathbf{s}_{\text{trg}}), \mathbf{s}_{\text{src}}, \mathbf{s}_{\text{trg}}) - b)^2 + (D(X_{\text{src}}, \mathbf{s}_{\text{trg}}, \mathbf{s}_{\text{src}}) - a)^2 \tag{4}$$

In [13], the authors set the scalar coefficients to be $\lambda_{\text{id}} = 5$, and $\lambda_{\text{cyc}} = 10$. The original study [13] does not mention how a and b are set (despite these greatly affecting training); we treat them as hyperparameters. Note that the true target spectrogram X_{trg} does not appear in any of the equations – this is what allows StarGAN-VC2 to be trained with non-parallel data where the source utterance X_{src} has no corresponding utterance from the target speaker.

StarGAN-VC2 uses a specially designed 2-1-2D convolutional architecture for the generator, as well as a projection discriminator [19] which comprises of a convolutional network (to extract features) followed by an inner product with an embedding corresponding to the source/target speaker pair. For the generator, a new form of modulation-based conditional instance normalization was introduced in [13]. This allows the speaker identity (which is provided as a one-hot vector) to multiplicatively condition the channels of an input feature. According to [13], this special layer is a key component in achieving high performance in StarGAN-VC2.

We use these building blocks for our new zero-shot approach. Concretely, the one-hot speaker vectors in StarGAN-VC2 are replaced with continuous embedding vectors obtained from a separate speaker encoding network (which can be applied to arbitrary speakers), as outlined in Sect. 3.

2.2 AutoVC

Zero-shot voice conversion was first introduced in 2019 with the AutoVC model [24], which remains one of only a handful of models that can perform zero-shot conversion (see e.g. [25] for a very recent other example). For AutoVC, zero-shot conversion is achieved by using an autoencoder with a specially designed bottleneck layer which forces the network's encoder to only retain linguistic content in its encoded latent representation. The model then uses a separate recurrent speaker encoder model $E(X)$, originally proposed for speaker identification [35], to extract a speaker embedding s from an input spectrogram. These speaker embeddings are then used to supply the missing speaker identity information to the decoder which, together with the linguistic content from the encoder, allows the decoder to synthesize an output spectrogram for an unseen speaker.

Formally, the full encoder-decoder model is trained to primarily minimize two terms. The first term is an L_2 reconstruction loss between the decoder output spectrogram $X_{\mathrm{src} \to \mathrm{src}}$ and input spectrogram X_{src}, with the source speaker's encoding (from the speaker encoder) provided to both the encoder and decoder. The second term is an L_1 loss between the speaker embedding of the decoder output $E(X_{\mathrm{src} \to \mathrm{src}})$ and the original speaker embedding $s_{\mathrm{src}} = E(X_{\mathrm{src}})$. The encoder and decoder consists of convolutional and Long Short-Term Memory (LSTM) [8] recurrent layers which are carefully designed to ensure that no speaker identity information is present in the encoder output.

As with StarGAN-VC and StarGAN-VC2, a corresponding parallel target utterance X_{trg} does not appear in any of the loss terms, allowing AutoVC to be trained without parallel data. Zero-shot inference is performed by using the speaker encoder to obtain embeddings for new utterances from unseen speakers, which is then provided to the decoder instead of the embedding corresponding to the source speaker, causing the decoder to return a converted output. We use this same idea of using an encoding network to obtain embeddings for unseen speakers in our new GAN-based approach, which we describe next.

3 StarGAN-ZSVC

While StarGAN-VC and StarGAN-VC2 allows training with non-parallel data and runs sufficiently fast, it is limited in its ability to only perform voice conversion for speakers seen during training: while parallel X_{src} and X_{trg} utterance pairs are not required, the model can only synthesize speech for target speaker identities (specified as one-hot vectors) seen during training. This could preclude the use of these models in many practical situations where zero-shot conversion is required between unseen speakers. Conversely, AutoVC allows for such zero-shot prediction and is trained on non-parallel data, but it is implemented with a slow vocoder and its performance suffers when trained on very little data. Combining the strengths of both of these methods, we propose the *StarGAN zero-shot voice conversion* model – StarGAN-ZSVC.

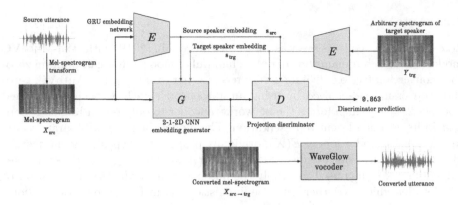

Fig. 1. The StarGAN-ZSVC system framework. The speaker encoder network E and the WaveGlow vocoder are pretrained on large speech corpora, while the generator G and discriminator D are trained on a 9-min subset of the VCC dataset. During inference, arbitrary utterances for the source and target speaker are used to obtain source and target speaker embeddings, $\mathbf{s}_{\mathrm{src}}$ and $\mathbf{s}_{\mathrm{trg}}$.

3.1 Overcoming the Zero-Shot Barrier

To achieve voice conversion between multiple speakers, the original StarGAN-VC2 model creates an explicit embedding vector for each source-target speaker pairing, which is incorporated as part of the generator G and discriminator D. This requires that each source-target speaker pairing is seen during training so that the corresponding embedding exists and has been trained – prohibiting zero-shot voice conversion. To overcome this hurdle, we instead infer separate source and target speaker embeddings, $\mathbf{s}_{\mathrm{src}}$ and $\mathbf{s}_{\mathrm{trg}}$, using a speaker encoder network E – similar to the approach followed in AutoVC (Sect. 2.2).

This framework is shown in Fig. 1. Utterances from unseen speakers (i.e. X_{src} and Y_{trg}) are fed to the speaker encoder E, yielding embeddings for these new speakers, which are then used to condition G and D, thereby enabling zero-shot conversion. The generator uses these embeddings to produce a converted Mel-spectrogram $X_{\mathrm{src} \rightarrow \mathrm{trg}}$ from a given source utterance's Mel-spectrogram X_{src}.

E is trained on a large corpus using a GE2E loss [35] which aims to simultaneously maximize distances between embeddings from different speakers while minimizing the distances between embeddings from utterances of the same speaker. NVIDIA's WaveGlow [23] is used, which does not require any speaker information for vocoding and thus readily allows zero-shot conversion.

3.2 Overcoming the Speed Barrier

The speed of the full voice conversion system during inference is bounded by (a) the speed of the generator G; (b) the speed of converting the utterance between time and frequency domains, consisting of the initial conversion from time-domain waveform to Mel-spectrogram and the speed of the vocoder; and (c) the speed of the speaker encoder E. To ensure that the speed of the full system is at least real-time, each subsystem needs to be faster than real-time.

(a) **Generator Speed.** For the generator G to be sufficiently fast, we design it to only include convolution, linear, normalization, and upscaling layers as opposed to a recurrent architecture like those used in AutoVC [24]. By ensuring that the majority of layers are convolutions, we obtain better-than real-time speeds for the generator.

(b) **Vocoder and Mel-Spectrogram Speed.** The choice of vocoder greatly affects computational cost. Higher-quality methods, such as those from the WaveNet family [21], are typically much slower than real-time, while purely convolutional methods such as MelGAN [15] are much faster but has poorer quality. Often the main difference between the slower and faster methods is again the presence of traditional recurrent layers in the vocoder architecture.

We opt for a reasonable middle-ground choice with the WaveGlow vocoder, which does have recurrent connections but does not use any recurrent layers with dense multiplications such as LSTM or Gated Recurrent Unit (GRU, another kind of recurrent cell architecture [1]) layers. We specifically use a pretrained WaveGlow network, as provided with the original paper [23]. Furthermore, the speed of the Mel-spectrogram transformation for the input audio is well faster than real-time due to the efficient nature of the fast Fourier transform and the multiplication by Mel-basis filters.

(c) **Speaker Encoder Speed.** The majority of research efforts into obtaining speaker embeddings involve models using slower recurrent layers, often making these encoder networks the bottleneck. We also make use of a recurrent stacked-GRU network as our speaker embedding network E. However, we only need to obtain a single speaker embedding to perform any number of conversions involving that speaker. We therefore treat this as a preprocessing step where we apply E to a few arbitrary utterances from the target and source speakers, averaging the results to obtain target and source speaker embeddings, and use those same embeddings for all subsequent conversions.

We also design the speaker embeddings to be 256-dimensional vectors of unit length. If we were to use StarGAN-ZSVC downstream for data augmentation (where we want speech from novel speakers), we could then simply sample random unit-length vectors of this dimensionality to use with the generator.

3.3 Architecture

With the previous considerations in mind, we design the generator G, discriminator D, and encoder network E, as shown in Fig. 2. The generator and discriminator are adapted from StarGAN-VC2 [13], while the speaker encoder is

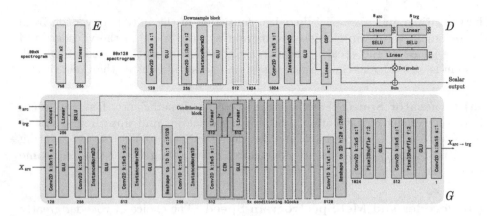

Fig. 2. StarGAN-ZSVC's network architectures. The speaker encoder E is a recurrent network similar to that used in the original GE2E paper, while the generator G and discriminator D are modified versions from the original StarGAN-VC2 architecture. Within layers, k and s represent kernel size and stride (for convolutions), f is the scaling factor (for pixel shuffle), and h and c are the height and channels of the output (for reshape layers). A number alongside a layer indicates the number of output channels (for convolutions), or output units (for linear and GRU layers). GLU layers split the input tensor in half along the *channels* dimension. GSP, GLU, and SELU indicate global sum pooling, gated linear units, and scaled exponential linear units, respectively.

adapted from the original model proposed for speaker identification [35]. Specifically, for E we use a simple stacked GRU model, while for D we use a projection discriminator [19]. For G, we use the 2-1-2D generator from StarGAN-VC2 with a modified central set of layers, denoted by the *Conditional Block* in the figure.

These conditional blocks are intended to provide the network with a way to modulate the channels of an input spectrogram, with modulation factors conditioned on the specific source and target speaker pairing. They utilize a convolutional layer followed by a modified conditional instance normalization layer [5] and a gated linear unit [4].

The modified conditional instance normalization layer performs the following operation on an input feature vector $\mathbf{f}$:

$$\mathrm{CIN}(\mathbf{f}, \gamma, \beta) = \gamma \left(\frac{\mathbf{f} - \mu(\mathbf{f})}{\sigma(\mathbf{f})} \right) + \beta \tag{5}$$

where $\mu(\mathbf{f})$ and $\sigma(\mathbf{f})$ are respectively the scalar mean and standard deviation of vector $\mathbf{f}$, while γ and β are computed using two linear layers which derive their inputs from the speaker embeddings, as depicted in Fig. 2. The above is computed separately for each channel when the input feature contains multiple channels.

For the discriminator, the source and target speaker embeddings are also fed through several linear layers and activation functions to multiply with the pooled output of D's main branch.

4   Experimental Setup

We compare StarGAN-ZSVC to other voice conversion models using the voice conversion challenge (VCC) 2018 dataset [17], which contains parallel recordings of native English speakers from the United States. Importantly, we *do not* train StarGAN-ZSVC or the AutoVC model (to which we compare) using parallel input-output examples. However, the traditional baseline models (below) do require parallel data. All training and speed measurements are performed on a single NVIDIA RTX 2070 SUPER GPU.

4.1   Dataset

The VCC 2018 dataset was recorded from 8 speakers, each speaking 81 utterances from the same transcript. 4 speakers are used for training and 4 for testing. To emulate a low-resource setting, we use a 9-min subset of the VCC 2018 training dataset for StarGAN-ZSVC and AutoVC. This corresponds to 90% of the utterances from two female (F) and two male (M) speakers (VCC2SF1, VCC2SF2, VCC2SM1, and VCC2SM2). This setup is in line with existing evaluations on VCC 2018 [13], allows for all combinations of inter- and intra-gender conversions, and allows for zero-shot evaluation on the 4 remaining unseen speakers.

In contrast to StarGAN-ZSVC and AutoVC, some of the baseline models only allow for one-to-one conversions, i.e. they are trained on parallel data and can only convert from seen speaker A to seen speaker B. We therefore train the baseline models on a single source-target speaker mapping (from VCC2SF1 to VCC2SM2), using 90% of the parallel training utterances for this speaker pair.

All utterances are resampled to 22.05 kHz and then converted to log Mel-spectrograms with a window and hop length of 1024 and 256 samples, respectively. During training, for each batch we randomly sample a k-frame sequence from each spectrogram, where k is randomly sampled from multiples of 32 between 96 to 320 (inclusive). This is done for all models to make it robust to utterance length, with the exception of StarGAN-ZSVC, which requires fixed-size input for its discriminator. This leads to slightly worse performance for StarGAN-ZSVC on long or silence-padded sequences. For a fair comparison, we therefore only consider non-silent frames of the target utterance.

4.2   Speaker Encoder and Vocoder Setup

The same WaveGlow vocoder is used to produce output waveforms for all networks to ensure a fair comparison. The WaveGlow model is pretrained on a large external corpus, as provided by the original paper [23]. However, since all models use log Mel-spectrogram inputs and produce log Mel-spectrogram outputs, we rather perform all quantitative comparisons on the spectrograms of each utterance (instead of waveforms), in order to minimize the vocoder's confounding effect.

Our WaveGlow implementation takes approximately 240 ms to produce one second of vocoded audio (taking a spectrogram as input). For the full voice conversion system to be faster than real-time, this means that the combined inference speed of the remaining sub-networks needs to be well under $700\,\mathrm{ms/s}$, or preferably significantly faster if used for data augmentation.

The speaker encoder is trained on 90% of the utterances from a combined set consisting of the VCTK [34], VCC 2018 [17], LibriSpeech [22], and the English CommonVoice 2020-06 datasets.[1] It is trained with the Adam optimizer [14] for 8 epochs with 8 speakers per batch, and 6 utterances per speaker in each batch. We start with a learning rate of 4×10^{-4} and adjust it down to 3×10^{-7} in the final epoch. Embeddings for speakers are precomputed by taking the average embedding over 4 arbitrary utterances for each speaker.

4.3   Baseline Models

We train 4 baseline models for comparison, all using the Adam optimizer. The first three are traditional one-to-one conversion models, consisting of a simple linear model, a DBLSTM model [31], and a UNet model [26]. The final model that we compare to is the AutoVC model, which is able to do zero-shot many-to-many conversion (Sect. 2.2). We compare AutoVC to StarGAN-ZSVC on all variants of seen/unseen source/target pairings. Each network is trained according to the method developed by Smith [29] by evaluating the decrease in loss every few hundred epochs for different learning rates, and updating the learning rate to correspond to the largest decrease in loss. This process is repeated until the validation loss begins to increase, after which training is terminated.

All one-to-one models are trained in the same way, taking the source spectrogram X_{src} as input and trained with an L_1 loss (which we found to produce better results than the L_2 loss) to predict the ground-truth target spectrogram X_{trg}. The linear model consists of 4 convolutional layers with output channels and kernel sizes of (200, 5), (200, 5), (100, 3), and (1, 3), respectively. The DBLSTM model is based on the original paper [31], but we do not use any time-alignment techniques (such as dynamic time warping). The model consists of 4 stacked bidirectional LSTM layers with a hidden size of 256 and a dropout of 0.3, followed by a final linear projection layer to bring the output dimension back to 80. The network is trained with a batch size of 8. The UNet model is built based on the structure of XResNet [7] using the method defined in the Fast.ai library [9].

Finally, AutoVC is trained using the same loss function as in the original paper [24]. It is trained with a batch size of 4 for 4700 epochs. The speaker encoder used is the pretrained encoder E described above.

4.4   StarGAN-ZSVC Training

We train StarGAN-ZSVC using the same Adam optimizer and learning rate scheduling technique of Smith [29]. Furthermore, we employ several tricks for successfully training GANs: (i) gradients in G and D are clipped to have a maximum norm of 1; (ii) the discriminator's learning rate is made to always

---

[1] Available under a CC-0 license at https://commonvoice.mozilla.org/en/datasets.

be half of the generators learning rate; (iii) the number of iterations training the discriminator versus generator is updated every several hundred epochs to ensure that the discriminator's loss is always roughly a factor of 10 lower than the adversarial term of the generator's loss; and (iv) dropout with a probability of 0.3 is added to the input of D after the first 3000 epochs (if added earlier it causes artifacts and destabilizes training).

The loss function used is the same as that of StarGAN-VC2, with the exception that the term $\mathcal{L}_{\text{cyc}}$ (see Sect. 2.1) is squared in our model, which we found to give superior results. We set $a = 1$, and $b = 0$ for the LSGAN constants, and $\lambda_{\text{cyc}} = 10$, $\lambda_{\text{id}} = 5$ for loss coefficients, being adjusted downwards during training in the same manner as in [13].

4.5 Evaluation

We compare converted output spectrograms to their ground-truth target spectrograms on the test dataset using several objective metrics. To account for different speaking rates, we first use dynamic time warping (DTW) to align the converted spectrogram to the target spectrogram, and then perform comparisons over non-silent regions of the *target* utterance. Non-silent regions are defined as those 80-dimensional spectrogram frames where the mean vector element value is greater than $-10\,\text{dB}$.

In addition to computing the mean absolute error (MAE) and mean square error (MSE) between spectrograms, we also compute a *cosine similarity* by finding the cosine distance between each 80-dimensional source/target frame pair of the Mel-spectrograms and then computing the mean cosine distance over all non-silent frames (after DTW alignment). This metric, denoted as $\cos(\theta)$, gives an additional measure of conversion quality.

Finally, to quantitatively measure speaker similarity (i.e. determining whether the generated spectrogram sounds like the target speaker), we define a new metric using the speaker encoder. We compute speaker embeddings for the target and output converted spectrograms using the speaker encoder E. The norm of the difference between these vectors, $\|E(X_{\text{src}\rightarrow\text{trg}}) - E(X_{\text{trg}})\| = e_{\text{norm}}$, is then used as a measure of speaker similarity, with a smaller norm corresponding to greater similarity between the converted and target spectrogram.

We also perform a subjective listening test with 12 proficient English speakers to assess how well StarGAN-ZSVC compares to AutoVC across various zero-shot settings. Each participant rated the naturalness of 144 utterances from 1 (bad) to 5 (excellent) where the utterance order and naming is randomized. The 144 utterances consist of 8 converted utterances for each seen/unseen source/target speaker pairing, for both AutoVC and StarGAN-ZSVC. A further 14 utterances are included to find a baseline rating for raw and vocoded audio. The ratings for each subset are averaged to find a mean opinion score (MOS), which serves as a measure of conversion quality.

5   Experiments

We perform two sets of experiments. First we perform an evaluation on seen speakers, where we compare StarGAN-ZSVC to all other models to obtain an indication of both speed and performance. We then compare StarGAN-ZSVC with AutoVC for zero-shot voice conversion, looking at both the output and cyclic reconstruction error. We encourage the reader to listen to the demo samples[2] for the zero-shot models.

5.1   Seen-to-Seen Conversion

In the first set of comparisons, we evaluate performance for test utterances where other utterances from both the source and target speaker have been seen during training. I.e., while the models have not been trained on these exact test utterances, they have seen the speakers during training. There is, however, a problem in directly comparing the one-to-one models (traditional baselines) to the many-to-many models (AutoVC and StarGAN-ZSVC). The one-to-one models are trained on parallel data, always taking in utterances from one speaker as input (VCC2SF1 in our case) and always producing output from a different target speaker (VCCSM2).

In contrast, the many-to-many models are trained without access to parallel data, taking in input utterances from several speakers (4 speakers, including VCC2SF1 and VCCSM2 in our case, as explained in Sect. 4.1). This means that the one-to-one and many-to-many models observe very different amounts of data. Moreover, while the data for both the one-to-one and many-to-many models are divided into a 90%–10% train-test split, the same exact splits aren't used in both setups; this is because the former requires parallel utterances, and the split is therefore across utterance *pairs* and not just individual utterances. To address this, we evaluate the many-to-many models in two settings: on the exact same test utterances as those from the test split of the one-to-one models, as well as on all possible source/target speaker utterance pairs where the source utterance is in the test utterances for the 4 seen training speakers. In the former case, it could happen that the many-to-many model actually observes one of the test utterances during training. Nevertheless, reporting scores for both settings allows for a meaningful comparison.

The results of this evaluation on seen speakers are given in Table 1. The results indicate that AutoVC appears to be the best in this evaluation on seen speakers. However, this comes at a computational cost: the linear and StarGAN-ZSVC models are a factor of 5 or more faster than the models relying on recurrent layers like DBLSTM and AutoVC.

---

[2] https://rf5.github.io/sacair2020/.

Table 1. Objective evaluation results when converting between speakers where both the source and target speaker are seen during training. For all metrics aside from cosine similarity, lower is better. Speed is measured as the time (in milliseconds) required to convert one second of input audio. The first StarGAN-ZSVC and AutoVC entries correspond to evaluations on the one-to-one test utterances, while the final two starred entries correspond to metrics computed when using test utterances from all seen training speakers for the many-to-many models.

Model	MAE	MSE	$\cos(\theta)$	e_{norm}	Speed (ms/s)
Linear	1.277	2.689	0.980	0.860	**0.15**
DBLSTM	1.329	3.102	0.982	0.496	12.52
UNet	1.370	3.347	0.980	0.545	100.5
AutoVC	**0.993**	**1.756**	**0.987**	**0.259**	10.99
StarGAN-ZSVC	1.092	2.101	0.977	0.513	1.88
AutoVC*	**1.000**	**1.783**	**0.987**	0.321	10.99
StarGAN-ZSVC*	1.008	1.863	0.983	**0.321**	1.88

5.2 Zero-Shot Conversion

Next we compare StarGAN-ZSVC and AutoVC in zero-shot settings, where either the source, target, or both source and target speaker are unseen during training. Many-to-many models can also be used in a cyclic manner; we use such cyclic reconstruction as another objective evaluation metric, where we compare how well the original spectrogram is reconstructed when performing this cyclical mapping of converting from the source speaker to the target speaker and back again. Results for zero-shot conversion are shown in Table 2.

Table 2. Objective evaluation results for zero-shot voice conversion for AutoVC and StarGAN-ZSVC. The *prediction* metrics compare the predicted output to the ground truth target, while the *reconstruction* metrics compare the cyclic reconstruction $X_{src\rightarrow trg\rightarrow src}$ with the original source spectrogram. e_{norm} indicates the vector norm of the speaker embeddings for the compared spectrograms, with lower values indicating closer speaker identities.

Setting	Model	Prediction			Reconstruction		
		MAE	$\cos(\theta)$	e_{norm}	MAE	$\cos(\theta)$	e_{norm}
Seen-to-unseen	AutoVC	1.246	**0.982**	0.742	1.178	0.976	0.392
	StarGAN-ZSVC	**1.030**	**0.982**	**0.705**	**0.197**	**0.997**	**0.124**
Unseen-to-seen	AutoVC	1.014	**0.986**	**0.328**	1.201	0.975	**0.753**
	StarGAN-ZSVC	**0.974**	0.985	0.380	**0.921**	**0.986**	0.760
Unseen-to-unseen	AutoVC	1.238	0.981	0.746	1.340	0.968	0.827
	StarGAN-ZSVC	**1.079**	**0.982**	**0.742**	**0.921**	**0.986**	**0.760**

The performance for AutoVC and StarGAN-ZSVC are similar on most metrics for the unseen-to-seen case. But for the seen-to-unseen case and the unseen-to-unseen case (where both the target and source speakers are new) StarGAN-ZSVC achieves both better prediction and reconstruction scores. This, coupled with its fast inference speed (Sect. 5.1), enables it to be used efficiently and effectively for downstream data augmentation purposes.

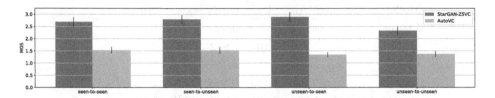

Fig. 3. Mean opinion score for naturalness for AutoVC and StarGAN-ZSVC in various source/target seen/unseen speaker pairings with 95% confidence intervals shown.

The results of the subjective evaluation are given in Fig. 3. To put the values into context, the MOS for the raw source utterances and vocoded source utterances included in the analysis are 4.86 and 4.33 respectively – these serve as an upper bound for the MOS values for both models. Figure 3 largely supports the objective evaluations, providing further evidence that StarGAN-ZSVC outperforms AutoVC in zero-shot settings. Interestingly, it would appear that StarGAN-ZSVC also appears more natural in the traditional seen-to-seen case. This evaluation indicates that, for human listeners, StarGAN-ZSVC appears more natural in the low-resource context considered in this paper.

6   Conclusion

This paper aimed to improve recent voice conversion methods in terms of speed, the use of non-parallel training data, and zero-shot prediction capability. To this end, we adapted the existing StarGAN-VC2 system by using a speaker encoder to generate speaker embeddings which are used to condition the generator and discriminator network on the desired source and target speakers. The resulting model, StarGAN-ZSVC, can perform zero-shot inference and is trainable with non-parallel data. In a series of experiments comparing StarGAN-ZSVC to the existing zero-shot voice conversion method AutoVC, we demonstrated that StarGAN-ZSVC is at least five times faster than AutoVC, while yielding better scores on objective and subjective metrics in a low-resource zero-shot voice conversion setting.

For future work, we plan to investigate whether scaling StarGAN-ZSVC up to larger datasets yields similar performance to existing high-resource voice conversion systems, and whether the system could be applied to other tasks aside from pure voice conversion (such as emotion or pronunciation conversion).

References

1. Cho, K., et al.: Learning phrase representations using RNN encoder-decoder for statistical machine translation. In: EMNLP (2014)
2. Choi, Y., Choi, M., Kim, M., Ha, J.W., Kim, S., Choo, J.: StarGAN: unified generative adversarial networks for multi-domain image-to-image translation. In: IEEE CVPR (2018)
3. Chorowski, J., Weiss, R.J., Bengio, S., van den Oord, A.: Unsupervised speech representation learning using WaveNet autoencoders. arXiv e-prints arXiv:1901.08810 (2019)
4. Dauphin, Y.N., Fan, A., Auli, M., Grangier, D.: Language modeling with gated convolutional networks. In: Precup, D., Teh, Y.W. (eds.) PMLR (2017)
5. Dumoulin, V., Shlens, J., Kudlur, M.: A learned representation for artistic style. In: ICLR (2017)
6. Erro, D., Moreno, A.: Weighted frequency warping for voice conversion. In: INTERSPEECH (2007)
7. He, T., Zhang, Z., Zhang, H., Zhang, Z., Xie, J., Li, M.: Bag of tricks for image classification with convolutional neural networks. In: IEEE CVPR (2019)
8. Hochreiter, S., Schmidhuber, J.: Long short-term memory. Neural Comput. **9**, 1735–1780 (1997)
9. Howard, J., Gugger, S.: DynamicUnet: create a U-Net from a given architecture (2020). https://docs.fast.ai/vision.models.unet#DynamicUnet. Accessed 8 Aug 2020
10. Huang, C., Lin, Y.Y., Lee, H., Lee, L.: Defending Your Voice: Adversarial Attack on Voice Conversion. arXiv e-prints arXiv:2005.08781 (2020)
11. Kameoka, H., Kaneko, T., Tanaka, K., Hojo, N.: StarGAN-VC: non-parallel many-to-many voice conversion using star generative adversarial networks. In: IEEE SLT Workshop (2018)
12. Kameoka, H., Kaneko, T., Tanaka, K., Hojo, N.: ACVAE-VC: non-parallel voice conversion with auxiliary classifier variational autoencoder. IEEE Trans. Audio Speech Lang. Process. **27**(9), 1432–1443 (2019)
13. Kaneko, T., Kameoka, H., Tanaka, K., Hojo, N.: StarGAN-VC2: rethinking conditional methods for StarGAN-based voice conversion. In: INTERSPEECH (2019)
14. Kingma, D.P., Ba, J.: Adam: A Method for Stochastic Optimization. arXiv e-prints arXiv:1412.6980 (2014)
15. Kumar, K., et al.: MelGAN: generative adversarial networks for conditional waveform synthesis. In: NeurIPS (2019)
16. Lal Srivastava, B.M., Vauquier, N., Sahidullah, M., Bellet, A., Tommasi, M., Vincent, E.: Evaluating voice conversion-based privacy protection against informed attackers. In: ICASSP (2020)
17. Lorenzo-Trueba, J., et al.: The voice conversion challenge 2018: promoting development of parallel and nonparallel methods. In: Odyssey Speaker and Language Recognition Workshop (2018)
18. Mao, X., Li, Q., Xie, H., Lau, R.Y., Wang, Z., Smolley, S.P.: Least squares generative adversarial networks. In: ICCV (2017)
19. Miyato, T., Koyama, M.: cGANs with projection discriminator. In: ICLR (2018)
20. Morise, M., Yokomori, F., Ozawa, K.: WORLD: a vocoder-based high-quality speech synthesis system for real-time applications. IEICE Trans. Inf. Syst. **E99.D**(7), 1877–1884 (2016)

21. van den Oord, A., et al.: WaveNet: A Generative Model for Raw Audio. arXiv e-prints arXiv:1609.03499 (2016)
22. Panayotov, V., Chen, G., Povey, D., Khudanpur, S.: Librispeech: an ASR corpus based on public domain audio books. In: IEEE ICASSP (2015)
23. Prenger, R., Valle, R., Catanzaro, B.: WaveGlow: a flow-based generative network for speech synthesis. In: IEEE ICASSP (2019)
24. Qian, K., Zhang, Y., Chang, S., Yang, X., Hasegawa-Johnson, M.: AutoVC: zero-shot voice style transfer with only autoencoder loss. In: PMLR (2019)
25. Rebryk, Y., Beliaev, S.: ConVoice: Real-Time Zero-Shot Voice Style Transfer with Convolutional Network. arXiv e-prints arXiv:2005.07815 (2020)
26. Ronneberger, O., Fischer, P., Brox, T.: U-Net: convolutional networks for biomedical image segmentation. In: Navab, N., Hornegger, J., Wells, W.M., Frangi, A.F. (eds.) MICCAI 2015. LNCS, vol. 9351, pp. 234–241. Springer, Cham (2015). https://doi.org/10.1007/978-3-319-24574-4_28
27. Shuang, Z.W., Bakis, R., Shechtman, S., Chazan, D., Qin, Y.: Frequency warping based on mapping formant parameters. In: INTERSPEECH (2006)
28. Sisman, B., Yamagishi, J., King, S., Li, H.: An Overview of Voice Conversion and its Challenges: From Statistical Modeling to Deep Learning. arXiv e-prints arXiv:2008.03648 (2020)
29. Smith, L.N.: Cyclical learning rates for training neural networks. In: IEEE WACV (2017)
30. Stylianou, Y., Cappe, O., Moulines, E.: Continuous probabilistic transform for voice conversion. IEEE Trans. Speech Audio Process. 6(2), 131–142 (1998)
31. Sun, L., Kang, S., Li, K., Meng, H.: Voice conversion using deep Bidirectional Long Short-Term Memory based Recurrent Neural Networks. In: IEEE ICASSP (2015)
32. Suundermann, D., Strecha, G., Bonafonte, A., Höge, H., Ney, H.: Evaluation of VTLN-based voice conversion for embedded speech synthesis. In: INTERSPEECH (2005)
33. Toda, T., Black, A.W., Tokuda, K.: Voice conversion based on maximum-likelihood estimation of spectral parameter trajectory. IEEE Trans. Audio Speech Lang. Process. 15(8), 2222–2235 (2007)
34. Veaux, C., Yamagishi, J., Macdonald, K.: CSTR VCTK Corpus: English Multi-speaker Corpus for CSTR Voice Cloning Toolkit (2017). http://homepages.inf.ed.ac.uk/jyamagis/page3/page58/page58.html. Accessed 1 Sep 2020
35. Wan, L., Wang, Q., Papir, A., Moreno, I.L.: Generalized end-to-end loss for speaker verification. In: ICASSP (2018)
36. Zhao, Y., et al.: Voice Conversion Challenge 2020: Intra-lingual semi-parallel and cross-lingual voice conversion. arXiv e-prints arXiv:2008.12527 (2020)
37. Zhizheng, W., Haizhou, L.: Voice conversion versus speaker verification: an overview. APSIPA Trans. Sig. Inf. Process. 3, e17 (2014)

Learning to Generalise in Sparse Reward Navigation Environments

Asad Jeewa[1,2(✉)] [iD], Anban W. Pillay[1,2] [iD], and Edgar Jembere[1,2] [iD]

[1] School of Mathematics, Statistics and Computer Science,
University of KwaZulu-Natal, Westville 4000, South Africa
asad.jeewa@gmail.com, {pillayw4,jemberee}@ukzn.ac.za
[2] Centre for Aritificial Intelligence Research, Cape Town, South Africa

Abstract. It is customary for RL agents to use the same environments for both training and testing. This causes the agents to learn specialist policies that fail to generalise even when small changes are made to the training environment. The generalisation problem is further compounded in sparse reward environments. This work evaluates the efficacy of curriculum learning for improving generalisation in sparse reward navigation environments: we present a manually designed training curriculum and use it to train agents to navigate past obstacles to distant targets, across several hand-crafted maze environments. The curriculum is evaluated against curiosity-driven exploration and a hybrid of the two algorithms, in terms of both training and testing performance. Using the curriculum resulted in better generalisation: agents were able to find targets in more testing environments, including some with completely new environment characteristics. It also resulted in decreased training times and eliminated the need for any reward shaping. Combining the two approaches did not provide any meaningful benefits and resulted in inferior policy generalisation.

Keywords: Generalisation · Curriculum learning · Sparse rewards · Navigation

1 Introduction

A fundamental challenge in reinforcement learning (RL) is that of generalisation [7]. It is customary for RL agents to use the same environments for both training and testing [8], as is the case for the Arcade Learning Environment [3], the classic RL benchmark. Agents therefore exhibit breakthrough results on very specific tasks but fail to generalise beyond the training environment [28]. Making small changes to the environment or task often leads to a dramatic decrease in performance [41,42]. This is because agents tend to memorise action sequences and therefore overfit to the training environments [7].

The generalisation problem is compounded in sparse reward environments. RL agents learn behaviour based solely on rewards received through interactions

© Springer Nature Switzerland AG 2020
A. Gerber (Ed.): SACAIR 2020, CCIS 1342, pp. 85–100, 2020.
https://doi.org/10.1007/978-3-030-66151-9_6

with an environment [31]. However, many environments have extrinsic rewards that are sparsely distributed, meaning that the environments does not return any positive or negative feedback to the agent on most timesteps. These environments are prevalent in the real-world [29] and training RL agents in them remains a major challenge [2]. There are various novel approaches to learning in these environments [2] but they tend to emphasise learning specialist polices that fail to generalise to unseen testing environments [7].

This research focuses on policy generalisation in sparse reward navigation environments. Policy generalisation refers to the extent to which a policy transfers to unseen environments within the same domain [8] without any additional training or fine-tuning. This is a difficult task since it is only possible for agents to learn on a small subset of possible states but it is desirable that they should be able to generalise and produce a good approximation over a larger state space [38]. In this work, agents are required to learn to navigate to distant targets across multiple environments, with different characteristics or obstacle configurations.

This work focuses on two approaches. The first technique is curriculum learning. When it is difficult for an agent to learn a task directly, a training curriculum can be designed to gradually increase an agent's knowledge over time. The curriculum imposes an order on training [14]: the agent is trained on a series of simpler tasks that progressively gets more difficult [25]. This enables it to learn "skills" that can be transferred to solve difficult tasks [25]. In this manner, the curriculum can be used to bypass the sparse rewards problem [12]. Curriculum learning has been shown to decrease training times as well as improve generalisation [4,12].

The second approach introduces intrinsic rewards to augment sparse extrinsic rewards. Intrinsic rewards are generated by the agent itself, instead of relying on feedback from the environment. Curiosity is a type of intrinsic reward that encourages an agent to find "novel" states [29] and has been used to learn policies that generalise to unseen environments.

In this research, we investigate the problem of generalisation in sparse reward navigation environments by evaluating the efficacy of curriculum learning for improving generalisation in this domain. A manually-designed curriculum for sparse reward navigation environments is presented and used to train agents in a suite of hand-crafted environments. Both training and testing performance of the curriculum is empirically compared and contrasted to two baseline algorithms: curiosity-driven exploration [29] and a hybrid approach that combines the curriculum with curiosity. The policies are evaluated in multiple testing environments that are either variations of the training environments or include entirely new characteristics.

The task, algorithms and environments are formally defined in Sect. 3. The benefits and limitations of the curriculum are discussed in Sect. 4: using the curriculum resulted in polices that generalised better than curiosity as well as decreased training times. Section 5 summarises the findings and discusses directions for future work.

2   Related Work

Generalisation remains a fundamental RL problems since agents tend to memorise trajectories from their training environments instead of learning transferable skills [7]. Classic RL benchmarks like the Arcade Learning Environment (ALE) [3] focus on creating specialist agents that perform well in a single environment. New benchmarks have been proposed to focus research on generalisation. The ProcGen Benchmark [7] uses procedural generation to generate new environments. The inherent diversity in the generated environments demands that agents learn robust polices in order to succeed. A similar framework is presented in [19] with larger scale three-dimensional environments.

Justesen et al. [20] however, highlighted limitations of procedural generation: it is difficult to automatically scale the difficulty of the task [20] and the distribution of the procedurally generated environments is often different to that of human-generated environments. Procedurally generating environments may lead to overfitting to the distribution of the generated environments [20]. A novel approach that uses reinforcement learning to learn a policy for generating environments shows promising results in [23].

Our work is inspired by Savinov et al. [32]. The authors emphasised the need for separate training and testing environments and investigated generalisation in custom maze environments with random goal placements. The aims of the study were different but the principles were incorporated into the curriculum defined in Subsect. 3.3. Similar findings were highlighted in other studies [8,42].

Curriculum learning was shown to decrease training times and improve generalisation across multiple common datasets in [4]. The main idea is to split a complex task into smaller, easier-to-solve sub-problems and controlling the curriculum to ensure that the task is never too difficult for the agent [17]. Previous work manually generated training curricula for various tasks [22,34]. A limitation of this approach is the requirement of expert domain knowledge [39]. Various studies attempted to alleviate this problem by presenting novel techniques for automatically generating a curriculum [12,24,39]. Florensa et al. [12] presented a method for automatically generating a curriculum that exhibited promising results in sparse reward navigation environments. The maze environments from the study have been incorporated into this study. The curriculum in this work is manually designed though only general concepts, such as environment size and obstacle configuration, were varied so as to ensure it did not require significant fine-tuning or expert knowledge.

Curriculum learning is an implicit form of generalisation [4]. Closely related to curriculum learning is hierarchical reinforcement learning. Tessler et al. [40] presented a framework that enabled agents to transfer "skills" learnt from easy sub-tasks to difficult tasks requiring multiple skills. Agents learnt "high-level" actions that pertain to walking and movement and used these skills to learn difficult navigation tasks faster in [13]. Our curriculum has been designed to implicitly learn in this manner since there are no obstacles in the early stages of training, thereby allowing agents to focus on locomotion.

The sparse reward problem is well-studied in reinforcement learning. Many novel approaches emphasise learning specialist polices and do not focus on generalisation [7]. Reward shaping augments the reward signal with additional rewards to enable learning in sparse reward environments. It can have a detrimental effect on training if it is used incorrectly and can change the optimal policy or the definition of the task [9,26,28]. Manually engineering reward functions for each new environment is difficult [9,15]. Alternatively, reward functions were recovered from demonstrations in [15,36,37]. Shaped rewards can result in specialist policies that generalise poorly [15]. The problem was investigated in [16] where agents learnt polices that were optimised for single training environments. A major benefit of our curriculum is that it does not require any reward shaping.

An alternative to "shaping" an extrinsic reward is to supplement it with intrinsic rewards [27] such as curiosity. Curiosity-Driven Exploration by Self-Supervised Prediction [29] formally defined a framework for training curious agents. Curiosity empowers the agent by giving it the capability of exploration, enabling it to reach far away states that contain extrinsic rewards. A well-known limitation of the approach is that agents often find a source of randomness in an environment that allows it to inadvertently satiate its curiosity [5]. There are various other novel approaches [6,33].

Curiosity has been chosen as a baseline as it has shown promising generalisation capabilities in previous studies [5,29]. Agents struggled to generalise to environments with different textures in [5,29]. This is not relevant to this study since agents observations are vector rather than visual representations (see Subsect. 3.1).

To our knowledge, curriculum learning has not been evaluated extensively with regards to generalisation in sparse reward navigation environments.

3   Methodology

3.1   The Task

The goal of the agent is to navigate from its starting point to a fixed distant target, with obstacles or walls placed along its route. The agent is required to learn foresight: it needs to learn to move further away from the target in the present, in order to find the target in the future. The task is a variation of the classic point-mass navigation task in various studies [10,11]. We consider an agent interacting with an environment in discrete time steps. At each time step t, the agent gets an observation o_t of the environment and then takes an action a_t from a set of actions A.

The observation set O comprises the coordinates of the agent's current position, the coordinates of the target, the distance to the goal and rays that extend in 8 directions, at $45°$ intervals. These short rays provide essential feedback to the agent by enabling it to detect walls and targets that are in its vicinity and therefore adapt its policy accordingly.

The rays take on additional importance when agents are placed in previously unseen environments since they enable the agents to learn robust policies: when an agent detects an obstacle in its vicinity, it needs to learn to move away from the obstacle, in the direction of an open path. If an agent executes memorised actions, it will move directly into walls and never reach its destination.

The ray length was tuned to balance the difficulty of the task: if the rays are too long, the agent unrealistically detects objects that are far away but if it is too short, the agent is unable to detect anything except that which is immediately in front of it. This is analogous to the field of view. The observations were stacked to equip the agents with a small memory of the immediate past. The previous ten observations were stored at any given time.

The action set a_t allows the agent to move in eight directions: forwards, backwards, sideways as well as diagonally, unlike the standard Gridworld task [42].

By default, before any training modifications are made, the environments are all sparse reward environments since the agent only receives a +1 reward for finding the target. The starting positions of the agent and the target are far away from each other, on different ends of the environment. The agents do not receive any intermediate rewards and incur a small penalty on every timestep, to encourage them to find the target in the shortest possible time.

3.2 Environments

There are multiple environments and each varies in terms of the configuration of walls and obstacles (see Fig. 1). This is to deter agents from learning an optimal policy in one single environment, rather learning the "skill" of finding a target in an arbitrary navigation environment. The predefined environments were carefully designed to represent high-level features or environment characteristics that include dead-ends and multiple paths to the target. We theorise that introducing agents to numerous environment features in training enables them to learn a flexible policy that enables them to find targets when similar features are found in new environments. The environments were divided into a set of training and testing environments. The generalisability of the agents was evaluated in the testing environments.

The training environments were further divided into three categories: *Obstacle* environments (see Fig. 1a) contain only a single obstacle that varies in terms of size and orientation. The sizes range from a scale of 0 to 3 and the orientation is defined as any angle from $0°$, in $45°$ increments. The size of the agent and ray length are also depicted in Fig. 1a to illustrate the scale of the task.

Maze environments have multiple obstacles and were subdivided based on difficulty. There are *Standard* mazes in Fig. 1b and *Difficult* mazes in Fig. 1c. *Difficult* mazes have multiple obstacles that span more than half the width of the entire environment. They also include more complex versions of some of the *Standard* mazes, by manipulating the size of each obstacle in an environment. The "u-maze" from [11] was also incorporated into this group. The difficult mazes were deliberately designed to test the boundaries of the algorithms and to identify limitations.

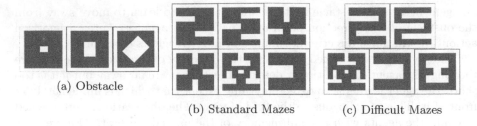

(a) Obstacle   (b) Standard Mazes   (c) Difficult Mazes

Fig. 1. Training environments

The testing environments were divided into two categories: *Orientation* and *New*. *Orientation* testing environments were created by rotating the training mazes by 90° and without changing the overall structure of the obstacles. *New* testing environments have different obstacle configurations to the training environments. New features or environment characteristics, such as bottlenecks or repeated obstacles, were incorporated into this group. This allowed us to analyse whether the agents were able to learn advanced skills and further assess the extent of the generalisation. Both these categories were further subdivided into *Standard* and *Difficult* subcategories, as per the definition used for the training environments. An illustration of the *Orientation* environments are shown in Fig. 2a. Both the *Standard New* and *Difficult New* groups, depicted in Fig. 2b and c respectively, contain three mazes each. The "spiral-maze", a commonly used maze seen in [11], was incorporated into the difficult category.

(a) Orientation   (b) Standard New   (c) Difficult New

Fig. 2. Testing environments

3.3   Algorithms

Curriculum Learning. A curriculum was manually designed to enable agents to learn the task of finding distant targets across multiple sparse reward navigation environments (see Algorithm 1). This is difficult since agents cannot optimise a policy for any specific environments and when the environments are large, with multiple obstacles (the most difficult version of the task), the reward feedback is sparse.

The curriculum has been designed to act as a means of bypassing the sparse rewards problem. It also improves generalisation by exposing agents to a diverse set of environments during training.

Algorithm 1. Manually-Designed Curriculum

Input: Obstacle Environments O, Obstacle Max Scale $S_{obstacle}$, Maze Environments M, Environment Max Scale $S_{environment}$, Reward Threshold $R_{threshold}$, Number Consecutive Episodes $n_{consecutive}$

for $i \leftarrow 1$ to $S_{environment}$ **do**

    Reset episode count

    $r_{average} = 0$

    repeat (for each episode)

        $r_{average} \leftarrow$ average episodic reward from previous $n_{consecutive}$ episodes

        Sample an obstacle environment from O

        Sample scale from $\{0, 1, 2, \ldots, S_{obstacle}\}$

        Sample angle from $\{0°, 45°, 90°, 135°, \ldots, 315°\}$

        Sample agent and target starting positions

    until $r_{average} < R_{threshold}$

    Reset episode count

    $r_{average} = 0$

    repeat (for each episode)

        $r_{average} \leftarrow$ average episodic reward from previous $n_{consecutive}$ episodes

        Sample a maze environment from M

        Sample agent and target starting positions

    until $r_{average} < R_{threshold}$

end for

Environment parameters are varied over time to control the difficulty of the task to ensure that the current task is never too difficult for the agent. The first parameter is the environment size: decreasing the size, while keeping the agent size and speed the same, decreases the sparsity of rewards since the goal and target are closer to each other in smaller environments. The second parameter is the obstacle configuration, which is varied through changing the number and size of obstacles: either single obstacles or multiple obstacles in a maze-like structure.

In the early stages of training, the environments are small and contain a single obstacle or none at all. This was achieved by assigning O, in Algorithm 1, to the obstacle environments in Fig. 1a. Agents are able to learn how to control themselves by navigating around the environment to nearby targets. When the average reward (over the past 5000 consecutive episodes) reaches a predefined threshold, the difficulty is increased. The first adjustment is to increase the size and number of obstacles, through randomly sampling maze environments from Fig. 1b and in Fig. 1c. When the agent reaches the same predefined reward threshold, the environment size is increased. This two-fold difficulty adjustment keeps occurring until the agent progresses to large maze environments with multiple obstacles. This ensures that the curriculum only progresses when the agent has succeeded in its current task.

Randomly sampling environments is an important aspect of the curriculum. It is also essential that the set of training environments is diverse and incorporates a wide array of obstacle configurations [7]. This deters agents from memorising the dynamics of any particular training environment, instead learning how to navigate past arbitrary obstacles to find distant targets. This is analogous to supervised learning i.e. training on a diverse training set al.lows for a more generalised model that does not overfit to training data. Specifically, overfitting means memorising a policy that is optimised for the training environments, resulting in poor performance in the testing environments. Similarly, policy memorisation refers to a policy that optimises the dynamics of a particular environment by memorising actions that lead to success, resulting in poor performance even when subtle changes are made to the environment [41].

The maximum environment size ($S_{environment}$ in Algorithm 1) was carefully tuned to ensure that the task is a sparse rewards problem. This was verified by running an agent trained with policy gradient on the sparse reward function (+1 for finding the target), with no exploration strategy, and observing that it was not possible for it to find the target, after a large number of training steps [16].

Inspired by various other work [21,32,42], the last aspect of the curriculum attempts to bypass the sparse rewards problem by "densifying" the training environment. The starting locations of both the agent and target are randomised at the start of every episode. This means that the target is often close to the agent, resulting in frequent feedback that enables meaningful learning. This also encourages the agent to explore different parts of the environments.

Baseline Algorithms. We compare the performance of the curriculum to curiosity-driven exploration defined by Pathak et al. in [29]. This equips the agent with an intrinsic reward that allows it to explore the training environments by seeking "novel" states, thereby gaining an understand of the dynamics of the various environments. A reward is generated through a prediction error: agents are trained to predict the next state as well as actions taken in between states. In this way, the reward only captures surprising states that have come about directly as a result of the agents actions. Curiosity has shown promising generalisation capabilities in previous studies [5,29].

In the curiosity setting, the curriculum defined in Subsect. 3.3 is omitted i.e. the size of the environment is fixed at the largest configuration and a training maze is randomly sampled from Fig. 1b and c on each episode. Training also occurs under the dense reward setting with random target and agent starting locations.

The final approach combines the curiosity reward with the hand-crafted curriculum which we term "Hybrid": Agents are trained using the curriculum from Subsect. 3.3 and the reward function is augmented with a curiosity signal. Both algorithms have been shown to improve generalisation individually [5,6,12] and it was therefore necessary to investigate if there were any merits to combining them.

3.4 Experimental Design

We evaluated the performance of the curriculum by comparing it to curiosity-driven exploration [29] and a hybrid "curiosity-curriculum" approach. All policies are represented by neural networks with Proximal Policy Optimisation (PPO) [35] being used as an optimiser. PPO is robust [35] and requires lesser hyperparameter tuning when compared to similar methods [5]. However, an arbitrary policy gradient method could have been: the focus of this work is rather on the comparison of different training methods so consistency in the optimisation method is more important.

We defined baseline hyperparameters for each algorithm by training agents in the easiest version of the tasks. The hyperparameters were then carefully tuned and optimised by observing the training process and then tweaking the relevant parameters as required. The networks have two hidden layers, each with 256 units. The swish activation function [30] was used. The learning rate and entropy coefficient were fixed at 3.0×10^{-4} and 0.01 respectively, along with a batch size of 256 and a buffer size of 5120. All agents were trained for 20 million training steps. This was carefully tuned to ensure that the agents had sufficient time to learn. However, it was observed that agents tended to overfit to the training environments when the steps were too high [42]. After tuning the hyperparameters independently for each algorithm, the agents were trained on a cluster of machines on the Centre for High Performance Computing [1], using the Unity ML-Agents platform [18]. The polices for each algorithm were then evaluated against each other. The codebase and further details are available at https://github.com/AsadJeewa/Learning-to-Generalise-in-Sparse-Reward-Navigation-Environments.

4   Results and Discussion

Analysis is performed in three stages: the first stage compares the training performance of each algorithm. Since the agents were trained under a dense rewards setting, with randomised agent and target starting positions for each episode, it is necessary to evaluate the algorithms under a sparse reward setting. This was achieved by positioning the agent and target at distant locations in every training environment, fixed at points that make the task as difficult as possible.

We perform a critical evaluation of the generalisability of each algorithm in the unseen testing environments. The last stage performs trajectory analysis to understand the strengths and limitations of each algorithm. It provides insight into the intricacies of how agents move within different environments.

4.1   Training Performance

The training curves are depicted in Fig. 3a i.e. the average episodic reward of the agents over time, with a smoothing factor of 0.2. For each algorithm, we performed five independent runs and computed the mean learning curve and standard deviation. Twenty independent instances of the environment were used for more efficient data collection during training.

The dashed line depicts the point at which both the curriculum and hybrid agents progressed to the final lesson, which corresponds to the training environments of the curiosity-driven agent.

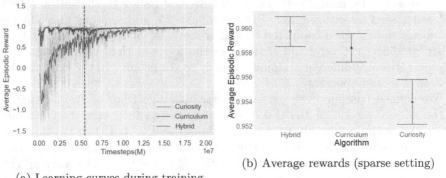

(a) Learning curves during training

(b) Average rewards (sparse setting)

Fig. 3. Training performance for all algorithms

Figure 3 highlights the benefits of using the curriculum. The learning curve never drops significantly since the agents' task is never too difficult. The curriculum advances quickly in the early stages of training when the task is easier. The sudden drops in reward are indicative of points at which the task is made more difficult but the fact that the curve peaks very quickly thereafter, indicates that knowledge is being transferred between tasks. In all runs, it was noted that the curriculum agent converged significantly faster than the curiosity agent.

A major benefit of the curriculum is that there is no reward shaping necessary. This is due to the manner in which the curriculum was designed that ensures that the agents always receive sufficient reward feedback during training. We performed an empirical investigation into various different shaped rewards and found no performance improvements. Rather, the motivations of the agents became polluted [9,26]. For example, when an agent was rewarded for moving closer to the target, it lacked the foresight to move past obstacles. Shaping rewards also resulted in more specialist policies that work well in some environments, but poorly in others. Reward shaping also requires additional information which may not be available in the real-world.

The curiosity curve shows rewards slowly increasing as training progresses. The hybrid training curve is very similar to the curriculum agent. When the curiosity strength was varied, the curves still followed a similar pattern. This indicates that the curiosity rewards had little effect on the training process when coupled with the curriculum.

Figure 3b illustrates that, for all algorithms, the agents were able to efficiently find the target in all training environments, under the sparse reward setting. All algorithms have an average reward that approaches a maximum possible reward of +1. These results act as a validation of each algorithm since it indicates that all agents have obtained sufficient knowledge of the task and are able to find targets across a diverse set of mazes. This allowed us to perform a fair comparison of the generalisation capabilities of each algorithm in the testing environments. Error bars are depicted with a confidence interval of 95%.

4.2 Generalisability

The best performing training run from Subsect. 4.1 was selected for each algorithm. The average reward was then analysed for each of the different groups of testing environments. Each algorithm was run for 1000 episodes, with a random testing environment being sampled at the start of the episode, from the corresponding testing group. This is necessary due to the stochastic nature of the polices: the agents sometimes succeed and fail in the same testing environment. This results in vastly different episodic rewards and a large number of episodes is therefore necessary to stabilise the average rewards.

When analysing the results, there are certain important considerations that need to be made. The performance of each algorithm is often different i.e. agents succeed and fail in different testing environments. There are instances when one algorithm enabled agents to navigate to the target in a short time, but another resulted in agents only finding the target after a large number of episode steps or never at all. We wish to investigate this phenomenon further in future work.

The task is not trivial since it as analogous to placing a human or vehicle in a new environment and only equipping them with information about its current location, destination and the ability to "see" what's around it. It does not have any knowledge of the dynamics of the environment that it is placed in. This means that some "exploration" is necessary and it is expected that agents will move into obstacles as they try to advance towards the goal. It is not possible to solve the generalisation problem completely: it was not expected that the agents would obtain expert performance in the testing environments. The goal is rather to transfer some knowledge that can be reused in the environments.

The policies are used "as-is" and there is no fine-tuning for any of the testing environments, as is the case in other studies [29]. It is definitely possible to improve the results in each testing environment by fine-tuning the policy though that is not the aim of this study. This work rather investigated the extent to which the learned policy generalised.

Lastly, the sample size in the testing environment groups is fairly small. There are only three environments in some groups. In future work, we wish to investigate whether the results hold when increasing the size of the groups.

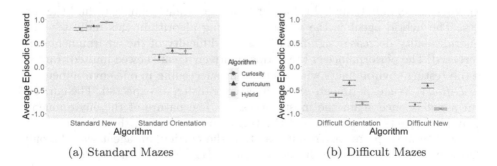

(a) Standard Mazes   (b) Difficult Mazes

Fig. 4. Generalisability in the maze testing environments

The average episodic rewards are in the range $[-1, 1)$. A successful run is one in which agents are able to navigate to the target. The faster an agent finds the target, the higher the reward it receives. An average reward approaching one therefore indicates that the agents successfully found the targets on all runs. A score below one indicates that on most runs, the agents were unable to find the target, across all environments, with zero representing an inflection point.

The results highlight an expected gap between training and testing performance. However, they also indicate that some generalisation has taken place.

Standard Mazes. The experiments that we conducted indicate good performance for all algorithms in the standard mazes. Figure 4a illustrates that the algorithms preformed similarly in the *Standard New* environments. Notably, all the agents were able to consistently navigate to the target in all three environments. This is promising since the obstacle configurations are completely different to the training environments. This indicates that the policy is robust and generalises well (in these environments). On average, the hybrid agents found the targets marginally faster.

The *Standard Variation* results depict that all algorithms are able to succeed on most runs. The curriculum agent was marginally the most successful across the six environments but the performance is once again similar for all algorithms. It is encouraging that the agents succeed in some environments however, we theorise that the results can be improved by fine-tuning the set of training and testing environments, or procedurally generating training mazes to improve the robustness of the policies.

Difficult Mazes. While the results of the algorithms in the standard mazes showed similar performance, the agents trained using the curriculum performed best in the difficult mazes.

The *Difficult Orientation* results in Fig. 4b indicate that the agents weindicate that the agents were re unable to find the target on most runs. However, some transfer has taken place. The curriculum obtained the highest average reward: the result is statistically significant under a 95% confidence interval. Interestingly, both the curriculum and hybrid agents succeeded in two of the five environments but the hybrid agent took significantly longer to find the targets. The hybrid agent is the worst performing algorithm; this indicates that generalisability decreases significantly as the difficulty of the environments are increased. The performance of the curiosity-driven agent showed limited transfer to the testing environments with agents only succeeding in one environment.

Difficult New experiments show the least transfer, as expected. The curriculum agent is once again the most successful. The nature of the environments mean that agents are able to find the targets on some runs, though not consistently. The most promising result was that the curriculum agent was the only algorithm that succeeded in the "spiral-maze" [11] depicted in Fig. 2c.

4.3   Trajectory Analysis

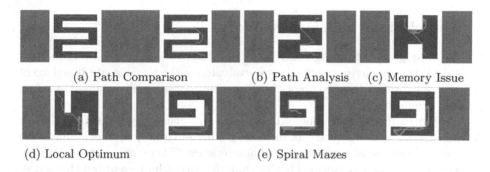

(a) Path Comparison   (b) Path Analysis   (c) Memory Issue

(d) Local Optimum   (e) Spiral Mazes

Fig. 5. Walkthrough trajectories

We performed trajectory analysis by analysing the movement patterns of the trained agents across the different environments, as per [32]. It was often observed that the curriculum agents tended to move in a more directed manner than the curiosity-driven agents. The curriculum agents also tended to "stick" to the walls for a longer time, using them to guide it to the target. An example of this is depicted in Fig. 5a. The trail of a curiosity-driven agent is shown in red, on the left, and that of the curriculum agent is in blue. There is further proof of this in Fig. 5b. This figure also highlights common behaviour of the curriculum agents: they initially attempted to move directly towards the goal, along the shortest possible path, but when the agents detected an obstacle, they adapted to move around it. The highlights the robustness of the policy.

A limitation of all the algorithms is that it was sometimes observed that the agents repeatedly move along a similar path and only make slight advancements towards the target, over a long period of time. However, the agents often still find their way to the target, as shown in Fig. 5c. In an attempt to alleviate this problem, we would like to look into different methods for increasing the "memory" of the agents. The number of stacked observations could be increased, so that agents can "remember" more of their previous failures, or recurrent architectures could be used.

Figure 5d shows an example of an environment in which the curriculum agent failed to find the target. The agent was progressing towards the target but then got stuck in a local optimum and kept repeating the same actions, until the maximum episode steps was reached. It is possible that the agents would eventually have found its way to the target. This result points to some memorisation in the policy. We theorise that improving the memory of the agent would also alleviate this problem.

The most promising result is shown in Fig. 5e. The spiral maze is difficult because the agent needs to learn a very specific trajectory in order to find the target. The curriculum agent was the only agent that succeeded in this environment. This further highlights the robustness of the curriculum: it was able to continuously adapt its actions as it observed the environment. The curiosity agents, depicted on the left in Fig. 5e and the hybrid agents (on the far right) both got stuck in local optima and failed to reach the target.

5   Conclusions and Future Work

We have designed a training curriculum that improves generalisation in sparse reward navigation environments. It was evaluated against a curiosity-based agent [29] and a hybrid of the two algorithms, in a suite of manually-designed navigation environments.

The curriculum agents showed the most promising generalisation results. Agents were able to find targets in more testing environments, including some with completely new environment characteristics. There are certain environments when curiosity performed better than the curriculum agent but the performance of the agents were more erratic i.e. they sometimes performed excellently and sometimes very poorly within the same environments. Curriculum learning proved to be more a robust approach. It also resulted in decreased training times and eliminated the need for any reward shaping.

Combining curiosity with the curriculum provided no meaningful benefits. The training performance was very similar to the curriculum agent and it exhibited inferior policy generalisation in the difficult maze testing environments.

There are limitations to the curriculum, as indicated by the generalisation gap between the training and testing environments. Agents sometimes get stuck in local optimums and also repeated the same movement patterns in an episode. There is some memorisation occurring since the agents perform excellently in the training environments and struggle in some testing environments. However, the results are promising, since it shows clear evidence of knowledge transfer to unseen environments.

In future work, we propose further increasing the diversity in the training environments and fine-tuning the curriculum to further improve the results. We also wish to investigate the effects of increasing the memory of agents to deter them from repeating trajectories in testing environment. Another interesting direction is to perform further large scale analysis of the algorithms by increasing the number of testing environments, either manually or by procedurally generating them [7].

References

1. Centre for high performance computing. https://www.chpc.ac.za/
2. Andrychowicz, M., et al.: Hindsight experience replay. In: Advances in Neural Information Processing Systems, pp. 5048–5058 (2017)
3. Bellemare, M.G., Naddaf, Y., Veness, J., Bowling, M.: The arcade learning environment: an evaluation platform for general agents. J. Artif. Intell. Res. **47**, 253–279 (2013)
4. Bengio, Y., Louradour, J., Collobert, R., Weston, J.: Curriculum learning. In: Proceedings of the 26th Annual International Conference on Machine Learning, ICML 2009, pp. 41–48. Association for Computing Machinery, Montreal (2009). https://doi.org/10.1145/1553374.1553380

5. Burda, Y., Edwards, H., Pathak, D., Storkey, A., Darrell, T., Efros, A.A.: Large-scale study of curiosity-driven learning. In: International Conference on Learning Representations (2019). https://openreview.net/forum?id=rJNwDjAqYX
6. Burda, Y., Edwards, H., Storkey, A., Klimov, O.: Exploration by random network distillation. arXiv preprint arXiv:1810.12894 (2018)
7. Cobbe, K., Hesse, C., Hilton, J., Schulman, J.: Leveraging procedural generation to benchmark reinforcement learning. arXiv preprint arXiv:1912.01588, p. 27 (2019)
8. Cobbe, K., Klimov, O., Hesse, C., Kim, T., Schulman, J.: Quantifying generalization in reinforcement learning. arXiv preprint arXiv:1812.02341, p. 8 (2018)
9. Devlin, S.M., Kudenko, D.: Dynamic potential-based reward shaping (2012). http://eprints.whiterose.ac.uk/75121/
10. Duan, Y., Chen, X., Houthooft, R., Schulman, J., Abbeel, P.: Benchmarking deep reinforcement learning for continuous control. In: International Conference on Machine Learning, pp. 1329–1338 (2016). http://proceedings.mlr.press/v48/duan16.html, ISSN: 1938–7228 Section: Machine Learning
11. Florensa, C., Held, D., Geng, X., Abbeel, P.: Automatic goal generation for reinforcement learning agents. In: International Conference on Machine Learning, pp. 1515–1528 (2018). http://proceedings.mlr.press/v80/florensa18a.html. ISSN: 1938–7228 Section: Machine Learning
12. Florensa, C., Held, D., Wulfmeier, M., Zhang, M., Abbeel, P.: Reverse curriculum generation for reinforcement learning. arXiv:1707.05300 [cs] (2018)
13. Frans, K., Ho, J., Chen, X., Abbeel, P., Schulman, J.: Meta learning shared hierarchies. arXiv:1710.09767 [cs] (2017)
14. Hacohen, G., Weinshall, D.: On the power of curriculum learning in training deep networks. arXiv:1904.03626 [cs, stat] (2019)
15. Hussein, A., Elyan, E., Gaber, M.M., Jayne, C.: Deep reward shaping from demonstrations. In: Proceedings of the 2017 International Joint Conference on Neural Networks (IJCNN), pp. 510–517. IEEE (2017)
16. Jeewa, A., Pillay, A., Jembere, E.: Directed curiosity-driven exploration in hard exploration, sparse reward environments. In: Davel, M.H., Barnard, E. (eds.) Proceedings of the South African Forum for Artificial Intelligence Research, Cape Town, South Africa, 4–6 December 2019, CEUR Workshop Proceedings, vol. 2540, pp. 12–24. CEUR-WS.org (2019). http://ceur-ws.org/Vol-2540/FAIR2019_paper_42.pdf
17. Jiang, L., Meng, D., Zhao, Q., Shan, S., Hauptmann, A.G.: Self-paced curriculum learning. In: Proceedings of the Twenty-Ninth AAAI Conference on Artificial Intelligence (2015). https://www.aaai.org/ocs/index.php/AAAI/AAAI15/paper/view/9750
18. Juliani, A., et al.: Unity: a general platform for intelligent agents. arXiv:1809.02627 [cs, stat] (2018)
19. Juliani, A., et al.: Obstacle tower: a generalization challenge in vision, control, and planning. arXiv:1902.01378 [cs] (2019)
20. Justesen, N., Torrado, R.R., Bontrager, P., Khalifa, A., Togelius, J., Risi, S.: Illuminating generalization in deep reinforcement learning through procedural level generation. arXiv:1806.10729 [cs, stat] (2018)
21. Kang, B., Jie, Z., Feng, J.: Policy optimization with demonstrations. In: International Conference on Machine Learning, pp. 2469–2478 (2018). http://proceedings.mlr.press/v80/kang18a.html
22. Karpathy, A., van de Panne, M.: Curriculum learning for motor skills. In: Kosseim, L., Inkpen, D. (eds.) AI 2012. LNCS (LNAI), vol. 7310, pp. 325–330. Springer, Heidelberg (2012). https://doi.org/10.1007/978-3-642-30353-1_31

23. Khalifa, A., Bontrager, P., Earle, S., Togelius, J.: PCGRL: Procedural content generation via reinforcement learning. arXiv:2001.09212 [cs, stat] (2020)
24. Matiisen, T., Oliver, A., Cohen, T., Schulman, J.: Teacher-student curriculum learning. In: IEEE Transactions on Neural Networks and Learning Systems, pp. 1–9 (2019). https://doi.org/10.1109/TNNLS.2019.2934906
25. Narvekar, S., Stone, P.: Learning curriculum policies for reinforcement learning. arXiv:1812.00285 [cs, stat] (2018)
26. Ng, A.Y., Harada, D., Russell, S.: Policy invariance under reward transformations: theory and application to reward shaping. ICML **99**, 278–287 (1999)
27. Oudeyer, P.Y., Kaplan, F.: What is intrinsic motivation? A typology of computational approaches. Front. Neurorobotics **1**, 6 (2009)
28. Packer, C., Gao, K., Kos, J., Krähenbühl, P., Koltun, V., Song, D.: Assessing generalization in deep reinforcement learning. arXiv:1810.12282 [cs, stat] (2019)
29. Pathak, D., Agrawal, P., Efros, A.A., Darrell, T.: Curiosity-driven exploration by self-supervised prediction. In: Proceedings of the IEEE Conference on Computer Vision and Pattern Recognition Workshops (CVPRW 2017), pp. 488–489. IEEE, Honolulu (2017). https://doi.org/10.1109/CVPRW.2017.70, http://ieeexplore.ieee.org/document/8014804/
30. Ramachandran, P., Zoph, B., Le, Q.V.: Searching for activation functions. arXiv:1710.05941 [cs] (2017)
31. Ravishankar, N.R., Vijayakumar, M.V.: Reinforcement learning algorithms: survey and classification. Indian J. Sci. Technol. **10**(1), 1–8 (2017). https://doi.org/10.17485/ijst/2017/v10i1/109385, http://www.indjst.org/index.php/indjst/article/view/109385
32. Savinov, N., Dosovitskiy, A., Koltun, V.: Semi-parametric topological memory for navigation. arXiv:1803.00653 [cs] (2018)
33. Savinov, N., et al.: Episodic curiosity through reachability. arXiv:1810.02274 [cs, stat] (2019)
34. Schmidhuber, J.: POWERPLAY: training an increasingly general problem solver by continually searching for the simplest still unsolvable problem. arXiv:1112.5309 [cs] (2012)
35. Schulman, J., Wolski, F., Dhariwal, P., Radford, A., Klimov, O.: Proximal policy optimization algorithms. arXiv:1707.06347 [cs] (2017)
36. Suay, H.B., Brys, T.: Learning from demonstration for shaping through inverse reinforcement learning, p. 9 (2016)
37. Suay, H.B., Brys, T., Taylor, M.E., Chernova, S.: Reward shaping by demonstration. In: Proceedings of the Multi-Disciplinary Conference on Reinforcement Learning and Decision Making (RLDM) (2015)
38. Sutton, R.S., Barto, A.G.: Reinforcement Learning, Second Edition: An Introduction. MIT Press, Cambridge (2018). google-Books-ID: uWV0DwAAQBAJ
39. Svetlik, M., Leonetti, M., Sinapov, J., Shah, R., Walker, N., Stone, P.: Automatic curriculum graph generation for reinforcement learning agents. In: Proceedings of the Thirty-First AAAI Conference on Artificial Intelligence (2017). https://www.aaai.org/ocs/index.php/AAAI/AAAI17/paper/view/14961
40. Tessler, C., Givony, S., Zahavy, T., Mankowitz, D.J., Mannor, S.: A deep hierarchical approach to lifelong learning in minecraft. arXiv:1604.07255 [cs] (2016)
41. Ye, C., Khalifa, A., Bontrager, P., Togelius, J.: Rotation, translation, and cropping for zero-shot generalization. arXiv:2001.09908 [cs, stat] (2020)
42. Zhang, C., Vinyals, O., Munos, R., Bengio, S.: A study on overfitting in deep reinforcement learning. arXiv:1804.06893 [cs, stat] (2018)

Evaluation of a Pure-Strategy Stackelberg Game for Wildlife Security in a Geospatial Framework

Lisa-Ann Kirkland[1]([⊠]) [iD], Alta de Waal[1,2] [iD], and Johan Pieter de Villiers[1] [iD]

[1] University of Pretoria, Pretoria, South Africa
lisakirkland25@gmail.com, {alta.dewaal,pieter.devilliers}@up.ac.za
[2] Centre for Artificial Intelligence (CAIR), Pretoria, South Africa

Abstract. Current research on wildlife security games has minimal focus on performance evaluation. The performance of the rangers is evaluated by assessing their game utility, sometimes in comparison with their maximin utility, and other times in comparison with their real-world utility when the game is implemented in a wildlife park. Currently no evaluation framework exists, and this paper proposes an evaluation suite to address this. The movements of the wildlife, the rangers, and the poachers are simulated over a grid of cells corresponding to the wildlife park, where cells containing geographical obstacles are excluded. Poaching and arrest frequency are the primary evaluation measures used. Firstly, we develop a null game to act as a baseline. Typically, one would expect random behaviour of all agents in the null game. However, we simulate random movement for the rangers but more intelligent movement for the poachers. The motivation for this design is to assess whether executing the Stackelberg game yields significantly better ranger performance than random movement, while keeping the poachers' behaviour consistent. The intelligent poachers move by taking their geographical preferences into account and learn from poaching and arrest events. Secondly, we propose that the rangers act as the Stackelberg follower instead of the leader. We formulate a simple pure-strategy Stackelberg game and implement four variations of the game within the framework. The results of the simulations show that the rangers perform better than random when using the Stackelberg game and perform best when acting as the follower.

Keywords: Evaluation · Wildlife security · Game theory · Stackelberg

1 Introduction

Rhino poaching continues to be a major problem in South Africa. Although rhino deaths started decreasing in 2015, the number of poaching activities inside and adjacent to the Kruger National Park (KNP) has only decreased from 2 466 in 2015 to 2 014 in 2019 [3,4]. Anti-poaching units offer an attempt to combat rhino poaching [15] and to facilitate such efforts, this paper focuses on

© Springer Nature Switzerland AG 2020
A. Gerber (Ed.): SACAIR 2020, CCIS 1342, pp. 101–118, 2020.
https://doi.org/10.1007/978-3-030-66151-9_7

wildlife security games [23]. These games make use of the Stackelberg Security Game (SSG) [5], the current game-theoretic approach in security domains. In the domain of wildlife security, the attackers are poachers, the defenders are rangers and the targets to protect are moving animals. SSGs are used to optimally allocate limited ranger resources in a wildlife park where attacks on the animals occur frequently. To our knowledge, there is currently no evaluation framework for wildlife security games and there are inconsistencies in the evaluation. Evaluating the games based on expected utility is difficult because it is based on the location of the wildlife animals, who are constantly moving. This paper introduces a framework which simulates the movements of the poachers, rangers, and wildlife to address this. The simulation studies are intended to provide the rangers with an estimate of the average behaviour in one month. We propose clear evaluation metrics for the rangers to assess their performance, which allows them to decide on the best strategy for real-world implementation to combat the poachers. Furthermore, we propose acting as the Stackelberg follower instead of the leader in this domain. A simple pure-strategy Stackelberg game is designed and implemented within the framework to test this idea.

The SSG is an extensive form game wherein the defenders act first and the attackers follow. The game can be represented by a game tree where the branches are the actions of the agents and their payoffs for each combination of actions are given at the terminal nodes. The SSG assumes that attackers conduct surveillance on the defenders to obtain complete knowledge of their mixed-strategy and then respond with a pure-strategy by attacking a single target [21]. A pure-strategy for each agent consists of the cross product of the set of actions available to them at each of their information states. A pure-strategy equilibrium provides the optimal action to take at each of their nodes in the tree. A mixed-strategy is a probability distribution over the set of pure-strategies. A Green Security Game (GSG), which includes protection of wildlife, fisheries, and forests, has frequent attacks on targets. Attackers can therefore not afford much time to conduct extensive surveillance to learn the mixed-strategy of the defenders [10]. Furthermore, there could be many attackers present at any given time [17] so assuming a pure-strategy response for the attackers is not viable. Attackers in this domain often return to sites of past success [13] and since attacks occur frequently, the defenders can gather enough observational data to learn the mixed-strategy of the attackers. Thus, we propose that the defenders could perform better when acting as the Stackelberg follower. There is not always an advantage in terms of payoffs to being the Stackelberg leader [16], so it is reasonable to reverse the roles of the defender and the attacker in the domain of GSGs. Although the follower in SSGs acts with a pure-strategy, this is only necessary to ease the computation of the leader's optimisation problem [18]. However, we do not need to find an optimal strategy for the attackers since we learn this from the data. We only need to solve the follower's problem, which is computationally much simpler, to find the defenders' best response to the mixed-strategy of the attacker.

A sensible question is whether we should use the Stackelberg model at all. The Stackelberg duopoly game originates from economics where two firms share the market for a certain product [20]. The price of the product depends on the quantities produced by both firms and each firm's profit depends on this price and the cost per unit of production. The problem is to determine what quantity of the product each firm must produce to maximise their profit. The Cournot duopoly game solves this problem when both firms make their decision at the same time and the Nash equilibrium (NE) is for them to produce the same quantity [7]. In the Stackelberg duopoly, the leader has an advantage and can choose to produce more than the Cournot quantity which will increase their profits. The follower's best response is to produce less than the Cournot quantity which decreases their profit. However, in security games the payoffs are structured differently: defenders do not wish to share the targets with the attackers but instead want to prevent the attackers from making any attacks on the targets. It has been shown that the Stackelberg equilibrium and the NE for the defenders are interchangeable [24]. The SSG model therefore yields the NE mixed-strategy for the defenders and a pure-strategy for the attackers, which results in a defender payoff that may be higher than the NE payoff. However, the attackers' best response to this mixed-strategy has the same maximal value (their NE payoff) for any pure-strategy in the support of their optimal mixed-strategy [18] so they have no reason not to deviate and choose a pure-strategy which may result in a defender payoff that is lower than the NE payoff. When computing optimal strategies to commit to, it is often assumed that the follower will break ties in the leader's favour (to maximise the leader's payoff) [6] but this is not a reasonable assumption in security domains. The Stackelberg model thus seems to have a follower's advantage in GSGs. By acting as the follower, the defenders can learn the mixed-strategy of the attackers from past observations. They can then choose a mixed-strategy best response that secures their own NE payoff but yields an attacker payoff that is lower than the NE payoff.

In Sect. 2 we provide a brief overview of current research about wildlife security and how the performance of games is evaluated. Section 3 describes the null game, which serves as a baseline model. The formulation of a simple wildlife security game, where both the rangers and the poachers execute a pure-strategy, is described in Sect. 4. Variations of the simple game are implemented within the framework in Sect. 5 and compared with the null game and each other. We conclude the paper in Sect. 6 with some remarks and suggestions for future research, and thereafter provide a summary of input parameters in an Appendix.

2   Related Work

The Bayesian SSG has become the standard approach for security games and handles uncertainty around the attackers' payoffs by assuming different types of attackers with a Bayesian *a priori* distribution assumption [18]. Uncertainties due to the attackers' bounded rationality and limited observations are addressed by using robust algorithms [19]. The algorithms are evaluated by assessing the defenders' reward against two baselines: the uniform strategy, which assigns equal probability of taking each strategy; and the maximin strategy, which maximises the minimum reward of the defenders irrespective of the attackers' actions.

The first application of the Bayesian SSG for wildlife security is the PAWS algorithm [23]. Since the targets to protect are moving animals whose location is not always known, the wildlife park is divided into a grid of cells which become the new targets. Available poaching data is utilised to learn a behavioural model for the poachers to account for their bounded rationality. Evaluation of the SSG algorithm is achieved by comparing the cumulative expected utility of the rangers over 30 simulated rounds of the game against the maximin strategy on a grid of 64 cells. Different behavioural models are compared in Yadav et al. [22] where the models are learned using data from a wildlife park in Indonesia and their predictive performance is tested using ROC curves. The SSG algorithm is evaluated on 25 randomly selected grid cells, where the rangers' maximum regret of the optimal strategy is compared to that of the real world.

The work in Kar et al. [13] follows a similar approach to that of Yadav et al. [22] by comparing different behavioural models. However, they develop a computer game with a 5×5 grid over a Google Maps view of the wildlife park. A probability heat map of the rangers' mixed-strategy is overlayed onto the grid and the wildlife is arranged in four different payoff structures. On average 38 human subjects played as the attackers in 5 rounds of each game to learn the behavioural models and the defenders' utility against these subjects is compared for evaluation. Although there is some similarity to this work, no movements of the wildlife, the rangers or the poachers are considered.

In our earlier work [14], a null game is designed where the rangers and the poachers both act randomly. Thus, the uniform strategy [19] is similar to this null game. Yet none of the research on wildlife security use the uniform strategy for comparison and the maximin strategy is the only baseline model considered. While evaluating models by simulating repeated instances of the game or by applying the game to real-world data is valid, the data used only provides a snapshot of the situation. Since the wildlife are constantly foraging for food, the poachers foraging for wildlife and the rangers foraging for poachers, it becomes important to know more about their spatial and temporal movements [15]. Measuring the expected utility is useful for comparison but since it is calculated based on the locations of the wildlife, who are constantly moving, the actual number of wildlife poached is more valuable. The evaluation framework presented in this paper allows for including real-world data and is supposed to offer an alternative to implementation in a wildlife park.

3   The Null Game

3.1   Geographical Features

Our previous null game [14] focuses on a grid of cells and follows the routes of a herd of wildlife, one group of rangers and one group of poachers until the poachers are arrested or leave the park. It is assumed that 10 games occur within a month, and for each month we record the number of poaching events and the number of times the poachers leave or are arrested. The monthly cycle is simulated for 1 000 Monte Carlo repetitions and the averages over the simulations provide the measures of performance. Some simulations on ways to move are compared and movement towards a destination provides the smoothest and most realistic movement for the rangers and the poachers. The start and destination cells for the rangers and the poachers are chosen completely randomly. Although the grid cells are supposed to correspond to a map of the wildlife park, the game does not take any geographical features into account. We modify that game to incorporate geographical information into the framework. Figure 1 shows a map of the KNP and a subarea used to demonstrate how the algorithm works. Currently we use the public shapefiles in the SANParks data repository [2] for the KNP. The **geopandas** Python library [1] is utilised so that geographical data can be used, and distances can be calculated within the actual wildlife park. Two classes are created, a **Park** class and an **Agent** class. Within the **Park** class, all the geographical information is collected. A grid is also calculated, based on how large the cells should be, for either the whole park or a subarea of the park.

Two attributes are created for the **Agent** class to exclude cells in the grid, corresponding to areas where the agent cannot go. The first restricts agents from entering areas which contain geographical obstacles such as steep mountains, dense vegetation, rivers, and dams. The second restricts an agent to stay within a specific area. For example: you might want to restrict the wildlife to stay within an area defined by a census or home range analysis; ranger patrols might need to stay within a certain distance from their patrol huts; or poachers might need to stay close enough to their homes. Figure 2 shows a grid of 566 cells that are 1.5 × 1.5 km in size, for the subarea in Fig. 1, where the cells excluded are white.

Fig. 1. Map and subarea of the Kruger National Park. The map on the left illustrates the geographical information used within the framework, while the subarea shown on the right will be the focus of this study.

3.2   Poacher Movement

The null game serves as a baseline model, so that when compared with other games, the performance of the rangers' success in protecting wildlife and arresting poachers can be assessed. We would like to know whether executing the GSG helps the rangers to perform better than when they execute random motion. However, in our previous attempt to construct a realistic baseline model, both the rangers and the poachers moved from a random starting cell towards a random destination cell (uniform game). This makes it difficult to assess whether the rangers' performance improves when both the rangers and the poachers act according to the GSG since the poachers' strategy improves at the same time as the rangers' strategy. Thus, in the baseline model, the random rangers need to compete with more intelligent poachers, those who learn, to truly evaluate any performance increase of the rangers when they act according to the GSG.

In a game theory algorithm, we would use information about an agent's preferences to try and quantify their payoffs. Similarly, we can use this information to determine how an intelligent agent might move through the wildlife park. Another two attributes were created for this: one for features they dislike and how far they would like to stay away from them; and one for features they like and how near they would like to stay to them. For example: the poachers would probably like to avoid any entrance gates to the park since rangers often conduct searches there; they would likely stay away from main roads, camps and picnic spots to avoid being identified by the public; they might prefer to stay near to the park border to make escape easier; and they would possibly like to stay near to water sources since it is likely that they might find wildlife there. These preferences are implemented by increasing or decreasing selection weights for each cell. For each feature, each cell starts with a weight of $w = 0.5$. If it is a feature that the poachers would like to stay d km away from, then the weight starts decreasing for cells that are within d km away and continues to decrease as the cells get nearer to the feature: if a cell c_i has minimum distance d_i km from the feature, then its weight will be $w = w \times [1 - (d - d_i)/d]$. Similarly, if it is a feature that the poacher would like to stay d km near to, then the weight increases more for cells c_i which are nearer to that feature: $w = w \times [1 + (d - d_i)/d]$. The weights are increased or decreased in this manner for each feature that the poacher has preferences for. Figure 2 shows the cell selection weights for a poacher who dislikes being 2 km from camps, 3 km from roads and 5 km from gates, and who likes being within 15 km of dams and water and within 30 km of the border. The weights are depicted by a colour scale, where darker colours indicate higher values.

Along with moving towards their preferences, the poachers also learn from events that occur. The poachers begin in a random cell, either on the border of the park or at the edge of the grid and proceed towards a random destination cell. If they reach the destination cell with no event, then they head off on a new trajectory back towards the start cell and we record that they left before poaching. If they leave safely without being arrested, then they continue to use that point of entry because they assume there is low risk in being arrested there.

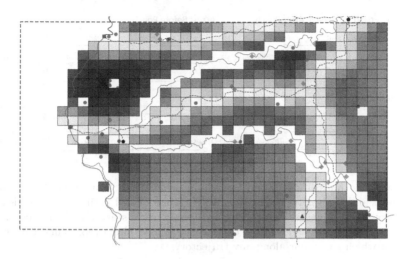

Fig. 2. Poacher allowed cells and cell selection weights. The cells excluded for the poachers are shown in white and the selection weights are depicted by a colour scale where darker colours represent higher values.

The poachers can either encounter wildlife for poaching on their trajectory towards the destination cell or on their way back to the start. We assume that once the wildlife has been poached, that they would like to exit promptly before being arrested. Thus, after a poaching occurs while going towards the destination, they change direction and head back towards the start cell. Furthermore, since they know where the wildlife are likely to be, they want to return to that area, so the poaching cell becomes their new destination cell. If the poachers encounter the wildlife while going towards the start, then they continue on the same trajectory towards the start after the poaching event. They would also adopt the poaching cell as their new destination cell when re-entering the park in this event. We do not allow for a second poaching event once on the trajectory towards the start cell after a poaching, they can only poach again after re-entry to the park. We record that the poachers left after poaching if they leave the park safely in the past two events described. However, if they are arrested before reaching the start cell then we record that they were arrested after poaching. Of course, the poachers could also be arrested without having poached any wildlife and in this case, we record that they were arrested before poaching. After being arrested, the poachers must re-enter the park, but they will choose a new random entry point since they did not have success going towards the current start cell. Figure 3 demonstrates the different scenarios that occur during one game.

The two attributes describing the poachers' preferences can be helpful in making the wildlife movement more realistic as well. Some examples include wildlife wanting to stay near water; liking specific types of vegetation for grazing; enjoying mud baths or shady areas; and wanting to avoid camp areas where there are lots of people. The null game is thus simulated with better movement for the

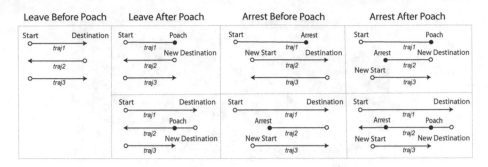

Fig. 3. Scenarios that can occur and how the poachers learn from events. Trajectories continue back and forth between the start and destination cell until the game ends after a specified number of moves. An open circle represents the start of each trajectory and an arrow represents the end of that trajectory. A solid circle represents a poach or arrest event which can occur along any trajectory.

wildlife as well, where the destination cell is chosen as a random cell near water and movement is based on the preferences specified.

The game continues with the wildlife, rangers and poachers moving back and forth between their start and destination cells and ends after a specified number of moves. For example, considering a grid with 1 km^2 cells, a person could walk 100 km in 20 h at a speed of 5 km/h. Allowing short stops to rest or eat, 100 moves would consume an entire day. Thirty such games could be played per month and the games are simulated for a specified number of months to determine their average monthly behaviour. The number of poaching events and arrest events per month are recorded and are used to calculate the poach frequency per day and arrest frequency per day, so that games of different lengths can be compared. When these measures are similar, we consider two secondary measures: the average number of moves for each arrest and the average distance between the poachers and rangers for games with no arrests. For further understanding and analysis, we also record how many times the agents reach their start cell or destination cell to keep track of their trajectories. The `movingpandas` Python library [12] is utilised to store trajectories which can be easily analysed and plotted after the simulation.

4   Simple Security Game

As a start, we would like to implement the simplest security game within the framework to demonstrate whether there are any improvements in the performance of the rangers. We consider the traditional Stackelberg Game, where the follower observes the leader's pure-strategy and reacts with his best response pure-strategy. As an example, to explain how the game works, we consider the wildlife park being divided into only two grid cells. The idea can easily be extrapolated to use all the cells provided in the grid. Before we continue to develop the game, we first make the following assumptions:

- there is only one group of rangers and one group of poachers, where each group acts together and they cannot split up;
- the park is divided into two grid cells;
- the rangers act as the leader and commit to protecting a single grid cell;
- the poachers observe which cell the rangers protect and react by attacking a single grid cell; and
- the rangers and the poachers act to maximise their own expected utility.

With these assumptions set clearly, we can identify the components of the game. We know that the agents are the rangers and the poachers, and that the actions are the coverage of the two grid cells by these agents. We do not yet know what the payoffs are, but we know that the outcome will include the number of rhino saved and/or poached and whether the poacher is arrested. For this example, we have two rhinos in grid cell 1 which is 500 m from the border and one rhino in grid cell 2 which is on the border. The four possible events are shown in Fig. 4. For the outcomes of each event, the solid rhinos represent the number of rhinos saved and the dotted rhinos represent the number of rhinos poached. If the rangers and the poachers are in the same grid cell, then the poachers are arrested and no rhinos are poached.

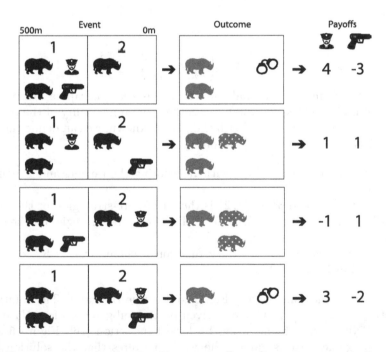

Fig. 4. Game events and outcomes. For events, the policeman represents the rangers, the gun represents the poachers and the solid (black) rhino depicts the animals in each grid cell. For outcomes, the solid (green) rhino depicts the saved rhinos, the dotted (red) rhino depicts the poached rhinos and an arrest is represented by handcuffs. (Color figure online)

In order to solve the game, we need to define the pure-strategies for each agent and quantify the outcomes as payoffs. Since the rangers act first, they have one information state and their pure-strategies are just their actions, cell 1 and cell 2, given by the set $S^R = \{1, 2\}$. Because the poachers observe the rangers' action, they have two information states: $P.1$ when the rangers go to cell 1 and $P.2$ when the rangers go to cell 2. The pure-strategies of the poachers thus need to specify what action to take at each information state, and are given by the set $S^P = \{(i, j) : \text{for } i, j = 1, 2\}$, which means cell i at $P.1$ and cell j at $P.2$. To calculate the payoffs, let the value of a rhino be 1 and the value of an arrest be 2. A poached rhino will count as negative for the rangers and an arrest will count as negative for the poachers. The payoffs can also include an agent's preferences, so let the penalty for the poachers be -1 for every cell that is 500 m away from the border. Let $u^R\left(S_i^R, S_{j.i}^P\right)$ be the payoff for the rangers and $u^P\left(S_i^R, S_{j.i}^P\right)$ be the payoff for the poachers when the rangers are are in cell i and the poachers are in cell $j.i$, where S_i^R is the ith element in S^R and $S_{j.i}^P$ is the jth element of S^P with the action at information state $P.i$. Then the payoffs are calculated as:

$$u^R\left(S_i^R, S_{j.i}^P\right) = \begin{cases} r_i + a_i + 2 & \text{if } i = j.i \\ r_i + a_i - a_{j.i} & \text{if } i \neq j.i \end{cases} \tag{1}$$

and

$$u^P\left(S_i^R, S_{j.i}^P\right) = \begin{cases} p_{j.i} - 2 & \text{if } i = j.i \\ p_{j.i} + a_{j.i} & \text{if } i \neq j.i \end{cases}, \tag{2}$$

where a_i is the number of animals in cell i, r_i is the geographic utility of the rangers in cell i (0 in this example), $p_{j.i}$ is the geographic utility of the poachers in cell $j.i$, and 2 is for an arrest. With the payoffs known, we can define the game mathematically as $G = \langle A, S, U \rangle$, where

- $A = \{R, P\}$ is the set of agents with R denoting the rangers and P denoting the poachers;
- $S = \{S^R, S^P\}$, where $S^R = \{1, 2\}$ is the set of pure-strategies for the rangers and $S^P = \{(1, 1), (1, 2), (2, 1), (2.2)\}$ is the set of pure-strategies for the poachers; and
- $U = \{u^R, u^P\}$ is the set of utility functions, where $u^R, u^P : S^R \times S^P \to \mathbb{R}$ are defined in Eqs. 1 and 2.

We construct the game tree in Fig. 5 to describe the game. The solution to a pure-strategy Stackelberg Game is given by the Subgame Perfect Nash equilibrium (SPNE) and is found using backward induction [16]. Figure 5 shows the three subgames in this game. The SPNE requires that the solution has a Nash equilibrium (NE) in each subgame, even if it is never reached. The backward induction process for finding the SPNE is presented visually in Fig. 5 with thick lines representing the optimal strategies for each agent. Let $\hat{S}^R$ denote the optimal strategy for the rangers and $\hat{S}^P$ the optimal strategy for the poachers.

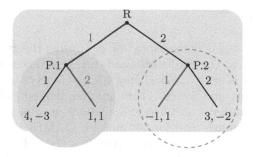

Fig. 5. Stackelberg game tree and subgames. The rangers have one information state and the poachers have two information states ($P.1$ and $P.2$). The payoffs are shown at the terminal nodes with the rangers' payoffs first. There are 3 subgames and the thick lines indicate the backward induction process for finding the SPNE.

The SPNE is $\hat{S}^R = 1, \hat{S}^P = (2,1)$, thus the rangers go to cell 1 and the poachers to cell 2, with payoffs of 1 for the rangers and 1 for the poachers.

   The game can also be written as the normal form representation in Table 1 and the SPNE is a subset of the NE for the normal form game. Finding all NE for this normal form game includes the SPNE above, as well as an equilibrium where at information state $P.2$ the poachers execute a mixed-strategy by choosing each cell with probability 0.5. If the roles were reversed and the rangers were to act as the follower then the SPNE is $\hat{S}^R = (1,2), \hat{S}^P = 2$ so the rangers and the poachers both go to cell 2 and the payoffs are 3 for the rangers and -2 for the poachers. This example thus shows a follower's advantage since both agents receive a higher payoff when they follow than when they lead. The use of the SPNE is just for demonstration in this article. In practice, it would be preferred to solve for an optimal mixed-strategy for the rangers, which is a probability distribution over their set of pure-strategies. This mixed-strategy could then be utilised, for example, over the duration of one month in which a random strategy is selected from this distribution every day.

Table 1. Normal form of the Stackelberg game. The rangers are the row player and have two pure-strategies. The poachers are the column player and have 4 pure-strategies, where (i, j) means i at $P.1$ and j at $P.2$. The body of the table shows the payoffs at each combination of their strategies, where the rangers' payoffs are given first.

R	P			
	$(1,\ 1)$	$(1,\ 2)$	$(2,\ 1)$	$(2,\ 2)$
1	$4, -3$	$4, -3$	$1,\ 1$	$1,\ 1$
2	$-1,\ 1$	$3, -2$	$-1,\ 1$	$3, -2$

5   Experiments

We perform simulations for the subarea in Fig. 1, using the grid shown in Fig. 2. The poachers' entry is at the border cells and their preferences are as described in Sect. 3.2. The wildlife is set to dislike being 1 km near to camps and prefer being within 10 km of dams and water. There are 566 allowed cells for each agent, after excluding geographical obstacles. Simulations are run with 200 moves per game, 10 games per month, and for 500 months. GAME1 is the uniform game, with random movement for all agents. GAME2 is the null game, with random movement for the rangers, intelligent movement for the poachers and improved animal movement. The poach frequency per day and arrest frequency per day are the primary measures for assessing the rangers' performance. We also consider the average number of moves to make an arrest and the average distance between the rangers and the poachers when there are no arrests. Since the distributions of these measures are skewed, we report on the median and calculate the bootstrap standard error (SE) of the median using 1 000 bootstrap samples. Furthermore, we do pairwise comparisons of the games for each measure and test the general hypothesis of identical populations using Mood's median test [11]. Table 2 shows the median for each measure, with bootstrap SE of the median in brackets, and the superscripts indicate where Mood's median test is non-significant. As can be expected, the random rangers have poorer performance against the intelligent poachers than against the random poachers since the poach frequency per day is significantly higher in GAME2 than in GAME1. Figure 6 shows the trajectories for a single round of the null game.

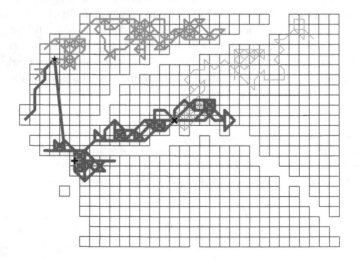

Fig. 6. Trajectories for a single round of the null game. The lines represent the movements of the wildlife (green, narrow line), the rangers (blue, medium line) and the poachers (red, thick line). A black * represents a capture event, a black X represents a poaching event and a black + represents a leaving event. (Color figure online)

Next, we implement the pure-strategy Stackelberg Game, as described in Sect. 4. A `Game` class was created with methods to calculate the strategies, payoffs, and game solution. The rangers are set to like being within 10 km of dams and water since that is likely where the wildlife can be found. The poachers' preferences are as described in Sect. 3.2. For each agent, based on the agent's geographical preferences, each allowed cell has a selection weight which aids in determining the movement into the next cell and a utility which aids in selecting the destination cell. The wildlife is set to dislike being 1 km near to camps and like being within 10 km of dams and water. Figure 7 shows a colour scale of the wildlife preferences as well as a simulated collection of wildlife sightings that serves as an animal density estimate. The payoffs for the rangers and the poachers are calculated using the animal densities (with a weight of 5), their utility based on geographical preferences (with a weight of 2) and arrests when they are in the same cell (with a weight of 40). We perform the following simulations of the pure-strategy Stackelberg game:

- GAME3 the rangers as the Stackelberg leader against the intelligent poachers;
- GAME4 the rangers as the Stackelberg leader against the poachers as the Stackelberg follower;
- GAME5 the rangers as the Stackelberg follower against the intelligent poachers; and
- GAME6 the rangers as the Stackelberg follower against the poachers as the Stackelberg leader.

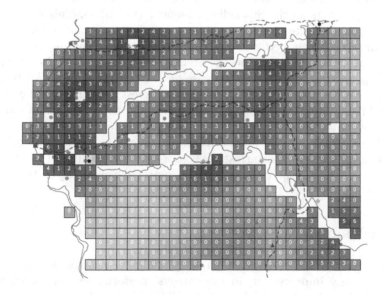

Fig. 7. Wildlife density estimates and cell selection weights. The numbers indicate how many wildlife have been sighted in each cell and the selection weights are depicted by a colour scale where darker colours represent higher values.

Table 2. Median and bootstrap SE in brackets for evaluation measures. A superscript i means the null hypothesis for Mood's median test that the medians are the same is not rejected, at a significance level of $\alpha = 0.05$, when compared pairwise with GAMEi.

	Poach Freq per Day	Arrest Freq per Day	Ave Moves for Arrests	Ave Distance (km) for Non-arrests
GAME1	0.067 (0.006) [4,6]	0.067 (0.001) [2,3]	78.0 (2.1)	10.4 (0, 1)
GAME2	0.083 (0.016) [3,5]	0.067 (0.001) [1]	67.6 (2.7) [3,4,5]	11.8 (0.1) [3,6]
GAME3	0.067 (0.016) [2,5]	0.067 (0.013) [1]	66.8 (2.4) [2,4,5]	11.4 (0.2) [2,4,6]
GAME4	0.033 (0.015) [1,6]	0.167 (0.008) [5]	62.8 (2.3) [2,3,5]	11.1 (0.2) [3,6]
GAME5	0.067 (0.005) [2,3]	0.133 (0.016) [4]	67.4 (1.2) [2,3,4]	9.5 (0.1)
GAME6	0.067 (0.005) [1,4]	0.267 (0.016)	49.8 (1.5)	11.6 (0.2) [2,3,4]

The results for the Stackelberg games are shown in Table 2. When comparing GAME3 and GAME5 with GAME2 (null game), we have a direct comparison of the rangers' performance since the only difference between the games is the movement of the rangers. The poach frequency per day is lower in GAME3 and GAME5 than in GAME2, and the arrest frequency per day is significantly higher in GAME5 than in GAME2. Thus, the rangers perform better than random when playing the Stackelberg game as the leader or the follower against the intelligent poachers. When comparing GAME3 with GAME4, where the rangers act as the Stackelberg leader, they perform better in GAME4 since the poach frequency per day is significantly lower and the arrest frequency per day is significantly higher. Thus, comparison of the rangers' performance against the intelligent poachers (GAME3) represents a worse case for the rangers than against the poachers as the Stackelberg follower (GAME4). This is reasonable when trying to select the better game since we would not want to have an optimistic estimate of their performance. Similarly, when comparing GAME5 and GAME6, where the rangers acts as the Stackelberg follower, GAME5 against the intelligent poacher represents a worse case for the rangers than GAME6 against the poachers as the Stackelberg leader since the arrest frequency per day is much higher and the average moves for an arrest is much lower in GAME6. Comparing GAME4 and GAME6, there is no significant difference in poach frequency per day but GAME6 has a much higher arrest frequency per day and a much lower average number of moves for arrests. Thus, when both agents act according to the Stackelberg game, the rangers perform better when acting as the follower than as the leader.

6   Conclusions

The null game presented in this paper provides a realistic baseline model for assessing any improvement in the rangers' performance. Improved ranger performance is defined as having fewer wildlife poached and more poachers arrested. The primary performance measures of poach frequency per day and arrest frequency per day thus directly address the objectives of the rangers. As expected, the rangers have poorer performance against the intelligent poachers than against the random poachers in the null game. Implementing the simple Stackelberg security game shows that even this simple game-theoretic algorithm results in a significant improvement for the rangers. An Appendix is provided in Sect. 7 containing a summary of the classes, attributes and simulation parameters required for the null game and the pure-strategy Stackelberg games.

Utilising better geographic data is expected to alleviate the problem with back and forth movement around cells that are excluded due to geographical obstacles. The next step would be to incorporate time into the simulation. For example, the poachers' re-entry into the park after an arrest could be delayed; the visibility of the agents could be increased during dry seasons or nights when it is full moon; rivers might be easily crossed during dry seasons; and where there is dense vegetation or steep mountains the speed of the agents could be decreased within that region instead of excluding those cells.

Further improvements can be implemented to make the null game more realistic. Including multiple groups of rangers, multiple groups of poachers, and multiple herds of wildlife would be a valuable improvement. Utilising an animal movement model for different types of wildlife instead of simulating the movements of the wildlife could also improve the framework considerably. Alternatively, we could design routes for each of the wildlife, the poachers, and the rangers using imaging software to identify sand trails [15], using routes uncovered by poacher tracking [8], or using road segments to define routes [9]. The routes can then be used for their movement within the framework and as their set of strategies in the GSG algorithm.

Since the framework is designed to compare and evaluate different wildlife security games, another task would be to include game-theoretic algorithms discussed in current research within the framework. We would like to test the idea of the rangers acting as the Stackelberg follower against the current algorithms. Observed data can be utilised in a Bayesian network to learn the poachers' mixed-strategy and the rangers' mixed-strategy best response can be calculated.

7 Appendix

The evaluation framework is developed in Python 3.8. It utilises the **geopandas** [1] library to handle geographical information and the **movingpandas** [12] library to store, plot and analyse the trajectories in each simulation. Table 3 provides a summary of the classes, attributes and simulation parameters used in the framework. For the uniform game, the **move_type** is set to **"random"** for all agents but for the null game it is set to **"intelligent"** for the poachers. The **Park** class has methods to calculate the grid, the cells on the edge of the grid, and the cells on the park border. The **Agent** class has methods to find the agent's allowed cells and calculate their geographical selection weights and utilities. Furthermore, it contains methods to find their start cell, destination cell and calculate the next cell to move into. The **Game** class is more useful for the security games as it contains methods to calculate strategies, payoffs, and the game solution. For the null game, it just collects the agents and whether the

Table 3. Summary of classes, attributes and simulation parameters.

Class	Attribute	Description
Park	`boundary`	`GeoDataFrame` of park boundary (polygon)
	`trees`	`GeoDataFrame` of areas with dense vegetation (polygons)
	`mountains`	`GeoDataFrame` of areas with steep mountains (polygons)
	`roads`	`GeoDataFrame` of main roads (lines)
	`rivers`	`GeoDataFrame` of main rivers (lines)
	`dams`	`GeoDataFrame` of dams (points)
	`water`	`GeoDataFrame` of water holes, fountains and drinking troughs (points)
	`camps`	`GeoDataFrame` of main rest camps (points)
	`picnic`	`GeoDataFrame` of picnic spots (points)
	`gates`	`GeoDataFrame` of public gates (points)
	`custom`	dictionary of the form `{"name": GeoDataFrame}`
	`subarea`	latitude and longitude bounds of park subarea
	`cell_x_length`	horizontal length of grid cells (meters)
	`cell_y_length`	vertical length of grid cells (meters)
Agent	`name`	name of the agent
	`park`	park object
	`grid_type`	`"full"` / `"bounded"`
	`move_type`	`"random"` / `"intelligent"` / `"game"`
	`area_out`	list of feature names for areas to stay out of
	`area_within`	list of feature names for areas to stay within
	`dislikes`	dictionary of feature names and distances (meters) to stay away, eg. `{"name": distance}`
	`likes`	dictionary of feature names and distances (meters) to stay near, eg. `{"name": distance}`
Game	`name`	name of the game
	`wildlife`	agent object for wildlife herd
	`ranger`	agent object for rangers
	`poacher`	agent object for poachers
	`poacher_entry`	`"edge"` / `"border"`
	`game_type`	`"null"` / `"stackel_lead"` / `"stackel_follow"`
	`sightings`	`GeoDataFrame` of wildlife sightings (points)
Sim	`game`	game object to simulate
	`seed`	sets the random seed
	`end_moves`	number of moves until the game ends
	`games_pm`	number of games to simulate per month
	`months_total`	number of months to simulate

poachers' entry point should be a cell on the edge of the grid or on the border of the park. The `Sim` class has methods to simulate a single game and to simulate games for a number of months. Additionally, to evaluate the simulations, there are methods for calculating the median of the performance measures, bootstrap standard errors of the median and p-values for Mood's median test.

References

1. GeoPandas 0.7.0. https://geopandas.org/
2. SANParks Data Repository. http://dataknp.sanparks.org/sanparks/
3. Minister Molewa highlights progress on Integrated Strategic Management of Rhinoceros (2017). https://www.environment.gov.za/mediarelease/molewa_progressonintegrated_strategicmanagement_ofrhinoceros
4. Department of Environment, Forestry and Fisheries report back on rhino poaching in South Africa in 2019 (2020). https://www.environment.gov.za/mediarelease/reportbackon2019_rhinopoachingstatistics
5. An, B., Tambe, M.: Stackelberg security games (SSG) basics and application overview. In: Abbas, A.E., Tambe, M., von Winterfeldt, D. (eds.) Improving Homeland Security Decisions, pp. 485–507. Cambridge University Press, Cambridge (2017). https://doi.org/10.1017/9781316676714.021
6. Conitzer, V., Sandholm, T.: Computing the optimal strategy to commit to. In: Proceedings of the 7th ACM Conference on Electronic Commerce, pp. 82–90 (2006). https://dl.acm.org/doi/10.1145/1134707.1134717
7. Cournot, A.A.: Researches Into the Mathematical Principles of the Theory of Wealth. Macmillan, New York (1897). https://www3.nd.edu/~tgresik/IO/Cournot.pdf
8. De Oude, P., Pavlin, G., De Villiers, J.P.: High-level tracking using bayesian context fusion. In: FUSION 2018, 21st International Conference on Information Fusion, pp. 1415–1422. IEEE (2018). https://doi.org/10.23919/ICIF.2018.8455342
9. Fang, F., et al.: Deploying PAWS: field optimization of the protection assistant for wildlife security. In: AAAI 2016, Proceedings of the 30th AAAI Conference on Artificial Intelligence, pp. 3966–3973. AAAI Press (2016). https://dl.acm.org/doi/10.5555/3016387.3016464
10. Fang, F., Stone, P., Tambe, M.: When security games go green: designing defender strategies to prevent poaching and illegal fishing. In: IJCAI 2015, Proceedings of the 24th International Joint Conference on Artificial Intelligence, pp. 2589–2595. AAAI Press (2015). https://dl.acm.org/doi/10.5555/2832581.2832611
11. Gibbons, J.D., Chakraborti, S.: Nonparametric Statistical Inference, 4th edn. CRC Press, Boca Raton (2003). https://doi.org/10.4324/9780203911563
12. Graser, A.: MovingPandas: efficient structures for movement data in Python. J. Geogr. Inf. Sci. **7**(1), 54–68 (2019). https://doi.org/10.1553/giscience2019_01_s54
13. Kar, D., Fang, F., Fave, F.D., Sintov, N., Tambe, M.: "A game of thrones": When human behavior models compete in repeated stackelberg security games. In: AAMAS 2015, Proceedings of the 14th International Conference on Autonomous Agents and Multiagent Systems, pp. 1381–1390. IFAAMAS (2015). https://dl.acm.org/doi/10.5555/2772879.2773329
14. Kirkland, L., de Waal, A., de Villiers, J.P.: Simulating null games for uncertainty evaluation in green security games. In: FUSION 2019, 22nd International Conference on Information Fusion, pp. 1–8. IEEE (2019). https://ieeexplore.ieee.org/document/9011280

15. Lemieux, A.M. (ed.): Situational Prevention of Poaching. Routledge, London (2014). https://doi.org/10.4324/9780203094525
16. Myerson, R.B.: Game theory: Analysis of Conflict. Harvard University Press, Cambridge (1991). https://doi.org/10.2307/j.ctvjsf522
17. Nguyen, T.H., et al.: CAPTURE: a new predictive anti-poaching tool for wildlife protection. In: AAMAS 2016, Proceedings of the 15th International Conference on Autonomous Agents & Multiagent Systems, pp. 767–775. IFAAMAS (2016). https://dl.acm.org/doi/abs/10.5555/2936924.2937037
18. Paruchuri, P., Pearce, J.P., Marecki, J., Tambe, M., Ordonez, F., Kraus, S.: Playing games for security: an efficient exact algorithm for solving Bayesian Stackelberg games. In: AAMAS 2008, Proceedings of the 7th International Conference on Autonomous Agents and Multiagent Systems, vol. 2, pp. 895–902. IFAAMAS (2008). https://dl.acm.org/doi/10.5555/1402298.1402348
19. Pita, J., Jain, M., Tambe, M., Ordóñez, F., Kraus, S.: Robust solutions to Stackelberg games: addressing bounded rationality and limited observations in human cognition. Artif. Intell. **174**(15), 1142–1171 (2010). https://doi.org/10.1016/j.artint.2010.07.002
20. von Stackelberg, H.: Market Structure and Equilibrium. Springer, Berlin (2011). https://doi.org/10.1007/978-3-642-12586-7
21. Tambe, M.: Security and game theory: algorithms, deployed systems, lessons learned. Cambridge University Press, Cambridge (2011). https://doi.org/10.1017/CBO9780511973031
22. Yadav, A., Nguyen, T.H., Fave, F.D., Tambe, M., Agmon, N.: Handling payoff uncertainty with adversary bounded rationality in green security domains. In: BECIS 2015, Workshop on Behavioral, Economic and Computational Intelligence for Security, pp. 1–16 (2015). https://teamcore.seas.harvard.edu/publications/handling-payoff-uncertainty-green-security-domains-adversary-bounded-0
23. Yang, R., Ford, B., Tambe, M., Lemieux, A.: Adaptive resource allocation for wildlife protection against illegal poachers. In: AAMAS 2014, Proceedings of the 13th International Conference on Autonomous Agents and Multi-Agent Systems, pp. 453–460. IFAAMAS (2014). https://dl.acm.org/doi/10.5555/2615731.2615805
24. Yin, Z., Korzhyk, D., Kiekintveld, C., Conitzer, V., Tambe, M.: Stackelberg vs. Nash in security games: interchangeability, equivalence, and uniqueness. In: AAMAS2010, Proceedings of the 9th International Conference on Autonomous Agents and Multiagent Systems, vol. 1, pp. 1139–1146. IFAAMAS (2010). https://dl.acm.org/doi/10.5555/1838206.1838360

An Analysis of Deep Neural Networks for Predicting Trends in Time Series Data

Kouame Hermann Kouassi[1,2]($\boxtimes$) (iD) and Deshendran Moodley[1,2] (iD)

[1] University of Cape Town, 18 University Avenue Rondebosch,
Cape Town 7700, South Africa
ksskou001@myuct.ac.za, deshen@cs.uct.ac.za
[2] Centre for Artificial Intelligence Research, 18 University Avenue Rondebosch,
Cape Town 7700, South Africa

Abstract. Recently, a hybrid Deep Neural Network (DNN) algorithm, TreNet was proposed for predicting trends in time series data. While TreNet was shown to have superior performance for trend prediction to other DNN and traditional ML approaches, the validation method used did not take into account the sequential nature of time series datasets and did not deal with model update. In this research we replicated the TreNet experiments on the same datasets using a walk-forward validation method and tested our best model over multiple independent runs to evaluate model stability. We compared the performance of the hybrid TreNet algorithm, on four datasets to vanilla DNN algorithms that take in point data, and also to traditional ML algorithms. We found that in general TreNet still performs better than the vanilla DNN models, but not on all datasets as reported in the original TreNet study. This study highlights the importance of using an appropriate validation method and evaluating model stability for evaluating and developing machine learning models for trend prediction in time series data.

Keywords: Time series trend prediction · Deep neural networks · Ensemble methods · Walk-forward validation

1 Introduction

With the advent of low cost sensors and digital transformation, time series data is being generated at an unprecedented speed and volume in a wide range of applications in almost every domain. For example, stock market fluctuations, computer cluster traces, medical and biological experimental observations, sensor networks readings, etc., are all represented in time series. Consequently, there is an enormous interest in analyzing time series data, which has resulted in a large number of studies on new methodologies for indexing, classifying, clustering, summarizing, and predicting time series data [10,11,16,23,25].

Centre for Artificial Intelligence Research (CAIR).

In certain time series prediction applications, segmenting the time series into a sequence of trends and predicting the slope and duration of the next trend is preferred over predicting just the next value in the series [16,23]. Piecewise linear representation [10] or trend lines can provide a better representation for the underlying semantics and dynamics of the generating process of a non-stationary and dynamic time series [16,23]. Moreover, trend lines are a more natural representation for predicting change points in the data, which may be more interesting to decision makings. For example, suppose a share price in the stock market is currently rising. A trader in the stock market would ask "How long will it take and at what price will the share price peak and when will the price start dropping?" Another example application is for predicting daily household electricity consumption. Here the user may be more interested in identifying the time, scale and duration of peak or low energy consumption.

While deep neural networks (DNNs) has been widely applied to computer vision, natural language processing (NLP) and speech recognition, there is limited research on applying DNNs for time series prediction. In 2017, Lin et al. [16] proposed a novel approach to directly predict the next trend of a time series as a piecewise linear approximation (*trend line*) with a slope and a duration using a hybrid neural network approach, called TreNet. The authors showed that TreNet outperformed SVR, CNN, LSTM, pHHM [23], and cascaded CNN and RNN.

However, the study had certain limitations.

Inadequacy of Cross-validation: The study used standard cross-validation with random shuffling. This implies that data instances, which are generated after a given validation set, are used for training [1].

No Model Update: In real world applications where systems are often dynamic, models become outdated and must be updated as new data becomes available. TreNet's test error was estimated on a single hold-out set, which assumes that the system under consideration is static. TreNet's evaluation therefore does not provide a sufficiently robust performance measure for datasets that are erratic and non-stationary [1].

No Evaluation of Model Stability: DNNs, as a result of random initialisation and possibly other random parameter settings could yield substantially different results when re-run with the same hyperparameter values on the same dataset. Thus, it is crucial that the best DNN configurations should be stable, i.e. have minimal deviation from the mean test loss across multiple runs. There is no evidence that this was done for TreNet.

Missing Implementation Details: Important implementation details in the TreNet study are not stated explicitly. For instance, the segmentation method used to transform the raw time series into trend lines is not apparent. This questions the reproducibility of TreNet's study.

This paper attempts to address these shortcomings. Our research questions are:

1. Does a hybrid deep neural networks approach for trend prediction perform better than vanilla deep neural networks?

2. Do deep neural networks models perform better for trend prediction than simpler traditional machine learning (ML) models?
3. Does the addition of trend line features improve performance over local raw data features alone?

The remainder of the paper is structured as follows. We first provide a brief background of the problem and a summary of related work, followed by the experimental design. We then give a brief overview of the experiments, describe the experiments, present and discuss their results. Finally, we provide a summary and discussion of the key findings.

2 Background and Related Work

2.1 Background

The time series trend prediction problem is concerned with predicting the future evolution of the time series from the current time. This evolution is approximated as a succession of time-ordered piecewise linear approximations. The linear approximations indicate the *direction*, the *strength*, and the *length* of the upward/downward movement of the time series. The *slope* of the linear approximation determines the *direction* and the *strength* of the movement, and the number of time steps covered by that linear approximation, i.e. its *duration* determines its *length*. The formal problem definition is given below.

Problem Formulation: We define a univariate time series as $X = \{x_1, ..., x_T\}$, where x_t is a real-valued observation at time t. The trend sequence T for X, is denoted by $T = \{<l_1, s_1>, ..., <s_k, l_k>\}$, and is obtained by performing a piecewise linear approximation of X [10]. l_k represents the *duration* and is given by the number of data points covered by trend k and s_k is the slope of the trend expressed as an angle between -90 and $90°$. Given a historical time series X and its corresponding trend sequence T, the aim is to predict the *next trend* $<s_{k+1}, l_{k+1}>$.

2.2 Related Work

Traditional trend prediction approaches include Hidden Markov Models (HMM)s [19,23] and multi-step ahead predictions [2]. Leveraging the success of CNNs, and LSTMs in computer vision and natural language processing [3,7,14], Lin et al. [16] proposed a hybrid DNN approach, TreNet, for trend prediction. TreNet uses a CNN which takes in recent point data, and an LSTM which takes in historical trend lines to extract local and global features respectively. These features are then fused to predict the next trend. While the authors report a marked performance improvement when compared to other approaches, the validation method used in their experiments is questionable. More specifically it does not take into account the sequential nature of times series data. The data was first randomly shuffled, 10% of the data was held out for testing and a cross validation approach for training with the remainder of the data. Randomly shuffling the data and using a standard cross validation approach does not take into account the sequential nature of time series data and may give erroneous results [16]. A walk-forward validation with successive and overlapping partitioning (see Sect. 3.4) is better suited for evaluating and comparing model performance on time series data [18]. It maintains the order of a time series sequence and deals with changes in its properties over time [18]. To deal with this limitation we attempt to replicate the TreNet approach using a walk forward validation instead of random shuffling and cross validation.

Some follow-up research to TreNet added attention mechanisms [5,27], however, they not deal with trend prediction specifically. Another active and related field to trend prediction is the stock market direction movement, which is only concerned with the direction of the time series, it does not predict the strength and the duration of the time series [5,6,9,17,20,24]. Generally, the baseline methods used by prior work include neural networks, the naive last value prediction, ARIMA, SVR [16,26]. They do not include ensemble methods such as random forests, which are widely used particularly for stock market movement prediction [13,22].

3   Experimental Design

3.1   Datasets

Experiments were conducted on the four different datasets described below.

1. The *voltage dataset* from the UCI machine learning repository[1]. It contains 2075259 data points of a household voltage measurements of one minute interval. It is highly volatile but normally distributed. It follows the same pattern every year, according to the weather seasons as shown in Fig. 4 in the appendix. It corresponds to the power consumption dataset used by Lin et al. [16].
2. The *methane dataset* from the UCI machine learning repository[2]. We used a resampled set of size of 41786 at a frequency 1 Hz. The methane dataset is skewed to the right of its mean value and exhibits very sharp changes with medium to low volatility as shown in Fig. 5 in the appendix. It corresponds to the gas sensor dataset used by Lin et al. [16].
3. The *NYSE dataset* from Yahoo finance[3]. It contains 13563 data points of the composite New York Stock Exchange (NYSE) closing price from 31-12-1965 to 15-11-2019. Its volatility is very low initially until before the year 2000 after which, it becomes very volatile. It is skewed to the right as shown in Fig. 6 in the appendix. It corresponds to the stock market dataset used by Lin et al. [16].

---

[1] https://archive.ics.uci.edu/ml/datasets/individual+household+electric+power+consumption.

[2] https://archive.ics.uci.edu/ml/datasets/gas+sensor+array+under+dynamic+gas+mixtures.

[3] https://finance.yahoo.com.

4. The *JSE dataset* from Yahoo finance. It contains 3094 data points of the composite Johannesburg Stock Exchange (JSE) closing price from 2007-09-18 to 2019-12-31. Compared to the NYSE, this stock market dataset is less volatile and shows a symmetrical distribution around its mean value. However, it has a flat top and heavy tails on both sides as shown in Fig. 7 in the appendix.

The characteristics of the four datasets are summarised in Table 1.

Table 1. Summary of the characteristics of the datasets.

	Seasonality	Skewness	Volatility
Voltage	Seasonal	Symmetric	Very high
Methane	Non-seasonal	Right skewness	Medium to low
NYSE	Non-seasonal	Right skewness	Low to high
JSE	Non-seasonal	Almost symmetric	Medium to low

3.2 Data Preprocessing

The data preprocessing consists of three operations: missing data imputation, the data segmentation, and the sliding window operation. Each missing data point is replaced with the closest preceding non-missing value. The segmentation of the time series into trend lines i.e. piecewise linear approximations is done by regression using the bottom-up approach, similar to the approach used by Wang et al. [23]. The data instances, i.e. the input-output pairs are formed using a sliding window. The input features are the local data points $L_k = <x_{t_k-w}, ..., x_{t_k}>$ for the current trend $T_k = <s_k, l_k>$ at the current time t. The window size w is determined by the duration of the first trend line. The output is the next trend $T_{k+1} = <s_{k+1}, l_{k+1}>$. The statistics of the segmented datasets are provided in Table 7 in the appendix.

3.3 Learning Algorithms

The performance of seven ML algorithms, i.e. the hybrid TreNet approach, four vanilla DNN algorithms and two traditional ML algorithms were evaluated. These algorithms are described below.

TreNet: TreNet has a hybrid CNN which takes in raw point data, and LSTM which takes in trend lines as shown in Fig. 1. The LSTM consisted of a single LSTM layer, and the CNN is composed of two stacked [16] 1D convolutional neural networks without pooling layer. The second CNN layer is followed by a ReLU activation function. Each of the flattened output of the CNN's ReLU layer and the LSTM layer is projected to the same dimension using a fully connected layer for the fusion operation. The fusion layer consists of a fully connected layer that takes the element-wise addition of the projected outputs of the CNN and LSTM components as its input, and outputs the slope and duration values. A dropout layer is added to the layer before the output layer. The best TreNet hyperparameters for each dataset are shown in Table 9 in the appendix and compared to Lin et al.'s [16].

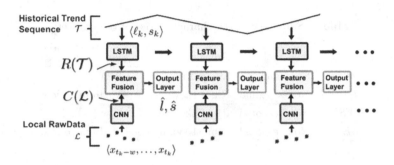

Fig. 1. Illustration of the hybrid neural network architecture [16]

Vanilla DNN Algorithms:

- *The MLP* consists of N number of fully connected neural network (NN) layers, where, $N \in [1, 5]$. Each layer is followed by a ReLU activation function to capture non-linear patterns. To prevent overfitting, a dropout layer is added after each odd number layer, except the last layer. For instance, if the number of layers $N = 5$, the layer 1 and layer 3 will be followed by a dropout layer.
- *The LSTM* consists of N LSTM layers, where $N \in [1, 3]$. Each layer is followed by a ReLU activation function to extract non-linear patterns, and a dropout layer to prevent overfitting. After the last dropout layer, a fully connected NN layer is added. This layer takes the feature representation extracted by the LSTM layers as its input and predicts the next trend. The LSTM layers are not re-initialised after every epoch.
- *The CNN* consists of N 1D-convolutional layer, where $N \in [1, 3]$. Each convolutional layer, which consists of a specified number of filters of a given kernel size, is followed by a ReLU activation function, a pooling layer, and a dropout layer to prevent overfitting. The final layer of the CNN algorithm is a fully connected neural network which takes the features extracted by the convolution, activation, pooling, and dropout operations as its input and predicts the next trend. The structure of a 1D-CNN layer is illustrated in Fig. 2.

The parameters of the vanilla DNN algorithms were tuned manually. The best values found for each algorithm on each dataset are shown in Table 10 in the appendix.

DNN Algorithm Training, and Initialisation: The equally weighted average slope and duration mean square error (MSE) is used as a loss function during training with the Adam optimizer [12]. To ensure robustness against random initialisation, the DNNs are initialised using the He initialisation technique [8] with normal distribution, fan-in mode, and a ReLU activation function.

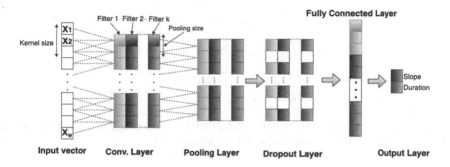

Fig. 2. The structure of a one layer 1D-convolution neural network.

Traditional ML Algorithms: The SVR and RF algorithms are implemented using Sklearn [21], but, GBM is implemented with LightGBM[4]. We tuned the *gamma* and *C* hyperparameters for the SVR; the *number of estimators*, the *maximum depth*, the *boostrap*, and *warm start* hyperparameters for the RF; as well as the *boostrap type*, the *number of estimators*, and the *learning rate* hyperparameters for the GBM, on the validation sets. Their best hyperparameter configurations per dataset are shown in Table 11 in the appendix. We use the MSE loss for the RF.

3.4   Model Evaluation with Walk-Forward Evaluation

The walk-forward evaluation procedure, with the successive and overlapping training-validation-test partition [18], is used to evaluate the performance of the models. The input-output data instances are partitioned into training, validation, and test sets in a successive and overlapping fashion [18] as shown in Fig. 3. For the methane and JSE datasets, the combined test sets make up 10% of their total data instances as per the original TreNet experiments; and 80% and 50% for the voltage and NYSE datasets respectively because of their large sizes. The partition sizes for each dataset are given in Table 8 in the appendix. We set the number of partitions to 8 for the voltage, 44 for methane, 5 for NYSE and, 101 for the JSE dataset. This determines the number of model updates performed for each dataset. For example, one initial training and 7 (8-1) model updates are performed for the voltage dataset. For DNN models, the neural networks

---

[4] https://lightgbm.readthedocs.io/en/latest/index.html

are initialised using the weights of the most recent model, during model update. This makes the training of the network faster without compromising its generalisation ability. More details about this technique which we refer to as *model update with warm-start* is given in Sect. A.2 in the appendix. The average root mean square error (RMSE), given in Eq. 1, is used as the evaluation metric.

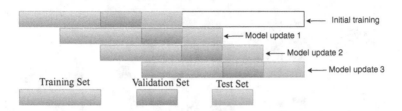

Fig. 3. An example of successive and overlapping training-validation-test partitioning with 4 partitions (1 initial training and 3 model updates)

$$RMSE = \sqrt{\frac{1}{T}\sum_{t=1}^{T}(y_t - y_t')^2} \qquad (1)$$

where, $y_t \rightarrow$ actual next trend, $y_t' \rightarrow$ predicted next trend, and $T \rightarrow$ number of data instances. For the DNN algorithms each experiment is run 10 times and the mean and the standard deviation across the 10 runs are reported. This provides a measure of the stability of the DNN configuration using different random seeds.

4   Experiments

We performed four experiments; each with four datasets. In experiment 1, we implement and evaluate a TreNet [16]. TreNet uses a hybrid deep learning structure, that combines both a CNN and an LSTM, and takes in a combination of raw data points and trend lines as its input. In experiment 2, we compared the TreNet results with the performance of vanilla MLP, CNN and LSTM structures on raw point data to analyse the performance improvement when using a hybrid approach with trend lines. In experiment 3, we evaluate the performance of three traditional ML techniques, i.e. SVR, RF, and GBM on raw point data to analyse the performance difference between DNN and non-DNN approaches. In experiment 4, we supplement the raw data features with trend lines features to evaluate the performance improvement over the raw data features alone for both DNN and non-DNN algorithms.

4.1   Experiment 1: Replicating TreNet with Walk-Forward Validation

We replicated the TreNet approach using a walk forward validation rather than random shuffling and cross validation used in the original TreNet experiments.

Table 2. Comparison of the slope (S), duration (D), and average (A) RMSE values achieved by our hybrid neural network's performance and Lin et al.'s results. The percentage improvement (% improv.) over the naive LVM

	Voltage			Methane			NYSE		
	S	D	A	S	D	A	S	D	A
Our LVM	17.09	86.51	51.80	28.54	152.86	90.70	127.16	0.33	63.75
Our TreNet	9.25	62.37	35.81	14.87	31.25	23.06	86.89	1.23	44.06
Our % improv.	**45.87**	27.90	30.87	**47.90**	**79.56**	**74.58**	**31.67**	−272.73	**30.89**
Lin et al.'s LVM	21.17	39.68	30.43	10.57	53.76	32.17	8.58	11.36	9.97
Lin et al.'s TreNet	12.89	25.62	19.26	9.46	51.25	30.36	6.58	8.51	7.55
Lin et al.'s % improv.	39.11	**35.43**	**36.71**	10.50	4.69	5.63	23.31	**25.09**	24.27

In order to compare our results with the original TreNet we use a similar performance measure to Lin et al. [16]. We measure the percentage improvement over a naive last value model (LVM). The naive last value model simply "takes the duration and slope of the last trend as the prediction for the next one" [16]. The use of a relative metric makes comparison easier, since the RMSE is scale-dependent, and the trend lines generated in this study may differ from Lin et al.'s [16]. Lin et al. [16] did not provide details of the segmentation method they used in their paper. Furthermore, the naive last value model does not require any hyper-parameter tuning, its predictions are stable and repeatable, i.e. does not differ when the experiment is rerun, and is only dependent on the characteristics of the dataset.

Table 2 shows the performance improvement on RMSE values over the LVM achieved by the TreNet implementation on each dataset. They are compared to the performance of the original TreNet on the three datasets they used in their experiments, i.e. the voltage, methane and NYSE datasets. The results of our experiment differ substantially from those reported for the original TreNet. Our TreNet models' percentage improvement over the naive LVM is 13.25 (**74.58**/5.63) and 1.27 (**30.89**/24.27) times greater than Lin et al.'s [16], on the methane and NYSE datasets respectively; but 1.19 (36.71/**27.90**) times smaller on the voltage dataset. The naive LVM performs better than our TreNet model on the NYSE for the duration prediction. The −272.73 % decrease in performance is due to two reasons. On the one hand, the model training, i.e. the loss minimisation was biased towards the slope loss at the expense of the duration loss. This is because the slope loss significantly greater compared to the duration loss, but, TreNet's loss function weights both equally. On the other hand, the durations of the trends in the NYSE dataset being very similar - with a standard deviation of 0.81 - makes the last value prediction model a favourably competitive model for the duration prediction.

The greater average improvement on the methane and NYSE is attributed to the use of the walk-forward evaluation procedure. The methane and NYSE datasets undergo various changes in the generating process because of the sudden changes in methane concentrations and the economic cycles for the NYSE. Thus, the use of the walk-forward evaluation ensures that the most recent and useful training set is used for a given validation/test set. However, given that Lin et al. [16] did not drop older data from the training data set, the network may learn long-range relationships that are not useful for the current test set. Furthermore, they used random shuffling which may most likely result in future data points being included in the training data. The smaller improvement of our TreNet model on the voltage dataset can be attributed to our use of a smaller window size for the *local raw data* fed into the CNN. We used 19 compared to their best value of 700 on the voltage dataset. This is one of the limitations of our replication of TreNet. For each dataset, we used the length of the first trend line as window size of the *local raw data* feature fed into the CNN, instead of tuning it to select the best value. The other limitation is the use of a sampled version of the methane dataset instead of the complete methane dataset.

4.2   Experiment 2: Trend Prediction with Vanilla DNN Algorithms

Given that we are now using a different validation method which yields different performances scores to the original TreNet, we checked whether the TreNet approach still outperforms the vanilla DNN algorithms. We implemented and tested three vanilla DNN models namely a MLP, LSTM, and CNN using only raw local data features.

Table 3 shows the average RMSE values for slope and trend predictions achieved by the vanilla DNNs and TreNet on each dataset across 10 independent runs. The deviation across the 10 runs is also shown to provide an indication of the stability of the model across the runs. We use the average slope and duration RMSE values as an overall comparison metric. The % improvement is the improvement of the best vanilla DNN model over TreNet. The best model is chosen based on the overall comparison metric.

In general TreNet still performs better than the vanilla DNN models, but does not outperform the vanilla models on all the datasets. The most noticeable case is on the NYSE, where the LSTM model outperforms the TreNet model on both the slope and duration prediction. This contradicts Lin et al. [16]'s findings, where TreNet clearly outperforms all other models including LSTM. On average, Lin et al.'s [16] TreNet model outperformed their LSTM model by 22.48%; whereas, our TreNet implementation underperformed our LSTM model by 1.31%. However, Lin et al. [16]'s LSTM model appears to be trained using trend lines only and not raw point data. This LSTM model uses *local raw data* features. It must also be noted that the validation method used here is substantially different from the one used by Lin et al. [16]. The large performance difference between TreNet and the vanilla models on the methane dataset is because for this dataset the raw local data features do not provide the global information about the time series since it is non-stationary. This is confirmed by the increase in the performance of the MLP (23.83%), LSTM (11.02%) and CNN (24.05%) after supplementing the raw data features with trend line features (see experiment 4 in Sect. 4.4).

Table 3. Comparison of the RMSE values achieved by the vanilla DNN models and TreNet. The % improvement (% improv.) is the improvement of the best vanilla DNN model over TreNet

	Voltage			Methane		
	Slope	Duration	Average	Slope	Duration	Average
MLP	**9.04 ± 0.06**	62.82 ± 0.04	35.93 ± 0.05	14.57 ± 0.10	49.79 ± 4.85	32.18 ± 2.48
LSTM	10.30 ± 0.0	62.87 ± 0.0	36.59 ± 0.0	**14.21 ± 0.19**	56.37 ± 1.77	35.29 ± 0.49
CNN	9.24 ± 0.10	62.40 ± 0.13	35.82 ± 0.12	15.07 ± 0.35	54.79 ± 4.55	34.93 ± 2.45
TreNet	9.25 ± 0.0	**62.37 ± 0.01**	**35.81 ± 0.01**	14.87 ± 0.40	**31.25 ± 2.62**	**23.06 ± 1.51**
% improv.	−0.11	−0.05	−0.03	**2.02**	−59.33	−39.55
	NYSE			JSE		
	Slope	Duration	Average	Slope	Duration	Average
MLP	90.76 ± 4.43	33.08 ± 42.08	61.92 ± 23.26	19.87 ± 0.01	12.51 ± 0.09	16.19 ± 0.05
LSTM	**86.56 ± 0.01**	**0.41 ± 0.08**	**43.49 ± 0.05**	19.83 ± 0.01	12.68 ± 0.01	16.25 ± 0.01
CNN	89.31 ± 1.38	12.21 ± 12.17	50.76 ± 6.78	19.90 ± 0.06	**12.48 ± 0.21**	16.19 ± 0.14
TreNet	86.89 ± 0.14	1.23 ± 0.38	44.06 ± 0.26	**19.65 ± 0.05**	12.49 ± 0.04	**16.07 ± 0.05**
% improv.	**0.38**	**66.67**	**1.29**	−1.12	−0.16	−0.75

4.3 Experiment 3: Traditional ML Models

Given the new validation method, we now compare the performance of DNN trend prediction models to the performance of traditional ML models. We implemented and tested three traditional ML models, i.e. radial-based SVR, RF, and GBM. To our knowledge, RF and GBM have not been used previously for trend prediction. Lin et al. [16] compared their approach against multiple SVR kernels that took in both local raw data and trend line features. In this experiment, our models take in only *local raw data* features without trend lines.

Table 4 shows the RMSE values achieved by the traditional ML algorithms and the best DNN models on each dataset. The best DNN model is TreNet on all datasets except on the NYSE, on which LSTM is the best model. The improvement (%) is the performance improvement of the best traditional ML model over the best DNN model, where, the best model is selected based on the equally weighted average slope and duration RMSE, i.e. average.

The best traditional ML algorithm underperformed the best DNN algorithm by 0.47% and 1.74% respectively on the (almost) normally distributed datasets such voltage and the JSE datasets. However, the RF model outperformed the best DNN model, i.e. TreNet by 33.04% on the methane dataset; while the SVR model matched the performance of the best DNN model, i.e. LSTM on the NYSE dataset. TreNet learns long-range dependencies from trend line features with its LSTM component. Although this is useful for stationary and less evolving time series such as the voltage and JSE datasets, it appears that it can be detrimental in the case of dynamic and non-stationary time series such as the methane dataset. This may explain why the traditional ML models, which do not keep long-term memory, performed better on this dataset.

Table 4. Comparison of the best DNN models (Best DNN) with the traditional ML algorithms. The % improvement (% improv.) is the performance improvement of the best traditional ML model over the best DNN model

	Voltage			Methane		
	Slope	Duration	Average	Slope	Duration	Average
RF	9.53 ± 0.0	63.11 ± 0.20	36.32 ± 0.10	10.09 ± 0.01	20.79 ± 0.01	15.44 ± 0.01
GBM	10.0 ± 0.0	62.67 ± 0.0	36.34 ± 0.0	13.05 ± 0.0	75.10 ± 0.0	44.08 ± 0.0
SVR	9.32 ± 0.0	62.58 ± 0.0	35.95 ± 0.0	14.98 ± 0.0	34.39 ± 0.0	24.69 ± 0.0
Best DNN	$\mathbf{9.25 \pm 0.0}$	$\mathbf{62.37 \pm 0.01}$	$\mathbf{35.81 \pm 0.01}$	14.87 ± 0.40	31.25 ± 2.62	23.06 ± 1.51
% improv.	-0.76	-0.34	-0.47	$\mathbf{32.15}$	$\mathbf{33.47}$	$\mathbf{33.04}$
	NYSE			JSE		
	Slope	Duration	Average	Slope	Duration	Average
RF	88.75 ± 0.17	$\mathbf{0.29 \pm 0.0}$	44.52 ± 0.09	20.21 ± 0.0	12.67 ± 0.0	16.44 ± 0.0
GBM	86.62 ± 0.0	0.42 ± 0.0	43.52 ± 0.0	20.08 ± 0.0	12.62 ± 0.0	16.35 ± 0.0
SVR	$\mathbf{86.55 \pm 0.0}$	0.42 ± 0.0	43.49 ± 0.0	20.01 ± 0.0	12.85 ± 0.0	16.43 ± 0.0
Best DNN	86.56 ± 0.01	0.41 ± 0.08	43.49 ± 0.05	$\mathbf{19.65 \pm 0.05}$	$\mathbf{12.49 \pm 0.04}$	$\mathbf{16.07 \pm 0.05}$
% improv.	$\mathbf{0.01}$	2.44	0.0	-2.19	-1.04	-1.74

The fact that the radial-based SVR performed better than TreNet on the NYSE dataset contradicts Lin et al. [16]'s results. We attribute this to the use of *local raw data* features alone, instead of *local raw data* plus *trend line* features used by Lin et al. [16].

4.4   Experiment 4: Addition of Trend Line Features

In this experiment, we supplement the raw data with trend line features to analyse whether this yields any performance improvement to the DNN and non-DNN models from Experiments 2 and 3. We did retain the hyperparameter values found using the *raw data* features alone for this experiment.

Table 5 shows the average performance improvement (%) after supplementing the raw data with trend line features. The negative sign indicates a drop in performance. The Average is the mean and the standard error of the improvements over the algorithm or the dataset. The actual RMSE values are shown in Table 12 and Table 13 in the appendix.

Table 5. Performance improvement after supplementing the raw data with trend line features.

	MLP	LSTM	CNN	RF	GBM	SVR	Average
Voltage	$\mathbf{0.03}$	0.0	-73.14	-0.13	$\mathbf{0.06}$	-0.36	-12.26 ± 12.18
Methane	$\mathbf{23.83}$	$\mathbf{11.02}$	$\mathbf{24.05}$	-4.47	$\mathbf{42.88}$	-6.28	$\mathbf{15.17 \pm 7.71}$
NYSE	$\mathbf{6.49}$	0.0	-1.00	$\mathbf{2.36}$	$\mathbf{0.23}$	-0.02	1.34 ± 1.12
JSE	-4.14	-1.17	-5.37	-7.60	$\mathbf{0.37}$	-10.96	-4.81 ± 1.70
Average	$\mathbf{6.55 \pm 6.16}$	$\mathbf{4.93 \pm 2.87}$	-13.87 ± 20.79	-2.46 ± 2.22	$\mathbf{10.89 \pm 10.67}$	-4.41 ± 2.62	

The addition of trend line features improved the performance of both DNN and non-DNN models 10 times out of 24 cases. In general, it improves the performance of dynamic and non-stationary time series such as the methane and NYSE datasets. This is because local raw data features do not capture the global information about the time series for non-stationary time series. Thus, the addition of trend line features brings new information to the models. In 12 out of 24 cases, the addition of trend line features reduced the performance of both DNN and non-DNN models except the GBM models. For these cases, the addition trend line features brings noise or duplicate information, which the models did not deal with successfully. This may be because the best hyperparameters for the raw data features alone may not be optimal for the raw data and the trend line features combined. For instance, DNN models are generally able to extract the true signal from noisy or duplicate input features, however, they are sensitive to the hyperparameter values.

The above results show that the addition of trend line features has the potential to improve the performance of both DNN and non-DNN models on non-stationary time series. This comes at the cost of additional complexities and restrictions. The first complexity is related to the model complexity because the bigger the input feature size, the more complex the model becomes. Secondly, the trend line features require the segmentation of the time series into trends, which brings new challenges and restrictions during inference. For instance, trend prediction applications that require online inference need an online segmentation method such as the one proposed by Keogh et al. [10]. It is therefore necessary to evaluate whether the performance gain over raw data features alone justifies these complexities and restrictions.

4.5   Summary of the Best Performing Trend Prediction Algorithms

Table 6 provides a summary of the best models and their average performance from all four experiments. The TreNet algorithm outperforms the non-hybrid algorithms on the voltage and JSE datasets, but the performance difference is marginal $< 1\%$. Interestingly, the traditional ML algorithms outperformed TreNet and the vanilla DNN algorithms on the methane and NYSE datasets.

The additional of trend lines to the point data (experiment 4) did not yield any substantial change in the results. It must be noted though that this was an exploratory experiment and that no hyper-parameter optimisation was done to cater for the introduction of a new input feature. It may well be the case that better models could be found of a new hyper-parameter optimisation process was undertaken.

It is clear from these results that TreNet generally performs well on most datasets. However, it is not the clear winner, and there are some dataset where traditional models can substantially outperform TreNet. It is also clear that models built with point data alone can generally reach the performance levels of TreNet.

Table 6. Average RMSE values (E) achieved by the hybrid algorithm, i.e. TreNet; and the best non-hybrid algorithm (A) with raw point data features alone (Pt) and with raw point data plus trend line features (Pt + Tr). The % change is with respect to the TreNet algorithm.

		% Change	Pt	Hybrid	Pt + T	% Change
Voltage	A	–	CNN	**TreNet**	MLP	–
	E	−0.03	35.82 ± 0.12	**35.81 ± 0.01**	35.92 ± 0.05	−0.31
Methane	A	–	**RF**	TreNet	RF	–
	E	**33.04**	**15.44 ± 0.01**	23.06 ± 1.51	16.13 ± 0.01	30.05
NYSE	A	–	SVR	TreNet	**GBM**	–
	E	**1.29**	43.49 ± 0.0	44.06 ± 0.26	**43.42 ± 0.0**	1.45
JSE	A	–	MLP	**TreNet**	GBM	–
	E	−0.75	16.19 ± 0.05	**16.07 ± 0.05**	16.29 ± 0.0	−1.37

5   Discussion and Conclusions

In this work, we identify and address some limitations of a recent hybrid CNN and LSTM approach for trend prediction, i.e. TreNet. We used an appropriate validation method, i.e. walk-forward validation instead of the standard cross-validation and also tested model stability. We compared TreNet to vanilla deep neural networks (DNNs) that take in point data features. Our results show that TreNet does not always outperform vanilla DNN models and when it does, the outperformance is marginal. Furthermore, our results show that for non-normally distributed datasets, traditional ML algorithms, such as Random Forests and Support Vector Regressors, can outperform more complex DNN algorithms. We highlighted the importance of using an appropriate validation strategy and testing the stability of DNN models when they are updated and retrained as new observations become available.

There are many avenues to probe the results of this work further. Firstly we only tested this on four datasets. While these included all three datasets used in the original TreNet paper [16], testing on more datasets is required to probe the generalisation of these findings. Secondly, there are some avenues that can be explored to improve on these results. Since the window size was fixed to the duration length of the first trend line, the effect of varying the window size could be tested. A sampled version of the methane dataset is used instead of the complete methane dataset and the full dataset could be used. Tuning the hyperparameters of the model after the addition of trend line features may increase the performance of the models. Finding the best hyper-parameter values for a particular time series required extensive experimentation, and often requires information about the characteristics of that time series. Automatic machine learning techniques [4, 15] could be explored for automating the feature selection, algorithm selection and hyperparameter configuration.

A   Appendix

A.1   Datasets

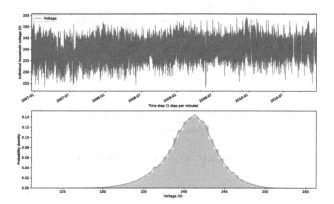

Fig. 4. Top - The individual household voltage dataset. Bottom - Probability distribution of the voltage dataset.

Table 7. Summary of the basic statistics of the segmented datasets and the input vector size per feature type.

	Voltage	Methane	NYSE	JSE
Number of local raw data points	2075259	41786	13563	3094
Number of trend lines	42280	4419	10015	1001
Mean ± deviation of the trend slope	-0.21 ± 10.41	0.17 ± 18.12	5.44 ± 81.27	0.21 ± 18.18
Mean ± deviation of the trend duration	50.08 ± 60.36	10.46 ± 67.03	2.35 ± 0.81	4.09 ± 5.23
Raw local data feature size	19	100	4	2
Raw local data + Trend line feature size	21	102	6	4
Number of data instances	42279	4418	10014	1001

A.2   Model Update with Warm-Start

The walk-forward evaluation procedure requires as many training episodes as the number of splits: one initial training and many model updates. This many training episodes can be computationally very expensive, particularly for deep neural networks. Thus, in this work, model update with warm start initialisation is used to reduce the training time of the neural network based algorithms.

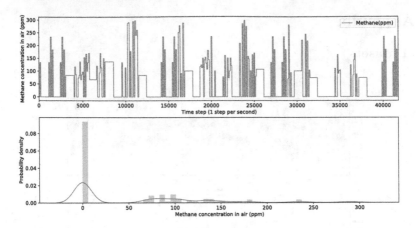

Fig. 5. Top - Methane concentration in air over time. Bottom - Probability distribution of the methane dataset.

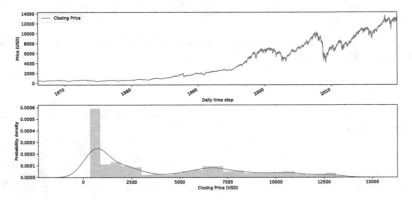

Fig. 6. Top - The composite New York Stock Exchange (NYSE) closing price dataset. Bottom - Probability distribution of the NYSE dataset.

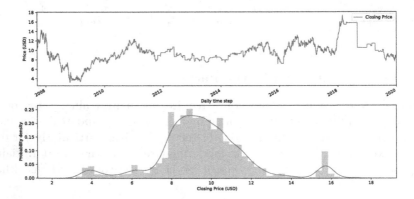

Fig. 7. Top - Composite Johannesburg Stock Exchange (JSE) closing price dataset. Bottom - Probability distribution of the JSE dataset.

Table 8. Summary of the data instance partitioning

	Voltage	Methane	NYSE	JSE
Number of data instances	42279	4418	10014	1001
Chosen total test sets percentage	80%	10%	50%	10%
Chosen test set size	4227	10	1001	1
Number of splits	8	44	5	101
Validation set size	4227	10	1001	1
Training set size	4227	3967	4008	899

That is, during model update, the new network is initialised with the weights of the previous model. In effect, the patterns learnt by the previous network are transferred to the new model, therefore, reducing the number of epochs required to learn the new best function. In practice, the walk-forward evaluation with warm start corresponds to performing the first training with the maximum number of epochs required to converge, then using a fraction of this number for every other update. This fraction - between 0.0 and 1.0 - becomes an additional hyperparameter dubbed *warm start*. The lowest value that out-performed the model update without warm-start is used as the best value, because this technique is essentially used to speed-up the model updates.

The speed-up, i.e. the expected reduction factor in the total number of epochs can be computed in advance using Eq. 4. The Eq. 4 is derived from Eq. 2 and Eq. 3.

$$E' = E + E \times (S - 1) \times \omega \tag{2}$$

$$E' = E \times (1 + (S - 1) \times \omega) \tag{3}$$

$$speed\text{-}up = \frac{E}{E'} = \frac{S}{1 + (S - 1) \times \omega} \tag{4}$$

Where, $E' \rightarrow$ *Total epochs with warm start*, $E \rightarrow$ *Epochs per split without warm-start*, $S \rightarrow$ *Number of data partition splits*, $\omega \rightarrow$ *warm-start fraction*.

A.3   Best Hyperparameters

Table 9. Our best TreNet hyperparameters found by manual experimentation. "?" means *unknown* and $S = \{300, 600, 900, 1200\}$

	Dropout	L2	LR	LSTM cells	CNN filters	Fusion layer	Batch Size	Epochs	Warm start
Voltage	0.0	5e−4	1e−3	[600]	[16, 16]	300	2000	100	0.2
Methane	0.0	5e−4	1e−3	[1500]	[4, 4]	1200	2000	2000	0.1
NYSE	0.0	0.0	1e−3	[600]	[128, 128]	300	5000	100	0.5
JSE	0.0	0.0	1e−3	[5]	[32, 32]	10	500	100	0.05
Lin et al. [16]	0.5	5e−4	?	[600]	[32, 32]	*From S*	?	?	*N/A*

A.4   Additional Results

Table 10. Hyperparameters optimised for the vanilla DNN algorithms and their best values found for each dataset

		Voltage	Methane	NYSE	JSE
MLP	Batch size	4000	250	5000	250
	Warm start	0.1	0.1	0.7	0.05
	Learning rate	1e−4	1e−3	1e−3	1e−3
	Dropout	0.0	0.0	0.0	0.0
	Weight decay	0.0	0.0	5e−4	0.0
	Number of epochs	10000	15000	500	100
	Layer configuration	[500, 400, 300]	[500, 400]	[500, 400, 300]	[100]
LSTM	Batch size	4000	2000	5000	1000
	Warm start	0.1	0.1	0.01	0.05
	Learning rate	1e−2	1e−4	1e−3	1e−3
	Dropout	0.0	0.0	0.5	0.5
	Weight decay	0.0	0.0	5e−5	0.0
	Number of epochs	1000	15000	100	100
	Cell configuration	[600]	[600, 300]	[100]	[100]
CNN	Batch size	2000	250	5000	1000
	Warm start	0.5	0.3	0.4	0.1
	Learning rate	1e−3	1e−3	1e−3	1e−3
	Dropout	0.0	0.0	0.0	0.0
	Weight decay	5e−5	5e−4	0.0	0.0
	Number of epochs	15000	1000	12000	100
	Filter configuration	[16]	[32, 32]	[32]	[32, 32]
	Kernel configuration	[2]	[2, 4]	[1]	[1, 1]
	Pooling type	Max	Max	Identity	Identity
	Pooling size	2	5	N/A	N/A

Table 11. Best hyperparameters of the traditional ML algorithms.

Algorithm	Hyperparameter	Voltage	Methane	NYSE	JSE
RF	Number of estimators	50	50	200	100
	Maximum depth	2	10	1	1
	Bootstrap	2000	False	True	False
	Warm start	False	False	True	True
GBM	Bootstrap type	gbdt	gbdt	gbdt	gbdt
	Number of estimators	1	10000	1	4
	Learning rate	2000	0.1	0.2	0.1
SVR	Gamma	0.1	1e−4	1e−1	1e−4
	C	4	10000	100	500

Table 12. Performance of vanilla DNN algorithms on raw data alone and raw data and trend line features.

	Voltage			Methane		
	Slope	Duration	Average	Slope	Duration	Average
Raw data	9.04 ± 0.06	62.82 ± 0.04	35.93 ± 0.05	14.57 ± 0.10	49.79 ± 4.85	32.18 ± 2.47
Raw data + Trend lines	**9.03 ± 0.06**	62.81 ± 0.04	**35.92 ± 0.05**	14.56 ± 0.19	**34.46 ± 2.79**	**24.51 ± 1.49**
	NYSE			JSE		
	Slope	Duration	Average	Slope	Duration	Average
Raw data	90.76 ± 4.43	33.08 ± 42.08	61.92 ± 23.26	19.87 ± 0.01	12.51 ± 0.09	16.19 ± 0.05
Raw data + Trend lines	90.45 ± 2.55	25.34 ± 24.09	57.90 ± 13.32	21.13 ± 0.30	12.59 ± 0.14	16.86 ± 0.22

MLP

	Voltage			Methane		
	Slope	Duration	Average	Slope	Duration	Average
Raw data	10.30 ± 0.0	62.87 ± 0.0	36.59 ± 0.0	**14.21 ± 0.19**	56.37 ± 1.77	**35.29 ± 0.68**
Raw data + Trend lines	10.30 ± 0.0	62.87 ± 0.0	36.59 ± 0.0	14.77 ± 0.51	**48.03 ± 5.74**	**31.40 ± 3.13**
	NYSE			JSE		
	Slope	Duration	Average	Slope	Duration	Average
Raw data	**86.56 ± 0.01**	0.41 ± 0.08	**43.49 ± 0.05**	19.83 ± 0.01	12.68 ± 0.01	16.26 ± 0.01
Raw data + Trend lines	**86.50 ± 0.01**	0.47 ± 0.03	**43.49 ± 0.02**	20.16 ± 0.03	12.74 ± 0.02	16.45 ± 0.03

LSTM

	Voltage			Methane		
	Slope	Duration	Average	Slope	Duration	Average
Raw data	**9.24 ± 0.10**	**62.40 ± 0.13**	**35.82 ± 0.12**	15.07 ± 0.35	54.79 ± 4.55	34.93 ± 2.45
Raw data + Trend lines	33.26 ± 19.41	90.78 ± 53.17	62.02 ± 36.29	15.14 ± 0.28	**37.92 ± 4.11**	**26.53 ± 2.20**
	NYSE			JSE		
	Slope	Duration	Average	Slope	Duration	Average
Raw data	89.31 ± 1.38	12.21 ± 12.17	50.76 ± 6.78	**19.90 ± 0.06**	**12.48 ± 0.21**	**16.19 ± 0.14**
Raw data + Trend lines	90.44 ± 1.74	14.05 ± 9.52	52.25 ± 5.63	21.41 ± 0.33	12.71 ± 0.15	17.06 ± 0.24

CNN

138   K. H. Kouassi and D. Moodley

Table 13. Performance of traditional ML algorithms on raw data alone and raw data and trend line features.

	Voltage			Methane		
	Slope	Duration	Average	Slope	Duration	Average
Local raw data	9.53 ± 0.0	63.11 ± 0.20	36.32 ± 0.10	10.09 ± 0.01	20.79 ± 0.01	15.44 ± 0.01
Local raw data + Trend lines	9.35 ± 0.0	63.19 ± 0.29	36.27 ± 0.15	11.53 ± 0.0	20.73 ± 0.01	16.13 ± 0.01
	NYSE			JSE		
	Slope	Duration	Average	Slope	Duration	Average
Local raw data	88.75 ± 0.17	0.29 ± 0.0	44.52 ± 0.09	20.21 ± 0.0	12.67 ± 0.0	16.44 ± 0.0
Local raw data + Trend lines	86.53 ± 0.01	0.41 ± 0.0	43.47 ± 0.01	22.68 ± 0.0	12.69 ± 0.0	17.69 ± 0.0

RF

	Voltage			Methane		
	Slope	Duration	Average	Slope	Duration	Average
Local raw data	10.0 ± 0.0	62.67 ± 0.0	36.34 ± 0.0	13.05 ± 0.0	75.10 ± 0.0	44.08 ± 0.0
Local raw data + Trend lines	10.01 ± 0.0	62.63 ± 0.0	36.32 ± 0.0	12.02 ± 0.0	38.34 ± 0.0	25.18 ± 0.0
	NYSE			JSE		
	Slope	Duration	Average	Slope	Duration	Average
Local raw data	86.62 ± 0.0	0.42 ± 0.0	43.52 ± 0.0	20.08 ± 0.0	12.62 ± 0.0	16.35 ± 0.0
Local raw data + Trend lines	86.42 ± 0.0	0.41 ± 0.0	43.42 ± 0.0	19.93 ± 0.0	12.65 ± 0.0	16.29 ± 0.0

GBM

	Voltage			Methane		
	Slope	Duration	Average	Slope	Duration	Average
Raw data	9.32 ± 0.0	62.58 ± 0.0	35.95 ± 0.0	14.98 ± 0.0	34.39 ± 0.0	24.69 ± 0.0
Raw data + Trend lines	9.54 ± 0.0	62.62 ± 0.0	36.08 ± 0.0	17.95 ± 0.0	34.52 ± 0.0	26.24 ± 0.0
	NYSE			JSE		
	Slope	Duration	Average	Slope	Duration	Average
Raw data	86.55 ± 0.0	0.42 ± 0.0	43.49 ± 0.0	20.01 ± 0.0	12.85 ± 0.0	16.43 ± 0.0
Raw data + Trend lines	86.54 ± 0.0	0.45 ± 0.0	43.50 ± 0.0	23.27 ± 0.0	13.19 ± 0.0	18.23 ± 0.0

SVR

References

1. Bergmeir, C., Benítez, J.M.: On the use of cross-validation for time series predictor evaluation. Inf. Sci. **191**, 192–213 (2012). https://doi.org/10.1016/j.ins.2011.12.028
2. Chang, L., Chen, P., Chang, F.: Reinforced two-step-ahead weight adjustment technique for online training of recurrent neural networks. IEEE Trans. Neural Netw. Learn. Syst. **23**(8), 1269–1278 (2012)
3. Chung, J., Gülçehre, Ç., Cho, K., Bengio, Y.: Empirical evaluation of gated recurrent neural networks on sequence modeling. CoRR abs/1412.3555 (2014)
4. Falkner, S., Klein, A., Hutter, F.: BOHB: robust and efficient hyperparameter optimization at scale. In: Proceedings of Machine Learning Research, PMLR, Stockholmsmässan, Stockholm Sweden, vol. 80, pp. 1437–1446, 10–15 July 2018. http://proceedings.mlr.press/v80/falkner18a.html
5. Feng, F., Chen, H., He, X., Ding, J., Sun, M., Chua, T.S.: Enhancing stock movement prediction with adversarial training. In: Proceedings of the Twenty-Eighth International Joint Conference on Artificial Intelligence, IJCAI-19, International Joint Conferences on Artificial Intelligence Organization, 7 July 2019, pp. 5843–5849. https://doi.org/10.24963/ijcai.2019/810

6. Guo, J., Li, X.: Prediction of index trend based on LSTM model for extracting image similarity feature. In: Proceedings of the 2019 International Conference on Artificial Intelligence and Computer Science, pp. 335–340. AICS 2019. ACM, New York (2019). https://doi.org/10.1145/3349341.3349427

7. Guo, T., Xu, Z., Yao, X., Chen, H., Aberer, K., Funaya, K.: Robust online time series prediction with recurrent neural networks. In: 2016 IEEE International Conference on Data Science and Advanced Analytics (DSAA), pp. 816–825 (2016). https://doi.org/10.1109/DSAA.2016.92

8. He, K., Zhang, X., Ren, S., Sun, J.: Delving deep into rectifiers: surpassing human-level performance on ImageNet classification (2015)

9. Kara, Y., Acar Boyacioglu, M., Baykan, Ö.K.: Predicting direction of stock price index movement using artificial neural networks and support vector machines: the sample of the Istanbul Stock Exchange. Expert Syst. Appl. **38**(5), 5311–5319 (2011). https://doi.org/10.1016/j.eswa.2010.10.027

10. Keogh, E., Chu, S., Hart, D., Pazzani, M.: An online algorithm for segmenting time series. In: Proceedings 2001 IEEE International Conference on Data Mining, pp. 289–296 (2001). https://doi.org/10.1109/ICDM.2001.989531

11. Keogh, E., Pazzani, M.: An enhanced representation of time series which allows fast and accurate classification, clustering and relevance feedback. In: KDD, vol. 98, pp. 239–243 (1998). https://doi.org/10.1.1.42.1358. http://www.aaai.org/Papers/KDD/1998/KDD98-041.pdf

12. Kingma, D.P., Ba, J.: Adam: a method for stochastic optimization (2014)

13. Kumar, I., Dogra, K., Utreja, C., Yadav, P.: A comparative study of supervised machine learning algorithms for stock market trend prediction. In: 2018 Second International Conference on Inventive Communication and Computational Technologies (ICICCT), pp. 1003–1007 (2018)

14. Lecun, Y., Bottou, L., Bengio, Y., Haffner, P.: Gradient-based learning applied to document recognition. Proc. IEEE **86**(11), 2278–2324 (1998)

15. Li, L., Jamieson, K., DeSalvo, G., Rostamizadeh, A., Talwalkar, A.: Hyperband: a novel bandit-based approach to hyperparameter optimization. J. Mach. Learn. Res. **18**(1), 6765–6816 (2017)

16. Lin, T., Guo, T., Aberer, K.: Hybrid neural networks for learning the trend in time series. In: IJCAI - Proceedings of the Twenty-Sixth International Joint Conference on Artificial Intelligence, pp. 2273–2279 (2017). https://doi.org/10.24963/ijcai.2017/316. https://www.ijcai.org/proceedings/2017/316

17. Liu, Q., Cheng, X., Su, S., Zhu, S.: Hierarchical complementary attention network for predicting stock price movements with news. In: Proceedings of the 7th ACM International Conference on Information and Knowledge Management, CIKM 2018, pp. 1603–1606. ACM, New York (2018). https://doi.org/10.1145/3269206.3269286. http://doi.acm.org/10.1145/3269206.3269286

18. Luo, L., Chen, X.: Integrating piecewise linear representation and weighted support vector machine for stock trading signal prediction. Appl. Soft Comput. **13**(2), 806–816 (2013). https://doi.org/10.1016/j.asoc.2012.10.026. http://www.sciencedirect.com/science/article/pii/S1568494612004796

19. Matsubara, Y., Sakurai, Y., Faloutsos, C.: AutoPlait: automatic mining of co-evolving time sequences. In: Proceedings of the 2014 ACM SIGMOD International Conference on Management of Data, SIGMOD 2014, pp. 193–204. Association for Computing Machinery, New York (2014). https://doi.org/10.1145/2588555.2588556

20. Nelson, D.M., Pereira, A.C., De Oliveira, R.A.: Stock market's price movement prediction with LSTM neural networks. In: Proceedings of the International Joint Conference on Neural Networks (DCC), May 2017 pp. 1419–1426 (2017). https://doi.org/10.1109/IJCNN.2017.7966019

21. Pedregosa, F., et al.: Scikit-learn: machine learning in Python. J. Mach. Learn. Res. **12**, 2825–2830 (2011)

22. Sharma, N., Juneja, A.: Combining of random forest estimates using LSboost for stock market index prediction. In: 2017 2nd International Conference for Convergence in Technology (I2CT), pp. 1199–1202 (2017)

23. Wang, P., Wang, H., Wang, W.: Finding semantics in time series. In: Proceedings of the 2011 International Conference on Management of Data - SIGMOD 2011, p. 385 (2011). https://doi.org/10.1145/1989323.1989364. http://portal.acm.org/citation.cfm?doid=1989323.1989364

24. Wen, M., Li, P., Zhang, L., Chen, Y.: Stock market trend prediction using high-order information of time series. IEEE Access **7**, 28299–28308 (2019). https://doi.org/10.1109/ACCESS.2019.2901842. https://ieeexplore.ieee.org/document/8653278/

25. Ye, L., Keogh, E.: Time series shapelets: a new primitive for data mining. In: Proceedings of the 15th ACM SIGKDD International Conference on Knowledge Discovery and Data Mining, KDD 2009, pp. 947–956. Association for Computing Machinery, New York (2009). https://doi.org/10.1145/1557019.1557122

26. Zhang, J., Cui, S., Xu, Y., Li, Q., Li, T.: A novel data-driven stock price trend prediction system. Expert Syst. Appl. **97**, 60–69 (2018). https://doi.org/10.1016/j.eswa.2017.12.026

27. Zhao, Y., Shen, Y., Zhu, Y., Yao, J.: Forecasting wavelet transformed time series with attentive neural networks. In: 2018 IEEE International Conference on Data Mining (ICDM), pp. 1452–1457 (2018)

Text-to-Speech Duration Models for Resource-Scarce Languages in Neural Architectures

Johannes A. Louw$^{(\boxtimes)}$ (iD)

Voice Computing Research Group, Next Generation Enterprises and Institutions,
CSIR, Pretoria, South Africa
jalouw@csir.co.za

Abstract. Sequence-to-sequence end-to-end models for text-to-speech have shown significant gains in naturalness of the produced synthetic speech. These models have an encoder-decoder architecture, without an explicit duration model, but rather a learned attention-based alignment mechanism, simplifying the training procedure as well as the reducing the language expertise requirements for building synthetic voices. However there are some drawbacks, attention-based alignment systems such as used in the Tacotron, Tacotron 2, Char2Wav and DC-TTS end-to-end architectures typically suffer from low training efficiency as well as model instability, with several approaches attempted to address these problems. Recent neural acoustic models have moved away from using an attention-based mechanisms to align the linguistic and acoustic encoding and decoding, and have rather reverted to using an explicit duration model for the alignment. In this work we develop an efficient neural network based duration model and compare it to the traditional Gaussian mixture model based architectures as used in hidden Markov model (HMM)-based speech synthesis. We show through objective results that our proposed model is better suited to resource-scarce language settings than the traditional HMM-based models.

Keywords: HMM · DNN · Speech synthesis · Duration modelling · Resource-scarce languages

1 Introduction

Deep neural network (DNN) based techniques applied to text-to-speech (TTS) systems have brought on dramatic improvements in the naturalness and intelligibility of synthesized speech. An example of the change in the landscape could be seen in the 2019 edition of the Blizzard Challenge [1], where the best perceptually judged entry was based on a long short-term memory (LSTM) - recurrent neural network (RNN) hybrid architecture [4] with WaveNet [22] as the vocoder. In fact, of the twenty one entries to the Blizzard Challenge 2019 that submitted an accompanying paper (on the Blizzard Challenge website[1]), one system

---

[1] http://festvox.org/blizzard/blizzard2019.html.

© Springer Nature Switzerland AG 2020
A. Gerber (Ed.): SACAIR 2020, CCIS 1342, pp. 141–153, 2020.
https://doi.org/10.1007/978-3-030-66151-9_9

was based on a traditional unit-selection architecture, one system was based on a hidden Markov model (HMM) - deep neural network (DNN) hybrid driven unit-selection architecture, one system was based on a HMM-DNN based hybrid architecture, whilst the other eighteen systems were based on some or other DNN architecture.

The current research in TTS is dominated by DNN-based architectures as can also be seen from the paper submissions to the 2019 edition of Speech Synthesis Workshop (SSW)[2]. According to [24], the success of these architectures in the improvement of the synthesized speech naturalness and intelligibility can be broadly attributed to the attention-based models (such as Tacotron [23] and Deep Convolutional TTS (DCTTS) [19]) as well as the use of neural network based vocoders (such as WaveNet [22])).

Many of the newer DNN-based sequence-to-sequence model architectures are what is known as "end-to-end" systems, in that they only require text and audio pairs (<text, audio>) for training. The traditional TTS architectures are usually based on a pipeline of a linguistic front-end and a waveform generation back-end, requiring specialized linguistic knowledge or engineering capabilities for building new voices.

A major challenge of the end-to-end architectures is the computational complexity and load, where for example the WaveNet vocoder achieves a 0.3× real time synthesis speed of 16-bit 24 kHz mono audio on a Nvidia P100 GPU, and WaveRNN [5], which aims to improve the synthesis speed, achieves a 4× real time speed of the same fidelity audio on the same hardware [5]. This improvement still represents a very high computational load. The training time and computational requirements is also something that needs to be taken into consideration, for example the Tacotron 2 architecture [16] takes on average 234 h[3] to train (at 32-bit floating point precision) whilst the WaveGlow vocoder [16] (WaveGlow is one of the newer vocoders that was developed to address the high computational requirements of WaveNet) takes on average 768 h (see Footnote 3) to train (also at 32-bit floating point precision). These performance numbers were obtained with one Nvidia V100 16G GPU, which at the time of writing costs in the region of $6000–$7000 each (excluding supporting hardware, importing costs and taxes).

Other challenges of the end-to-end models are that the attention-based alignment systems, such as used in the Tacotron, Tacotron-2, Char2Wav [18] and DC-TTS [19] architectures, typically suffer from low training efficiency as well as model instability [31]. The low training efficiency means that one requires more data than is usually available for low-resourced environments (DC-TTS in [19] used 24 h of data, which still resulted in reverbed quality synthesized speech). Model instability may happen due to inaccurate alignments by the attention mechanism, resulting in repeated, skipped or mispronounced phonemes or words.

---

[2] https://www.isca-speech.org/archive/SSW_2019/.
[3] https://github.com/NVIDIA/DeepLearningExamples/tree/master/PyTorch/SpeechSynthesis/Tacotron2#expected-training-time.

Recent neural acoustic models such as Fastspeech [14], FastSpeech 2 [13] and a bottleneck feed-forward neural network implemented in [8] have moved away from using attention mechanism to align the linguistic and acoustic encoding and decoding, and have rather reverted to using an explicit duration model for the alignment. With our focus being on developing and implementing DNN architectures for resource-scarce environments we are looking at duration models in this work, and in particular speaker specific or dependent models. We compare the traditional HMM-based duration models with a DNN-based model suitable for resource-scarce environments and report on objective measures between the two models and a reference data set.

The organisation of the paper is as follows: in Sect. 2 we give some background on duration modeling as well as an overview of the two approaches followed in this work. Section 3 details our experiments and results, and lastly a discussion and conclusion is presented in Sect. 4.

2   Duration Models

Duration models, or to be more precise, phonetic duration models are employed in a TTS pipeline architecture in order to inform the phonetic acoustic model of the number of acoustic frames for which it must generate acoustic parameters, or features, that will typically be synthesized by a downstream vocoder into synthetic speech.

Intonation, emphasis or prominence and phrasing are influenced by the duration of the different phonetic units of an utterance [20]. The dynamic properties of the phonetic unit durations and their relationships and interactions in an utterance are complex, for example if one talks faster then the factor of speed increase is not applied equally to all phonetic units.

Early formant and diphone based TTS systems used sets of deterministic rules [7] developed by linguistic experts. Some models used the syllable as the fundamental unit of duration [2], as syllables are believed to be the natural units of prosody [20]. Data driven techniques for phonetic duration modelling have become ubiquitous, including decision trees [15], neural networks [25] and genetic algorithms [11].

In this work we will be comparing an HMM- and DNN-based duration model in a resource-scarce setting.

2.1   HMM-Based Duration Models

The technique we describe here is based on the widely used *HMM-based Speech Synthesis System* (HTS) [28]. The fundamental unit of duration is a phoneme, and each phoneme is modelled as a 5-state left-to-right, with no skip, HMM. State duration densities are modeled by single Gaussian distributions.

The duration models are context dependent, with many contextual factors that influence the duration of the individual phonemes taken into account (e.g., phone and phone context identity factors, stress-related factors, locational factors). The contextual factors taken into account depend on their availability in the particular language in question, i.e. some resource-scarce languages for example might not have any available stress models.

During training, a decision-tree based context clustering technique is used to cluster states of the context dependent HMMs. The decision-tree has a question at each node which splits the context into two groups (i.e. a binary tree). The clustered context dependent states are tied (shared) and are reestimated with embedded training.

During synthesis, the target text to be synthesized is converted to a context-based label sequence by the TTS engine front-end. A sentence HMM is constructed by concatenating context dependent HMMs according to the label sequence. The state durations of the sentence HMM can then be determined from the total length of speech and the state duration densities.

The reason for the decision-tree based context clustering technique is to overcome data scarcity, as it is impossible to prepare a speech database which includes all combinations of contextual factors.

Figure 1 shows the synthesis steps, where the decision- or regression tree is used to select the context dependent HMMs based on the context labels of the target text. The HMMs are concatenated to form the HMM sentence, which can then used to determine the phoneme durations from the HMM state durations.

2.2   DNN-Based Duration Models

The DNN-based phonetic duration model used in this work is based on a stack of fully connected layers in a feed-forward neural network (FFNN), as given in Fig. 2. At the output is a linear layer, whilst the *rectified linear unit* (ReLU) activation function was used for the hidden layers. Batch normalization and dropout were used with each hidden layer of the network. The Adam optimisation algorithm [6] was used with a learning rate scheduler that lowers the learning rate when the validation loss reaches a plateau (the Adam optimisation algorithm adjusts the learning rate, it is the upper bound that we reduced). The weights and biases of all the layers were initialized using the *He-uniform distribution* [3]. The loss function was the mean squared error (MSE) on the predicted duration feature.

As with the HMM-based duration models of the previous section, the features used included many contextual factors that influence the duration of the individual phonemes.

During training the TTS engine front-end creates a contextual label sequence for each recording of the training data in the speech database. This contextual label sequence is then converted into a linguistic description feature vector, used as input to the FFNN. The ground truth duration of each phone unit in the contextual label sequence is taken from the recorded database and used as the output feature target of the FFNN.

During synthesis the TTS engine front-end creates a contextual label sequence for the target utterance. This contextual label sequence is then converted into a linguistic description feature vector, used as input to the FFNN, and the FFNN does a prediction of the duration at the output.

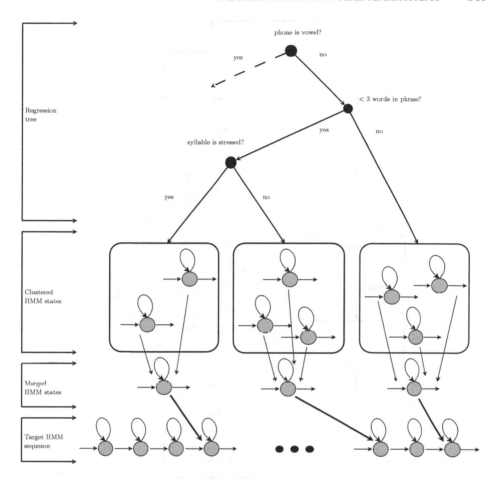

Fig. 1. HMM-based duration model.

3 Experimental Setup

3.1 Data

The data used in this work is a *subset* of an in-house single speaker Afrikaans female TTS corpus of duration 12:08:15.89. The corpus was recorded in a studio with a professional voice artist at a 44.1 kHz sampling rate with 16 bits precision. The subset used are recordings of the text of the *Lwazi II Afrikaans TTS Corpus* [12], consisting of 763 utterances of duration 00:56:30.29. This subset represents a small and phonetically balanced speech database as would be used for building HMM-based synthetic voices and attempting to build DNN-based synthetic voices.

The utterances were randomly split into training, validation and testing sets as given in Table 1. All audio was down-sampled to 16 kHz at 16 bits per sample

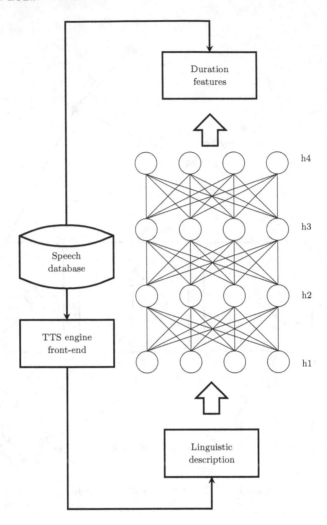

Fig. 2. DNN-based duration model.

and each utterance was normalised to the average power level of the subset (the 763 utterances).

Contextual Features. The text annotations of the speech database (Table 1) were tokenized and normalised with the Speect TTS engine front-end [10]. The context features used in this work is given in Table 2, and these features are the same as defined in [21], except for syllable stress, accent and ToBI (*Tones and Break Indices*) [17] tones which were not included due to it most probably not being available in resource-scarce settings. The context features of each utterance was also extracted using Speect.

Table 1. Speech database utterance splits as used in the experiments.

Set	# Utterances	Duration
Training	715	00:53:12.09
Validation	38	00:02:37.99
Test	10	00:00:40.21

Table 2. The linguistic context features as used in this work.

Context	Feature
Phoneme	The current phone
	The two preceding and succeeding phones
	The position of the current phone within the current syllable
Syllable	The number of phonemes within preceding, current, and succeeding syllables
	The position of the current syllable within the current word and phrase
	The number of preceding and succeeding stressed syllables within the current phrase
	The number of preceding and succeeding accented syllables within the current phrase
	The vowel identity within the current syllable
Word	Guessed part-of-speech (GPOS) of preceding, current, and succeeding words
	The number of syllables within preceding, current, and succeeding words
	The position of the current word within the current phrase
	The number of preceding and succeeding content words within the current phrase
	The number of words from the previous content word
	The number of words to the next content word
Phrase	The number of syllables within preceding, current, and succeeding phrases
	The position of the current phrase in major phrases
Utterance	The number of syllables, words, and phrases in the utterance

Reference Durations. The reference durations of the phone units in the speech database (Table 1) were obtained from a forced-alignment procedure using the HTK toolkit [27]. A frame resolution of 10 ms was used (hop size). A *silence* state was added between all words in the database in order to identify any pauses or phrase breaks which were recorded but not specifically annotated in

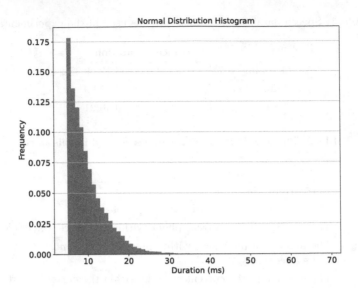

Fig. 3. The phone duration distribution of all the non-silent phones in the speech database.

the text with punctuation marks (based on work in [9]). Any non-annotated silence longer than 80 ms is marked as a pause and a phrase break is inserted into the utterance structure at this point. These phrase breaks have an influence on the context features as given in Table 2.

Figures 3 and 4 give the duration distributions of all the non-silent phones and the near-open front unrounded vowel (/æ/) respectively. Note that the minimum phone duration is 5 frames due to the use of a 5-state HMM model (see Sect. 2.1).

3.2   HMM-Based Duration Model

After the reference durations were extracted, a duration model was built based on the standard architecture of 5-state (excluding the emitting states), left-to-right HMM. The contextual features used were as defined in Table 2. The duration features were modelled by a single-component Gaussian. The decision trees state clustering was done using a minimum description length (MDL) factor of 1.0. Training of the model was done via custom scripts based on the standard demonstration script 2 available as part of HTS [30] (version 2.2).

Note that the model was only trained on the 715 training utterances of Table 1.

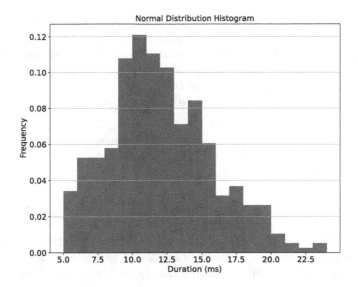

Fig. 4. The phone duration distribution of all the near-open front unrounded vowel (/æ/) in the speech database.

3.3 DNN-Based Duration Model

The contextual features of Table 2 were converted to a linguistic description vector containing a combination of binary encodings (for the phoneme identities and features) and positional information (as is done in [26]).

The input linguistic descriptions vector consisted of 375 features and was normalised to the range of [0.01, 0.99], whilst the output vectors (the reference durations) were normalised to zero mean and unit variance. TTS is a highly unbalanced mapping problem when viewed as a sequence-to-sequence mapping model [31] (mapping text to speech frames). The output speech sequence is much longer than the input text sequence. In order to add granularity on the text side, the durations are modeled in terms of their "HMM" states, i.e. as if the model consists of a number of HMM states. This has been proven to improve the quality of the synthesized speech [29]. The output vector has a normalised frame duration for each "state" of the HMM model (which was modelled using a 5-state left-to-right HMM).

Note that this model was also only trained on the 715 training utterances of Table 1, the same as the HMM model. Various model hyper-parameters in terms of the number of hidden layers and the number of units per hidden layer were trained and all the results are given in Table 3.

3.4 Results

The validation and test sets of Table 1 were synthesized with the HMM- and DNN-based duration models and the durations per phone unit were extracted.

Objective Measures. Two objective measures were used in order to evaluate how closely the models were able to predict the durations of the phonemes of the particular speaker. The Pearson correlation coefficient and the Root Mean Square Error (RMSE) between the predicted (y) and actual (x) durations (in terms of number of frames) were calculated.

The Pearson correlation coefficient (ρ) is given by:

$$\rho_{xy} = \frac{\sum_i (x_i - \bar{x})(y_i - \bar{y})}{\sqrt{\sum_i (x_i - \bar{x})^2}\sqrt{\sum_i (y_i - \bar{y})^2}} \tag{1}$$

and the RMSE by:

$$RMSE = \sqrt{\frac{\sum_i (x - y)^2}{T}} \tag{2}$$

where T is the number of frames. The results of the objective measurements on the synthesized durations of the validation and test sets of various architectures are given in Table 3. Higher correlation (ρ) is better whilst lower $RMSE$ (in terms of frames/phone) is better.

Table 3. Results of objective measurements for different model architectures. Root mean squared error ($RMSE$) is in units of frames per phone whilst the Pearson correlation coefficient (ρ) is dimensionless.

Architecture	Validation set		Test set	
	$RMSE$	ρ	$RMSE$	ρ
HMM, 5-state, single Gaussian	4.288	0.633	6.644	0.552
6 hidden layers, 128 units/layer	3.819	0.696	3.067	0.827
6 hidden layers, 256 units/layer	3.797	0.702	4.685	0.707
6 hidden layers, [512, 256, 128, 64, 32, 16] units	3.801	0.709	3.174	0.809
4 hidden layers, 128 units/layer	3.773	0.702	**2.905**	**0.832**
4 hidden layers, 256 units/layer	3.771	0.709	3.052	0.812
4 hidden layers, [128, 64, 32, 16] units	**3.739**	**0.720**	3.240	0.778

Figure 5 shows a visual comparison between the durations on a word level predicted by a HMM model, a DNN model and the reference recording.

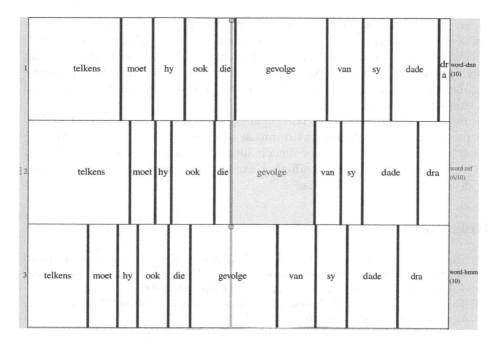

Fig. 5. A visual comparison of the duration prediction on the word level for the utterance *"Telkens moet hy die gevolge van sy dade dra"*. At the top is the DNN prediction, at the bottom the HMM prediction and in the middle the reference from the recorded speech.

4   Discussion and Conclusion

In this work we have developed an efficient feed-forward neural network for speaker dependent phonetic duration modeling in the context of resource-scarce text-to-speech settings. Our model trains in less than 2 h on a CPU and therefore can be easily adapted. Although not reported on, we have also applied this model on isiXhosa, isiZulu as well as Setswana corpora with similar success.

The importance of these types of explicit duration models have declined with the advent of the attention-based mechanisms in end-to-end neural speech synthesis architectures such as Tacotron, Tacotron 2 and Char2Wav. However, the challenges brought on with the attention-based mechanisms architectures and their unsuitability in resource-scarce environments have prompted the development of acoustic models such as Fastspeech and Fastspeech 2, which again use explicit duration models.

Our results show that a simple FFNN, with 4 hidden layers, can accurately predict phone unit duration and can reach a RMSE of 2.905 frames/phone on a speech database of less than 1 h in duration, with a high correlation over the whole sequence of phones.

It is interesting to note that larger networks do not necessarily perform better, which may be attributed to the lack of data for training the larger systems.

In contrast to our work, [20] mentioned that previous comparative studies between decision trees and neural networks found little difference in accuracy between either approach. We think that this may be due to the size of the dataset used for training, as it has been shown that neural networks with the appropriate architectures are much more data efficient than HMMs [29] and the dataset used in this work is particularly small.

Future work will include variants of output layers, such as a softmax function, to predict a region wherein the duration of a specific input may lie, such as done in [25]. The importance of specific linguistic features are also of particular interest, as eliminating hand crafted or expert developed features make it easier to develop voices in new languages.

References

1. Black, A.W., Tokuda, K.: The blizzard challenge-2005: evaluating corpus-based speech synthesis on common datasets. In: 9th European Conference on Speech Communication and Technology, pp. 77–80 (September 2005)
2. Campbell, W.N.: Syllable-based segmental duration. In: Talking Machines: Theories, Models, and Designs, pp. 211–224 (1992)
3. He, K., Zhang, X., Ren, S., Sun, J.: Delving deep into rectifiers: surpassing human-level performance on ImageNet classification. In: Proceedings of the IEEE International Conference on Computer Vision (ICCV) (December 2015)
4. Jiang, Y., et al.: The USTC system for blizzard challenge 2019. In: Blizzard Challenge Workshop 2019, Vienna, Austria (September 2019)
5. Kalchbrenner, N., et al.: Efficient Neural Audio Synthesis. arXiv e-prints arXiv:1802.08435 (February 2018)
6. Kingma, D.P., Ba, J.: Adam: a method for stochastic optimization. arXiv preprint arXiv:1412.6980 (2014)
7. Klatt, D.H.: Interaction between two factors that influence vowel duration. J. Acoust. Soc. Am. **54**(4), 1102–1104 (1973)
8. Louw, J.A.: Neural speech synthesis for resource-scarce languages. In: Barnard, E., Davel, M. (eds.) Proceedings of the South African Forum for Artificial Intelligence Research, Cape Town, South Africa, pp. 103–116 (December 2019)
9. Louw, J.A., Moodley, A., Govender, A.: The speect text-to-speech entry for the blizzard challenge 2016. In: Blizzard Challenge Workshop 2016, Cupertino, United States of America (September 2016)
10. Louw, J.A., van Niekerk, D.R., Schlünz, G.: Introducing the speect speech synthesis platform. In: Blizzard Challenge Workshop 2010, Kyoto, Japan (September 2010)
11. Morais, E., Violaro, F.: Exploratory analysis of linguistic data based on genetic algorithm for robust modeling of the segmental duration of speech. In: 9th European Conference on Speech Communication and Technology (2005)
12. van Niekerk, D., de Waal, A., Schlünz, G.: Lwazi II Afrikaans TTS Corpus (November 2015). https://repo.sadilar.org/handle/20.500.12185/443. ISLRN: 570–884-577-153-6
13. Ren, Y., Hu, C., Qin, T., Zhao, S., Zhao, Z., Liu, T.Y.: FastSpeech 2: Fast and High-Quality End-to-End Text-to-Speech. arXiv preprint arXiv:2006.04558 (2020)
14. Ren, Y., et al.: Fastspeech: fast, robust and controllable text to speech. In: Advances in Neural Information Processing Systems, pp. 3171–3180 (2019)

15. Riley, M.D.: Tree-based modelling for speech synthesis. In: The ESCA Workshop on Speech Synthesis, pp. 229–232 (1991)
16. Shen, J., et al.: Natural TTS Synthesis by Conditioning WaveNet on Mel Spectrogram Predictions. arXiv e-prints arXiv:1712.05884 (December 2017)
17. Silverman, K., et al.: ToBI: a standard for labeling English prosody. In: Proceedings of the 2nd International Conference on Spoken Language Processing (ICSLP), Alberta, Canada, pp. 867–870 (October 1992)
18. Sotelo, J., et al.: Char2wav: End-to-end speech synthesis. arXiv preprint arXiv:1609.03499 (2017)
19. Tachibana, H., Uenoyama, K., Aihara, S.: Efficiently trainable text-to-speech system based on deep convolutional networks with guided attention. arXiv e-prints arXiv:1710.08969 (October 2017)
20. Taylor, P.: Text-to-Speech Synthesis. Cambridge University Press, Cambridge (2009)
21. Tokuda, K., Nankaku, Y., Toda, T., Zen, H., Yamagishi, J., Oura, K.: Speech synthesis based on hidden Markov models. Proc. IEEE **101**(5), 1234–1252 (2013)
22. van den Oord, A., et al.: WaveNet: A generative model for raw audio. arXiv e-prints arXiv:1609.03499 (September 2016)
23. Wang, Y., et al.: Tacotron: Towards end-to-end speech synthesis. arXiv e-prints arXiv:1703.10135 (March 2017)
24. Watts, O., Henter, G.E., Fong, J., Valentini-Botinhao, C.: Where do the improvements come from in sequence-to-sequence neural TTS? In: 10th ISCA Speech Synthesis Workshop, ISCA, Vienna, Austria (September 2019)
25. Wei, X., Hunt, M., Skilling, A.: Neural network-based modeling of phonetic durations. arXiv preprint arXiv:1909.03030 (2019)
26. Wu, Z., Watts, O., King, S.: Merlin: an open source neural network speech synthesis system. In: SSW, pp. 202–207 (2016)
27. Young, S., et al.: The HTK Book, vol. 3, p. 175. Cambridge University Engineering Department, Cambridge (2002)
28. Zen, H., Tokuda, K., Masuko, T., Kobayasih, T., Kitamura, T.: A hidden semi-Markov model-based speech synthesis system. IEICE Trans. Inf. Syst. **E90–D**(5), 825–834 (2007)
29. Zen, H., Senior, A.: Deep mixture density networks for acoustic modeling in statistical parametric speech synthesis. In: 2014 IEEE International Conference on Acoustics, Speech and Signal Processing (ICASSP), pp. 3844–3848. IEEE (2014)
30. Zen, H., Tokuda, K., Masuko, T., Kobayasih, T., Kitamura, T.: A hidden semi-Markov model-based speech synthesis system. IEICE Trans. Infor. Sys. **E90–D**(5), 825–834 (2007)
31. Zhu, X., Zhang, Y., Yang, S., Xue, L., Xie, L.: Pre-alignment guided attention for improving training efficiency and model stability in end-to-end speech synthesis. IEEE Access **7**, 65955–65964 (2019)

Importance Sampling Forests for Location Invariant Proprioceptive Terrain Classification

Ditebogo Masha[1]($\boxtimes$) and Michael Burke[2]

[1] Department of Electrical and Electronics Engineering Science,
University of Johannesburg (UJ), Auckland Park, South Africa
201111866@student.uj.ac.za
[2] Institute of Perception, Action and Behaviour, School of Informatics,
University of Edinburgh, Edinburgh, UK
Michael.Burke@ed.ac.uk

Abstract. The ability for ground vehicles to classify the terrain they are traversing or have previously traversed is extremely important for manoeuvrability. This is also beneficial for remote sensing as this information can be used to enhance existing soil maps and geographic information system prediction accuracy. However, existing proprioceptive terrain classification methods require additional hardware and sometimes dedicated sensors to classify terrain, making the classification process complex and costly to implement. This work investigates offline classification of terrain using simple wheel slip estimations, enabling the implementation of inexpensive terrain classification. Experimental results show that slip-based classifiers struggle to classify the terrain surfaces using wheel slip estimates alone. This paper proposes a new classification method based on importance sampling, which uses position estimates to address these limitations, while still allowing for location independent terrain analysis. The proposed method is based on the use of an ensemble of decision tree classifiers trained using position information and terrain class predictions sampled from weak, slip-based terrain classifiers.

Keywords: Proprioceptive terrain classification · Random forests · Importance sampling · Autonomous ground vehicles

1 Introduction

Modern advancement in technology has exposed unmanned ground vehicles (UGVs) to terrain surfaces varying from uneven, potentially loose terrain with variable gradients in outdoor environments to indoor environments that are made up of materials consisting of different textures. For UGVs to adapt their driving strategies and maximise their performance, they need to be able to detect the terrain they are manoeuvring, classify it and then adjust their driving controls

© Springer Nature Switzerland AG 2020
A. Gerber (Ed.): SACAIR 2020, CCIS 1342, pp. 154–168, 2020.
https://doi.org/10.1007/978-3-030-66151-9_10

Fig. 1. Illustration of the terrain surfaces layout and the Packbot 510 UGV used for experiments. The top part is the carpet, grass and rocks are on the sides, while the surrounding area is the rubber.

to adapt to the type of terrain they are currently traversing. The ability for ground vehicles to classify the terrain they are traversing or have previously traversed is also beneficial for remote sensing [6], and the information can be used to enhance existing soil maps [21] and geographic information system (GIS) prediction accuracy [30].

Terrain classification is the process of determining into which terrain class category a specific terrain patch falls [10,18,23]. Commonly classified terrain surfaces for outdoor environments include dirt, sand, clay, asphalt, grass and gravel [22,29] while carpet, ceramic tiles and linoleum [14,26,29] are generally considered in indoor environments.

Terrain classification can be vision-based or through proprioception. Vision-based classification uses visual features, such as colour, texture and shape, obtained from sensors such as cameras and laser scanners [32]. Proprioceptive classification uses physical wheel-terrain interaction features that are extracted from a vehicle's sensors [5], and is sometimes also referred to as contact-based terrain classification [32].

A particularly interesting class of proprioceptive terrain classification relies on wheel-slip [11] and has been recommended as a simple and low-cost terrain analysis technique. However, this work shows that terrain classification using slip measurements can be unreliable, and that models trained to classify terrain using slip alone often suffer from over-fitting when applied in new terrains.

This paper proposed a method of addressing this limitation through importance sampling, which introduces position estimation into the classification process, while still allowing for location independent terrain classification. Here, we use a weak, probabilistic slip-based classifier to train an ensemble of classifiers using position information, thereby producing a terrain classifier conditioned on both slip and position measurements. Importantly, this process means that models do not need to be retrained for use in new locations.

2   Related Work

Proprioception for ground vehicles involves the sensing of the internal states of a vehicle using onboard sensors such as wheel encoders, accelerometers and rate traducers [17, 25]. Proprioceptive classifiers typically use these sensor measurements directly to classify the terrain being traversed [10]. The two most common proprioceptive terrain classification methods are vibration-based classification and traction-based classification.

Vibration-Based Terrain Classification. Vibration-based classification classifies terrain based on features extracted from vibrations induced by mechanically distinct terrains. The vibration features typically measured are characterised by the vertical, pitch and roll motions due to vertical wheel displacements [8, 9, 12, 13, 29]. Vibration-based terrain classification methods that use gyroscopes to measure terrain vibrations have been identified as the best performing terrain classifier for proprioceptive classification [23], when compared to accelerometer, current, voltage, microphone, wheel encoders, infrared and ultrasonic range sensors. A disadvantage for vibration-based classification is that its accuracy deteriorates at low speed due to the reduction of vibration amplitudes [4].

Traction-Based Terrain Classification. Traction-based classifiers use wheel torque and sinkage measurements to determine the minimum traction exerted at wheel-terrain interfaces and to label the terrain being traversed. Traction is a vehicular propulsive force produced by friction between a wheel and terrain, and since the frictional force produced depends on factors such as road conditions and road surface this can be used to classify different types of terrains [19, 31]. Brooks and Iagnemma [5] use a set of predefined thresholds of minimum traction available at the wheel-terrain interface to classify terrain.

Wheel Slip-Based Terrain Classification. Wheel slip has previously been proposed for proprioceptive terrain classification, as it occurs as a result of wheel terrain interaction. As UGVs traverse different terrain surfaces, the wheel terrain interaction creates a characteristic difference between actual and desired forward and rotational velocity values. This characteristic difference is as a result of slip that occurs as the wheels interacts with the terrain surface [11]. Wheel slip is relatively easy to measure, and as a result, provides a simple mechanism for terrain classification. Rotational slip estimation for tracked mobile robots [7] has been suggested as a feature for proprioceptive terrain classification [20].

Rotational slip estimation is an adaptive slip estimation approach that allows left and right track slip to be computed using only rotational velocity measurements from a rate gyroscope. Here, a recursive least squares estimation process is used to estimate states (1) and (2) using a sliding window of actual rotational velocities and velocity commands [7].

$$\phi_1 = \frac{s_1 - s_2}{l} \tag{1}$$

$$\phi_2 = 1 - \frac{s_1 + s_2}{2} \tag{2}$$

These states are related to the velocities of interest using

$$\omega_a = \phi_1 v_d + \phi_2 \omega_d \tag{3}$$

where ω_a is the measured rotational velocity, v_d is the commanded forward velocity and ω_d is the commanded rotational velocity. Slip estimates can be solved for using (1) and (2), given the estimated states. This paper uses rotational slip estimation for terrain classification.

A number of machine learning methods have been applied to terrain classification. Here, proprioceptive terrain measurements and associated terrain labels are used to train predictive models of terrain [5, 16, 24, 28]. However, these methods are vulnerable to over-fitting to collection conditions, and this work shows that machine learning terrain classification can easily fail to generalise in new locations. This paper shows how this limitation can be addressed using an importance sampling strategy.

3   Importance Sampling

Importance Sampling (IS) is a Monte Carlo sampling tool that is used to approximate a distribution when the only samples available are produced by a different distribution. Here, a new distribution is produced by sampling random draws from an existing distribution and computing a weighted average over the random draws, approximating a mathematical expectation with respect to a target distribution [2, 27]. Using IS, when given a random variable x with a probability of $p(x)$ and assuming we wish to compute an expectation $\mu_f = \mathbb{E}_p[f(X)]$ by sampling random draws $x^{(1)}, \ldots, x^{(m)}$ from $q(x)$, we can write

$$\mu_f = \int f(x)p(x)dx \tag{4}$$

For any probability density $p(x)$ that satisfies $q(x) > 0$, when $f(x)p(x) \neq 0$ we also have:

$$\mu_f = E_q[w(x)f(x)] \tag{5}$$

where $w(x) = \frac{p(x)}{q(x)}$. $\mathbb{E}_q[\cdot]$ denotes the expectation μ_f with respect to $q(x)$, this means that our expectation can be approximated using

$$\hat{\mu}_f \approx \frac{1}{m} \sum_{j=1}^{m} w(x^{(j)}) f(x^{(j)}) \tag{6}$$

To increase the accuracy of IS, for most x, $q(x)$ has to be approximately proportional to $p(x)$, thereby reducing variance in the estimate of μ_f. Importantly, IS is more than a variance reduction method as it is also used to investigate the properties of a distribution when sampling from another distribution of interest [27].

4   Importance Sampling Forests

We leverage this property to draw terrain class samples from a joint distribution conditioned on both position and slip, while still allowing for location independent terrain classification. In order to apply the importance sampling principle, we sample terrain labels from weak probabilistic slip classifiers (a decision tree), and use these to train new decision trees conditioned on vehicle position to produce an ensemble model over terrain classes. This can be considered a form of random forest [3]. Random forests are typically trained using bagging, where a subset of features are randomly sampled from a set, but here we train the forests (which we term importance sampling forests (ISF)) using labels sampled from a slip classifier. This can also be viewed as a form of boosting, an iterative training method where the weights of incorrectly classified samples are increased to make these more important in the next iteration, thereby reducing variance and bias and improving model performance [1,15]. The use of ISFs for terrain classification is shown in Algorithm 1.

Algorithm 1. Importance Sampling Forest Classifier

Input: Slip estimates, position estimates and terrain class labels
Output: Averaged terrain class probabilities and a trained ISF classifier

1: Let C_t be the terrain class at t
2: Let $\mathbf{x}_t$ be the position estimates at time t
3: Let $\mathbf{s}_t$ be the slip estimates at time t
4: Fit DT using slip estimates - $\mathbf{R}(C_t|\mathbf{s}_t)$
5: Initialise class label probabilities $\mathbf{q}(C_t|\mathbf{x}_t) = \mathbf{0}$
6: **for** i = 0 **to** I **do**
7:     Sample $j = 1 \ldots N$ labels $C^j \sim \mathbf{R}(C_t|\mathbf{s}_t)$ using DT class likelihood
8:     Fit position based DT classifier using samples $C^j \rightarrow \mathbf{q}^i(C_t|\mathbf{x}_t)$
9:     Add terrain sample probability predictions to list $\mathbf{q}(C_t|\mathbf{x}_t) = \mathbf{q}(C_t|\mathbf{x}_t) + \mathbf{q}^i(C_t|\mathbf{x}_t)$
10: **end for**
11: Average terrain class predictions $y_p = \frac{\mathbf{q}(C_t|\mathbf{x}_t)}{I}$

ISFs work by using terrain labels sampled from a pre-trained slip-based terrain classifier that is applied to a new set of slip estimates captured in a previously unseen terrain patch. The ISF classifier randomly draws new terrain labels C^j from the predicted output distribution $\mathbf{y}$ given by the $\mathbf{R}(C_t|\mathbf{s}_t)$ slip-based classifier. The new terrain label samples are then used, along with positions, $\mathbf{x}_t$, to train a number of position based terrain $\mathbf{q}(C_t|\mathbf{x}_t)$ classifiers.

The goal of the proposed ISF classification method is to find the expected terrain class C at position $\mathbf{x}_t$ with respect to the slip classifier distribution $\mathbf{R}(C|\mathbf{s}_t)$,

$$C(\mathbf{x}_t) = \int \mathbf{q}(C|\mathbf{x}_t, \mathbf{s}_t)\mathbf{R}(C|\mathbf{s}_t)d\mathbf{s}_t. \tag{7}$$

We accomplish this using an importance sampling forest,

$$C(\mathbf{x}_t) = \frac{1}{N}\sum_{i=1}^{N} \mathbf{q}^i(C|\mathbf{x}_t, \mathbf{s}_t) \tag{8}$$

where $\mathbf{q}^i(C|\mathbf{x}_t, \mathbf{s}_t)$ is a decision tree trained using class labels C^j sampled from the slip classifier class likelihood

$$C^j \sim \mathbf{R}(C|\mathbf{s}_t). \tag{9}$$

Importantly, the decoupling of position and slip measurements in the model above allows a slip-classifier to be applied in new locations, without needing to be retrained.

5   Experimental Results

We illustrate the use of ISFs on a terrain classification task using a Packbot 510 tracked robot.

5.1   Experimental Setup

A combination of indoor and outdoor terrain surfaces are used for testing (see Fig. 1), namely: rubber, carpet, rocks and grass. The Packbot 510 tracked mobile robot used for data collection is equipped with odometry sensing and a five degree of freedom manipulator. In addition to the standard platform configuration described above, it has been augmented with a mini-ITX computer, a 3D Velodyne LiDAR sensor and an inertial measuring unit (IMU).

The platform operates using an in-house autonomous 3D mapping application. Sensor data recorded included the pose estimate data obtained using a point-cloud-based iterative closest point localisation algorithm, desired forward and rotational velocities obtained from the path-following controller used on the platform, and actual forward and rotational velocity data obtained from a state estimation algorithm that fuses platform odometry data, IMU data and point-cloud-based localisation estimates.

Data was collected in a semi-autonomous mode, with user-defined goal points ensuring navigation trajectories crossed the terrain patches of interest. The platform controller ensured relatively smooth motion across the terrain. Motion involving spot turning is ignored, and forward velocity was kept relatively constant across the terrain.

After experimental setup and data preparation, rotational slip estimates [7] were estimated from the collected velocity data. The slip estimates were then labelled according to the terrain patch they were captured on.

Two different datasets were collected during different experimental runs on different days and for different terrain configurations. Figure 2 shows the terrain patch setup that was used to collect Dataset A, train the classifiers and also to perform the first test, which we refer to as Test A. Dataset A was split into 60% training, 10% validation and 30% test data.

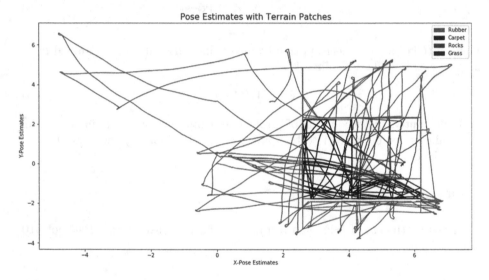

Fig. 2. The figure shows the positions on the four terrain surface patches where data was captured. (Yellow - Rubber, Red - Carpet, Blue - Rocks, Green - Grass.) (Color figure online)

Figure 3 shows the terrain setup that was used for Dataset B and to perform the second test, which we refer to as Test B. We trained support vector machines and decision trees[1] to predict terrain labels for given slip estimated using Dataset A, and report test accuracy on Test A. Model parameters were tuned to produce the best performance on the validation set.

We then tested these models on Dataset B, to illustrate the challenge of over-fitting to terrain configurations. We also used Test B to illustrate the value

---

[1] We also experimented with LSTM models, but these failed dismally, presumably due to a lack of data.

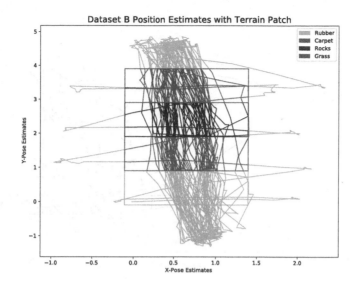

Fig. 3. Terrain layout where Dataset B was collected. The colour codes are still consistent with those of Fig. 2 (Color figure online).

of importance sampling forests, which allow for successful terrain classification across terrains without over-fitting.

5.2 Slip-Only Classification

When tested on Dataset A, both the support vector machine (Fig. 4) and decision tree (Fig. 5) seem to perform well, successfully classifying most terrain samples in the test set. These results agree with those typically seen in the literature, which has suggested that terrain classification using slip estimates alone is generally effective.

The DT returned a validation accuracy of 89%, and an accuracy score of 90% when Test A was conducted. However, when Test B is conducted, it is clear that the DT has over-fit to the terrain configuration of Test A. Similar results are seen for the SVM, as shown in Table 1.

When the trained decision tree classifier is used to classify the terrain patches contained in Dataset B, the classifier fails with a low accuracy score of 31%.

In order to address this over-fitting, a more conservative DT classifier was trained using training data from Dataset A. The classifier produced a validation accuracy of 65% and an accuracy score of 62% when Test A was conducted. Figure 7 shows the confusion matrix of the more conservative classifier, which is only weakly able to classify the terrain in Test B, as shown in Fig. 6.

The poor classification results obtained here seem to contradict findings in the literature about the efficacy of slip-based terrain classification, and highlight the importance of testing terrain classifiers under multiple conditions to avoid over-fitting.

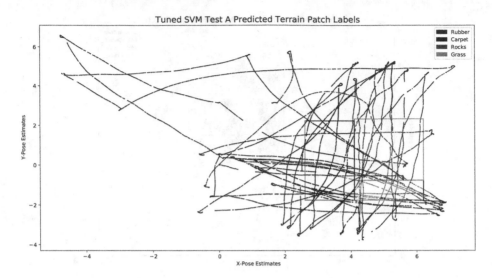

Fig. 4. The predicted labels for an SVM on Test A terrain seem to indicate that the terrain is generally classified correctly.

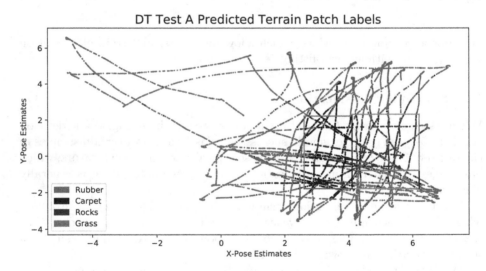

Fig. 5. The labels predicted by the DT classifier for Test A at position estimates corresponding to the test data seem to show successful terrain classification.

5.3   ISF Classifier Performance

We tested the performance of the proposed importance sampling forest model using the more conservative, but less accurate slip prediction model described above.

When the ISF terrain classification method was used to predict the terrain type, the classifier returned an accuracy score of 94% for Test A. Figure 8 shows

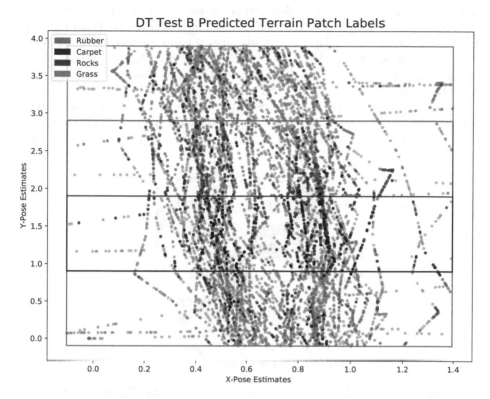

Fig. 6. The predicted labels by the DT classifier for Test B terrain patch classification at position estimates corresponding to the test data show that the slip-based terrain classification fails to classify the terrain patches particularly well.

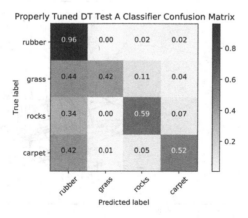

Fig. 7. The figure shows the performance of the properly tuned, conservative DT classifier when Test A is performed. The classifier obtains an accuracy score of 62%.

the confusion matrix when Test A position estimates were used to improve the performance of the previously trained slip-based terrain classifier. From the plot, we can see that the method accurately classifies the terrain patches. Though the accuracy of rubber dropped from 95% to 90%, the overall performance of the classifier improved significantly. The improvement can also be noted in Fig. 9, where the terrain patches can be clearly seen.

When Test B position estimates were used to classify the terrain using importance sampled forests and slip classifiers trained using dataset A, the new classifier returned an accuracy score of 97%. Figure 10 shows the confusion matrix

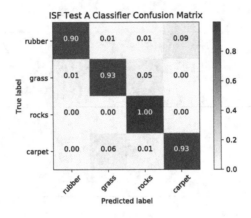

Fig. 8. The plot shows the level of improvement from the classifier with an accuracy score of 53% to an accuracy score of 94% when ISF and Test A pose estimations are used. Rock, grass and carpet have improved from a classification accuracy of less than 45%, while rubber dropped from an accuracy of 95%.

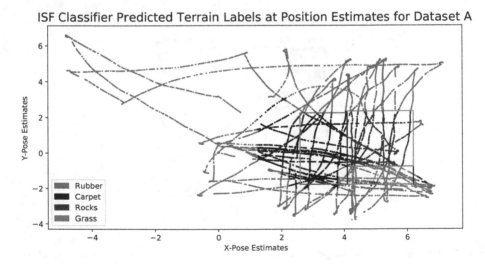

Fig. 9. The figure shows the Dataset A ISF terrain predictions.

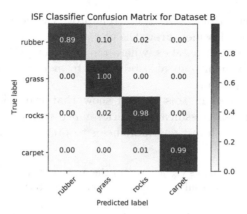

Fig. 10. The figure shows the level of improvement from the classifier with an accuracy score of 41% to an accuracy score of 97% when ISF and Test B pose estimations are used to re-train the classifier for classification.

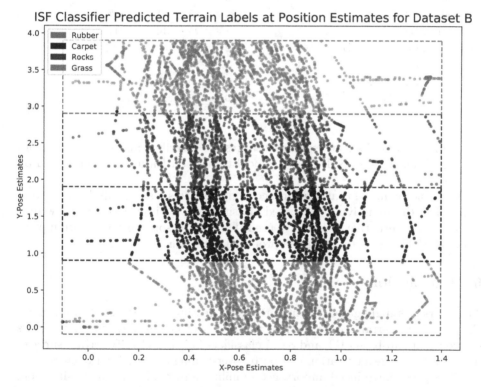

Fig. 11. The figure shows the Test B terrain patch label layout using the ISF terrain classifier. The terrain patches can be clearly noted. This is in stark comparison with the base slip classifier used for prediction, as shown in Fig. 6.

when Test B position estimates are used to improve the performance of the previously trained terrain classifier. From the plot, we can see that the method accurately classifies the terrain patches, where the classifier performance improved. The dramatic improvement can also be noted from Fig. 11, where the terrain patches can be clearly seen.

The results presented in this section show that the ISF classifier is able to dramatically increase classification performance through the use of spatial smoothing, and that the forest ensemble helps to prevent over-fitting.

Table 1. The table summarises (% accuracy) the average performance of all the classifiers' Test A and Test B results, while also comparing terrain-wise Test A and B performance.

Terrain type/Classifier methods	Rubber	Grass	Rocks	Carpet	Average accuracy
Train A SVM Test A	90	91	86	89	89%
Train A SVM Test B	100	0	0	0	Failed
Train A DT Test A	92	83	83	81	85%
Train A DT Test B	79	1	25	14	31%
Train A Conservative DT Test A	96	42	59	52	62%
Train A Conservative DT Test B	34	87	22	22	41%
Train A ISF Test A	90	93	100	93	**94%**
Train A ISF Test B	89	100	98	99	**97%**

Table 1 summarises the experimental results described above. Here, the convention Train A, Test B denotes a model trained on Dataset A, and tested on Dataset B.

It should be noted that importance sampling forests are inexpensive to compute when the underlying slip-based classifier is a decision tree, but slow dramatically if alternative models are used. For this reason, we do not attempt to improve SVM classifiers using the proposed approach.

6   Conclusions

This work has highlighted the importance of testing terrain classification models in multiple terrain configurations to avoid over-fitting. Experimental results showed that slip-based DT and SVM classifiers failed to classify terrain surfaces due to a loss of generalisation caused by over-tuning of model parameters.

This paper introduced importance sampling forests for terrain classification, a technique that uses sampled labels from a probabilistic slip-based terrain classifier to train position conditioned terrain classification models. This produces an ensemble terrain classifier, which allows for terrain classification that incorporates spatial information. Importantly, this approach means that the slip-based classifier can incorporate position information in new locations, as it is location invariant.

Experiments showed that the ISF terrain classification algorithm produced substantial improvements in terrain classification using simple slip measurements and proved to be highly effective across terrain configurations.

References

1. Akar, Ö., Güngör, O.: Classification of multispectral images using random forest algorithm. J. Geodesy Geoinf. **1**(2), 105–112 (2012)
2. Bishop, C.M.: Pattern Recognition and Machine Learning. Information Science and Statistics. Springer, New York (2006)
3. Breiman, L.: Random forests. Mach. Learn. **45**(1), 5–32 (2001)
4. Brooks, C.A., Iagnemma, K.: Vibration-based terrain classification for planetary exploration rovers. IEEE Trans. Rob. **21**(6), 1185–1190 (2005). https://doi.org/10.1109/TRO.2005.855994
5. Brooks, C.A., Iagnemma, K.: Self-supervised terrain classification for planetary surface exploration rovers. J. Field Robot. **29**(3), 445–468 (2012)
6. Brooks, C.A., Iagnemma, K.D.: Self-supervised classification for planetary rover terrain sensing. In: IEEE Aerospace Conference Proceedings, pp. 1–9 (2007). https://doi.org/10.1109/AERO.2007.352693
7. Burke, M.: Path-following control of a velocity constrained tracked vehicle incorporating adaptive slip estimation. In: Proceedings of the IEEE International Conference on Robotics and Automation, pp. 97–102 (2012). https://doi.org/10.1109/ICRA.2012.6224684
8. Collins, E.G., Coyle, E.J.: Vibration-based terrain classification using surface profile input frequency responses. In: 2008 IEEE International Conference on Robotics and Automation, pp. 3276–3283 (2008). https://doi.org/10.1109/ROBOT.2008.4543710
9. Coyle, E.: Fundamentals and methods of terrain classification using proprioceptive sensors. Ph.D. thesis, The Florida State University (2010)
10. Coyle, E., Collins, E.G., Roberts, R.G.: Speed independent terrain classification using singular value decomposition interpolation. In: 2011 IEEE International Conference on Robotics and Automation (ICRA), pp. 4014–4019. IEEE (2011)
11. Ding, L., Gao, H., Deng, Z., Yoshida, K., Nagatani, K.: Slip ratio for lugged wheel of planetary rover in deformable soil: definition and estimation. In: 2009 IEEE/RSJ International Conference on Intelligent Robots and Systems, IROS 2009, pp. 3343–3348. IEEE (2009)
12. DuPont, E.M., Moore, C.A., Collins, E.G., Coyle, E.: Frequency response method for terrain classification in autonomous ground vehicles. Auton. Robot. **24**(4), 337–347 (2008). https://doi.org/10.1007/s10514-007-9077-0
13. DuPont, E.M., Roberts, R.G., Selekwa, M.F., Moore, C.A., Collins, E.G.: Online terrain classification for mobile robots. Dyn. Syst. Control Parts A and B. **2005**, 1643–1648 (2005). https://doi.org/10.1115/IMECE2005-81659
14. Giguere, P., Dudek, G.: Surface identification using simple contact dynamics for mobile robots. In: 2009 IEEE International Conference on Robotics and Automation (2009). https://doi.org/10.1109/ROBOT.2009.5152662
15. Gislason, P.O., Benediktsson, J.A., Sveinsson, J.R.: Random forests for land cover classification. Pattern Recogn. Lett. **27**(4), 294–300 (2006)
16. Gonzalez, R., Iagnemma, K.: DeepTerramechanics: Terrain Classification and Slip Estimation for Ground Robots via Deep Learning. arXiv preprint arXiv:1806.07379 (2018)

17. Howard, A., Turmon, M., Matthies, L., Tang, B., Angelova, A., Mjolsness, E.: Towards learned traversability for robot navigation: from underfoot to the far field. J. Field Robot. **23**(11–12), 1005–1017 (2006). https://doi.org/10.1002/rob.20168
18. Iagnemma, K., Shibly, H., Dubowsky, S.: On-line terrain parameter estimation for planetary rovers. In: Proceedings of the IEEE International Conference on Robotics and Automation, vol. 3, pp. 3142–3147 (2002). https://doi.org/10.1109/ROBOT.2002.1013710
19. Kuntanapreeda, S.: Traction control of electric vehicles using sliding-mode controller with tractive force observer. Int. J. Veh. Technol **2014**, 1+ (2014). https://doi.org/10.1155/2014/829097
20. Masha, D., Burke, M., Twala, B.: Slip estimation methods for proprioceptive terrain classification using tracked mobile robots. In: 2017 Pattern Recognition Association of South Africa and Robotics and Mechatronics (PRASA-RobMech), pp. 150–155. IEEE (2017)
21. Moore, I.D., Gessler, P.E., Nielsen, G.Æ., Peterson, G.: Soil attribute prediction using terrain analysis. Soil Sci. Soc. Am. J. **57**(2), 443–452 (1993)
22. Ojeda, L., Borenstein, J., Witus, G.: Terrain trafficability characterization with a mobile robot. In: Proceedings of the SPIE Defense and Security Conference, Unmanned Ground Vehicle Technology VII, vol. 5804, pp. 235–243 (2005). https://doi.org/10.1117/12.601499
23. Ojeda, L., Borenstein, J., Witus, G., Karlsen, R.: Terrain characterization and classification with a mobile robot. J. Field Robot. **23**(2), 103–122 (2006). https://doi.org/10.1002/rob.20113
24. Otsu, K., Ono, M., Fuchs, T.J., Baldwin, I., Kubota, T.: Autonomous terrain classification with co-and self-training approach. IEEE Robot. Autom. Lett. **1**(2), 814–819 (2016)
25. Overholt, J.L., Hudas, G.R., Gerhart, G.R.: Defining proprioceptive behaviors for autonomous mobile robots. In: Unmanned Ground Vehicle Technology IV, vol. 4715, pp. 287–295. International Society for Optics and Photonics (2002). https://doi.org/10.1117/12.474460
26. Tick, D., Rahman, T., Busso, C., Gans, N.: Indoor robotic terrain classification via angular velocity based hierarchical classifier selection. In: Proceedings of the IEEE International Conference on Robotics and Automation, pp. 3594–3600 (2012). https://doi.org/10.1109/ICRA.2012.6225128
27. Tokdar, S.T., Kass, R.E.: Importance sampling: a review. Wiley Interdisc. Rev. Comput. Stat. **2**(1), 54–60 (2010). https://doi.org/10.1002/wics.56
28. Valada, A., Burgard, W.: Deep spatiotemporal models for robust proprioceptive terrain classification. Int. J. Robot. Res. **36**(13–14), 1521–1539 (2017). https://doi.org/10.1177/0278364917727062
29. Weiss, C., Frohlich, H., Zell, A.: Vibration-based terrain classification using support vector machines. In: 2006 IEEE/RSJ International Conference on Intelligent Robots and Systems, pp. 4429–4434 (2006). https://doi.org/10.1109/IROS.2006.282076
30. Yanar, T.A., Akyürek, Z.: The enhancement of the cell-based GIS analyses with fuzzy processing capabilities. Inf. Sci. **176**(8), 1067–1085 (2006). https://doi.org/10.1016/j.ins.2005.02.006
31. Yoshida, K., Watanabe, T., Mizuno, N., Ishigami, G.: Slip, traction control, and navigation of a lunar rover. In: i-SAIRAS 2003, p. 8579 (2003)
32. Zou, Y., Chen, W., Xie, L., Wu, X.: Comparison of different approaches to visual terrain classification for outdoor mobile robots. Pattern Recogn. Lett. **38**, 54–62 (2014)

Hybridized Deep Learning Architectures for Human Activity Recognition

Bradley Joel Pillay[1,2]([✉]) [iD], Anban W. Pillay[1,2] [iD], and Edgar Jembere[1,2] [iD]

[1] School of Mathematics, Statistics and Computer Science, University of KwaZulu-Natal, Westville Campus, Private Bag X54001, Durban 4000, South Africa
bradleyjoelpillay@gmail.com, {pillayw4,jemberee}@ukzn.ac.za
[2] Centre for AI Research (CAIR), Cape Town, South Africa

Abstract. Human activity recognition using video data has been an active research area in computer vision for many years. Various approaches were introduced to efficaciously recognize human activities. This study focuses on identifying activities performed by single individuals using visual information from short video clips. Several deep learning techniques are exploited to develop an architecture to effectively solve the human activity recognition task. The architecture hybridizes a two-stream neural network with a multi-layer perception (MLP). The two-stream neural network is a temporal segment network (TSN) which consists of a spatial and a temporal stream. The architecture adopts Octave Convolution neural networks as frame-level feature extractors in the temporal segment network (TSN). The optical flow calculations were performed using the FlowNet 2.0 algorithm, which serves as inputs to the temporal stream. This newly developed architecture was trained and evaluated on the KTH human activity dataset. The results obtained are competitive to existing state-of-the-art results.

Keywords: Human activity recognition · Octave convolution · Temporal segment network

1 Introduction

The recognition of human activity involves a process of identifying the actions and goals of individuals from a series of observations of the activities performed. The application of this recognition task can be utilized in multiple domains that aim to monitor the actions of human beings; such examples include detecting foul play in sports and abnormal activity for security purposes. There exists various investigations using two different categories of data, viz. video and sensor data, to solve the human activity recognition problem. Some video data may contain depth information, which is referred to as RGB-D data. This type of data is collected using special RGB-D camera devices. The sensor data used in

The support of the Centre for High Performance Computing (CHPC) is gratefully acknowledged.

A. Gerber (Ed.): SACAIR 2020, CCIS 1342, pp. 169–182, 2020.
https://doi.org/10.1007/978-3-030-66151-9_11

human activity recognition are generally collected from wearable devices, motion sensors, and body heat-sensors.

There are two aspects to human activity recognition: action classification and action detection [2]. Action detection refers to identifying activities of interest [3]. In contrast, action classification aims to classify an action that is being performed in each video snippet. The action classification problem needs to also solve the action representation sub-problem. The action representation problem deals with finding the best features to use to train a classifier.

Many approaches have been introduced to solve the human activity recognition problem. Traditional image processing techniques require the extraction of good feature descriptors, which is essential for successful classifications. However, the application of deep learning techniques has demonstrated tremendous performance improvements over traditional techniques. A particular advantage of deep learning approaches is its automatic feature extraction abilities [4].

In this paper, a hybrid deep learning architecture, utilizing a Temporal Segment Network (TSN), Octave Convolutional Neural Network (OctConv), and a Multi-Layer Perceptron (MLP), is proposed as a solution to the human activity recognition problem. The TSN and MLP are hybridized. The OctConv is used as a convolutional neural network (CNN). Other convolutional neural network models and various multi-layer perceptrons were implemented and evaluated before we settled on this architecture.

The rest of the paper is organised as follows. Section 2 presents a review of the literature on human activity recognition from video. The proposed architecture is described in Sect. 3. The methods, including the dataset, experimental design, and evaluation metrics are discussed in Sect. 4. The results obtained using the KTH dataset are presented and discussed in Sect. 5. Concluding remarks and pointers to future work are given in Sect. 6.

2 Literature Review

The three most popular deep learning models developed for human activity recognition are recurrent neural networks, 3D convolutional neural networks, and two-stream convolutional neural networks [2]. Many of the deep learning models for action recognition requires two types of input sequences: spatial and temporal sequences [2]. A two-stream convolutional neural network processes these two types of inputs independently. The features extracted from the sequences are fused using a fusion strategy.

A temporal segment network (TSN) is composed of a spatial and a temporal stream [6]. A TSN model operates on a sequence of short snippets that are sparsely sampled from the video instead of working on individual frames or a stack of frames. The study in [5], conducted with a TSN and a two-stream inflated 3D convolution network (I3D), demonstrated that two-stream networks obtain better results for motion that occurs over a short duration. The results presented in this study show that the TSN model yields slightly better results than the I3D model. The disadvantage of using a CNN in these two-stream networks, is that they fail to model longer-term temporal variations.

A deep adaptive temporal pooling module was proposed by [8] to capture long-term temporal information in CNNs. This module was coupled with a TSN model and has obtained state-of-the-art performance on the UCF101 and HMDB51 human activity video datasets. Hybridizing a 3D-CNN with a long short-term memory network (LSTM) has proven to provide an effective representation for long-term motion and modelling of sequential data [7]. Another study [9], took a similar hybridization approach but evaluated the proposed model on the KTH dataset. The results obtained are close to the current performances of state-of-the-art deep learning models.

A long-term motion descriptor, called the sequential Deep Trajectory Descriptor (sDTD), was proposed to effectively capture motion information [18]. The study proposed a model a three-stream framework that processes static spatial features, short-term motion, and long-term motion in the videos. A CNN-RNN architecture was utilised to model the long-term motion representation. The Deep Trajectory Descriptor (DTD) was initially proposed by [19] to describe the motion between video frames for action recognition. It is considered to be a much more powerful representation of dense trajectories. The model proposed in [18] was evaluated on the KTH, HMDB51, and UCF101 datasets, and was able to achieve state-of-the-art performance on the KTH dataset at the time of its study.

Stable spatio-temporal features was investigated in [10]. This study used the pairwise local binary pattern (P-LBP) and the scale-invariant feature transform (SIFT) handcrafted features to train a multi-layer perceptron (MLP). The MLP was also evaluated on the KTH dataset, and produced promising results. Handcrafted features are mainly utilised for training traditional classifiers. The MBH [20], and SIFT3D [21] are spatio-temporal handcrafted features which were proposed to better represent both motion and appearance information of videos. Other spatio-temporal features were extracted using the Haralick feature extraction technique on co-occurrence matrices that were applied to optical flow representations [22,23]. Boundary co-ordinates and shape moments were combined as features and used to train traditional classifiers [24]. These handcrafted features are commonly used to train such popular classifiers as Support Vector Machines [22–24], Naïve Bayes [24], and Bags-of-words [22].

Most architectures deal with recognising activities performed by a single individual. A model called stagNet was introduced to recognise both group and individual activities [26]. This model used a spatio-temporal attention mechanism and a semantic graph model. The proposed framework was compared to existing state-of-the-art approaches and evaluated on four public benchmarked datasets, viz. the Collective Activity dataset, the New Collective Activity Dataset, the UCLA Courtyard dataset, and the Volleyball dataset. The stagNet model is capable of learning spatio-temporal representation more accurately because of its semantic graph architecture. The Volleyball dataset results show that stagNet can extract and model spatio-temporal relationships much better than existing RNN-related models. The overall results of the StagNet architecture were very competitive on all four datasets.

Since deep learning is known for its automatic feature extraction abilities [4], this study considers a two-stream deep learning model as a feature extractor to train a simple multi-layer perceptron (MLP) model.

3 Architecture

The proposed architecture is given in Fig. 1. The architecture is based on the hybridization of a two-stream network and a multi-layer perceptron. The two-stream network employed is a Temporal Segment Network (TSN). A temporal segment network framework performs video-level predictions utilizing the visual information of entire videos [6]. The TSN is composed of two streams, namely a spatial stream and a temporal stream. The model operates on a sequence of short snippets sparsely sampled from the video instead of working on individual frames or frame stacks. A video V is divided into k segments $\{V_1, V_2, \ldots, V_k\}$ of equal durations. Short snippets consisting of x consecutive frames are randomly chosen from each segment V_k. An optical flow operator is applied to these sequential frames and the optical flow result is fed into the temporal stream.

Similarly, a random frame is selected from each segment V_k and input into the spatial stream. The class scores assigned to the different snippets are fused by a segmental consensus function to produce a class score, which is the video-level predicted class. The predictions obtained from the spatial and temporal streams are combined to produce the entire video's final prediction. Traditionally, a TSN is trained using three segments and then tested using 25 segments. However, this TSN uses ten video segments during training, validation, and testing. The consistency scheme was adopted from [8] to obtain more temporal information. Both the spatial stream and temporal stream requires an input size of 224 × 224. The frames chosen for the spatial stream are randomly cropped and horizontally flipped. These are the same parameters that are employed by [8]. Once the video is split into ten segments, an RGB video frame is randomly chosen from each segment and is input to the spatial CNN model.

Convolutional Neural Networks are popular and powerful deep learning algorithms in image processing. A few pre-trained CNN models were investigated to determine the best candidate for both the spatial and temporal streams. These CNNs include AlexNet, VGG-16, SqueezeNet, ResNet50, and OctResNet50 models. The AlexNet CNN consists of five convolutional layers, where some are followed by max-pooling layers [11]. It is then followed by three fully connected layers, where the final layer is constructed with 1000 neurons. These fully connected layers utilize a dropout technique to reduce overfitting. The AlexNet CNN was known as one of the best CNN models to produce high classification accuracies on the ImageNet dataset.

A study was conducted on the impact of increasing the depths of a CNN architecture [12]. It investigated these architectures' performances with various depths of 16 to 19 weight layers and utilizing convolutional filters. The model with a depth of 16 layers is called the VGG-16. The VGG model achieves better results than AlexNet as the depth increases. Another deep CNN model,

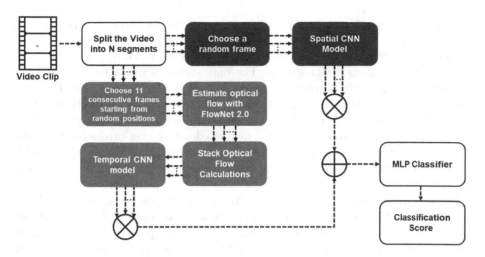

Fig. 1. Visual representation of the proposed architecture

SqueezeNet, was proposed with the intention to reduce the network's parameters so that it can easily be deployed with low memory requirements and can efficiently be transferred over a computer network [13]. This CNN model has approximately 5 MB of parameters and was able to produce the same level of accuracy as AlexNet when evaluated on the ImageNet dataset. The study also demonstrated that both the AlexNet and SqueezeNet model parameter size could be significantly reduced while maintaining accuracy by using a deep compression technique proposed by [14].

A deep residual learning framework, ResNet, was proposed in [15]. The study demonstrated that these networks are easily optimized and achieve higher accuracies with increased depths. These accuracy levels are competitive with state-of-the-art. An Octave Convolution (OctConv) was proposed in [1], to increase the efficiency in CNN models. This convolution operator was designed to easily replace vanilla convolutions in existing CNN models without adjusting any aspects of the network architecture. The study claims that this OctConv boosts accuracy for both image and video recognition tasks with much lower memory and computational cost. Evaluating the OctConv in ResNet CNN models (OctResNet) has shown significant accuracy improvements over the original ResNet models' performances.

When a performance comparison was completed on the selected CNN models, the OctResNet50 model produced the best results compared to the other CNN models when building the proposed architecture. These results are presented and discussed in Sect. 6. Hence, the OctResNet50 model was chosen for both the spatial and temporal stream. The OctResNet50 CNN model was pre-trained on the ImageNet dataset [1]. The output layer of the CNN model produces the classification score for the potential classes. These scores from all segments are fused using average fusion to form a single vector as the feature representation of the spatial stream component.

The temporal stream input consists of 11 consecutive video frames that are randomly chosen from each segment. The optical flow is estimated by using the FlowNet 2.0 algorithm to produce ten optical flow calculations [16]. FlowNet is an optical flow estimation algorithm that utilizes deep neural networks [16]. FlowNet 2.0 is the most recent version to date and focused on quality and speed improvements. The newer version has decreased estimation errors by over 50% than compared to the original. However, it is slower than the original architecture but outperforms all other optical flow algorithms in terms of accuracy. FlowNet 2.0 has also investigated ways to be able to work with small motions by introducing a subnetwork. The FlowNet 2.0 algorithm has experimented on motion segmentation and action recognition, and the optical flow estimations have proven to be very reliable. Overall, FlowNet 2.0 performs just as well as existing state-of-the-art methods. Due to its speed and performance accuracy, it was the preferred optical flow method in our architecture.

The ten optical flow calculations produced by the FlowNet 2.0 algorithm are stacked together and fed into the temporal CNN model. Another separate pre-trained OctResNet50 model trained on the ImageNet dataset was also employed as the temporal CNN model [1]. The output of the temporal stream's CNN model is the classification scores for the potential action classes. These scores from each segment are fused by the average fusion technique to produce a single feature representation vector of the temporal stream. The weighted average fusion is applied to the spatial and temporal stream's features. The spatial and temporal weight was set to 1 and 1.5, respectively. This weighting strategy was adopted from [8].

Once the weighted fusion was calculated, this served as input to a multi-layer perceptron (MLP) trained using backpropagation. This MLP consisted of an input layer with six neurons, a single hidden layer with 12 neurons, and an output layer with six neurons. ReLU was the activation function in the MLP. Each output neuron of the MLP carries a score that is associated with a potential classification class label.

This proposed architecture is different from other existing architectures in that it utilizes models that were introduced in very recent years by various research works. These models are employed in the two-stream network segment of this proposed architecture. This architecture stands out from the other two-stream architectures because it uses the multi-layer perceptron (MLP) as a classifier and the two-stream model as a feature extractor. Typical two-stream models use the respective streams' fused outputs as decision variables for the final classification result. However, this architecture uses the output as a feature vector that serves as an input to the MLP classifier. This hybridization of a two-stream model and an MLP have significantly increased the classification accuracies, which are presented and discussed in Sect. 5.

4   Methods

4.1   Dataset

The KTH human activity video dataset was used to validate the proposed architecture [17]. The dataset consists of 599 video clips containing six categories of actions, with approximately 100 videos per category. The six actions are: handwaving, boxing, handclapping, walking, jogging, and running. Example images of these activities is given in Fig. 2. Each category contains videos that were recorded by 25 different subjects in 4 different scenarios. All the video clips have a fixed frame rate of 25 fps and a resolution of 160 × 120 pixels.

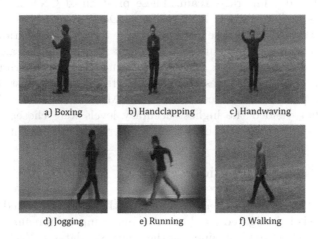

Fig. 2. Sample frames of actions from the KTH video dataset

4.2   Evaluation Metrics

A confusion matrix is commonly used to evaluate the performance of any classification model. Since this human activity recognition task is a classification problem, a confusion matrix was used to assess the performance of the architecture. From the confusion matrix, we can gather the True Positive (TP), True Negative (TN), False Positive (FP), and False Negative (FN) values to perform various statistical calculations such as Precision, Recall, Accuracy, and the F1-score. Most human activity recognition research reports the Precision value as the true accuracy performance of their classification model, even though there is an accuracy calculation formula to calculate the model's overall accuracy. The precision is a ratio of the number of correctly predicted classes that are positive. The precision and accuracy can be calculated using Eq. 1 and 2, respectively.

$$Precision = \frac{TP}{TP + FP} \tag{1}$$

$$Accuracy = \frac{TP + TN}{TP + TN + FP + FN} \qquad (2)$$

Unless stated otherwise, Eq. 1 was also used to report the accuracy of the model instead of using Eq. 2. The use of precision calculations is to maintain a fair comparison with other existing architecture results.

4.3 Experimental Design

The KTH dataset was divided into three sets, where 70% of the clips were chosen for training, 10% for validation, and 20% for testing. Some pre-trained CNN models trained on the ImageNet dataset were selected as candidate CNN models for the spatial and temporal stream. These pre-trained CNN models include AlexNet, VGG-16, SqueezeNet, ResNet50, and OctResNet50. Each stream was independently trained with these models, and the top two, best performing CNN models were chosen as candidate CNN models for the spatial and temporal streams. A combination of the selected CNN models was experimented with to observe which TSN produces the best results. Then the best TSN model was hybridized and experimented with various MLP architectures. The hybrid architecture that yielded the highest accuracy levels were chosen as the final architecture design. The results of the steps undertaken are presented in Sect. 5.

5   Results and Discussion

The result presented below in Table 1 and 2 are the results obtained by the various CNN models investigated for the spatial and temporal stream, respectively. These CNN models were pre-trained on the ImageNet dataset. Each of the CNN models was trained on the KTH dataset for 100 epochs. The overfitting was avoided by using the best saved model. This approach saves the weights of the models at the end of an iteration if the accuracy on the validation set is better than what was previously achieved by the model. The best models are used during the testing phase to obtain the final accuracy values.

It is noted that the VGG-16 and OctResNet50 were the top two best performing models in the spatial stream. Both the ResNet50 and OctResNet50 models have performed competitively in the temporal stream. After determining the top two best performing CNN models for the spatial and temporal stream, the combination of the models' performances is explored. The results obtained by this investigation are presented in Table 3. The best performing spatial and temporal CNN models were first chosen, but they yielded poor results. The best performing spatial CNN model and second-best temporal CNN model were chosen, but they also displayed poor results. The OctResNet50 spatial model with the ResNet50 temporal model has produced significantly better results. The results improved even more, when the OctResNet50 temporal model was employed instead. This version of the TSN model was selected to develop a hybrid architecture with an MLP.

Table 1. Spatial stream's CNN models and results

CNN models	Results	
	Loss	Accuracy
AlexNet	0.9385	53.25%
VGG-16	**0.7854**	**61.75%**
SqueezeNet	0.9049	58.00%
ResNet50	0.9934	51.42%
OctResNet50	**0.8574**	**60.25%**

Table 2. Temporal stream's CNN models and results

CNN models	Results	
	Loss	Accuracy
AlexNet	0.7981	69.75%
VGG-16	0.8592	75.83%
SqueezeNet	0.6627	75.08%
ResNet50	**0.5436**	**77.67%**
OctResNet50	**0.5224**	**78.00%**

Three different MLP architectures were experimented with the selected TSN model. All of them had one hidden layer. These networks varied by the number of neurons found in that layer and the type of activation function utilised. The different MLP architectures are defined in Table 4. Table 5 demonstrates the differences in the accuracy levels for each proposed hybrid architecture. The proposed TSN model hybridized with the first version of the MLP demonstrated significant improvements over the non-hybridized TSN model.

Table 3. Classification accuracies obtained by the various versions of the TSN model

Two-stream models	Accuracy
VGG-16 Spatial + OctResNet50 Temporal	60.00%
VGG-16 Spatial + ResNet50 Temporal	58.33%
OctResNet50 Spatial + OctResNet50 Temporal	**82.50%**
OctResNet50 Spatial + ResNet50 Temporal	80.00%

The first MLP version was adjusted by increasing the number of neurons to produce the second version. After replacing the first version of the MLP with the second version, the hybrid architecture showed greater accuracy levels. Further adjusting the MLP model by replacing the ReLU activation function with a Sigmoid function has shown a significant drop in accuracy levels than

Table 4. Different MLP architecture definitions

MLP version	Number of inputs	Number of neurons in the single hidden layer	Number of outputs	Activation function
1	6	3	6	ReLU
2	6	12	6	ReLU
3	6	12	6	Sigmoid

when utilizing the second version of the MLP. The hybridized architecture with the second MLP version has also displayed the potential of obtaining better accuracies. Therefore, it was decided to train that architecture by another 50 epochs further, bringing it to a total of 150 epochs. Increasing the number of training epochs for the hybrid TSN and MLP version 2 architecture has shown an increase in the accuracy levels. The accuracy levels are very competitive to the current existing state-of-the-art results.

Table 5. Accuracy levels for the different hybrid architecture models

Hybrid architecture	Number of epochs trained	Accuracy levels
Proposed TSN + MLP version 1	100	*88.33%*
Proposed TSN + MLP version 2	**100**	**96.67%**
Proposed TSN + MLP version 3	100	91.67%
Proposed TSN + MLP version 2	**150**	**97.50%**

The accuracy results of five independent runs of the proposed TSN model hybridised with the MLP version 2 architecture is presented in Table 6. Each of the independent runs reported was trained for 150 epochs. Saving the best model was also used to avoid overfitting of the model. It can be seen that the architecture produced accuracy levels that are above 90%. The highest accuracy level that the architecture produced is 97.5%. The standard deviation was calculated over the five independent runs and produced a value of 2.15. This value is small, which indicates that the accuracy levels are close to the mean and that high precision exists. The t-test was performed on the accuracy values to determine if the difference in performance is statistically significant. The t-test significance level was set to 0.05, and the two-tailed hypothesis was used. The t-test produced a t-value of -0.001863 and a p-value of 0.998603. This result proves that the difference in performances is not statistically significant.

The architecture was trained using a Nvidia V100 16 GB GPU and 10 CPUs on a high-performance computer. The training took approximately 3.5 h to complete for 150 epochs per independent run, which is equivalent to about 0.175 s to process a single video.

Table 6. Results from five independent runs of the best selected hybrid architecture

Independent run no.	Accuracy (%)
1	94.17
2	96.67
3	97.50
4	91.67
5	93.33
Mean	**94.67**
Standard deviation	**2.15**

The current state-of-the-art precision rate is 99.8%, which was achieved by [25], and the proposed architecture in this paper has achieved a precision value of 97.50%. The state-of-the-art method produces an accuracy rate of 99.80%, which is slightly better than the proposed architecture's accuracy value of 99.17%. Other evaluation metrics are reported and compared to the current state-of-the-art results in Table 7. The comparison of the proposed architecture's result to existing state-of-the-art results are given in Table 8.

A confusion matrix was compiled from the results obtained by hybrid TSN, and MLP version 2 is displayed in Table 9 below. Three out of six actions were successfully detected and classified, viz. handwaving, running, and walking. The remaining three categories had only one misclassification per category. The Boxing action was classified as walking, and both the handclapping and jogging were misclassified as boxing.

Table 7. Statistical analysis of the results obtained on the KTH dataset

Method	Measures				
	FPR	FNR (%)	Precision (%)	Recall (%)	CRR (%)
Khan et al. [25]	0.00	0.2	99.8	99.7	99.8
Proposed architecture	0.01	2.5	97.5	97.5	99.5

Table 8. Comparision of state-of-the-art results on the KTH video dataset

Author	Year	Accuracy (%)
Jaouedi et al. [27]	2019	96.30%
Shi et al. [18]	2017	96.83%
Tong et al. [28]	2017	97.17%
Shao et al. [29]	2016	97.50%
Proposed architecture	**2020**	**97.50%**
Khan et al. [25]	2019	99.80%

Table 9. Confusion matrix obtained by the proposed architecture on the KTH dataset.

Predicted class labels	Actual class labels					
	Boxing	Handclapping	Handwaving	Jogging	Running	Walking
Boxing	**19**	1	0	1	0	0
Handclapping	0	**19**	0	0	0	0
Handwaving	0	0	**20**	0	0	0
Jogging	0	0	0	**19**	0	0
Running	0	0	0	0	**20**	0
Walking	1	0	0	0	0	**20**

6   Conclusion and Future Work

In this paper, a deep learning architecture was proposed to effectively classify human actions. The proposed architecture was developed with commonly known deep learning algorithms, such as TSN, MLP, and CNN models. The OctResNet50 model employed was pre-trained on the ImageNet dataset and utilized as the frame-level feature extractor in the TSN model. An MLP architecture was hybridized with the TSN to produce the final proposed architecture. This architecture was trained and evaluated using the KTH human activity dataset. The results obtained are very competitive to existing state-of-the-art architectures. In future work, this architecture can be investigated using various other datasets. An emphasis can also be placed on improving the spatial stream's accuracy levels, which can enhance the overall results. An investigation can also be carried out on increasing the depth of the MLP and employing an optimisation technique to find optimal weights for the MLP network.

References

1. Chen, Y., et al.: Drop an octave: reducing spatial redundancy in convolutional neural networks with octave convolution. In: Proceedings of the IEEE International Conference on Computer Vision, pp. 3435–3444 (2019)
2. Zhang, H.B., et al.: A comprehensive survey of vision-based human action recognition methods. Sensors **19**(5), 1005 (2019)
3. Kang, S.M., Wildes, R.P.: Review of action recognition and detection methods. arXiv preprint arXiv:1610.06906 (2016)
4. Chandni, Khurana, R., Kushwaha A.K.S: Delving deeper with dual-stream CNN for activity recognition. In: Khare, A., Tiwary, U., Sethi, I., Singh, N. (eds.) Recent Trends in Communication, Computing, and Electronics. LNEE, vol. 524, pp. 333–342. Springer, Singapore (2019). https://doi.org/10.1007/978-981-13-2685-1_32
5. Bilkhu, M., Ayyubi, H.: Human Activity Recognition for Edge Devices. arXiv preprint arXiv:1903.07563 (2019)
6. Wang, L., et al.: Temporal segment networks: towards good practices for deep action recognition. In: Leibe, B., Matas, J., Sebe, N., Welling, M. (eds.) ECCV 2016. LNCS, vol. 9912, pp. 20–36. Springer, Cham (2016). https://doi.org/10.1007/978-3-319-46484-8_2

7. Arif, S., Wang, J., Ul Hassan, T., Fei, Z.: 3D-CNN-based fused feature maps with LSTM applied to action recognition. Fut. Internet **11**(2), 42 (2019)
8. Song, S., Cheung, N.M., Chandrasekhar, V., Mandal, B.: Deep adaptive temporal pooling for activity recognition. In: Proceedings of the 26th ACM International Conference on Multimedia, pp. 1829–1837 (October 2018)
9. Baccouche, M., Mamalet, F., Wolf, C., Garcia, C., Baskurt, A.: Sequential deep learning for human action recognition. In: Salah, A.A., Lepri, B. (eds.) HBU 2011. LNCS, vol. 7065, pp. 29–39. Springer, Heidelberg (2011). https://doi.org/10.1007/978-3-642-25446-8_4
10. Ullah, M., Ullah, H., Alseadonn, I.M.: Human action recognition in videos using stable features. Sig. Image Process. Int. J. (SIPIJ) **8**(6), 1–10 (2017)
11. Krizhevsky, A., Sutskever, I., Hinton, G.E.: ImageNet classification with deep convolutional neural networks. In: Advances in Neural Information Processing Systems, pp. 1097–1105 (2012)
12. Simonyan, K., Zisserman, A.: Very deep convolutional networks for large-scale image recognition. In: 3rd International Conference on Learning Representations (2015)
13. Iandola, F.N., Han, S., Moskewicz, M.W., Ashraf, K., Dally, W.J., Keutzer, K.: SqueezeNet: AlexNet-level accuracy with 50x fewer parameters and <0.5 MB model size. arXiv preprint arXiv:1602.07360 (2016)
14. Han, S., Mao, H., Dally, W.: Deep compression: compressing deep neural network with pruning, trained quantization and Huffman coding. In: 4th International Conference on Learning Representations (2016)
15. He, K., Zhang, X., Ren, S., Sun, J.: Deep residual learning for image recognition. CoRR abs/1512.03385 (2015)
16. Ilg, E., Mayer, N., Saikia, T., Keuper, M., Dosovitskiy, A., Brox, T.: Flownet 2.0: evolution of optical flow estimation with deep networks. In: Proceedings of the IEEE Conference on Computer Vision and Pattern Recognition, pp. 2462–2470 (2017)
17. Schuldt, C., Laptev, I., Caputo, B.: Recognizing human actions: a local SVM approach. In: 2004 Proceedings of the 17th International Conference on Pattern Recognition, ICPR 2004, vol. 3, pp. 32–36. IEEE (August 2004)
18. Shi, Y., Tian, Y., Wang, Y., Huang, T.: Sequential deep trajectory descriptor for action recognition with three-stream CNN. IEEE Trans. Multimedia **19**(7), 1510–1520 (2017)
19. Shi, Y., Zeng, W., Huang, T., Wang, Y.: Learning deep trajectory descriptor for action recognition in videos using deep neural networks. In: 2015 IEEE International Conference on Multimedia and Expo (ICME), pp. 1–6. IEEE (June 2015)
20. Dalal, N., Triggs, B., Schmid, C.: Human detection using oriented histograms of flow and appearance. In: Leonardis, A., Bischof, H., Pinz, A. (eds.) ECCV 2006. LNCS, vol. 3952, pp. 428–441. Springer, Heidelberg (2006). https://doi.org/10.1007/11744047_33
21. Scovanner, P., Ali, S., Shah, M.: A 3-dimensional sift descriptor and its application to action recognition. In: Proceedings of the 15th ACM International Conference on Multimedia, pp. 357–360. ACM (September 2007)
22. Caetano, C., dos Santos, J.A., Schwartz, W.R.: Optical flow co-occurrence matrices: a novel spatiotemporal feature descriptor. In: 2016 23rd International Conference on Pattern Recognition (ICPR), pp. 1947–1952. IEEE (December 2016)
23. Al-Akam, R., Paulus, D.: Dense 3D optical flow co-occurrence matrices for human activity recognition. In: Proceedings of the 5th International Workshop on Sensor-Based Activity Recognition and Interaction, p. 16. ACM (September 2018)

24. Samir, H., El Munim, H.E.A., Aly, G.: Suspicious human activity recognition using statistical features. In: 2018 13th International Conference on Computer Engineering and Systems (ICCES), pp. 589–594. IEEE (December 2018)
25. Khan, M.A., Akram, T., Sharif, M., Javed, M.Y., Muhammad, N., Yasmin, M.: An implementation of optimized framework for action classification using multilayers neural network on selected fused features. Pattern Anal. Appl. **22**(4), 1377–1397 (2019)
26. Qi, M., Wang, Y., Qin, J., Li, A., Luo, J., Van Gool, L.: stagNet: an attentive semantic RNN for group activity and individual action recognition. In: IEEE Transactions on Circuits and Systems for Video Technology (2019)
27. Jaouedi, N., Boujnah, N., Bouhlel, M.S.: A new hybrid deep learning model for human action recognition. J. King Saud Univ. Comput. Inf. Sci **32**(4), 447–453 (2020)
28. Tong, M., Wang, H., Tian, W., Yang, S.: Action recognition new framework with robust 3D-TCCHOGAC and 3D-HOOFGAC. Multimedia Tools Appl. **76**(2), 3011–3030 (2017)
29. Shao, L., Liu, L., Yu, M.: Kernelized multiview projection for robust action recognition. Int. J. Comput. Vis. **118**(2), 115–129 (2016)

DRICORN-K: A Dynamic RIsk CORrelation-driven Non-parametric Algorithm for Online Portfolio Selection

Shivaar Sooklal[1]([✉])[ID], Terence L. van Zyl[2][ID], and Andrew Paskaramoorthy[1][ID]

[1] School of Computer Science and Applied Mathematics,
University of the Witwatersrand, Johannesburg, South Africa
shivaarsooklal.108@gmail.com, andrew.paskaramoorthy@wits.ac.za
[2] Institute for Intelligent Systems, University of Johannesburg,
Johannesburg, South Africa
tvanzyl@uj.ac.za

Abstract. Online Portfolio Selection is regarded as a fundamental problem in Computational Finance. Pattern-Matching methods, and the CORN-K algorithm in particular, have provided promising results. Despite making notable progress, there exists a gap in the current state of the art – systematic risk is not considered. The lack of attention to systematic risk could lead to poor investment returns, especially in volatile markets. In response to this, we extend the CORN-K algorithm to present DRICORN-K – a Dynamic RIsk CORrelation-driven Non-parametric algorithm. DRICORN-K continuously adjusts a portfolio's market sensitivity based on the current market conditions. We measure market sensitivity using the β measure. DRICORN-K aims to take advantage of upward market trends and protect portfolios against downward market trends. To this end, we implement a number of market classification methods. We find that an exponentially weighted moving linear regression method provides the best classification of current market conditions. We further conducted an empirical analysis on five real world stock indices: the JSE Top 40, Bovespa, DAX, DJIA and Nikkei 225 against twelve state of the art algorithms. The results show that DRICORN-K can deliver improved performance over the current state of the art, as measured by cumulative return, Sharpe ratio and maximum drawdown. The experimental results lead us to conclude that the addition of dynamic systematic risk adjustments to CORN-K can result in improved portfolio performance.

Keywords: Online portfolio selection · Pattern-matching ·
Non-parametric learning · Systematic risk

1 Introduction

Online Portfolio Selection is regarded as a fundamental problem at the intersection of Computer Science and Finance. Online Portfolio Selection algorithms

© Springer Nature Switzerland AG 2020
A. Gerber (Ed.): SACAIR 2020, CCIS 1342, pp. 183–196, 2020.
https://doi.org/10.1007/978-3-030-66151-9_12

construct portfolios to maximise an investor's cumulative performance, often measured without reference to risk. This is achieved by specifying procedures to update portfolios sequentially as market information arrives. These online algorithms stand in contrast to batch optimisation procedures that are fundamental in the finance literature [1].

There are several approaches to Online Portfolio Selection, as described by Li and Hoi [2]. Online Portfolio Selection algorithms can be categorised into: Follow-the-Winner [3], Follow-the-Loser [4,5], Pattern-Matching [6–9], and Meta-Learning [10] approaches. Of the above algorithms, Pattern-Matching approaches are based on the most plausible assumptions. Further empirical studies on Pattern-Matching algorithms have shown that they outperform these other approaches [6–9]. In particular, the CORN-K (CORrelation-driven Nonparametric learning) algorithm, presented by Li et al. [8], has provided promising results.

Despite CORN-K's successes, there are gaps in its implementation: 1) it does not take risk into account during its portfolio optimisation and 2) it does not try to take advantage of this risk in varying market conditions. Both of these can lead to poor investment returns, especially in volatile markets. Additionally, it can result in inferior risk-adjusted returns by not adjusting for current market conditions [11].

Wang et al. [9] aims to address the first gap by penalising risky portfolios during portfolio optimisation. Although [9] presents improved results over CORN-K in volatile markets, their approach is focused on limiting downside risk, and thus does not address the second gap.

In this paper, we address the above issues by extending the CORN-K algorithm to present DRICORN-K (a Dynamic RIsk CORrelation-driven Nonparametric algorithm) by:

1. incorporating a systematic risk measure, β, into portfolio optimisation, and
2. classifying the current market trend, which will allow us to penalise high-risk portfolios when the market is bearish (decreasing), and reward high-risk portfolios when the market is bullish (increasing).

We evaluate DRICORN-K on five real world stock indices selected for their diverse characteristics: the JSE Top 40, Bovespa, DAX, DJIA and Nikkei 225. DRICORN-K delivers improved performance over the current state of the art, as measured by cumulative return, Sharpe ratio and maximum drawdown.

The remainder of this paper is as follows. The Online Portfolio Selection problem is formally described in Sect. 2. A discussion on Pattern-Matching approaches is presented in Sect. 3. This is followed by a discussion of the CORN-K algorithm and introduction of DRICORN-K in Sect. 4. The datasets are presented in Sect. 5 and experiments with results in Sect. 6.

2   The Online Portfolio Selection Problem

In a financial market, consider a portfolio containing m assets invested for n consecutive trading periods [2,4,6,9]. Let $\mathbf{x}_t = (x_{(t,1)}, \ldots, x_{(t,m)}) \in \mathbb{R}^m_+$ represent the price relative vector for the tth trading period, whose i^{th} component is $x_{(t,i)} = \frac{P(t,i)}{P(t-1,i)}$ where $P(t,i)$ is the closing price of the ith asset in the tth trading period. Define a market window $\mathbf{X}_{t-w}^t = (\mathbf{x}_{t-w}, \ldots, \mathbf{x}_t)$, where w is the given window size. Next, define a portfolio $\mathbf{b}_t = (b_{(t,1)}, \ldots, b_{(t,m)})$ where $b_{(t,i)}$ is the proportion of the portfolio invested in the ith asset for the tth trading period, and $b_{(t,i)} \geq 0$ and $\sum_i b_{(t,i)} = 1$. Thus the total return after t trading periods is defined as $S_t = \prod_{j=1}^{t} \mathbf{b}_j \cdot \mathbf{x}_j$.

An Online Portfolio Selection algorithm, $\mathcal{A}$, specifies the sequence of portfolios $\mathbf{B} = (\mathbf{b}_1, \ldots, \mathbf{b}_n)$ which aims to maximise S_n given a set of conditions based on the chosen performance measure. Examples of performance measures include the Sharpe ratio [3–5,8,9], maximum drawdown [5,8,9], and annual percentage yield or total cumulative wealth [4,8,10]. The maximisation of the performance measure is executed by learning each $\mathbf{b}_t$ sequentially at the beginning of period t based on the market window $\mathbf{X}_{t-w}^{t-1}$. The decision criteria for choosing a specific $\mathbf{b}_t$ is based on the implemented algorithm, $\mathcal{A}$.

The following assumptions are made with regard to the above Online Portfolio Selection problem [2]:

1. Transaction costs do not exist.
2. The market is liquid; each asset is arbitrarily divisible, and desired quantities can be bought and sold at the most recent closing price of any given trading period.
3. Market behaviour is not affected by any decision made by the Online Portfolio Selection algorithm (i.e. online investors are *price-takers*).

3   Pattern-Matching Approaches

Online Portfolio Selection approaches can be classified by the portfolio update scheme that they implement [2]. Follow-the-Winner algorithms increase the portfolio proportion of successful assets, while Follow-the-Loser algorithms increase the proportion of less successful assets. Pattern-Matching algorithms construct portfolios based on matching historical patterns of assets. Meta-Learning algorithms are formed by combining the above strategies.

Follow-the-Winner and Follow-the-Loser approaches base their decisions on the prevailing direction of the market. In this way, they assume the market will continue in its current trend or mean revert respectively, and select portfolios accordingly [2]. Pattern-Matching approaches find past market windows that match the prevailing market window, and select assets that have delivered the best performance in prior matching intervals [2,8]. The underlying assumption of each approach can lead to major losses if it is not realised.

Pattern-Matching approaches are typically non-parametric unsupervised learning techniques [2,8,12,13]. This is beneficial in high-dimensional contexts where the probability of backtest overfitting may be significant. Non-parametric models incur lower bias as a result of not fitting parameters with the data, which may lead to better generalisation.

Pattern-Matching approaches generally consist of two stages:

1. finding similar market windows, and
2. portfolio optimisation.

The first stage identifies the set of past market windows that are most similar to the current market window. The second stage learns an optimal portfolio based on the set obtained in the first stage.

Various algorithms use different metrics to determine the similarity between the past and current market windows. Examples include Györfi et al. [6] and Györfi et al. [7], which use Euclidean distance measures to determine similarity. Although these measures indicate "closeness", they do not include information on the direction that the market windows are moving in. This can cause the algorithm to use market windows that are uninformative, or even adverse. As a means to overcome this limitation, a measure that can indicate the "closeness" and direction of market windows could be used instead [8].

4   Correlation-Driven Non-parametric Learning Algorithms

4.1   CORN-K

The CORN-K algorithm [8] uses the Pearson product-moment correlation coefficient to measure the similarity between two given market windows. This enables CORN-K to extract information on the "closeness" and direction of market windows. Due to the steps required to calculate this coefficient, it reflects market-wide similarity during the windows under question. The choice was influenced by the Anticor algorithm in Borodin et al. [4] which tries to find statistical relations between pairs of stocks, and thus does not indicate market-wide similarity as a whole. Li et al. [8] thus found it more natural to use their chosen coefficient, as market windows (by definition) contain price relative vectors for each asset, and thus, the entire market.

As input, the algorithm takes in $\mathbf{X}_1^T = (\mathbf{x}_1, \cdots, \mathbf{x}_T)$: the sequence of historical price relative vectors over T consecutive trading periods, W: the maximum window size for experts, P: the maximum number of correlation coefficient thresholds, K: the number or percentage of experts to select the TOP-K experts.

For each trading period t, CORN-K determines the expert portfolio, $\mathcal{E}_t(w, \rho)$, for each (w, ρ) combination, where $w \in \{1, 2, \cdots, W\}$ and $\rho \in \{0, \frac{1}{P}, \frac{2}{P}, \cdots, \frac{P-1}{P}\}$.

Each expert is determined using a pattern-matching process. CORN-K obtains the set of all trading periods, $\mathcal{C}_t(w, \rho)$, whose trailing market windows are similar to the current market window. CORN-K measures similarity between market windows using the Pearson product-moment correlation coefficient, and creates $\mathcal{C}_t(w, \rho)$ for a given t as follows:

$$\mathcal{C}_t(w, \rho) = \left\{ w < i < t-1 \mid \frac{\text{cov}\left(\mathbf{X}_{i-w}^{i-1}, \mathbf{X}_{t-w}^{t-1}\right)}{\text{std}\left(\mathbf{X}_{i-w}^{i-1}\right) \text{std}\left(\mathbf{X}_{t-w}^{t-1}\right)} \geq \rho \right\} \tag{1}$$

CORN-K then searches for the optimal portfolio, $\mathcal{E}_t(w,\rho)$, based on $\mathcal{C}_t(w,\rho)$ as follows:

$$\mathcal{E}_t(w,\rho) = \arg \max_{\mathbf{b} \in \Delta_\mathbf{m}} \prod_{i \in \mathcal{C}_t(w,\rho)} (\mathbf{b} \cdot \mathbf{x}_i) \tag{2}$$

After obtaining the set of all experts for a given trading period t (i.e. $\mathcal{E}_t(w,\rho) \quad \forall w,\rho$), CORN-K creates an ensemble of the TOP-K experts according to the following formula:

$$\mathbf{b}_t = \frac{\sum_{w,p} q(w,\rho)s_{t-1}(w,\rho)\mathcal{E}_t(w,\rho)}{\sum_{w,p} q(w,\rho)s_{t-1}(w,\rho)} \tag{3}$$

where $q(w,\rho)$ represents the probability distribution function, and $s_{t-1}(w,\rho) = \prod_{j=1}^{t-1} \mathcal{E}_t(w,\rho) \cdot \mathbf{x}_j$ represents the total wealth achieved by $\mathcal{E}_t(w,\rho)$.

Wang et al. [9] extended the CORN-K algorithm by penalising risky portfolios during portfolio optimisation to create a risk-averse CORN-K algorithm. The risk penalty is measured by the standard deviation of returns of the portfolio under question. They modify Eq. (2), opting to use the log of cumulative returns instead, and create each expert as follows:

$$\mathcal{E}_t(w,\rho,\lambda) = \arg \max_{\mathbf{b} \in \Delta_\mathbf{m}} \frac{\sum_{i \in \mathcal{C}_t(w,\rho)} \log\left(\mathbf{b}^T \mathbf{x}_i\right)}{|\mathcal{C}_t(w,\rho)|} - \lambda\sigma_t(w,\rho) \tag{4}$$

where λ is their risk-aversion coefficient, $|\mathcal{C}_t(w,\rho)|$ is the size of $\mathcal{C}_t(w,\rho)$, and $\sigma_t(w,\rho) = \text{std}\left(\log\left(\mathbf{b}^T\mathbf{x}_i\right)\right)|_{i \in \mathcal{C}_t(w,\rho)}$ is their risk measure.

Although [9] presents improved results over CORN-K in volatile markets, the risk-averse CORN-K algorithm can result in an overly-conservative approach that avoids exploiting upside risk. In particular, it may be beneficial to increase portfolio risk when markets are bullish.

In financial theory, risk is decomposed into *systematic* and *idiosyncratic* components. Idiosyncratic risk is risk experienced by a specific company or industry, and can be diversified away. Systematic risk is inherent in the entire market and is undiversifiable. Thus, the risk of a diversified portfolio is almost entirely due to market movements, which can be exploited by adjusting the portfolio's market sensitivity according to market conditions.

4.2   DRICORN-K

We extend the risk-averse CORN-K algorithm to exploit upside risk while hedging downside risk. This is achieved by considering an alternative risk measure, *beta* (β), which reflects the sensitivity of a portfolio to the overall market. DRICORN-K penalises high-beta portfolios when the market is bearish, and rewards high-beta portfolios when the market is bullish.

The two key components of DRICORN-K are measuring the market sensitivity associated with a portfolio, and determining the current market conditions.

For a specific portfolio, $\mathbf{b}$, β is calculated as follows:

$$\beta_{\mathbf{b}} = \frac{\text{cov}(R_{\mathbf{b}}, R_m)}{\text{var}(R_m)} \tag{5}$$

where $R_{\mathbf{b}}$ and R_m are the daily returns on $\mathbf{b}$ and the market portfolio respectively. Thus, the β can be interpreted in the same manner as a regression coefficient in a linear regression model. That is, β indicates the magnitude and direction in which the portfolio moves relative to the market.

We incorporate β by extending the objective function in the portfolio optimisation step, based on the current market condition, as follows:

$$\mathcal{E}_t(w, \rho, \lambda) = \arg\max_{\mathbf{b} \in \Delta_m} \prod_{i \in \mathcal{C}_t(w,\rho)} (\mathbf{b} \cdot \mathbf{x}_i) \pm \lambda \beta_{\mathbf{b}} \tag{6}$$

where λ, the coefficient of β, is a hyperparameter. The $\lambda\beta_{\mathbf{b}}$ term is added when the market appears bullish, and subtracted when the market appears bearish.

The second component task of DRICORN-K is to classify whether the current market appears bullish (increasing) or bearish (decreasing).

We implemented seven methods for classifying whether a market is expected to be bullish or bearish. These include methods based on pure price changes; current vs. lagged moving average analysis on cumulative returns; and moving linear regression analysis on price relative vectors. For the price change methods, the market condition is classified based on the magnitude of market price change in the period of interest. The current moving average (CMA) vs. lagged moving average (LMA) (of cumulative returns) methods classify the market condition based on the relationship between their values. Alternatively, the moving linear regression methods classify the market condition based on the gradient of the regression line fitted to the price relative vectors over the previous two months. These methods are summarised in Table 1 and described further in Sect. 6.1.

Table 1. Market movement classification methods

Category	Description	Market movement		
		Decline	Rise	Stationary
Price Changes	Price change >20% (over past month)	Negative price change	Positive price change	No price change
	Price change >20%, from peak or trough (over past two months)			
Current Moving Average (CMA) vs. Lagged Moving Average (LMA)	Uniform Weighting	CMA < LMA	CMA > LMA	CMA = LMA
	Arithmetic Weighting			
	Exponential Weighting			
Moving Linear Regression	Uniform Weighting	Negative gradient	Positive gradient	Zero gradient
	Exponential Weighting			

5   Datasets

5.1   Training

We tuned the hyperparameters, and identified which market classification method to use, using a training dataset. Our training dataset consisted of 28 stocks over 504 trading days. This dataset was generated through simulation, using linear functions of an autoregressive (AR) model.

We initially use trading data on the NASDAQ index, from 2016 to 2018 to create the price relative vectors. We confirmed that this time series was stationary using the ADF test. Using the partial autocorrelation function (PACF), we selected an order of 6 for our autoregressive model, expressed as:

$$M_t = c_0 + c_1 M_{t-1} + c_2 M_{t-2} + c_3 M_{t-3} + c_4 M_{t-4} + c_5 M_{t-5} + c_6 M_{t-6} \qquad (7)$$

where each M_t represents an element of the price relative vector, and each c_i is an empirically determined coefficient. This model was used to generate a synthetic price relative vector over 504 trading days, $\mathbf{M} = (M_1, \ldots, M_{504})$, which represented our simulated market.

Using this simulated market data generator, we simulated the price relative vectors of 28 virtual stocks. In order to ensure that our training dataset would exhibit DRICORN-K's functionality, we required 75% of the stocks to be positively correlated with the simulated market, and the other 25% to be negatively correlated using the following formula:

$$\text{stock}_i = \gamma_i \mathbf{M} + \epsilon_i \qquad (8)$$

with γ_i as either positive or negative (representing positive or negative correlation to the simulated market respectively) being sampled from a uniform distribution; ϵ_i represents added white noise, sampled from a normal distribution, $\mathcal{N}(0, \sigma_i^2)$, where σ_i was sampled from a uniform distribution.

5.2   Testing

We tested DRICORN-K on the five real world indices, the JSE Top 40, Bovespa, DAX, DJIA and Nikkei 225, described in Table 2.

For each index, we downloaded individual stock datasets on the available top 30 index constituents, as of September 2020, from Yahoo Finance[1]. These time series were combined, cleaned and then used to create the price relative vectors required by the algorithms.

The datasets were also chosen to interrogate the performance of DRICORN-K, and the other algorithms, under various markets and market conditions. For each dataset, we selected a time period in which the index displayed a certain trend or pattern we wished to explore.

---

[1] https://finance.yahoo.com.

The JSE Top 40 index displayed an oscillatory pattern during the selected timeframe. It contained upward and downwards trends, but overall, it traded sideways.

The Bovespa index displayed a general upward trend throughout its timeframe with a sharp decline, and subsequent recovery, around March 2020.

The DAX index displayed an overall downward trend across the selected timeframe. This is indicative of a bear market.

Although it contained short market rises and declines, the DJIA index traded relatively sideways during the selected time period.

The Nikkei 225 index displayed peaks and troughs during its timeframe. There was a large decline at the beginning of the time period, and a large incline towards the end of the time period.

By testing DRICORN-K, and other algorithms, on these datasets, we hope to analyse their performance, strengths, weaknesses, and ability to generalise across various markets experiencing different economic conditions.

Table 2. Test datasets

Dataset	Country	Timeframe	# Trading days	# Assets
JSE Top 40	South Africa	22/05/2014–22/05/2018	998	29
Bovespa	Brazil	01/01/2016–01/01/2020	992	27
DAX	Germany	07/02/2000–07/02/2004	996	23
DJIA	US	14/01/1999–14/01/2003	1003	26
Nikkei 225	Japan	11/08/2014–11/08/2018	997	30

6   Experiments

6.1   Market Classification Metrics

We implemented the seven different market classification methods summarised in Table 1. Using our training dataset, we identified the approach that works best in the DRICORN-K algorithm. The hyperparameters of each market classification method were tuned using the simulated dataset from Sect. 5.1. Each method is classified under one of three categories:

Price Changes: The first approach checks whether the current market price has changed by more than 20%, compared to the previous month's price. The second approach checks whether the current market price has changed by more than 20% of its highest or lowest recorded price, over the past two months. A negative (positive) price change is classified as a declining (rising) market, while no price change is classified as a stationary market. These methods assume that price changes alone can indicate the current trend of the market.

Current Versus Lagged Moving Average: The lagged moving average (LMA) had a lag of one month. If the current moving average (CMA) is less (greater) than the LMA, the market is regarded as declining (rising), and if CMA = LMA, the market is regarded as stationary. We interpret these methods as lagging indicators of market movements. We implemented three versions of this type, each with a different weighting of the past trading periods. In our first approach, we implemented a uniform weighting, which assumes that each past trading period in the window contributes equally in determining the current trend of the market. For our second and third approaches, we implemented an arithmetic and an exponential weighting. These assume that more recent trading periods have a greater influence on the market trend [14], with the difference being that older trading period weightings are "eroded" quicker when using the exponential weighting.

Moving Linear Regression: A negative gradient indicates a declining market, a positive a rising market, and zero indicating a stationary market. We implemented two methods with different weightings of price relative vectors used in the regression process. The first method implements a uniform weighting, while the second implements an exponential weighting. The first method assumes that each trading period has an equal influence in determining the market trend, while the second method assumes that more recent periods have a greater influence [14].

Through empirical analysis on our training dataset, we found that the approach using moving linear regression with exponential weighting performed best. This identified method was selected to be used in DRICORN-K going forward.

6.2 Implementation

We implemented DRICORN-K, and other algorithms, using the toolbox presented by Li et al. [15]. For all implemented algorithms, we used their respective default parameters. For DRICORN-K, we used $W = 5$, $P = 10$, $K = 10\%$, $\lambda = 0.001$. In our market classification method (moving linear regression with exponential weighting) we used a smoothing factor of 0.6 and a market window size of two months.

6.3 Performance Measures

We used the following measures to capture the performance of the algorithms:

– Cumulative Return (CR)

$$S_n = \prod_{j=1}^{n} \mathbf{b}_j \cdot \mathbf{x}_j \tag{9}$$

where S_n is the cumulative return after n trading periods, $\mathbf{b}_j$ is the resulting portfolio at period j, and $\mathbf{x}_j$ is the price relative vector at period j.
Generally, the higher the cumulative return, the more preferable the Online Portfolio Selection algorithm.

– Annualised Sharpe Ratio (SR), [16]

$$\mathbf{SR}_n = \frac{\mathbf{APY}_n - R_f}{\sigma_p} \tag{10}$$

where $\mathbf{SR}_n$ is the annualised Sharpe Ratio after n periods, $\mathbf{APY}_n$ is the Annualised Percentage Yield (see note below), R_f is the risk-free rate of return, and σ_p is the annualised standard deviation of daily returns.
To calculate $\mathbf{SR}_n$, we set $R_f = 4\%$. To obtain σ_p, we multiplied the calculated standard deviation of daily returns by $\sqrt{252}$, as we assumed that there is an average of 252 trading days in a year.

• Note:
Annualised Percentage Yield (APY)

$$\mathbf{APY}_n = (S_n)^{\frac{1}{y}} - 1 \tag{11}$$

where S_n is the total return after n trading periods, and y is the number of years corresponding to n. APY is the rate of return achieved, taking into account the impact of compounding. Generally, the higher the APY, the more preferable the Online Portfolio Selection algorithm.

The Sharpe Ratio measures risk-adjusted return. Generally, the higher the annualised Sharpe Ratio, the more preferable the Online Portfolio Selection algorithm.

– Maximum Drawdown (MDD)

$$\mathbf{MDD}(n) = \sup_{q \in (0,n)} \left[\sup_{r \in (0,q)} \mathbf{S}(r) - \mathbf{S}(q) \right] \tag{12}$$

where $\mathbf{S}(j) = \{S_0, \dots, S_j\}$
MDD is a risk evaluation that measures the maximum decline from a historical peak of the total wealth (S) achieved by the algorithm. The smaller the MDD, the more risk-tolerable the Online Portfolio Selection algorithm.

Regarding the performance measures, there are some interesting points to consider when evaluating DRICORN-K's performance. Cumulative return is simply a measure of the change in absolute wealth. It does not take risk and other market properties into account. Thus, this measure alone does not accurately portray DRICORN-K's performance, as it does not take the algorithm's risk-adjusting ability into account. The Sharpe ratio provides insight on risk-adjusted returns, by providing a "return per unit risk" value. This unit of risk is standard deviation of daily returns (σ_p). DRICORN-K may receive a low SR value, as its daily returns may have been volatile. However, this was the intention of DRICORN-K – to increase risk (volatility) when the market is bullish, and become conservative when the market is bearish. This results in its daily returns having an erratic appearance, resulting in a higher σ_p value, yielding a lower SR. The MDD value specifically measures the degree of downside risk of an algorithm. Although this is an important measure, and investors are mainly concerned with downside risk, it does not provide an indication of upside risk of an algorithm. A key idea in DRICORN-K is to take advantage of upside risk, when the market is bullish, thus increasing returns while taking on relatively "safe risk".

Table 3. Results: performance measures for each of the twelve algorithms compared to DRICORN-K in five markets with varying conditions

Category	Algorithm	Dataset														
		JSE Top 40			Bovespa			DAX			DJIA			Nikkei 225		
		CR	SR	MDD	CR	SR	MDD	CR	SR	MDD	CR	SR	MDD	CR	SR	MDD
Benchmarks	UBAH	1.23	0.08	**0.17**	2.59	1.00	0.28	0.77	−0.28	0.64	1.06	−0.12	0.34	1.51	0.40	**0.19**
	UCRP	1.33	0.22	0.23	2.78	1.16	**0.24**	1.76	0.31	0.49	1.24	0.07	0.31	1.58	0.46	0.20
Follow-the-Winner	UP	1.33	0.22	**0.22**	2.78	1.17	**0.24**	1.77	0.31	0.49	1.24	0.07	0.31	1.58	0.46	**0.20**
	EG	1.32	0.21	0.22	2.77	1.16	0.24	1.83	0.33	0.49	1.23	0.06	**0.31**	1.57	0.46	0.20
	ONS	1.56	0.17	0.75	4.20	**1.33**	0.27	1.02	−0.08	0.57	3.28	**1.20**	0.34	1.59	0.36	0.28
Follow-the-Loser	ANTICOR2	1.42	0.16	0.44	**6.35**	**1.46**	0.30	4.74	**0.92**	0.44	4.75	1.01	0.42	1.61	0.37	0.25
	PAMR2	1.68	0.22	0.63	0.77	−0.21	0.66	4.32	0.83	**0.31**	5.94	1.08	0.59	0.94	−0.18	0.60
	CWMR-StdDev	1.69	0.22	0.64	0.89	−0.13	0.66	5.52	**1.00**	**0.31**	6.16	**1.09**	0.61	0.93	−0.20	0.62
	OLMAR2	1.89	0.26	0.70	3.55	0.58	0.49	4.05	0.58	0.50	**6.41**	0.94	0.60	1.13	−0.03	0.62
Pattern-Matching	B^K	1.15	−0.03	0.29	2.87	0.89	0.31	**7.75**	0.64	0.67	1.20	0.03	**0.30**	1.34	0.18	0.27
	B^{NN}	1.02	−0.20	0.31	**4.83**	1.02	0.33	1.76	0.08	0.82	1.82	0.37	0.36	1 56	0.33	0.28
	CORN-K	**2.33**	**0.69**	0.34	3.16	0.72	0.44	2.04	0.18	0.82	2.18	0.51	0.46	**3.02**	**1.20**	0.25
	DRICORN-K	**2.00**	**0.57**	0.40	3.24	0.76	0.39	**5.93**	0.43	0.68	2.76	0.71	0.39	**2.77**	**1.07**	0.29

6.4 Algorithms

We tested DRICORN-K against twelve Online Portfolio Selection algorithms. These algorithms are categorised as follows:

- **Benchmarks:** Uniform Buy And Hold (UBAH), Uniform Constant Rebalanced Portfolios (UCRP)
- **Follow-the-Winner:** Universal Portfolios (UP), Exponential Gradient (EG), Online Newton Step (ONS)
- **Follow-the-Loser:** Anti Correlation (ANTICOR2), Passive Aggressive Mean Reversion (PAMR2), Confidence Weighted Mean Reversion (CWMR-StdDev), Online Moving Average Reversion (OLMAR2)
- **Pattern-Matching:** Non-parametric Kernel-based Log-optimal (B^K), Non-parametric Nearest Neighbor Log-optimal (B^{NN}), Correlation-driven Non-parametric Top-K (CORN-K)

This allowed us to position DRICORN-K's performance relative to the current state of the art, while gaining valuable insight on each algorithm's behaviour in various markets.

6.5   Results

The results of these experiments can be seen in Table 3, where the performance measures for each algorithm tested on the five datasets are displayed. The top two performances on each dataset are marked in bold. In Fig. 1 we display the

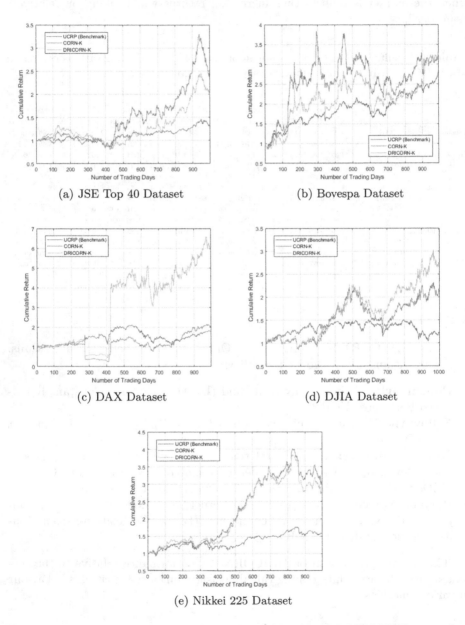

(a) JSE Top 40 Dataset

(b) Bovespa Dataset

(c) DAX Dataset

(d) DJIA Dataset

(e) Nikkei 225 Dataset

Fig. 1. Cumulative returns achieved by UCRP, CORN-K and DRICORN-K across five datasets.

cumulative returns achieved by UCRP, CORN-K and DRICORN-K across five datasets. The initial wealth for each algorithm is set to 1.

In Table 3, we observe varying results across the different datasets, particularly in the Follow-the-Winner and Follow-the-Loser categories. Their results seem to depend on the market conditions within the particular dataset. Follow-the-Winner strategies seem to perform well when the market is on an overall upward trend, while Follow-the-Loser strategies seem perform well when the market data contains large downward trends. This observation implies that these strategies do not generalise well to varying market conditions, compared to Pattern-Matching strategies. The Pattern-Matching strategies, CORN-K and DRICORN-K in particular, do not show vast changes in performance when tested on datasets of varying market conditions. This generalisability of Pattern-Matching strategies serves as further support over Follow-the-Winner and Follow-the-Loser strategies.

As seen in Table 3, DRICORN-K consistently outperforms the market benchmarks. DRICORN-K does not always outperform the other Online Portfolio Selection algorithms, in terms of the selected performance measures. Nonetheless, it does perform well and offers advantages in the form of generalisability. On majority of the datasets, it outperforms CORN-K, by displaying higher CR and SR, and lower MDD.

In Fig. 1, we see that, in general, DRICORN-K's cumulative return over time is less sensitive than that of CORN-K, particularly on market declines. DRICORN-K also appears to increase its systematic risk on market inclines, aiming to take advantage of bullish trends. This can, in some cases, result in DRICORN-K becoming increasingly correlated with the market. The result of this is suboptimal returns, in comparison to other Online Portfolio Selection algorithms that outperform the market.

7   Conclusion

In this paper we extended the CORN-K algorithm to present DRICORN-K – a Dynamic RIsk CORrelation-driven Non-parametric algorithm. The extensions included incorporating a systematic risk measure, β, into portfolio optimisation; and classifying the current market trend, which allowed us to penalise high-risk portfolios when the market was bearish, and reward high-risk portfolios when the market was bullish. These extensions were in response to CORN-K not taking risk into account during its portfolio optimisation, and not trying to exploit this risk in varying market conditions. Empirical experiments on various datasets lead us to conclude that, bearing in mind the performance measures' interpretations, our dynamic systematic risk adjustments to CORN-K can result in improved portfolio performance, while generalising across various markets.

Future work includes improving the methods used to classify market conditions using time series analysis, and to incorporate other market- and stock-related factors into the portfolio optimisation stage. These factors include size premiums, value premiums and momentum.

References

1. Paskaramoorthy, A.B., Gebbie, T.J., van Zyl, T.L.: A framework for online investment decisions. Invest. Anal. J. **49**, 215–231 (2020)
2. Li, B., Hoi, S.: Online portfolio selection: a survey. ACM Comput. Surv. **46**, 12 (2012)
3. Agarwal, A., Hazan, E., Kale, S., Schapire, R.E.: Algorithms for portfolio management based on the newton method. In: Proceedings of the 23rd International Conference on Machine Learning, pp. 9–16 (2006)
4. Borodin, A., El-Yaniv, R., Gogan, V.: Can we learn to beat the best stock. J. Artif. Intell. Res. **21**, 579–594 (2004)
5. Li, B., Zhao, P., Hoi, S.C.H., et al.: PAMR: passive aggressive mean reversion strategy for portfolio selection. Mach. Learn. **87**, 221–258 (2012). https://doi.org/10.1007/s10994-012-5281-z
6. Györfi, L., Lugosi, G., Udina, F.: Nonparametric kernel-based sequential investment strategies. Math. Finan. Int. J. Math. Stat. Finan. Econ. **16**(2), 337–357 (2006)
7. Györfi, L., Udina, F., Walk, H., et al.: Nonparametric nearest neighbor based empirical portfolio selection strategies. Stat. Decis. **26**(2), 145–157 (2008)
8. Li, B., Hoi, S.C.H., Gopalkrishnan, V.: CORN: correlation-driven nonparametric learning approach for portfolio selection. ACM Trans. Intell. Syst. Technol. (TIST) **2**(3), 1–29 (2011)
9. Wang, Y., Wang, D., Zheng, T.F.: Racorn-k: risk-aversion pattern matching-based portfolio selection. In: 2018 Asia-Pacific Signal and Information Processing Association Annual Summit and Conference (APSIPA ASC), pp. 1816–1820. IEEE (2018)
10. Das, P., Banerjee, A.: Meta optimization and its application to portfolio selection. In: Proceedings of the 17th ACM SIGKDD International Conference on Knowledge Discovery and Data Mining, pp. 1163–1171 (2011)
11. Gooding, A.E., O'Malley, T.P.: Market phase and the stationarity of beta. J. Financ. Quant. Anal. **12**(5), 833–857 (1977)
12. Snow, D.: Machine learning in asset management–part 1: portfolio construction–trading strategies. J. Financ. Data Sci. **2**(1), 10–23 (2020)
13. Snow, D.: Machine learning in asset management–part 2: portfolio construction–weight optimization. J. Financ. Data Sci. **2**(1), 10–23 (2020)
14. James, F.E.: Monthly moving averages-an effective investment tool? J. Financ. Quant. Anal. **3**(3), 315–326 (1968)
15. Li, B., Sahoo, D., Hoi, S.C.H.: OLPS: a toolbox for on-line portfolio selection. J. Mach. Learn. Res. **17**(1), 1242–1246 (2016)
16. Sharpe, W.F.: Mutual fund performance. J. Bus. **39**(1), 119–138 (1966)

Knowledge Representation
and Reasoning

Cognitive Defeasible Reasoning: the Extent to Which Forms of Defeasible Reasoning Correspond with Human Reasoning

Clayton Kevin Baker[✉][iD], Claire Denny[iD], Paul Freund[iD],
and Thomas Meyer[iD]

University of Cape Town and CAIR, Cape Town, South Africa
{bkrcla003,dnncla004,frnpau013}@myuct.ac.za, tmeyer@cs.uct.ac.za

Abstract. Classical logic forms the basis of knowledge representation and reasoning in AI. In the real world, however, classical logic alone is insufficient to describe the reasoning behaviour of human beings. It lacks the flexibility so characteristically required of reasoning under uncertainty, reasoning under incomplete information and reasoning with new information, as humans must. In response, non-classical extensions to propositional logic have been formulated, to provide non-monotonicity. It has been shown in previous studies that human reasoning exhibits non-monotonicity. This work is the product of merging three independent studies, each one focusing on a different formalism for non-monotonic reasoning: KLM defeasible reasoning, AGM belief revision and KM belief update. We investigate, for each of the postulates propounded to characterise these logic forms, the extent to which they have correspondence with human reasoners. We do this via three respective experiments and present each of the postulates in concrete and abstract form. We discuss related work, our experiment design, testing and evaluation, and report on the results from our experiments. We find evidence to believe that 1 out of 5 KLM defeasible reasoning postulates, 3 out of 8 AGM belief revision postulates and 4 out of 8 KM belief update postulates conform in both the concrete and abstract case. For each experiment, we performed an additional investigation. In the experiments of KLM defeasible reasoning and AGM belief revision, we analyse the explanations given by participants to determine whether the postulates have a normative or descriptive relationship with human reasoning. We find evidence that suggests, overall, KLM defeasible reasoning has a normative relationship with human reasoning while AGM belief revision has a descriptive relationship with human reasoning. In the experiment of KM belief update, we discuss counter-examples to the KM postulates.

Keywords: Non-monotonic reasoning · Defeasible reasoning · Belief revision · Belief update · Survey · Google forms · Mechanical turk

---

Supported by Centre for Artificial Intelligence Research (CAIR).

A. Gerber (Ed.): SACAIR 2020, CCIS 1342, pp. 199–219, 2020.
https://doi.org/10.1007/978-3-030-66151-9_13

1   Introduction

It is well-documented that human reasoning exhibits flexibility considered key to intelligence [21], yet fails to conform to the prescriptions of classical or propositional logic [25] in the Artificial Intelligence (AI) community. The AI community, therefore, seeks to incorporate such flexibility in their work [21]. Non-classical or non-monotonic logic is flexible by nature. Whereas classical reasoning is enough to describe systems with a calculated output in an efficient way, how humans reason is non-classical because humans are known to reason in different ways [25]. The problem is that non-monotonic reasoning schemes have been developed for and tested on computers, but not on humans. There is a need to investigate whether there exists a correspondence between non-monotonic reasoning and human reasoning and, if so, to what extent it exists. This problem is important because we can gain insight into how humans reason and incorporate this into building improved non-monotonic AI systems. An issue which needs to be considered is that humans are diverse subjects: some reason normatively while others reason descriptively. In the case of normative reasoning, a reasoner would conclude that a certain condition *should be* the case or that the condition is usually the case. In the case of descriptive reasoning, a reasoner would make a bold claim that a certain condition *is* exactly true or exactly false. We emphasise that a thorough investigation needs to be done to determine the extent of the correspondence between non-monotonic reasoning and how humans reason.

We propose this work as a contribution towards solving this problem. While acknowledging that this work falls within a broader research paradigm towards this goal [21,24,25], what differentiates this work is that it is, to our knowledge, the first work with an explicit view towards testing each of these particular formal non-monotonic frameworks: KLM defeasible reasoning [13], AGM belief revision [1], and KM belief update [11]. We report on these frameworks in a paper due to the close theoretical links between the frameworks' domains. Postulates for defeasible reasoning and belief revision may be translated from the one context to the other [5]. Using such translations, KLM defeasible reasoning [13] can be shown to be the formal counterpart of AGM belief revision [8]. This does not hold for KM belief update [11]. Belief update is commonly considered a necessarily distinct variant of belief revision for describing peoples' beliefs in certain domains [11].

In Sect. 2, we describe related work and the formalisms of non-monotonic reasoning under investigation in our study. We end this section with our problem statement. In Sect. 3, we describe the design and implementation of three distinct surveys, one for each formalism of non-monotonic reasoning in our study. Each survey seeks to determine the extent of correspondence between the postulates of that formalism and human reasoning. In Sect. 4, we describe the methods used to analyse our survey results. We present our results, discussion and conclusions in Sect. 5. Lastly, we propose the track for future work in Sect. 6.

2 Background

Humans are known to reason differently about situations in everyday life and this reasoning behaviour can be compared to the paradigm of non-monotonic reasoning in AI. Non-monotonic reasoning is the study of those ways of inferring additional information from given information that does not satisfy the monotonicity property, which is satisfied by all methods based on classical logic [13]. Said otherwise, non-monotonic logic fails the principle that whenever x follows from a set A of propositions then it also follows from every set B with $B \subseteq A$ [18]. With non-monotonic reasoning, a conclusion drawn about a particular situation does not always hold i.e. in light of newly gained, valid information, previously valid conclusions have to change. This type of reasoning is described in the context of AI [23]. We consider three forms of non-monotonic reasoning, namely defeasible reasoning, belief revision and belief update. The latter two are both forms of *belief change* [11], wherein there exists a belief base and a belief set [6]. Explicit knowledge the agent has about the world resides in the belief base, whereas both the explicit knowledge the agent has about the world and the inferences derived from it reside in the belief set.

2.1 Defeasible Reasoning

Defeasible reasoning occurs when the evidence available to the reasoner does not guarantee the truth of the conclusion being drawn [21]. A defeasible statement has two identifiable parts: an antecedent or premises and a consequence or conclusion [7]. With classical reasoning, we proceed from valid premises to a valid conclusion and this conclusion will never change. With defeasible reasoning, we can proceed from valid premises to a valid conclusion also. However, in light of new valid information, the previously valid conclusion is allowed to change. Either the conclusion will be supported by the new information or the conclusion will be defeated by the new information. This defeasible reasoning behaviour applies to many aspects of the everyday life of humans, where the information available to the reasoner is often incomplete or contains errors. As such, defeasible information often involves information that is considered typical, normal or plausible. We shall now illustrate this with an example. Consider the following statements: *employees pay tax* and *Alice is an employee*. From the statements given, can we conclude that *Alice pays tax*? In the classical case, we can only conclude that *Alice pays tax*. Using defeasible reasoning, we can also conclude that *Alice pays tax*. However, should we receive additional information about Alice that she is not a typical employee, we can change our conclusion to be *Alice does not pay tax*. In this case, we have to amend our premises to account for the defeasible information viz. *employees typically pay tax* and *Alice is not a typical employee*.

2.2 Belief Revision

In belief revision, conflicting information indicates flawed prior knowledge on the part of the agent, forcing the retraction of conclusions drawn from it [11,19]. Information is then taken into account by selecting the models of the new information closest to the models of the base, where a model of information μ is a state of the world in which μ is true [11]. An example of this reasoning pattern will now be described. Consider the same statements used above in the defeasible reasoning example. Using the reasoning pattern of belief revision, we can infer from our beliefs that Alice does pay tax. Suppose we now receive new information: *Alice does not pay tax*. This is inconsistent with our belief base, so a decision must be made regarding which beliefs to retract prior to adding the new information into our beliefs. We could revise our beliefs to be that *employees pay tax* and *Alice does not pay tax*. In [4], this decision is proposed to be influenced by whether we believe some statements more strongly than others. In [1], it is proposed to be influenced by closeness (the concept of minimal change), in that we aim to change as little about our existing knowledge as we can do without having conflicting beliefs.

2.3   Belief Update

In belief update, conflicting information is seen as reflecting the fact that the world has changed, without the agent being wrong about the past state of the world. To get an intuitive grasp of the distinction between belief update and revision, take the following example adapted from [11]. Let b be the proposition that the book is on the table, and m be the proposition that the magazine is on the table. Say that our belief set includes $(b \wedge \neg m) \vee (\neg b \wedge m)$, that is the book is on the table or the magazine is on the table, but not both. We send a student in to report on the state of the book. She comes back and tells us that the book is on the table, that is b. Under the AGM [1] postulates for belief revision proposed in [1], we would be warranted in concluding that $b \wedge \neg m$, that is, the book is on the table and the magazine is not. But consider if we had instead asked her to ensure that the book was on the table. After reporting, we again are faced with the new knowledge that b. This time adding the new knowledge corresponds to the case of belief update. And here it seems presumptuous to conclude that the magazine is not on the table [11]. Either the book was already on the table and the magazine was not, in which case the student would have done nothing and left, or the magazine was on the table and the book not, in which case the student presumably would have simply put the book on the table and left the magazine similarly so. As these examples are formally identical, there is a need for different formalisms to accommodate both cases.

2.4   Problem Statement

We propose a first study to address the gap between the postulates of KLM [13] defeasible reasoning, AGM [1] belief revision and KM [11] belief update, and human reasoning.

Research Question: To what extent do the postulates of defeasible reasoning, belief revision and belief update correspond with human reasoning?

We have investigated three approaches to non-monotonic reasoning: the KLM [13] defeasible reasoning approach, the AGM [1] belief revision approach and the KM [11] belief update approach. In additional investigations, the reasoning style of participants, normative or descriptive, was identified in the cases of defeasible reasoning and belief revision. For belief update, the additional investigation was to find counter-examples to the KM [11] postulates.

3   Implementation

In this section, we describe the design and implementation of three surveys: one each for defeasible reasoning, belief revision, and belief update. We also describe our implementation strategy and expected challenges. Finally, we document our testing and evaluation strategy. The major reason for our choice of the survey as a testing instrument was its ease of integration with Mechanical Turk, which was the channel we had chosen for sourcing our participants. Moreover, the web-based survey is a common tool used in sociological research, such that "it might be considered an essential part of the sociological toolkit" [32]. Future work may look towards testing our research questions in a non-survey environment.

3.1   Survey Designs

Each of the three surveys focused on testing a particular formalism of non-monotonic reasoning: survey 1 tested defeasible reasoning, survey 2 tested belief revision and survey 3 tested belief update. 30 responses were wanted per survey. Participants were asked whether they accepted the conclusions proposed by the postulates of the formalism of non-monotonic reasoning in question, and were asked to give an explanation for their answer. The postulates were presented in concrete and abstract form. The concrete part of the survey consisted of the translations of all the postulates into English sentences. The abstract part consisted of the translations of all the postulates into variables, denoted by capital letters from the English alphabet. The logical behaviour of the postulates was maintained in the translations of these postulates from propositional logic to their concrete and abstract forms, respectively. For a particular postulate in the concrete case, the premises and conclusion were substituted with sentences from the English language. In the abstract case, the premises and conclusion were substituted by variables using letters from the English alphabet. Together, the premises and conclusion for each postulate created a story for the participant to read. The stories used in the concrete part of the survey were designed to mimic an environment in which a general reasoner might find himself. For example, some of the stories related to reasoning about students and homework, whilst others related to reasoning about the weather. The stories used in the abstract part were less verbose as no context was given to indicate the meaning of the variables used. An example of a concrete, story-style or real-world question would be: *If Cathy has a cake to bake, will she use an oven?*. An example of an abstract question would be: given the following, *If A then B*, and *If C then A*, can we say that *If C then B*? The survey questions can be navigated to by means of Appendix A for reference.

Survey 1. This survey tested participants' ability to reason defeasibly. Participants were asked whether they accepted the conclusions proposed by the KLM [13] postulates of defeasible reasoning and were required to provide explanations for their reasoning. We refer to the KLM [13] postulates of *Left Logical Equivalence* (LLE), *Right Weakening* (RW), *And*, *Or* and *Cautious Monotonicity* (CM), included in Appendix A for reference. The KLM [13] postulates were presented as textual stories containing a set of information, or premises, and a proposed conclusion. For each postulate, the stories were included in concrete and abstract form. The concrete form of the postulates was kept separately from the abstract form. The concrete part of the survey was presented to participants first. The abstract part was presented next. For both the concrete and abstract parts, the order of the postulates was randomised. Crucial to this study, the explanations given by participants were used to identify whether they reasoned normatively or descriptively. This survey also tested participants' ability to reason defeasibly in a broader sense. In particular, additional defeasible reasoning postulates were presented to participants. This was done by presenting each postulate in concrete and abstract form and asking participants to reason as before. In the concrete case only, participants' ability to reason under two distinctive subcategories of defeasible reasoning, prototypical reasoning and presumptive reasoning, was tested. Prototypical reasoning [17] suggests each reasoning scenario assumes a model with certain typical features, whereas presumptive reasoning [31] suggests that an argument may have multiple possible consequences. As an avenue for future work, the ability for participants to reason prototypically and presumptively could be tested in greater detail with scope to include testing participants' ability to reason in the abstract case.

Survey 2. The questions in this survey were developed to test whether postulates of a specific formalisation of the process of belief revision feature in cognitive reasoning. The formalisation used is that of the eight-postulate approach as proposed by Alchourrón, Gärdenfors and Makinson (AGM) [1]. We refer to the eight-postulate approach as the AGM [1] postulates of *Closure, Success, Inclusion, Vacuity, Consistency, Extensionality, Super-expansion* and *Sub-expansion*, included in Appendix A for reference. Two types of questions were developed: concrete and abstract. This involved designing scenarios in which to ground the concrete questions. Five such scenarios were designed. Abstract questions were developed directly based on the formal postulates. The abstract questions were included to test the postulates without having the agent's knowledge of the world hindering their answers and to have questions which are less semantically loaded [16] than real-world concrete questions. The benefit of abstract examples is further discussed by Pelletier and Elio [21]. The concrete questions started as abstract representations explicitly requiring the application of one or some of the formal postulates to obtain the desired answer. These representations were then elaborated in the context of a scenario. The scenarios designed are: linguists, smoking, wildlife, bag of stationery and, acrobats. The scenarios designed are inspired by the literature and the researcher's knowledge of the world.

Survey 3. The questions in this survey were developed to test the KM approach [11] to belief update. The KM [11] postulates we used are included as postulates *U1*, *U2*, *U3*, *U4*, *U5*, *U6*, *U7* and *U8* in Appendix A. These postulates mirrored the eight-postulate approach for belief revision, with the core difference between the postulates for revision and the postulates for update being the type of knowledge referred to: static knowledge for revision and dynamic knowledge for update. The questions in this survey were broken into three sets. The first consisted of abstract questions, in which the KM [11] postulates were presented and participants were asked to rate their agreement with the postulates on a linear or Likert scale with extremal points "strongly agree" and "strongly disagree". The postulates were presented using non-technical language. The second set of questions were concrete questions that were meant to be confirming instances of each of the eight KM postulates, where participants were asked to answer either *Yes* or *No*, and motivate their answer. The third set followed the same format as the second but was meant to present counter-examples to the postulates, with the counter-examples largely sourced from the literature. The first counter-example was based on the observation that updating p by $p \vee q$ does not affect the KM approach [9], which seems counter-intuitive. The second was based on the observation that updating by an inclusive disjunction leads to the exclusive disjunction being believed in the right conditions (a modification of the checkerboard example in [9]), which again seems counter-intuitive. The third was based on the observation that sometimes belief revision semantics seem appropriate in cases corresponding to the way that belief update is commonly, and has been here, presented in [15]. The final is an example testing a counter-intuitive result of treating equivalent sentences as leading to equivalent updates.

3.2   Mechanical Turk

Mechanical Turk (MTurk) is a service provided by Amazon that serves as an interface between service *Requesters* and a network of *Workers*. It addresses three problems [10]. It is used by software developers to incorporate human intelligence into software applications. It is used by business people to access a large network of human intelligence to complete tasks such as conducting market research. It is used by people looking to earn money to find work that can be done anywhere and at any time, using skills they already have. We used MTurk for access to its network of people to complete our surveys, which were hosted on Google Forms. An advantage is that its network of Workers includes people from a large range of ages, education levels and places [26]. Such places include the United States of America, India, Pakistan, the United Kingdom and the Philippines [26].

Although we did not set out to target a specific population of reasoners, MTurk offered a choice of up to 3 different qualifications that our Workers must satisfy. For the defeasible reasoning survey, Workers were required to be Master Workers, a qualification assigned by MTurk to top Workers who consistently submit high-quality results. Workers were required to have a HIT Approval Rate (%) for all Requesters' HITs ≥ 97, and have more than 0 HITs approved. For the belief revision survey, two MTurk qualifications and one internal qualification was used to recruit participants. Workers were required to have a HIT Approval Rate (%) for all Requesters' HITs > 98, and have more than 5000 HITs approved. The required number of HITs approved was varied, between 1000 and 5000, to allow for a diverse sample of respondents. We created one internal qualification to ensure that the 30 respondents were unique across all of the published batches of the survey. This qualification was called *Completed my survey already* and assigned to Workers which have submitted a response in a previous batch, including the batch of the trial HIT. For the belief update survey, a single qualification was used: only Master Workers were allowed to participate in the survey.

3.3 Google Forms

Google Forms is an application which allows users to create and disseminate free online surveys. Research performed in 2018 revealed that the recent surge of low-quality qualitative data from MTurk is primarily due to international Turkers (workers on MTurk) [30] using Virtual Private Networks or Virtual Private Servers to waive qualifications required to complete surveys [12]. This motivated including a checkpoint within the surveys themselves, considering the surveys were answered online. The checkpoint comprised custom *captchas* and an attention check, designed to be an indicator of the respondent's suitability to take the survey. In this context, suitability comprises four requirements: *(i)* the response is not generated by a bot, *(ii)* the respondent is not using a script, *(iii)* the respondent can understand English, *(iv)* the respondent reads questions in full. Requirements *i* and *ii* address that the respondent must be a human. Requirement *iii* addresses that the survey questions are in English and require English answers. This limits the survey's population of potential respondents, as the respondent's English proficiency may affect their performance on the HIT e.g. in their interpretation of double negatives. A *Human Intelligence Task* (HIT) is any activity that can be performed on a computer by a human actor e.g. writing an essay. MTurk offered varying ages, backgrounds and other such contextual factors, resulting in it also presenting the challenge of verifying English proficiency levels, as understanding English is a broad classification.

We sought to clarify whether their understanding of a question posed in English was sufficient to answer correctly a trick question. We considered two options: to create a separate, qualifying HIT or include the qualifier as part of the survey. We chose the latter. Finally, requirement *iv* addresses that the respondent must be paying attention and reading all the information presented as prior knowledge before answering a question. If the respondent failed to meet requirement *iv*, we would lack cause to believe our assumption of what comprises their prior knowledge in later questions would not be violated.

3.4   Testing and Evaluation

Each of our surveys were evaluated by a group of both laypeople and experts for clarity. Each of our surveys were also published on MTurk as a trial HIT. The results of the trial HITs were used to gauge how Turkers might respond to the final survey.

Feedback from Groups of Laypeople and Experts. We asked a variety of experts and non-experts to evaluate our survey for coherence, clarity and other desirable characteristics of questions, more examples of which can be found in [14]. One of the authors evaluated each of the three surveys. We also approached an expert in psychology and an expert in philosophy, at the University of Cape Town, however they were not available to evaluate our surveys. The remaining experts who evaluated the survey questions included one Masters student in Computer Science, as well as two Computer Science Honours students also conducting studies on non-monotonic reasoning forms. One of the surveys was evaluated by an international doctoral student in language and African studies. Based on the suggestions from experts and laypeople, a variety of changes were made to the surveys.

Trial HITs. A trial of the surveys was conducted, *(i)* to gain familiarity with the MTurk service and platform and *(ii)* to test the survey and its questions on a sample of Turkers. It involved three separate postings of the survey links as HITs on the site, each requiring five responses. The HIT was created with certain specifications accordingly. Workers were compensated R30 (above the South African hourly minimum wage) for completing the tasks, and the tasks included a time estimate, all of which were under an hour. We did not restrict workers by location, but required that they should have completed a certain number of HITs previously, and have a certain approval rating ($\geq 95\%$) for their tasks, as recommended by Amazon to improve response quality [29]. A Turker's approval rating refers to the percentage of their tasks that have been approved or accepted by the Requesters who published them. Based on the results from the trial survey, changes were made for the final experiments. The changes included increasing both the compensation and the estimated completion time.

3.5   Ethical, Professional and Legal Issues

Ethical issues are those which require a choice to be made between options based on whether they evaluate as ethical or unethical. Professional issues here refer to those which pertain to ethical standards and rules that the profession of Computer Science has for its members, particularly with respect to research. Ethical and professional issues thus overlap. Legal issues refer to those which involve the law. As this project involved experiments with people, ethical clearance was obtained from the University of Cape Town Faculty of Science Human Research Ethics Committee before proceeding with the experiments. The primary issue in the experiments was the use of MTurk, in particular, whether Workers were being paid a fair wage for their work. Per [2], the following three steps were taken to mitigate these concerns. First, workers were paid more than the South African minimum wage for an hour's work. Second, in the title of the task, the estimated amount of time needed for the task was clearly stated. Finally, there is a section in the survey which gives an overview of what the research concerns, placing the work in context. Workers were also required to give their informed consent to participate in the study. This was achieved by having a consent form at the start of the survey, whereby workers could either agree to participate in the research and then continue to the rest of the survey, or they could decline to participate and be thanked for their time. Contact details of the researchers were also provided. Before the data-handling, all survey responses were anonymised. We also did not collect names, cellphone numbers or email addresses from our participants. The only personal contact information we collected from each participant was their Amazon Turk *WorkerID*. To view our survey questions, raw collected data and the codebooks used for data analysis, click here.

4   Methods of Analysis

Responses were rejected if the participant failed the checkpoint section in the survey. In our analysis, we reference applying a baseline of 50% to our results. The choice of 50% as a baseline was arbitrary, but it served as a tool to evaluate the meaning of our results. As a starting point for evaluation and a baseline for agreement, it was basic and could be improved upon in future work.

4.1   Survey 1

The defeasible reasoning survey had 30 responses, which were downloaded from Google Forms. One response was rejected due to the participant submitting twice. Coding of participant responses was performed using Microsoft Excel functions. The coding spreadsheet is included in our Github repository, referenced in Appendix A. For this survey, we assumed that the KLM [13] postulate of *Reflexivity*, the idea that a proposition x defeasibly entails itself, holds for all human reasoners and therefore it was not tested. Feedback from our supervisor indicated that a few survey questions were not appropriate models of the KLM [13] postulates they intended to test, as they used the word *some* in the conclusion. These were questions 6 and 7, referring to the KLM [13] postulates of *Right Weakening* and *And*, respectively. In the following, we state question 6 as was presented in the survey, as an example, to clarify. The given information was presented as a numbered list and the conclusion was phrased as a question. Question 6, testing *Right Weakening*, asked: given i) no police dogs are vicious and ii) highly trained dogs are typically police dogs, can you conclude that *some* highly trained dogs are vicious? We draw the reader's attention to the fact that the word *some* is not part of the definition of the KLM [13] postulates. Thus, we have removed the responses to these questions in our analysis of the results.

Quantitative Data. In our collected data, participant agreement with the postulates, the *Yes* or *No* responses, were considered quantitative data. This agreement was measured using a hit rate. The hit rate (%) for each postulate was calculated as with the formula: $\frac{\text{number of Yes responses}}{\text{total number of responses}} \times 100$. Hit rates were measured for each postulate in the concrete and the abstract case. A postulate with a hit rate of $\geq 50\%$ in both the concrete and abstract case was said to have agreement with the participants in this survey. We plotted the concrete and abstract hit rate for each defeasible reasoning postulate as well as the concrete hit rates for prototypical reasoning and presumptive reasoning, in Fig. 1. Where no data was available, this was indicated by a blank in the figure.

Qualitative Data. In our collected data, the explanations given by participants were considered qualitative data. We have identified four main emerging themes for participant explanations. The theme *Support* refers to an explanation which contained only information given in the question. The theme *Speculative* refers to an explanation for which there is partial support from the given information, but also in which external information, not present in the question, is considered. *Technical* refers to an explanation which contains the phrase *typically, but not always*. The theme *Other* refers to explanations which did not fit into any of the above categories and often contained explanations which were vague or explanations quoted from an external source but contained nonsensical words. After identifying these four themes, we have pooled the explanations from the *Support* and *Technical* themes and qualified these together as normative. We have qualified explanations fitting the *Speculative* theme as descriptive.

4.2   Survey 2

The belief revision survey had 40 participants, as 10 responses were rejected; 30 responses were used. Analysis of the Questions section of the survey, for both the trial and final survey, comprised finding the modal answer and hit rate for each closed question and performing qualitative analysis on the open questions. The data was downloaded from Google Forms and Mechanical Turk.

Quantitative Data. The modal answer and hit rate (%) for closed questions were calculated by applying Microsoft Excel functions to the data. A hit indicates success. In this context, success is defined as both the respondent and the application of the belief revision postulates obtaining the same answer. The hit rate is thus calculated for each question as $\frac{\text{number of successes}}{\text{no. of responses}} \times 100$. The analysis of the results employs a baseline of a hit rate of 50% to indicate overall success.

Qualitative Data. The qualitative analysis was performed in NVivo, a qualitative data analysis software package, and made use of *Tesch's Eight Steps in the Coding Process* [3]. In this process, a combination of pre-determined and emerging codes were used. Codes on topics expected to be found were taken from literature, based on the theory being empirically tested. These include the eight postulates of belief revision as proposed by Alchourrón, Gärdenfors and Makinson [1]: closure, success, inclusion, vacuity, consistency, extensionality, super-expansion, sub-expansion. Other pre-determined codes include: normative and descriptive. Emerging codes are those which were not anticipated at the beginning, or are both unusual and of interest. They are developed solely on the basis of the data collected from respondents by means of the survey. An example of an emerging code used in the trial of this study is *It is stated*. This code represents the respondent taking a passive approach to their response. Other examples would be *real-world influence* and *likelihood*.

Pre-determined codes *normative* and *descriptive* refer to the reasoning style identified in responses to open questions. A normative style involves making value judgements [20], commenting on whether something is the way it should be or not. This includes implied judgements through the use of emotive language. A descriptive style, in contrast, does not - it involves making an observation, commenting on how something is [20].

4.3 Survey 3

Quantitative Data. The belief update survey had 34 participants, of which 4 responses were rejected. For the quantitative data, two forms of analysis were chosen, corresponding to the two different forms of quantitative data (ordinal and binary) gathered. For the ordinal (Likert-type) data, the median is an appropriate measure of central tendency [28], and thus was chosen, and for the binary data, the hit rate as above was chosen. Relating this back to the research question, a postulate was seen as confirmed if it saw both a hit rate $\geq 50\%$ for the confirming concrete example, and a median value of agree or better.

Qualitative Data. For the qualitative data, emerging codes were developed for Sect. 2 on a *per question* basis. This was so as to better interpret the quantitative results, and, in particular with the counter-examples, to see whether the reasons given by participants for their answers matched the theory behind the objections as given in the literature. Similar to the belief revision case, a common code was *new information should be believed*, which corresponds to the case of simply believing new information.

5   Results, Discussion and Conclusions

To answer our research question, we found several correspondences between the KLM [13] approach for defeasible reasoning, the AGM [1] approach for belief revision and the KM [11] approach for belief update, and how our participants reasoned. For defeasible reasoning, there was correspondence with one KLM [13] postulate (refer to Fig. 1): *Or*. For belief revision, there was correspondence with three AGM [1] postulates (refer to Fig. 2): *Success*, *Vacuity* and *Closure*. For belief update, there was correspondence with four KM [11] postulates (refer to

Fig. 3): *U1*, *U3*, *U4* and *U6*. For each of the three surveys, we present additional results that are of importance. Our surveys were designed separately and contained slightly differing methodologies, so we have not attempted a holistic comparison of the results. Future work might do so. Discussion of less expected results from each survey can be found at either of the links in Appendix Sect. A.1, in the respective individual papers.

5.1 Additional Results for KLM Defeasible Reasoning

The KLM [13] postulate *Or* shows agreement with our participants, suggested by both the concrete and abstract hit rates being ≥50% (concrete hit rate 75,86%, abstract hit rate 58,62%). In addition to *Or*, 2 out of 5 KLM [13] postulates show agreement in the concrete case only: *Left Logical Equivalence* (55,17%) and *Cautious Monotonicity* (72,41%). Across all KLM [13] postulates tested in this study, where both concrete and abstract hit rates were present, we observed the pattern that the concrete hit rate was always higher than abstract hit rate. The additional defeasible reasoning postulates we have investigated were *Rational Monotonicity*, *Transitivity* and *Contraposition*, included in Appendix A for reference. The defeasible reasoning postulate of *Transitivity* shows acceptance by our survey participants (concrete 72,41%, abstract 65,52%). In the case of *Contraposition*, a change in hit rate pattern was observed: it was the only postulate for which neither hit rate exceeded the baseline hit rate ≥50%, suggesting a negative relationship with our participants' reasoning, and it was the only postulate for which the abstract hit rate (41,38%) was higher than the concrete hit rate (17,24%). We observed that *Rational Monotonicity* had the largest difference between hit rates. The difference between the concrete and abstract hit rates for *Rational Monotonicity* was 65,51%, with a significant agreement in the concrete case (concrete 72,41%). In our investigation of participant agreement with prototypical reasoning and presumptive reasoning, we also observed strong agreement in the concrete case with both concrete hit rates ≥85%. Our additional investigation sought to identify whether participants reasoned normatively or descriptively. We found that across the majority of KLM [13] postulates and additional defeasible reasoning postulates, participants explained their acceptance or disagreement using a normative reasoning style. This can be explained by (1) participants relying mainly on the information given in the study and (2) participants accepting the information given in the study as plausible.

5.2 Additional Results for AGM Belief Revision

The hit rates were taken as indications of the type of relationship between human reasoning and the relevant AGM [1] postulates. For the concrete and abstract questions for postulates *Success* (concrete hit rate 90%, abstract hit rate 76.67%), *Closure* (concrete 100%, abstract 53.33%) and *Vacuity* (concrete 50%, abstract 56.67%), the hit rates obtained were ≥50%, suggesting a positive relationship between human reasoning and those postulates. Postulates *Extensionality* (concrete 26.67%, abstract 40%), *Super-expansion* (concrete 38.33%, abstract 36.67%) and *Consistency* (concrete 50%, abstract 36.67%) received hit rates ≤50%, suggesting a negative relationship. Postulates *Sub-expansion* (concrete 76.67%, abstract 40%) and *Inclusion* (concrete 23.33%, abstract 60%) had discrepancies of >30% between the hit rates for their concrete and abstract questions, and their relationships to human reasoning thus found to be inconclusive. Through an additional investigation, we found that participants have a predominantly descriptive relationship with belief revision when postulates are presented both in concrete and abstract form. The balance of descriptive and normative reasoning styles of respondents in their responses became more even for the abstract questions, perhaps suggesting an increasing reliance on perceived rules in situations to which humans are less able to relate.

5.3   Additional Results for KM Belief Update

When reporting the abstract results in this section, the first number indicates the median of the participants' attitudes towards the postulate if 0 = strongly disagree and 5 = strongly agree. The subsequent percentage is the percentage of people who agreed or strongly agreed with the postulate. The concrete questions and counter-examples were sometimes tested using multiple questions. The hit rate for such postulates refers to the question with the lowest percentage of conformance with the postulate. $U1$ (concrete 90%, abstract: 4; 76.7%), $U3$ (concrete 76.7%, abstract: 4; 56.7%), $U4$ (concrete 66.7%, abstract: 4; 76.7%) and $U6$ (concrete 76.7%, abstract: 4; 66.7%) saw hit rates uniformly >50%. $U2$ (concrete 76.7%, abstract: 3; 50%) and $U5$ (concrete 90%, abstract: 3; 50%) saw a neutral median abstract Likert score; with a correspondingly split abstract hit rate. $U7$ (concrete 76.7%, abstract: 2.5; 36.7%) and $U8$ (concrete 90%, abstract: 3; 43.3%) saw an abstract hit rate of <50%. Qualitatively, all postulates excluding $U5$ and $U7$, saw codes such that the majority reason for agreement with the concrete questions was theoretically in accordance with the postulate. All of the counter-examples examined saw hit rates >50%. The first counter-example (hit rate 63.3%) followed from $U2$. The second counter-example (83.3%) follows from the set of $U1$, $U4$, and $U5$. The third counter-example (60%) was against $U8$. The final counter-example (70%) follows independently from $U4$, and the set of $U1$ and $U6$. Although implicated theoretically, qualitative analysis suggested participants still reasoned in accordance with $U1$ in the counter-examples.

6   Future Work

Our results suggest that the models of KLM defeasible reasoning [13], AGM belief revision [1] and KM belief update [11] are not yet a perfect fit with human reasoning because participants failed to reason in accordance with many of the postulates of these models. A larger participant pool is required to confirm our results. In future work, it may be interesting to add blocks to the study, in the form of different control groups e.g. paid reasoners as opposed to unpaid reasoners, to explore the effects of different circumstances on cognitive reasoning and which logic form is most closely resembled in each such block.

A   Appendix: Supplementary Information

A.1   External Resources

We have created a GitHub repository which contains additional resources for this project. In this repository, we include our survey questions, our raw data and the codebooks used for our data analysis. As mentioned in the abstract, this work is the product of merging three independent papers: one each for KLM [13] defeasible reasoning, AGM belief revision [1] and KM belief update [11]. These independent papers are also included in the GitHub repository. The GitHub repository can be accessed by clicking here. In addition, a summary of our project work is also showcased on our project website which can be viewed by clicking here.

A.2   Defeasible Reasoning

KLM Postulates. Table 1 presents the KLM postulates. For ease of comparison, we present the postulates translated in a manner similar to [27]. We write $C_n(S)$ to represent the smallest set closed under classical consequence containing all sentences in S, and $D_C(S)$ to represent the resulting set if defeasible consequence is used instead. $D_C(S)$ is assumed defined only for finite S. $C_n(\alpha)$ is an abbreviation for $C_n(\{\alpha\})$, and $D_C(\alpha)$ is an abbreviation for $D_C(\{\alpha\})$.

Table 1. KLM postulates

1	Reflexivity	$\alpha \in D_C(\alpha)$
2	Left Logical Equivalence	If $\alpha \equiv \phi$ then $D_C(\alpha) = D_C(\phi)$
3	Right Weakening	If $\alpha \in D_C(\phi)$ and $\gamma \in C_n(\alpha)$ then $\gamma \in D_C(\phi)$
4	And	If $\alpha \in D_C(\phi)$ and $\gamma \in D_C(\phi)$ then $\alpha \wedge \gamma \in D_C(\phi)$
5	Or	If $\alpha \in D_C(\phi)$ and $\alpha \in D_C(\gamma)$ then $\alpha \in D_C(\phi \vee \gamma)$
6	Cautious Monotonicity	If $\alpha \in D_C(\phi)$ and $\gamma \in D_C(\phi)$ then $\gamma \in D_C(\phi \wedge \alpha)$

Reflexivity states that if a formula is satisfied, it follows that the formula can be a consequence of itself. *Left Logical Equivalence* states that logically equivalent formulas have the same consequences. *Right Weakening* expresses the fact that one should accept as plausible consequences all that is logically implied by what one thinks are plausible consequences. *And* expresses the fact that the conjunction of two plausible consequences is a plausible consequence. *Or* says that any formula that is, separately, a plausible consequence of two different formulas, should also be a plausible consequence of their disjunction. *Cautious Monotonicity* expresses the fact that learning a new fact, the truth of which could have been plausibly concluded, should not invalidate previous conclusions.

Additional Postulates. Table 2 presents additional defeasible reasoning postulates. *Cut* expresses the fact that one may, in his way towards a plausible conclusion, first add an hypothesis to the facts he knows to be true and prove the plausibility of his conclusion from this enlarged set of facts and then deduce (plausibly) this added hypothesis from the facts. *Rational Monotonicity* expresses the fact that only additional information, the negation of which was expected, should force us to withdraw plausible conclusions previously drawn. *Transitivity* expresses that if the second fact is a plausible consequence of the first and the third fact is a plausible consequence of the second, then the third fact is also a plausible consequence of the first fact. *Contraposition* allows the converse of the original proposition to be inferred, by the negation of terms and changing their order.

Table 2. Additional postulates

1	Cut	If $\alpha \in D_C(\phi \wedge \gamma)$ and $\gamma \in D_C(\phi)$ then $\alpha \in D_C(\phi)$
2	Rational Monotonicity	If $\alpha \notin D_C(\phi \wedge \gamma)$ and $\neg\phi \notin D_C(\gamma)$ then $\alpha \notin D_C(\gamma)$
3	Transitivity	If $\alpha \in D_C(\phi)$ and $\gamma \in D_C(\alpha)$ then $\gamma \in D_C(\phi)$
4	Contraposition	If $\alpha \in D_C(\phi)$ then $\neg\phi \in D_C(\neg\alpha)$

A.3   Belief Revision

AGM Postulates. Table 3 presents the AGM postulates. $K * \alpha$ is the sentence representing the knowledge base after revising the knowledge base K with α. We assume that K is a set that is closed under classical deductive consequence.

Table 3. AGM postulates

1	Closure	$K * \alpha = C_n(K * \alpha)$
2	Success	$\alpha \in K * \alpha$
3	Inclusion	$K * \alpha \subseteq C_n(K \cup \{\alpha\})$
4	Vacuity	If $\neg\alpha \notin K$ then $C_n(K \cup \{\alpha\}) \subseteq K * \alpha$
5	Consistency	$K * \alpha = C_n(\alpha \wedge \neg\alpha)$ only if $\models \neg\alpha$
6	Extensionality	If $\alpha \equiv \phi$ then $K * \alpha = K * \phi$
7	Super-expansion	$K * (\alpha \wedge \phi) \subseteq C_n(K * \alpha \cup \{\phi\})$
8	Sub-expansion	If $\neg\phi \notin K$ then $C_n(K * \alpha \cup \{\phi\}) \subseteq K * (\alpha \wedge \phi)$

Closure implies logical omniscience on the part of the ideal agent or reasoner, including after revision of their belief set. *Success* expresses that the new information should always be part of the new belief set. *Inclusion* and *Vacuity* are motivated by the principle of minimum change. Together, they express that in the case of information α, consistent with belief set or knowledge base K, belief revision involves performing expansion on K by α i.e. none of the original beliefs need to be withdrawn. *Consistency* expresses that the agent should prioritise consistency, where the only acceptable case of not doing so is if the new information, α, is inherently inconsistent - in which case, success overrules consistency. *Extensionality* effectively expresses that the content i.e. the belief represented, and not the syntax, affects the revision process, in that logically equivalent sentences or beliefs will cause logically equivalent changes to the belief set. *Super-expansion* and *sub-expansion* is motivated by the principle of minimal change. Together, they express that for two propositions α and ϕ, if in revising belief set K by α one obtains belief set K' consistent with ϕ, then to obtain the effect of revising K with $\alpha \wedge \phi$, simply perform expansion on K' with ϕ. In short, $K * (\alpha \wedge \phi) = (K * \alpha) + \phi$.

Table 4. KM postulates

1	(U1)	$\alpha \in K \diamond \alpha$
2	(U2)	If $\alpha \in K$ then $K \diamond \alpha = K$
3	(U3)	$K \diamond \alpha = C_n(\alpha \wedge \neg\alpha)$ only if $\models \neg\alpha$ or $K = C_n(\alpha \wedge \neg\alpha)$
4,	(U4)	If $\alpha \equiv \phi$ then $K \diamond \alpha = K \diamond \phi$
5,	(U5)	$K \diamond (\alpha \wedge \phi) \subseteq C_n(K \diamond \alpha \cup \{\phi\})$
6	(U6)	If $\phi \in K \diamond \alpha$ and $\alpha \in K \diamond \phi$ then $K \diamond \alpha = K \diamond \phi$
7	(U7)	If K is complete then $K \diamond (\phi \vee \alpha) \subseteq C_n(K \diamond \alpha \cup K \diamond \phi)$
8.	(U8)	$K \diamond \alpha = \bigcap_{\phi \in K} C_n(\phi) \diamond \alpha$
9	(U*9)	$K \diamond \alpha = C_n(K \diamond \alpha)$

A.4   Belief Update

KM Postulates. Table 4 presents the KM postulates. For ease of comparison, the postulates have been rephrased as in the AGM paradigm [22]. We use $\diamond$ to represent the update operator. *U1* states that updating with the new fact must ensure that the new fact is a consequence of the update. *U2* states that updating on a fact that could in principle be already known has no effect. *U3* states the reasonable requirement that we cannot lapse into impossibility unless we either start with it, or are directly confronted by it. *U4* requires that syntax is irrelevant to the results of an update. *U5* says that first updating on α then simply adding the new information γ is at least as strong (i.e. entails) as updating on the conjunction of α and γ. *U6* states that if updating on α_1 entails α_2 and if updating on α_2 entails α_1, then the effect of updating on either is equivalent. *U7* applies only to complete knowledge bases, that is knowledge bases with a single model. If some situation arises from updating a complete K on α and it also results from updating that K from ϕ then it must also arise from updating that K on $\alpha \vee \phi$. *U8* is the disjunction rule. *U*9* is not necessary in the propositional formulation of the postulates and is listed for completeness. It was not tested in the survey.

A.5   Results

In Fig. 1, we show the Hit Rate (%) for each defeasible reasoning postulate. In Fig. 2, we show the Hit Rate (%) for each belief revision postulate. In Fig. 3, we show the Hit Rate (%) for each belief update postulate.

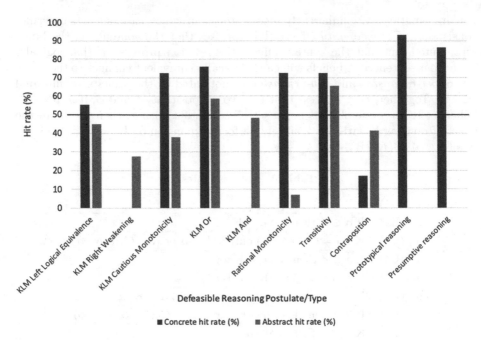

Fig. 1. Hit rate (%) for defeasible reasoning postulates

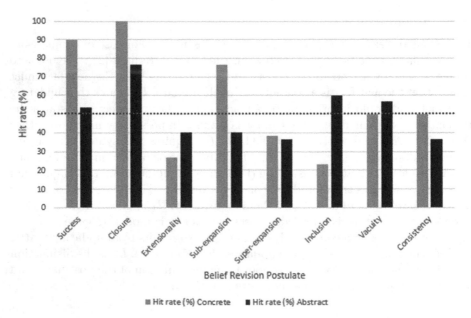

Fig. 2. Hit rate (%) for belief revision postulates

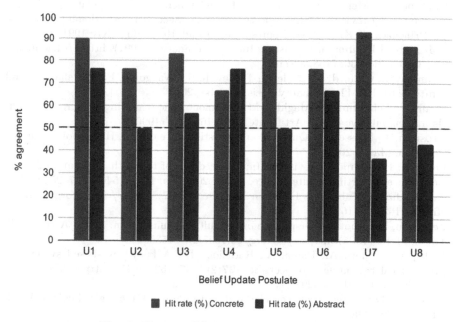

Fig. 3. Hit rate (%) for belief update postulates

References

1. Alchourrón, C.E., Gärdenfors, P., Makinson, D.: On the logic of theory change: partial meet contraction and revision functions. J. Symb. Logic **50**, 510–530 (1985). https://doi.org/10.2307/2274239
2. Buhrmester, M.: M-turk guide (2018). https://michaelbuhrmester.wordpress.com/mechanical-turk-guide/
3. Creswell, J.W.: Research Design: Qualitative, Quantitative, and Mixed Methods Approaches, vol. 4, pp. 245–253. SAGE Publications, Thousand Oaks (2014)
4. Darwiche, A., Pearl, J.: On the logic of iterated belief revision. Artif. Intell. **89**, 1–29 (1997). https://doi.org/10.1016/S0004-3702(96)00038-0
5. Gärdenfors, P., Makinson, D.: Nonmonotonic inference based on expectations. Artif. Intell. **65**(2), 197–245 (1994)
6. Gärdenfors, P.: Belief Revision: An Introduction, pp. 1–26. Cambridge University Press, Cambridge (1992). https://doi.org/10.1017/CBO9780511526664.001
7. Governatori, G., Terenziani, P.: Temporal extensions to defeasible logic. In: Orgun, M.A., Thornton, J. (eds.) AI 2007. LNCS (LNAI), vol. 4830, pp. 476–485. Springer, Heidelberg (2007). https://doi.org/10.1007/978-3-540-76928-6_49
8. Hansson, S.: A Textbook of Belief Dynamics: Theory Change and Database Updating. Kluwer Academic Publishers, Berlin (1999)
9. Herzig, A., Rifi, O.: Update operations: a review. In: Prade, H. (ed.) Proceedings of the 13th European Conference on Artificial Intelligence, pp. 13–17. John Wiley & Sons, Ltd., New York (1998)
10. Inc., A.M.T.: Faqs (2018). https://www.mturk.com/help

11. Katsuno, H., Mendelzon, A.O.: On the difference between updating a knowledge base and revising it. In: Proceedings of the Second International Conference on Principles of Knowledge Representation and Reasoning, KR 1991, pp. 387–394. Morgan Kaufmann Publishers Inc., San Francisco (1991). http://dl.acm.org/citation.cfm?id=3087158.3087197

12. Kennedy, R., Clifford, S., Burleigh, T., Jewell, R., Waggoner, P.: The shape of and solutions to the MTurk quality crisis, October 2018

13. Kraus, S., Lehmann, D., Magidor, M.: Nonmonotonic reasoning, preferential models and cumulative logics. Artif. Intell. **44**, 167–207 (1990)

14. Krosnich, J., Presser, S.: Question and questionnaire design. Handbook of Survey Research, March 2009

15. Lang, J.: Belief update revisited. In: Proceedings of the 20th International Joint Conference on Artificial Intelligence, IJCAI 2007, pp. 1534–1540, 2517–2522. Morgan Kaufmann Publishers Inc., San Francisco (2007). http://dl.acm.org/citation.cfm?id=1625275.1625681

16. Lehmann, D.: Another perspective on default reasoning. Ann. Math. Artif. Intell. **15**(1), 61–82 (1995). https://doi.org/10.1007/BF01535841

17. Lieto, A., Minieri, A., Piana, A., Radicioni, D.: A knowledge-based system for prototypical reasoning. Connect. Sci. **27**(2), 137–152 (2015). https://doi.org/10.1080/09540091.2014.956292

18. Makinson, D.: Bridges between classical and nonmonotonic logic. Logic J. IGPL **11**(1), 69–96 (2003)

19. Martins, J., Shapiro, S.: A model for belief revision. Artif. Intell. **35**, 25–79 (1988). https://doi.org/10.1016/0004-3702(88)90031-8

20. Over, D.: Rationality and the normative/descriptive distinction. In: Koehler, D.J., Harvey, N. (eds.) Blackwell Handbook of Judgment and Decision Making, pp. 3–18. Blackwell Publishing Ltd., United States (2004)

21. Pelletier, F., Elio, R.: The case for psychologism in default and inheritance reasoning. Synthese **146**, 7–35 (2005). https://doi.org/10.1007/s11229-005-9063-z

22. Peppas, P.: Belief revision. In: Harmelen, F., Lifschitz, V., Porter, B. (eds.) Handbook of Knowledge Representation. Elsevier Science, December 2008. https://doi.org/10.1016/S1574-6526(07)03008-8

23. Pollock, J.: A theory of defeasible reasoning. Int. J. Intell. Syst. **6**, 33–54 (1991)

24. Ragni, M., Eichhorn, C., Bock, T., Kern-Isberner, G., Tse, A.P.P.: Formal nonmonotonic theories and properties of human defeasible reasoning. Minds Mach. **27**(1), 79–117 (2017). https://doi.org/10.1007/s11023-016-9414-1

25. Ragni, M., Eichhorn, C., Kern-Isberner, G.: Simulating human inferences in light of new information: a formal analysis. In: Kambhampati, S. (ed.) Proceedings of the Twenty-Fifth International Joint Conference on Artificial Intelligence (IJCAI 16), pp. 2604–2610. IJCAI Press (2016)

26. Ross, J., Zaldivar, A., Irani, L., Tomlinson, B.: Who are the turkers? Worker demographics in Amazon mechanical turk, January 2009

27. Rott, H.: Change, Choice and Inference: A Study of Belief Revision and Nonmonotonic Reasoning. Oxford University Press (2001)

28. Sullivan, G., Artino, R., Artino, J.: Analyzing and interpreting data from likert-type scales. J. Grad. Med. Educ. **5**(4), 541–542 (2013)

29. Turk, A.M.: Qualifications and worker task quality best practices, April 2019. https://blog.mturk.com/qualifications-and-worker-task-quality-best-practices-886f1f4e03fc

30. TurkPrime: After the bot scare: Understanding what's been happening with data collection on mturk and how to stop it September 2018. https://blog.turkprime.com/after-the-bot-scare-understanding-whats-been-happening-with-data-collection-on-mturk-and-how-to-stop-it
31. Verheij, B.: Correct grounded reasoning with presumptive arguments. In: Michael, L., Kakas, A. (eds.) JELIA 2016. LNCS (LNAI), vol. 10021, pp. 481–496. Springer, Cham (2016). https://doi.org/10.1007/978-3-319-48758-8_31
32. Witte, J.: Introduction to the special issue on web surveys. Sociol. Methods Res. **37**(3), 283–290 (2009)

A Taxonomy of Explainable Bayesian Networks

Iena Petronella Derks[1](✉) (iD) and Alta de Waal[1,2] (iD)

[1] Department of Statistics, University of Pretoria, Pretoria, South Africa
inekederks1@gmail.com
[2] Center for Artificial Intelligence Research (CAIR), Pretoria, South Africa

Abstract. Artificial Intelligence (AI), and in particular, the explainability thereof, has gained phenomenal attention over the last few years. Whilst we usually do not question the decision-making process of these systems in situations where only the outcome is of interest, we do however pay close attention when these systems are applied in areas where the decisions directly influence the lives of humans. It is especially noisy and uncertain observations close to the decision boundary which results in predictions which cannot necessarily be explained that may foster mistrust among end-users. This drew attention to AI methods for which the outcomes can be explained. Bayesian networks are probabilistic graphical models that can be used as a tool to manage uncertainty. The probabilistic framework of a Bayesian network allows for explainability in the model, reasoning and evidence. The use of these methods is mostly ad hoc and not as well organised as explainability methods in the wider AI research field. As such, we introduce a taxonomy of explainability in Bayesian networks. We extend the existing categorisation of explainability in the model, reasoning or evidence to include explanation of decisions. The explanations obtained from the explainability methods are illustrated by means of a simple medical diagnostic scenario. The taxonomy introduced in this paper has the potential not only to encourage end-users to efficiently communicate outcomes obtained, but also support their understanding of how and, more importantly, why certain predictions were made.

Keywords: Bayesian network · Reasoning · Explainability

1 Introduction

Advances in technology have contributed to the generation of big data in nearly all fields of science, giving rise to new challenges with respect to explainability of models and techniques used to analyse such data. These models and techniques are often too complex; concealing the knowledge within the machine, hence decreasing the extent of interpretability of results. Subsequently, the lack of explainable models and techniques contribute to mistrust among users in fields of science where interpretability and explainability are indispensable.

© Springer Nature Switzerland AG 2020
A. Gerber (Ed.): SACAIR 2020, CCIS 1342, pp. 220–235, 2020.
https://doi.org/10.1007/978-3-030-66151-9_14

To elucidate the need for explainable models, consider the following three scenarios. Firstly, suppose a medical diagnosis system is used to determine whether a tumour sample is malignant or benign. Here, the medical practitioner must be able to understand how and why the system reached the decision, and, if necessary, inspect whether the decision is supported by medical knowledge [2]. Next, consider self-driving cars. In this context, the self-driving car must be able to process information faster than a human, such that accidents and fatalities can be avoided [21]. Suppose a self-driving car is involved in an accident, then the system must be able to explain that in order to avoid hitting a pedestrian, the only option was to swerve out of the way and, by coincidence, into another vehicle. Lastly, consider an online restaurant review system, where reviews are classified as positive or negative based on the words contained in the review. Here, the classifier simply returns whether a review is positive or negative, without explaining which words contributed to the classification. As such, negative reviews that are expressed in, for example, a sarcastic manner, might be classified as positive, resulting in a restaurant receiving a higher rating and more diners – who might experience bad service (or even food poisoning) as a result of mislabelled reviews.

Given its relevance in many application areas, the explainability problem has attracted a great deal of attention in recent years, and as such, is an open research area [24]. The manifestation of explainable systems in high-risk areas has influenced the development of explainable artificial intelligence (XAI) in the sense of prescriptions or taxonomies of explanation. These include fairness, accountability, transparency and ethicality [3,11,23]. The foundation of such a system should include these prescriptions such that a level of usable intelligence is reached to not only understand model behaviour [1] but also understand the context of an application task [14]. Bayesian networks (BNs) – which lie at the intersection of AI, machine learning, and statistics – are probabilistic graphical models that can be used as a tool to manage uncertainty. These graphical models allow the user to reason about uncertainty in the problem domain by updating ones beliefs, whether this reasoning occurs from cause to effect, or from effect to cause. Reasoning in Bayesian networks is often referred to as what-if questions. The flexibility of a Bayesian network allows for these questions to be predictive, diagnostic and inter-causal. Some what-if questions might be intuitive to formulate, but this is not always the case especially on a diagnostic and inter-causal level. This might result in sub-optimal use of explainability in BNs - especially on an end-user level. Apart from well-established reasoning methods, the probabilistic framework of a Bayesian network also allows for explainability in evidence. These include most probable explanation and most relevant explanation. To extend on the existing explainability methods, we propose an additional approach which considers explanations concerned with the decision-base.

In this paper, we research the current state of explainable models in AI and machine learning tasks, where the domain of interest is BNs. In the current research, explanation is often done by principled approaches to finding explanations for models, reasoning, and evidence. Using this, we are able to formulate a taxonomy of explainable BNs. We extend this taxonomy to include explanation of decisions. This taxonomy will provide end-users with a set of tools to better understand predictions made by BNs and will therefore encourage efficient communication between end-users. The paper is structured as follows. We first investigate the community and scope of explainability methods in Sect. 2. Thereafter, we introduce explanation in BNs, which includes the formulation of principled approaches, the theoretical properties associated therewith and a hands-on medical diagnosis example. Section 4 presents our newly formulated taxonomy of explainable BNs. The final section concludes the paper and includes a short discussion of future work.

2 Related Work

In application areas where erroneous decisions have a direct impact on livelihood, relying on systems where the predictions cannot be explained may not be an option. Explainability in such systems aids in establishing trust in not only circumstances where the system is used as a primary decision tool, but also cases where the system takes on a supportive role [28].

Over the past few years, explainability in AI systems has gained immense attention from the research community. This is reflected in the launch of various events and organisations. The Defense Advanced Research Projects Agency (DARPA) launched the Explainable Artificial Intelligence (XAI) initiative in 2016. The XAI programs intention is to encourage the production of AI techniques where emphasis is placed on developing more accurate and precise models, while still maintaining a high level of explainability. Ultimately, XAI systems must be able to explain their rationale and enable understanding [12]. Conferences, such as the International Joint Conferences on Artificial Intelligence (IJCAI) conducts workshops specifically focusing on XAI [26]. This topic has also made a noticeable appearance at the Neural Information Processing Systems (NeurIPS) conference, with panel discussions solely concentrating on XAI.

The scope of explainability is inherently linked to the complexity of the model, as well as the goal thereof. Usually, but not necessarily, there is a trade-off between model accuracy and explainability – the higher the accuracy, the lower the explainability [31]. For example, decision trees provide a clear explanation but are often less accurate than deep learning models, which are less transparent. It should be mentioned that this trade-off is also connected to the quality of data. AI and machine learning models that are transparent by design, such as linear regression, decision trees and k-nearest neighbours, convey a degree of explainability [1]. However, when AI and machine learning models do not provide clear explanations, separate explainability methods are applied to the model to gain meaningful explanations. Methods of explainability are not limited to the behaviour of the model or decision-making process as a whole, and may be applied to single instances, predictions or decisions [6]. These explanations can be in the form of visualisations or natural language [10]. Some of the existing explainability methods are layer-wise relevance propagation (LRP), which are often used in deep neural networks where the prediction made by the network is propagated back into the neural network using a set of predefined rules [27]. Another explainability method is local interpretable model-agnostic explanations (LIME). LIME methods can be used to explain prediction instances by attempting to understand the behaviour of the prediction function in the context of the prediction. Here, the user is able to obtain a local explanation for that particular instance. LIME can also be used to obtain explanations for the entire model by generating multiple instances [17]. Methods of explainability are also extended to document classifiers, where documents are classified based on predicted likelihood. Here, explanations can be produced based on a search through the text-space of possible word combinations – starting with a single word and expanding the number of words until an explanation is found [25].

Uncertainty is present in the majority of AI fields, such as knowledge representation, learning and reasoning [22]. Real-world data often contain noisy and uncertain observations close to the decision boundary, which may result in predictions that cannot be explained [7]. Probabilistic graphical models can be seen as uncertainty management tools as they are able to represent and reason with uncertainty. These probabilistic models are often employed to support decision making in various application fields, including legal and medical applications [29]. One such probabilistic model is BNs, which is capable of combining expert knowledge and statistical data, therefore allowing for complex scenarios to be modelled. However, not only are the inner workings of Bayesian networks complicated to most end-users [15], the explanation of probabilistic reasoning is challenging and as such results appear to be counter-intuitive or wrong [16]. Therefore, there exists a demand for explanation in Bayesian networks.

Explanation methods for Bayesian networks can be divided into three broad approaches. The first approach consists of presenting information contained in the knowledge base and is known as *explanation of the model*. There are two objectives associated with this type of explanation. Firstly, explanation of the model is used to assist application experts in the model-construction phase. Secondly, it is used for instructional purposes to offer knowledge about the domain [19]. The objective of the second approach is to justify the conclusion and how it was obtained. This approach is referred to as *explanation of reasoning* [9]. The final approach, *explanation of evidence*, is concerned with the treatment of the variables in the Bayesian network [13]. In explanation of evidence, also referred to as *abduction*, an explanation is seen as the configuration of a portion of the variables present in the Bayesian network, given evidence. Not included in the aforementioned explanation methods are techniques that describe whether the end-user is ready to make a decision, and if not, what additional information is required to better prepare for decision making. Techniques such as sensitivity analysis [4] and same-decision probability [5] provide the end-user with insight on decisions. We group these methods into a fourth approach, *explanation of decisions*. For the purpose of this paper, and accordingly, the formulation of the explainable taxonomy, we only consider explanation of reasoning, evidence, and decisions. Explanation of the model is excluded from this taxonomy – at the time being – as the intent of the taxonomy is to support understanding of how and why predictions were made and not on the model-construction itself.

3   Explainable Bayesian Networks

We adapt the XAI terminology to the scope of BNs by defining the term XBN and thereby referring to explainable BNs. To illustrate XBN in Bayesian networks, consider the Asia network from Lauritzen and Spiegelhalter (1988) [20] as an example.

Example Statement: Suppose a patient visits a doctor, complaining about shortness of breath (dyspnoea) (**D**). The patient is worried he might have lung cancer. The doctor knows that lung cancer is only one of the possible causes for dyspnoea, and other causes include bronchitis (**B**) and tuberculosis (**T**). From her training, the doctor knows that smoking increases the probability of lung cancer (**C**) and bronchitis. Both tuberculosis and lung cancer would result in an abnormal X-ray (**X**) result. Lastly, a recent visit to Asia might increase the probability of tuberculosis, as the disease is more prevalent there than the patient's country of origin.

From this example statement, the nodes and values are defined and then the graphical structure of the BN is constructed. This is followed by the quantification of the conditional probability tables (CPTs) for each node [18][1]. The final BN is illustrated in Fig. 1. Now that the domain and uncertainty are represented in the BN, we will look into how to use the BN. Reasoning in BNs takes place once we observe the value of one or more variables and we want to condition on this new information [18]. It is important to note that this information need not necessarily flow in the direction of the arcs, and therefore, reasoning can occur in the opposite direction of the arcs.

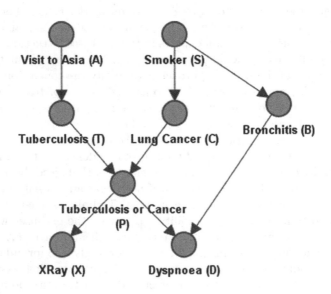

Fig. 1. Asia Bayesian network

---

[1] All BN models are constructed in BayesiaLab (www.bayesialab.com).

3.1   Explanation of Reasoning

Suppose during the doctor's appointment, the patient tells the doctor he is a smoker before any symptoms are assessed. As mentioned earlier, the doctor knows smoking increases the probability of the patient having lung cancer and bronchitis. This will, in turn, also influence the expectation of other symptoms, such as the result of the chest X-Ray and shortness of breath. Here, our reasoning is performed from new information about the causes to new beliefs of the effects. This type of reasoning is referred to as **predictive reasoning** and follows the direction of the arcs in the network. Through predictive reasoning, we are interested in questions concerning *what will happen*. In some cases, predictive reasoning is not of great insight and it is often required to reason from symptoms (effect) to cause, which entails information flow in the opposite direction to the network arcs. For example, bronchitis can be seen as an effect of smoking. Accordingly, we are interested in computing $P(S|B)$. This is referred to as **diagnostic reasoning** and is typically used in situations where we want to determine *what went wrong*. The final type of probabilistic reasoning in BNs is **inter-causal reasoning**, which relates to mutual causes of a common effect – typically indicated by a v-structure in the network. In other words, inference is performed on the parent nodes of a shared child node. Note that the parent nodes are independent of one another unless the shared child node is observed, a concept known as *d-separation*. From the Asia network, we observe a v-structure between Tuberculosis, Lung Cancer and Tuberculosis or Cancer (see Fig. 2a). Here, Tuberculosis is independent from Lung cancer. Suppose we observe the patient has either Tuberculosis or Cancer – indicated by the green (or light grey if viewed in grey-scale) bar in Fig. 2b – then this observation increases the probabilities of the parent nodes, Tuberculosis and Lung Cancer. However, if it is then revealed that the patient does, in fact, have Tuberculosis it, in turn, lowers the probability of a patient having Lung Cancer (see Fig. 2c). We can then say Lung Cancer has been *explained away*. It should be noted that the probabilistic reasoning methods discussed above can be used as is, or can be combined to accommodate the problem at hand.

3.2   Explanation of Evidence

Sometimes, users of the system find the results of reasoning unclear or questionable. One way to address this is to provide scenarios for which the reasoning outcomes are upheld. A fully specified scenario is easier to understand than a set of reasoning outcomes. Explanation of evidence methods are useful in specifying these scenarios. They are based on the posterior probability and the generalised Bayes factor. Firstly, we focus on methods that aim to find a configuration of variables such that the posterior probability is maximised given the evidence. Here, we consider the Most Probable Explanation (MPE), which is a special case of the Maximum A Posteriori (MAP). The MAP in a BN is a variable configuration which includes a subset of unobserved variables in the explanation set

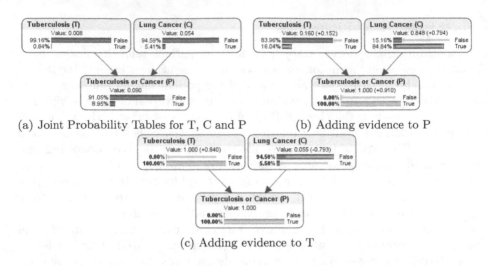

(a) Joint Probability Tables for T, C and P   (b) Adding evidence to P

(c) Adding evidence to T

Fig. 2. Belief updating for T, C and P

such that the posterior probability – given evidence – is maximised. Similarly, if the variable configuration consists of all variables present in the explanation set, we have an MPE solution [13]. However, in some real-world applications, the variable set often consists of a large number of variables, which may result in over-specified or under-specified explanations obtained from the MPE. In fact, only a few variables may be relevant in explaining the evidence. The next approach finds a single instantiation that maximises the generalised Bayes factor in a trans-dimensional space containing all possible partial instantiations. In other words, this approach aims to obtain an explanation only consisting of the most relevant variables in the BN, given the evidence. This approach is known as the Most Relevant Explanation (MRE) [32–34].

Most Probable Explanation. Let's first consider the MPE method. Recall that the MPE finds the complete instantiation of the target variables – which are defined to be unobserved – such that the joint posterior probability is maximised given evidence. Figure 3 shows the scenario (or case) that has the highest joint probability in the Asia network. Note here the probabilities are replaced by the likelihood of the variable state belonging to the most probable scenario, for example, if we look at the two possible states for Bronchitis, we see that 'False', i.e., the patient does not have bronchitis, is more probable. Suppose we discover the patient suffers from shortness of breath, we can then set the evidence for Dyspnoea as 'True' (illustrated in Fig. 4). By introducing this new evidence, we now observe a slightly different scenario, where it is more probable for the patient to be a smoker and have bronchitis. Notice here that variables that seem irrelevant to the evidence explanation, such as Visit to Asia and XRay, are included in the explanation. This could lead to overspecified hypotheses, especially in larger networks.

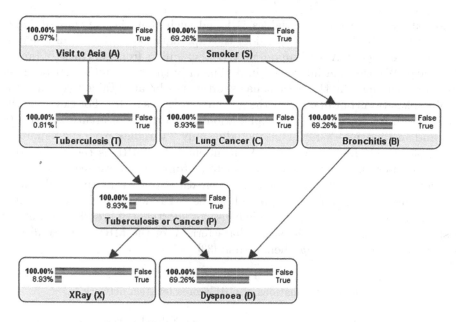

Fig. 3. Initial MPE for Asia Bayesian network

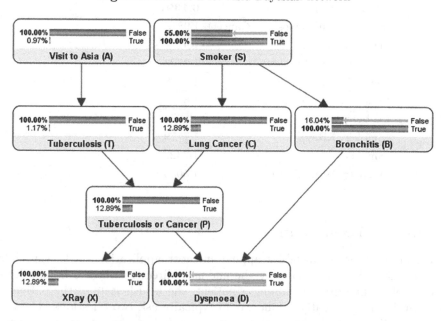

Fig. 4. Updated MPE for Asia Bayesian network

Most Relevant Explanation. To avoid an overspecified hypotheses, one approach is to trim or prune less relevant variables from the explanation. That is, instead of finding the complete instantiation of the target variables, a partial instantiation of the target variables is found such that the *generalised Bayes factor* is maximised. Let's first consider the explanations obtained from the generalised Bayes factor. Again, suppose the patient suffers from shortness of breath (evidence). We are then interested in finding only those variables that are relevant in explaining why the patient has shortness of breath. Table 1 contains the set of explanations obtained from the generalised Bayes factor. For example, the last entry shows that a possible explanation for shortness of breath is a trip to Asia and an abnormal X-ray. Thus including only 2 variables from the remaining 7 variables (excluding Dyspnoea). As mentioned, the MRE is the explanation that maximises the generalised Bayes factor. From Table 1 we see that having Bronchitis best explains the shortness of breath. Notice that this explanation does not include Smoking, as opposed to the MPE which included Smoking. Thus, although smoking is a probable cause for shortness of breath, it is not the most relevant cause. An interesting characteristic of the MRE is its ability to capture the *explaining away* phenomenon [33].

Table 1. Explanations of GBF scores for Asia network

Explanation	Generalised Bayes factor
(Bronchitis)	**6.1391**
(Smoker, Tuberculosis or Cancer)	1.9818
(Tuberculosis or Cancer)	1.9771
(Lung Cancer, Smoker)	1.9723
(Lung Cancer)	1.9678
(Smoker, Tuberculosis)	1.8896
(Tuberculosis)	1.8276
(Smoker, XRay)	1.7779
(Smoker)	1.7322
(Visit to Asia, XRay)	1.5635

3.3   Explanation of Decisions

Hidden or unobserved variables appear in most application fields, especially in areas where decisions made by the end-user directly influence human lives. For example, when first examining a patient, the health-state of the patient is unknown. In these situations, one would typically ask two questions. The first being *given the available information, are we ready to make a decision?* and secondly, *if we are not yet ready to make a decision, what additional information do we require to make an informed decision?*. To answer these questions, the authors of [5] propose a threshold-based notion, named *same-decision probability*, which provides the user with a confidence measure that represents the probability that a certain decision will be made, had information pertaining unknown variables been made available. Another possible threshold-based solution to this is sensitivity analysis [30]. In sensitivity analysis, the assessments for the conditional probabilities in the BN are systematically changed to study the effect on the output produced by the network. The idea is that some conditional probabilities will hardly influence the decisions, while others will have significant impact.

Same-Decision Probability. Suppose we are interested in making a decision on whether the patient is a smoker (Smoking), which is conditioned on evidence Tuberculosis or Cancer. We can then use the BN such that our decision pertaining to the hypothesis is supported on the basis that the belief in the hypothesis given some evidence exceeds a given threshold. Now, the patient may have access to information that is unknown to us, for example, the patient recently visited Asia and chose not to disclose this information. Therefore, we do not have access to the true state of this variable. The true state knowledge may confirm or contradict our decision based on the probability of smoking given some evidence and the patient visiting Asia. If we now compare this probability with some threshold, we have a degree of confidence in our original decision regarding smoking and the available evidence. Had the patient disclosed his trip to Asia, it is then unlikely that we would have made a different decision. Hence, we can make use of the same-decision probability (SDP). Consider now the BN given in Fig. 5. Notice here the addition of three nodes, *P(Smoker = True)*, *Decision Threshold* and *Decision*. Where *P(Smoker = True)* represents the hypothesis probability and the decision threshold is set to 55%. Suppose now we update our network such that Tuberculosis or Cancer (P) is True – to reflect the scenario discussed above. The hypothesis probability then increases from 50.00% to 84.35% (see Fig. 6). Our decision is confirmed given the threshold since the hypothesis probability now exceeds the given threshold value. From Table 2, the SDP before adding evidence for the 'True' state is 0.00%. After adding evidence, the SDP for our decision is 83.88%, indicating that our decision confidence is 83.88%[2].

Table 2. Decision confidence for Asia network

	States	Minimum	Maximum	Mean	Standard deviation
No evidence	False	100.00%	100.00%	100.00%	0.00%
	True	0.00%	0.00%	0.00%	0.00%
Evidence	False	0.00%	100.00%	16.12%	36.77%
	True	0.00%	100.00%	83.88%	36.77%

---

[2] The SDP scenario was constructed using the decision node functionality in Bayesialab. The decision nodes are indicated as green (or dark grey if viewed in grey-scale).

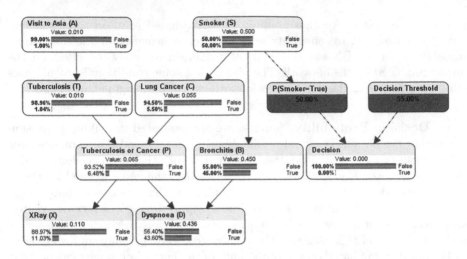

Fig. 5. Addition of decision node in Asia network

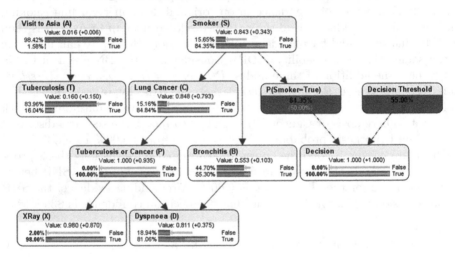

Fig. 6. Updated decision for Asia network

4   XBN in Action

The point of XBN is to explain the AI task at hand. In other words, the question the decision-maker seeks to answer, and not the technique in principle. Therefore, we need to be able to freely ask 'why' or 'what' and from this select a method that would best address the AI task. In Fig. 7 we present a taxonomy of XBN. The purpose of this taxonomy is to categorise XBN methods into four phases of BNs: The first phase involves the construction of the BN model. Explanation in the 'model' phase is critical when the model is based on expert knowledge. The second phase is reasoning, the third phase evidence, and the fourth decision. Explanation of the model and sensitivity analysis are illustrated in grey as it is out of scope for this paper. Although we define the taxonomy along these phases, we do acknowledge that not all phases are necessarily utilised by the decision-maker. For example, when using BNs to facilitate participatory modelling [8], the main emphasis is on explaining the model. Or, when using BNs as a classifier, the emphasis is on explaining the decisions. In this section, we present typical questions of interest to the decision-maker in each category of the XBN taxonomy.

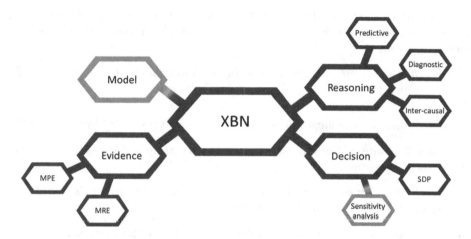

Fig. 7. A schematic view of XBN

4.1 Reasoning

Reasoning in the XBN taxonomy is concerned with the justification of a conclusion. Returning to our Asia example, the end-user might ask the following question,

> "*Given the patient recently visited Asia, how likely is an abnormal chest X-Ray?*"

Here, we are concerned with a single outcome: the X-Ray result. On the other hand, the doctor may have knowledge about symptoms presented by the patient and ask,

> "*What is the probability of a patient being a smoker, given that he presented shortness of breath?*"

We can extend this to a forensic context. Suppose a crime scene is investigated where a severely burned body is found. The forensic analyst can then ask,

> "*The burn victim is found with a protruded tongue, was the victim exposed to fire before death or after?*"

Consider now a financial service context where a young prospective home owner is declined a loan. The service provider can then ask,

"Did the prospective owner not qualify for the home loan because of his age?"

From these examples, we see that explanation of reasoning is used where questions are asked in the context of single variable outcomes for diagnosis.

4.2 Evidence

When we are interested in the subset of variables that describes specific scenarios, we use explanation of evidence methods. For example, in our Asia example the doctor may ask,

"Which diseases are most probable to the symptoms presented by the patient?"

or

"Which diseases are most relevant to the symptoms presented by the patient?"

In a forensic context, the forensic analyst investigating a crime scene may ask the following question,

"What are the most relevant causes of death, given the victim is found with a severely burned body and protruded tongue?"

Similarly this can be applied to fraud detection. Suppose the analyst investigates the credit card transactions of a consumer. The analyst can then ask,

"What are the most probable transaction features that contributed to the flagging of this consumer?"

Explanation of evidence can also be used to provide explanations for financial service circumstances. For example, if a prospective home owner is turned down for a loan, he may ask the service provider which features in his risk profile are more relevant (contributed most) to being turned down.

4.3 Decisions

Explanation of decisions typically asks the following questions *"Do we have enough evidence to make a decision?"*, and if not, *"what additional evidence is required to make a decision?"*. For example, in our Asia example we can ask,

"Do we have enough evidence on the symptoms presented to make a decision on the disease?"

or

"Since we are not yet able to determine the disease, what additional information – test, underlying symptoms, comorbidities – is required to make a decision?"

Applied to forensic investigations, this can be used to answer questions relating to crime scene investigations. The analyst may ask questions regarding the actual evidence collected from the crime scene, i.e., if enough evidence is collected to rule a crime as a homicide or what additional evidence is required to rule the crime as a homicide. Should they investigate further or is the evidence that is already collected enough to make an informed decision?

5 Conclusion

The development of AI systems has faced incredible advances in recent years. We are now exposed to these systems on a daily basis, such as product recommendation systems used by online retailers. However, these systems are also being implemented by medical practitioners, forensic analysts and financial services – application areas where decisions directly influence the lives of humans. It is because of these high-risk application areas that progressively more interest is given to the explainability of these systems.

This paper addresses the problem of explainability in BNs. We first explored the state of explainable AI and in particular BNs, which serves as a foundation for our XBN framework. We then presented a taxonomy to categorise XBN methods in order to emphasise the benefits of each method given a specific usage of the BN model. This XBN taxonomy will serve as a guideline, which will enable end-users to understand how and why predictions were made and will, therefore, be able to better communicate how outcomes were obtained based on these predictions.

The XBN taxonomy consists of explanation of reasoning, evidence and decisions. Explanation of the model is reserved for future work, since the taxonomy described in this paper is focused on how and why predictions were made and not on the model-construction phase. Other future research endeavours include the addition of more dimensions and methods to the XBN taxonomy – this involves more statistical-based methods and the incorporation of causability (which also addresses the quality of explanations) – as well as applying this taxonomy to real-world applications.

References

1. Barredo Arrieta, A., et al.: Explainable artificial Intelligence (XAI): concepts, taxonomies, opportunities and challenges toward responsible AI. Inf. Fusion **58**, 82–115 (2020). https://doi.org/10.1016/j.inffus.2019.12.012
2. Brito-Sarracino, T., dos Santos, M.R., Antunes, E.F., de Andrade Santos, I.B., Kasmanas, J.C., de Leon Ferreira, A.C.P., et al.: Explainable machine learning for breast cancer diagnosis. In: 2019 8th Brazilian Conference on Intelligent Systems (BRACIS), pp. 681–686. IEEE (2019)
3. Cath, C.: Governing artificial intelligence: ethical, legal and technical opportunities and challenges. Philos. Trans. R. Soc. Math. Phys. Eng. Sci. **376**(2133) (2018). https://doi.org/10.1098/rsta.2018.0080

4. Chan, H., Darwiche, A.: On the robustness of most probable explanations. In: Proceedings of the 22nd Conference on Uncertainty in Artificial Intelligence, UAI 2006, June 2012
5. Choi, A., Xue, Y., Darwiche, A.: Same-decision probability: a confidence measure for threshold-based decisions. Int. Int. J. Approximate Reasoning **53**(9), 1415–1428 (2012)
6. Das, A., Rad, P.: Opportunities and Challenges in Explainable Artificial Intelligence (XAI): A Survey. arXiv preprint arXiv:2006.11371 (2020)
7. De Waal, A., Steyn, C.: Uncertainty measurements in neural network predictions for classification tasks. In: 2020 IEEE 23rd International Conference on Information Fusion (FUSION), pp. 1–7. IEEE (2020)
8. Düspohl, M., Frank, S., Döll, P.: A review of Bayesian networks as a participatory modeling approach in support of sustainable environmental management. J. Sustain. Dev. **5**(12), 1 (2012). https://doi.org/10.5539/jsd.v5n12p1
9. Gallego, M.J.F.: Bayesian networks inference: Advanced algorithms for triangulation and partial abduction (2005)
10. Goebel, R., et al.: Explainable AI: the new 42? In: Holzinger, A., Kieseberg, P., Tjoa, A.M., Weippl, E. (eds.) CD-MAKE 2018. LNCS, vol. 11015, pp. 295–303. Springer, Cham (2018). https://doi.org/10.1007/978-3-319-99740-7_21
11. Greene, D., Hoffmann, A.L., Stark, L.: Better, nicer, clearer, fairer: a critical assessment of the movement for ethical artificial intelligence and machine learning. In: Proceedings of the 52nd Hawaii International Conference on System Sciences, pp. 2122–2131 (2019). https://doi.org/10.24251/hicss.2019.258
12. Gunning, D., Aha, D.W.: DARPA's explainable artificial intelligence program. AI Mag. **40**(2), 44–58 (2019)
13. Helldin, T., Riveiro, M.: Explanation methods for Bayesian networks: review and application to a maritime scenario. In: Proceedings of The 3rd Annual Skövde Workshop on Information Fusion Topics, SWIFT, pp. 11–16 (2009)
14. Holzinger, A., et al.: Towards the Augmented Pathologist: Challenges of Explainable-AI in Digital Pathology. arXiv preprint arXiv:1712.06657 pp. 1–34 (2017). http://arxiv.org/abs/1712.06657
15. Keppens, J.: Explaining Bayesian belief revision for legal applications. In: JURIX, pp. 63–72 (2016)
16. Keppens, J.: Explainable Bayesian network query results via natural language generation systems. In: Proceedings of the Seventeenth International Conference on Artificial Intelligence and Law, pp. 42–51 (2019)
17. Khedkar, S., Subramanian, V., Shinde, G., Gandhi, P.: Explainable AI in healthcare. In: Healthcare (April 8, 2019). 2nd International Conference on Advances in Science and Technology (ICAST) (2019)
18. Korb, K.B., Nicholson, A.E.: Bayesian Artificial Intelligence. CRC Press, Boca Raton (2010)
19. Lacave, C., Díez, F.J.: A review of explanation methods for Bayesian networks. Knowl. Eng. Rev. **17**(2), 107–127 (2002). https://doi.org/10.1017/S026988890200019X
20. Lauritzen, S.L., Spiegelhalter, D.J.: Local computations with probabilities on graphical structures and their application to expert systems. J. R. Stat. Soc. Seri. B (Methodological) **50**(2), 157–194 (1988)
21. Lawless, W.F., Mittu, R., Sofge, D., Hiatt, L.: Artificial intelligence, autonomy, and human-machine teams: interdependence, context, and explainable AI. AI Mag. **40**(3), 5–13 (2019)

22. Lecue, F.: On the role of knowledge graphs in explainable AI. Seman. Web **11**(1), 41–51 (2020)
23. Leslie, D.: Understanding artificial intelligence ethics and safety: A guide for the responsible design and implementation of AI systems in the public sector (2019). https://doi.org/10.5281/zenodo.3240529
24. Lipton, Z.C.: The mythos of model interpretability. Queue **16**(3), 31–57 (2018)
25. Martens, D., Provost, F.: Explaining data-driven document classifications. MIS Q. **38**(1), 73–100 (2014)
26. Miller, T., Weber, R., Magazzeni, D.: Proceedings of the IJCAI 2019 Workshop on Explainable AI (2019)
27. Montavon, G., Binder, A., Lapuschkin, S., Samek, W., Müller, K.-R.: Layer-wise relevance propagation: an overview. In: Samek, W., Montavon, G., Vedaldi, A., Hansen, L.K., Müller, K.-R. (eds.) Explainable AI: Interpreting, Explaining and Visualizing Deep Learning. LNCS (LNAI), vol. 11700, pp. 193–209. Springer, Cham (2019). https://doi.org/10.1007/978-3-030-28954-6_10
28. Samek, W., Müller, K.-R.: Towards explainable artificial intelligence. In: Samek, W., Montavon, G., Vedaldi, A., Hansen, L.K., Müller, K.-R. (eds.) Explainable AI: Interpreting, Explaining and Visualizing Deep Learning. LNCS (LNAI), vol. 11700, pp. 5–22. Springer, Cham (2019). https://doi.org/10.1007/978-3-030-28954-6_1
29. Timmer, S.T., Meyer, J.J.C., Prakken, H., Renooij, S., Verheij, B.: A two-phase method for extracting explanatory arguments from Bayesian networks. International Journal of Approximate Reasoning **80**, 475–494 (2017)
30. van der Gaag, L.C., Coupé, V.M.H.: Sensitivity analysis for threshold decision making with Bayesian belief networks. In: Lamma, E., Mello, P. (eds.) AI*IA 1999. LNCS (LNAI), vol. 1792, pp. 37–48. Springer, Heidelberg (2000). https://doi.org/10.1007/3-540-46238-4_4
31. Xu, F., Uszkoreit, H., Du, Y., Fan, W., Zhao, D., Zhu, J.: Explainable AI: a brief survey on history, research areas, approaches and challenges. In: Tang, J., Kan, M.-Y., Zhao, D., Li, S., Zan, H. (eds.) NLPCC 2019, Part II. LNCS (LNAI), vol. 11839, pp. 563–574. Springer, Cham (2019). https://doi.org/10.1007/978-3-030-32236-6_51
32. Yuan, C.: Some properties of most relevant explanation. In: ExaCt, pp. 118–126 (2009)
33. Yuan, C., Lim, H., Lu, T.C.: Most relevant explanation in Bayesian networks. J. Artif. Intell. Res. **42**, 309–352 (2011). https://doi.org/10.1613/jair.3301
34. Yuan, C., Liu, X., Lu, T.C., Lim, H.: Most relevant explanation: Properties, algorithms, and evaluations. In: Proceedings of the 25th Conference on Uncertainty in Artificial Intelligence, UAI 2009, pp. 631–638 (2009)

A Boolean Extension of KLM-Style Conditional Reasoning

Guy Paterson-Jones[1]([⊠])([iD]), Giovanni Casini[1,2]([iD]), and Thomas Meyer[1]([iD])

[1] CAIR and University of Cape Town, Cape Town, South Africa
guy.paterson.jones@gmail.com, tmeyer@cair.org.za
[2] ISTI-CNR, Pisa, Italy
giovanni.casini@isti.cnr.it

Abstract. Propositional KLM-style defeasible reasoning involves extending propositional logic with a new logical connective that can express defeasible (or conditional) implications, with semantics given by ordered structures known as ranked interpretations. KLM-style defeasible entailment is referred to as rational whenever the defeasible entailment relation under consideration generates a set of defeasible implications all satisfying a set of rationality postulates known as the KLM postulates. In a recent paper Booth et al. proposed PTL, a logic that is more expressive than the core KLM logic. They proved an impossibility result, showing that defeasible entailment for PTL fails to satisfy a set of rationality postulates similar in spirit to the KLM postulates. Their interpretation of the impossibility result is that defeasible entailment for PTL need not be unique. In this paper we continue the line of research in which the expressivity of the core KLM logic is extended. We present the logic Boolean KLM (BKLM) in which we allow for disjunctions, conjunctions, and negations, but not nesting, of defeasible implications. Our contribution is twofold. Firstly, we show (perhaps surprisingly) that BKLM is more expressive than PTL. Our proof is based on the fact that BKLM can characterise all single ranked interpretations, whereas PTL cannot. Secondly, given that the PTL impossibility result also applies to BKLM, we adapt the different forms of PTL entailment proposed by Booth et al. to apply to BKLM.

Keywords: Non-monotonic reasoning · Defeasible entailment

1 Introduction

Non-monotonic reasoning has been extensively studied in the AI literature, as it provides a mechanism for making bold inferences that go beyond what classical methods can provide, while retaining the possibility of revising these inferences in light of new information. In their seminal paper, Kraus et al. [14] consider a general framework for non-monotonic reasoning, phrased in terms of *defeasible, or conditional implications* of the form $\alpha \mathrel{|\!\sim} \beta$, to be read as "*If α holds, then typically β holds*". Importantly, they provide a set of *rationality conditions*,

© Springer Nature Switzerland AG 2020
A. Gerber (Ed.): SACAIR 2020, CCIS 1342, pp. 236–252, 2020.
https://doi.org/10.1007/978-3-030-66151-9_15

in the form of structural properties, that a reasonable form of entailment for these conditionals should satisfy, and characterise these semantically. Lehmann and Magidor [16] also considered the question of which entailment relations definable in the KLM framework can be considered to be the *correct* ones for non-monotonic reasoning. In general, there is a large class of entailment relations for KLM-style logics [9], and it is widely agreed upon that there is no unique best answer. The options can be narrowed down, however, and Lehmann et al. propose *Rational Closure* (RC) as the minimally acceptable form of rational entailment. Rational closure is based on the principle of *Presumption of Typicality* [15], which states that propositions should be considered typical unless there is reason to believe otherwise. For instance, if we know that birds typically fly, and all we know about a robin is that it is a bird, we should tentatively conclude that it flies, as there is no reason to believe it is atypical. While RC is not always appropriate, there is fairly general consensus that interesting forms of conditional reasoning should extend RC inferentially [9,15].

Since KLM-style logics have limited conditional expressivity (see Sect. 2.1), there has been some work in extending the KLM constructions to more expressive logics. Perhaps the main question is whether entailment relations resembling RC can also be defined for more expressive logics. The first investigation in such a direction was done by Booth and Paris [4], who consider an extension in which both positive ($\alpha \mathrel{|\!\sim} \beta$) and negative ($\alpha \mathrel{|\!\not\sim} \beta$) conditionals are allowed. Booth et al. [3] later considered a more expressive logic called *Propositional Typicality Logic* (PTL), in which propositional logic is extended with a modal-like typicality operator •. This typicality operator can be used anywhere in a formula, in contrast to KLM-style logics, where typicality refers only to the antecedent of conditionals of the form $\alpha \mathrel{|\!\sim} \beta$.

The price one pays for this expressiveness is that rational entailment becomes more difficult to pin down. This is shown by Booth et al. [2], who prove that several desirable properties of rational closure are mutually inconsistent for PTL entailment. They interpret this as saying that the correct form of entailment for PTL is contextual, and depends on which properties are considered more important for the task at hand.

In this paper we consider a different extension of KLM-style logics, which we refer to as *Boolean KLM* (BKLM), and in which we allow negative conditionals, as well as arbitrary conjunctions and disjunctions of conditionals. We do not allow the nesting of conditionals, though. We show, perhaps surprisingly, that BKLM is strictly more expressive than PTL by exhibiting an explicit translation of PTL knowledge bases into BKLM. We also prove that BKLM entailment is more restrictive than PTL entailment, in the sense that a stronger class of entailment properties are inconsistent for BKLM. In particular, attempts to extend rational closure to BKLM in the manner of LM-entailment as defined by Booth et al. [2], are shown to be untenable.

The rest of the paper is structured as follows. In Sect. 2 we provide the relevant background on the KLM approach to defeasible reasoning, and discuss various forms of rational entailment. We then define Propositional Typicality

Logic, and give a brief overview of the entailment problem for PTL. In Sect. 3 we define the logic BKLM, an extension of KLM-style logics that allows for arbitrary boolean combinations of conditionals. We investigate the expressiveness of BKLM, and show that it is strictly more expressive PTL by exhibiting an explicit translation of PTL formulas into BKLM. In Sect. 4 we turn to the entailment problem for BKLM, and show that BKLM suffers from stronger versions of the known impossibility results for PTL. Section 5 discusses some related work, while Sect. 6 concludes and points out some future research directions.

2   Background

Let $\mathcal{P}$ be a set of propositional atoms, and let $p, q, \ldots$ be meta-variables for elements of $\mathcal{P}$. We write $\mathcal{L}^{\mathcal{P}}$ for the set of propositional formulas over $\mathcal{P}$, defined by $\alpha ::= p \mid \neg\alpha \mid \alpha \wedge \alpha \mid \top \mid \bot$. Other boolean connectives are defined as usual in terms of $\wedge, \neg, \rightarrow$, and $\leftrightarrow$. We write $\mathcal{U}^{\mathcal{P}}$ for the set of valuations of $\mathcal{P}$, which are functions $v : \mathcal{P} \rightarrow \{0, 1\}$. Valuations are extended to $\mathcal{L}^{\mathcal{P}}$ in the usual way, and satisfaction of a formula α will be denoted $v \Vdash \alpha$. For the remainder of this paper we assume that $\mathcal{P}$ is finite, and drop the superscripts where there's no ambiguity.

2.1   The Logic KLM

Kraus et al. [14] study a conditional logic, which we refer to as KLM. It is defined by assertions of the form $\alpha \mathrel{\vert\!\sim} \beta$, which are read "if α, then typically β". For example, if $\mathcal{P} = \{b, f\}$ refers to the properties of being a bird and flying respectively, then $b \mathrel{\vert\!\sim} f$ states that birds typically fly. There are various possible semantic structures for this logic, but in this paper we are interested in the case of *rational* conditional assertions. The semantics for rational conditionals is given by *ranked interpretations* [16]. The following is an alternative, but equivalent definition of such a class of interpretations.

Definition 1. *A* ranked interpretation *$\mathcal{R}$ is a function from $\mathcal{U}$ to $\mathbb{N} \cup \{\infty\}$ satisfying the following convexity condition: if $\mathcal{R}(u) < \infty$, then for every $0 \leq j < \mathcal{R}(u)$, there is some $v \in \mathcal{U}$ for which $\mathcal{R}(v) = j$.*

Given a ranked interpretation $\mathcal{R}$, we call $\mathcal{R}(u)$ the *rank* of u with respect to $\mathcal{R}$. Valuations with a lower rank are viewed as being more typical than those with a higher rank, whereas valuations with infinite rank are viewed as being impossibly atypical. We refer to the set of *possible valuations* as $\mathcal{U}^{\mathcal{R}} = \{u \in \mathcal{U} : \mathcal{R}(u) < \infty\}$, and for any $\alpha \in \mathcal{L}$ we define $[\![\alpha]\!]^{\mathcal{R}} = \{u \in \mathcal{U}^{\mathcal{R}} : u \Vdash \alpha\}$.

Every ranked interpretation $\mathcal{R}$ determines a total preorder on $\mathcal{U}$ in the obvious way, namely $u \leq_{\mathcal{R}} v$ iff $\mathcal{R}(u) \leq \mathcal{R}(v)$. Writing the strict version of this preorder as $\prec_{\mathcal{R}}$, we note that it is *modular*:

Proposition 1. *$\prec_{\mathcal{R}}$ is modular, i.e. for all $u, v, w \in \mathcal{U}$, $u \prec_{\mathcal{R}} v$ implies that either $w \prec_{\mathcal{R}} v$ or $u \prec_{\mathcal{R}} w$.*

Lehmann et al. [16] define ranked interpretations in terms of modular orderings on $\mathcal{U}$. The following observation proves that the two definitions are equivalent:

Proposition 2. *Let $\mathscr{R}_1$ and $\mathscr{R}_2$ be ranked interpretations. Then $\mathscr{R}_1 = \mathscr{R}_2$ iff $\prec_{\mathscr{R}_1} = \prec_{\mathscr{R}_2}$.*

We define satisfaction with respect to ranked interpretations as follows. Given any $\alpha \in \mathcal{L}$, we say $\mathscr{R}$ *satisfies* α (written $\mathscr{R} \Vdash \alpha$) iff $[\![\alpha]\!]^{\mathscr{R}} = \mathcal{U}^{\mathscr{R}}$. Similarly, $\mathscr{R}$ satisfies a conditional assertion $\alpha \mathrel{\vert\!\sim} \beta$ iff $\min_{\leq_{\mathscr{R}}} [\![\alpha]\!]^{\mathscr{R}} \subseteq [\![\beta]\!]^{\mathscr{R}}$, or in other words iff all of the $\leq_{\mathscr{R}}$-minimal valuations satisfying α also satisfy β.

Example 1. Let $\mathscr{R}$ be the ranked interpretation below. Then $\mathscr{R}$ satisfies $\mathsf{p} \to \mathsf{b}$, $\mathsf{b} \mathrel{\vert\!\sim} \mathsf{f}$ and $\mathsf{p} \mathrel{\vert\!\sim} \neg\mathsf{f}$. Note that in our diagrams we omit rank ∞ for brevity, and represent a valuation as a string of literals, with $\overline{p}$ indicating the negation of the atom p.

2	pbf
1	$\overline{\mathsf{p}}\mathsf{b}\overline{\mathsf{f}}$, p$\overline{\mathsf{b}}\overline{\mathsf{f}}$
0	p$\overline{\mathsf{b}}$f, $\overline{\mathsf{p}}$bf, $\overline{\mathsf{p}}\overline{\mathsf{b}}$f

A useful simplification is the fact that classical statements (such as $\mathsf{p} \to \mathsf{b}$) can be viewed as special cases of conditional assertions in ranked interpretations:

Proposition 3 *[14, p. 174].* *For all $\alpha \in \mathcal{L}$, $\mathscr{R} \Vdash \alpha$ iff $\mathscr{R} \Vdash \neg\alpha \mathrel{\vert\!\sim} \bot$.*

In what follows we define a *knowledge base* to be a finite set of conditional assertions. The set of all ranked interpretations over $\mathcal{P}$ is denoted by RI, and we write $\text{MOD}(\mathcal{K})$ for the set of ranked models of a knowledge base $\mathcal{K}$. For any $U \subseteq \text{RI}$, we write $U \Vdash \alpha$ to mean $\mathscr{R} \Vdash \alpha$ for all $\mathscr{R} \in U$, and finally the set of formulas satisfied by the ranked interpretation $\mathscr{R}$ is denoted by $\text{sat}(\mathscr{R})$.

2.2 Propositional Typicality Logic

In this paper we are interested in looking at more expressive variations of KLM, as the syntax for conditionals in KLM is somewhat restrained. An early investigations in this direction was done by Booth and Paris [4], who consider an extension of KLM that permits both positive ($\alpha \mathrel{\vert\!\sim} \beta$) and negative ($\alpha \mathrel{\not\vert\!\sim} \beta$) conditionals.

A more recent variation of KLM is Propositional Typicality Logic (PTL), a logic for defeasible reasoning proposed by Booth et al. [2], in which propositional logic is enriched with a *typicality operator* •. The intuition behind a formula •α is that it is true whenever α is *typical* for the world in consideration. In contrast to KLM, however, the typicality operator can be placed anywhere in a formula, as well as nested. Formulas for PTL are defined by the grammar $\alpha ::= \top \mid \bot \mid p \mid \bullet\alpha \mid \neg\alpha \mid \alpha \wedge \alpha$, where p is any propositional atom, and other logical connectives can be defined as usual in terms of $\neg$ and $\wedge$. We denote the set of all PTL formulas by $\mathcal{L}^\bullet$.

Satisfaction for PTL formulas is defined with respect to a ranked interpretation $\mathscr{R}$. Given a valuation $u \in \mathcal{U}$ and formula $\alpha \in \mathcal{L}^\bullet$, we define $u \Vdash_\mathscr{R} \alpha$ inductively in the same manner as propositional logic, with an additional rule for the typicality operator: $u \Vdash_\mathscr{R} \bullet\alpha$ if and only if $u \Vdash_\mathscr{R} \alpha$ and there is no $v \prec_\mathscr{R} u$ such that $v \Vdash_\mathscr{R} \alpha$. We say that $\mathscr{R}$ *satisfies* the formula α, written $\mathscr{R} \Vdash \alpha$, iff $u \Vdash_\mathscr{R} \alpha$ for all $u \in \mathcal{U}^\mathscr{R}$. The following proposition explains why we are viewing PTL as an extension of KLM, rather than as a separate logic in its own right:

Proposition 4 *[3, Proposition 11]. A ranked interpretation $\mathscr{R}$ satisfies $\alpha \mathrel{|\!\sim} \beta$ iff it satisfies $\bullet\alpha \to \beta$.*

Proposition 4 can be rephrased as saying that every KLM knowledge base has an equivalent PTL knowledge base, in the sense that they share the same set of ranked models. Note, however, that the converse doesn't hold, which intuitively shows that PTL is strictly more expressive than KLM:

Proposition 5 *[3, Proposition 13]. For any $p \in \mathcal{P}$, the knowledge base consisting of $\bullet p$ has no equivalent KLM knowledge base.*

Later, we will show that there is a sense in which PTL is *not* maximally expressive for semantics given by ranked interpretations, a fact that may seem surprising in light of its unrestricted syntax.

2.3   The Entailment Problem

We now turn to a central question in non-monotonic reasoning, namely determining what forms of entailment are appropriate in a defeasible setting. In other words, we wish to understand what it means for a formula α to *follow* from a knowledge base $\mathcal{K}$. We will denote such a relation by $\mathcal{K} \mathrel{\approx\!\!\!|} \alpha$, to be read "$\mathcal{K}$ *defeasibly entails α*".

First steps toward the entailment problem for KLM-style logics were made by Kraus et al. [14], who argue that a defeasible entailment relation should satisfy all of the *rationality properties* listed below. Such relations are said to be *rational*, and one reason for their importance is that they can be characterised precisely by ranked interpretations:

$$(\text{Refl}) \quad \mathcal{K} \mathrel{\approx\!\!\!|} \alpha \mathrel{|\!\sim} \alpha \text{ for all } \alpha \in \mathcal{L}$$

$$(\text{Lle}) \quad \models \alpha \leftrightarrow \beta \text{ and } \mathcal{K} \mathrel{\approx\!\!\!|} \alpha \mathrel{|\!\sim} \gamma \text{ implies } \mathcal{K} \mathrel{\approx\!\!\!|} \beta \mathrel{|\!\sim} \gamma$$

$$(\text{Rw}) \quad \models \beta \to \gamma \text{ and } \mathcal{K} \mathrel{\approx\!\!\!|} \alpha \mathrel{|\!\sim} \beta \text{ implies } \mathcal{K} \mathrel{\approx\!\!\!|} \alpha \mathrel{|\!\sim} \gamma$$

$$(\text{And}) \quad \mathcal{K} \mathrel{\approx\!\!\!|} \alpha \mathrel{|\!\sim} \beta \text{ and } \mathcal{K} \mathrel{\approx\!\!\!|} \alpha \mathrel{|\!\sim} \gamma \text{ implies } \mathcal{K} \mathrel{\approx\!\!\!|} \alpha \mathrel{|\!\sim} \beta \wedge \gamma$$

$$(\text{Or}) \quad \mathcal{K} \mathrel{\approx\!\!\!|} \alpha \mathrel{|\!\sim} \gamma \text{ and } \mathcal{K} \mathrel{\approx\!\!\!|} \beta \mathrel{|\!\sim} \gamma \text{ implies } \mathcal{K} \mathrel{\approx\!\!\!|} \alpha \vee \beta \mathrel{|\!\sim} \gamma$$

$$(\text{Cm}) \quad \mathcal{K} \mathrel{\approx\!\!\!|} \alpha \mathrel{|\!\sim} \beta \text{ and } \mathcal{K} \mathrel{\approx\!\!\!|} \alpha \mathrel{|\!\sim} \gamma \text{ implies } \mathcal{K} \mathrel{\approx\!\!\!|} \alpha \wedge \beta \mathrel{|\!\sim} \gamma$$

$$(\text{Rm}) \quad \mathcal{K} \mathrel{\approx\!\!\!|} \alpha \mathrel{|\!\sim} \gamma \text{ implies } \mathcal{K} \mathrel{\approx\!\!\!|} \alpha \mathrel{|\!\sim} \neg\beta \text{ or } \mathcal{K} \mathrel{\approx\!\!\!|} \alpha \wedge \beta \mathrel{|\!\sim} \gamma$$

Proposition 6 *[16, Theorem 5]. A defeasible entailment relation $\mathrel{\vert\approx}$ is rational iff for each knowledge base $\mathcal{K}$, there is a ranked interpretation $\mathscr{R}_\mathcal{K}$ such that $\mathcal{K} \mathrel{\vert\approx} \alpha \mathrel{\vdash} \beta$ iff $\mathscr{R}_\mathcal{K} \Vdash \alpha \mathrel{\vdash} \beta$.*

Note that by Proposition 4, these rationality properties can be considered for PTL entailment relations as well, by replacing each instance of $\alpha \mathrel{\vdash} \beta$ with the equivalent $\bullet\alpha \to \beta$. An interesting consequence of an entailment relation being rational is *non-monotonicity*, which means that the following Tarskian definition of entailment fails to be rational [16]:

Definition 2. *A formula α is* rank entailed *by a knowledge base $\mathcal{K}$ (written $\mathcal{K} \mathrel{\vert\approx}_R \alpha$) iff $\mathscr{R} \Vdash \alpha$ for every ranked model $\mathscr{R}$ of $\mathcal{K}$.*

Despite this, it is generally agreed that defeasible entailment relations should extend rank entailment, a property known as *Ampliativity*. In the context of PTL entailment, Booth et al. [2] consider this, as well as a number of other desirable properties of defeasible entailment:

(INCLUSION) $\mathcal{K} \mathrel{\vert\approx} \alpha$ for all $\alpha \in \mathcal{K}$

(CUMULATIVITY) $\mathcal{K} \mathrel{\vert\approx} \alpha$ whenever $\mathcal{K} \mathrel{\vert\approx} \beta$ for all $\beta \in \mathcal{K}_2$ and $\mathcal{K}_2 \mathrel{\vert\approx} \alpha$

(AMPLIATIVITY) $\mathcal{K} \mathrel{\vert\approx} \alpha$ whenever $\mathcal{K} \mathrel{\vert\approx}_R \alpha$

(STRICT ENTAILMENT) for classical $\alpha \in \mathcal{L}$, $\mathcal{K} \mathrel{\vert\approx} \alpha$ iff $\mathcal{K} \mathrel{\vert\approx}_R \alpha$

(TYPICAL ENTAILMENT) for classical $\alpha \in \mathcal{L}$, $\mathcal{K} \mathrel{\vert\approx} \top \mathrel{\vdash} \alpha$ iff $\mathcal{K} \mathrel{\vert\approx}_R \top \mathrel{\vdash} \alpha$

(SINGLE MODEL) for all $\mathcal{K}$ there's some $\mathscr{R} \in \text{MOD}(\mathcal{K})$ such that
$$\mathcal{K} \mathrel{\vert\approx} \alpha \text{ iff } \mathscr{R} \Vdash \alpha$$

Proposition 6 states that the Single Model property is equivalent to being rational for KLM entailment relations, but note that the properties diverge for more expressive logics. Surprisingly, it turns out that a number of these properties are mutually inconsistent in the case of PTL entailment relations:

Proposition 7 *[2, Theorem 1]. There is no PTL entailment relation $\mathrel{\vert\approx}$ satisfying the Inclusion, Strict Entailment, Typical Entailment and Single Model properties.*

As a final remark on general entailment relations, we note that this list of properties is by no means exhaustive. Booth et al. [2] consider many variations of the above properties in the context of PTL entailment, whereas Casini et al. [9] study properties of extensions of *Rational Closure*, a well-known entailment relation for KLM.

2.4 Rational Closure

Given the failure of rank entailment to be rational, an interesting question is which rational entailment relation should be considered the right one for defeasible reasoning. In their seminal paper, Lehmann et at. [16] define *Rational Closure*, an entailment relation for KLM that is widely considered to be a minimal acceptable answer to this question [9]. In this section we give a semantic description of Rational Closure in terms of an ordering on ranked interpretations [12]:

Definition 3 *[12, Definition 7]. Given two ranked interpretations $\mathscr{R}_1$ and $\mathscr{R}_2$, we say $\mathscr{R}_1$ is preferred to $\mathscr{R}_2$ (written $\mathscr{R}_1 <_G \mathscr{R}_2$) iff for every $u \in \mathcal{U}$ we have $\mathscr{R}_1(u) \leq \mathscr{R}_2(u)$ and there is some $v \in \mathcal{U}$ s.t. $\mathscr{R}_1(v) < \mathscr{R}_2(v)$.*

Intuitively, the lower down a ranked interpretation $\mathscr{R}$ is with respect to the ordering $\leq_G$, the fewer exceptional valuations it has modulo the constraints of $\mathcal{K}$. The $\leq_G$-minimal ranked interpretations can therefore be thought of as the semantic counterpart to the *Presumption of Typicality* mentioned in the introduction. For the case of KLM knowledge bases containing positive and/or negative conditionals, it follows from the work of Booth and Paris [4] that there is always a unique minimal model:

Proposition 8. *Let $\mathcal{K} \subseteq \mathcal{L}^\sim$ be a knowledge base. Then if $\mathcal{K}$ is consistent, $\mathrm{MOD}(\mathcal{K})$ has a unique $\leq_G$-minimal element, denoted by $\mathscr{R}_{\mathcal{K}}^{RC}$.*

The Rational Closure of a knowledge base is defined to be (or rather, can be characterised as) the set of formulas satisfied by this minimal model:

Proposition 9 *[12, Theorem 2]. A conditional $\alpha \mathrel{|\!\sim} \beta$ is in the rational closure of a knowledge base $\mathcal{K} \subseteq \mathcal{L}^\sim$ (written $\mathcal{K} \approx_{RC} \alpha \mathrel{|\!\sim} \beta$) iff $\mathscr{R}_{\mathcal{K}}^{RC} \Vdash \alpha \mathrel{|\!\sim} \beta$.*

Rational Closure satisfies all of the properties given in Sect. 2.3, and has attractive properties in other respects [16]. Nevertheless, it has some well-known shortcomings, such as not providing for the inheritance of generic properties to exceptional individual - a property that is known as the *drowning effect*. To deal with some of these issues, various refinements of Rational Closure have been proposed, such as Lexicographic Closure [15], Relevant Closure [8] and Inheritance-Based Closure [7]. There is a general consensus that interesting forms of defeasible entailment should extend Rational Closure inferentially [9].

3   Boolean KLM

In this section we describe *Boolean* KLM (BKLM), an extension of KLM that permits arbitrary boolean combinations of defeasible conditionals. Syntactically, this goes beyond the extension of Booth and Paris [4] by allowing disjunctive as well as negative assertions in knowledge bases. BKLM formulas are defined by the grammar $A ::= \alpha \mathrel{|\!\sim} \beta \mid \neg A \mid A \wedge A$, with other boolean connectives defined as usual in terms of $\neg$ and $\wedge$. For convenience, we use $\alpha \mathrel{|\!\not\sim} \beta$ as a synonym for $\neg(\alpha \mathrel{|\!\sim} \beta)$, and write $\mathcal{L}^b$ for the set of all BKLM formulas. Hence, for example, $(\alpha \mathrel{|\!\sim} \beta) \wedge (\gamma \mathrel{|\!\not\sim} \delta)$ and $\neg((\alpha \mathrel{|\!\not\sim} \beta) \vee (\gamma \mathrel{|\!\sim} \delta))$ are valid BKLM formulas, but the nested conditional $\alpha \mathrel{|\!\sim} (\beta \mathrel{|\!\sim} \gamma)$ is not.

Satisfaction for BKLM is defined in terms of ranked interpretations, by extending KLM satisfaction in the obvious fashion, namely $\mathscr{R} \Vdash \neg A$ iff $\mathscr{R} \not\Vdash A$ and $\mathscr{R} \Vdash A \wedge B$ iff $\mathscr{R} \Vdash A$ and $\mathscr{R} \Vdash B$. This leads to some subtle differences between BKLM and the other logics described in this paper. For instance, care must be taken to apply Proposition 3 correctly when translating between propositional formulas and BKLM formulas. The propositional formula $\mathsf{p} \vee \mathsf{q}$ translates to the BKLM formula $\neg(\mathsf{p} \vee \mathsf{q}) \mathrel{|\!\sim} \bot$, and *not* to the BKLM formula $(\neg\mathsf{p} \mathrel{|\!\sim} \bot) \vee (\neg\mathsf{q} \mathrel{|\!\sim} \bot)$, as the following example illustrates:

Example 2. Consider the propositional formula $A = \mathsf{p} \vee \mathsf{q}$ and the BKLM formula $B = (\neg \mathsf{p} \mathrel{\vert\!\sim} \bot) \vee (\neg \mathsf{q} \mathrel{\vert\!\sim} \bot)$. If $\mathscr{R}$ is the ranked interpretation below, then $\mathscr{R}$ satisfies A but not B, as neither clause of the disjunction is satisfied.

1	$\mathsf{p\bar{q}}$
0	$\mathsf{\bar{p}q}$

To prevent possible confusion, we will avoid mixing classical and defeasible assertions in a BKLM knowledge base. For similar reasons, it's also worth noting the difference between boolean connectives in PTL and the corresponding connectives in BKLM. By Proposition 4, one might expect a BKLM formula such as $\neg(\mathsf{p} \mathrel{\vert\!\sim} \mathsf{q})$ to be equivalent to the PTL formula $\neg(\bullet\mathsf{p} \to \mathsf{q})$. This is not the case in general, however:

Example 3. Consider the formulas $A = \neg(\bullet\mathsf{p} \to \mathsf{q})$ and $B = \neg(\mathsf{p} \mathrel{\vert\!\sim} \mathsf{q})$, and let $\mathscr{R}$ be the ranked interpretation in the example above. Note that A is equivalent to $\bullet\mathsf{p} \wedge \neg\mathsf{q}$, which is not satisfied by $\mathscr{R}$. On the other hand, $\mathscr{R}$ satisfies B.

A natural question is how BKLM compares to PTL in terms of expressiveness. In the next two sections we show that BKLM is strictly more expressive than PTL, and detail an algorithm that converts PTL knowledge bases into equivalent BKLM knowledge bases.

3.1   Expressiveness of BKLM

Satisfaction for KLM, PTL and BKLM formulas is defined in terms of ranked interpretations. This allows us to compare their expressiveness directly, in terms of the sets of models that they can characterise. With the results mentioned earlier, we can already do this for KLM and PTL:

Example 4. Let $\mathcal{K} \subseteq \mathcal{L}^{\vert\!\sim}$ be a KLM knowledge base. Then the PTL knowledge base $\mathcal{K}' = \{\bullet\alpha \to \beta : \alpha \mathrel{\vert\!\sim} \beta \in \mathcal{K}\}$ has exactly the same ranked models as $\mathcal{K}$ by Proposition 4, and hence PTL is at least as expressive as KLM. Proposition 5 proves that PTL is strictly *more* expressive than KLM.

Our main result in this section is that BKLM is maximally expressive, in the sense that it can characterise *any* set of ranked interpretations. First, we recall that for every valuation $u \in \mathcal{U}$ there is a corresponding characteristic formula $\hat{u} \in \mathcal{L}$, which has the property that $v \Vdash \hat{u}$ iff $v = u$.

Lemma 1. *For any ranked interpretation $\mathscr{R}$ and valuations $u, v \in \mathcal{U}$, the following equivalences hold:*

1. $\mathscr{R} \Vdash \top \not\mathrel{\vert\!\sim} \neg\hat{u}$ *iff* $\mathscr{R}(u) = 0$.
2. $\mathscr{R} \Vdash \hat{u} \mathrel{\vert\!\sim} \bot$ *iff* $\mathscr{R}(u) = \infty$.
3. $\mathscr{R} \Vdash \hat{u} \vee \hat{v} \mathrel{\vert\!\sim} \neg\hat{v}$ *iff* $u \prec_{\mathscr{R}} v$ *or* $\mathscr{R}(u) = \mathscr{R}(v) = \infty$.

Note that this lemma holds even in the trivial case where $\mathcal{R}(u) = \infty$ for all $u \in \mathcal{U}$. For convenience, in later parts of the paper we will write $\alpha < \beta$ as a standard shorthand for the defeasible conditional $\alpha \vee \beta \mathrel{|\!\sim} \neg\beta$.

Lemma 2. *Let $\mathcal{R}$ be any ranked interpretation. Then there exists a formula $ch(\mathcal{R}) \in \mathcal{L}^b$ with $\mathcal{R}$ as its unique model.*

We refer to $ch(\mathcal{R})$ as the *characteristic formula* of $\mathcal{R}$. Taking a disjunction of characteristic formulas suffices to prove the following more general corollary:

Corollary 1. *Let $U \subseteq \mathrm{RI}$ be a set of ranked interpretations. Then there exists a formula $ch(U) \in \mathcal{L}^b$ with U as its set of models.*

In principle, this corollary shows that for any PTL knowledge base there exists some BKLM formula with the same set of models, and hence BKLM is at least as expressive as PTL. In the next section we make this relationship more concrete, by providing an explicit algorithm for translating PTL knowledge bases into BKLM.

3.2   Translating PTL Into BKLM

In Sect. 2.2, satisfaction for PTL formulas was defined in terms of the possible valuations of a ranked interpretation $\mathcal{R}$. In order to define a translation operator between PTL and BKLM, our main idea is to encode satisfaction with respect to a *particular* valuation $u \in \mathcal{U}$, by defining an operator $\mathrm{tr}_u : \mathcal{L}^\bullet \to \mathcal{L}^b$ such that for each $u \in \mathcal{U}^{\mathcal{R}}$, $\mathcal{R} \Vdash \mathrm{tr}_u(\alpha)$ iff $u \Vdash_{\mathcal{R}} \alpha$.

Definition 4. *We define tr_u by structural induction as follows, where $\alpha, \beta \in \mathcal{L}^\bullet$, $p \in \mathcal{P}$ and $u \in \mathcal{U}$:*

1. $tr_u(p) \stackrel{\text{def}}{=} \hat{u} \mathrel{|\!\sim} p$
2. $tr_u(\top) \stackrel{\text{def}}{=} \hat{u} \mathrel{|\!\sim} \top$
3. $tr_u(\bot) \stackrel{\text{def}}{=} \hat{u} \mathrel{|\!\sim} \bot$
4. $tr_u(\neg\alpha) \stackrel{\text{def}}{=} \neg tr_u(\alpha)$
5. $tr_u(\alpha \wedge \beta) \stackrel{\text{def}}{=} tr_u(\alpha) \wedge tr_u(\beta)$
6. $tr_u(\bullet\alpha) \stackrel{\text{def}}{=} tr_u(\alpha) \wedge \bigwedge_{v \in \mathcal{U}} \left[(\hat{v} < \hat{u}) \to \neg tr_v(\alpha) \right]$

Note that this is well-defined, as each case is defined in terms of strict subformulas. These translations can be viewed as analogues of the definition of PTL satisfaction - case 6 intuitively states that $\bullet\alpha$ is satisfied by a possible valuation u iff u is a minimal valuation satisfying α, for instance. The following lemma confirms that this intuition is correct:

Lemma 3. *Let $\mathcal{R}$ be a ranked interpretation, and $u \in \mathcal{U}^{\mathcal{R}}$ a valuation with $\mathcal{R}(u) < \infty$. Then for all $\alpha \in \mathcal{L}^\bullet$ we have $\mathcal{R} \Vdash tr_u(\alpha)$ if and only if $u \Vdash_{\mathcal{R}} \alpha$.*

A PTL formula $\alpha \in \mathcal{L}^\bullet$ is satisfied by a ranked interpretation $\mathscr{R}$ iff it is satisfied by every possible valuation of $\mathscr{R}$. By combining the translation operators in Definition 4 for each possible world, we can encode this statement as a BKLM formula as follows:

Definition 5. $tr(\alpha) \stackrel{\text{def}}{=} \bigwedge_{u \in \mathcal{U}} \left((\hat{u} \not\hspace{-0.5mm}\sim \bot) \to tr_u(\alpha) \right)$

Finally, we can prove that this translation does indeed result in an equivalent BKLM formula:

Lemma 4. *For all $\alpha \in \mathcal{L}^\bullet$ and any ranked interpretation $\mathscr{R}$, $\mathscr{R}$ satisfies α iff $\mathscr{R}$ satisfies $tr(\alpha)$.*

4   The Entailment Problem for BKLM

We now turn to the question of defeasible entailment for BKLM knowledge bases, and in particular whether interesting entailment relations resembling Rational Closure can be defined. As a first observation, Proposition 7 show that there can be no *exact* analogue of Rational Closure for PTL, and thus in light of our translation result there cannot be an exact analogue for BKLM either. In the case of PTL, however, we can get fairly close:

Proposition 10 *[5, Proposition 5.2]. Let $\mathcal{K} \subseteq \mathcal{L}^\bullet$ be a consistent PTL knowledge base. Then $\mathrm{MOD}(\mathcal{K})$ has a unique $\leq_G$-minimal element, denoted $\mathscr{R}_\mathcal{K}^{LM}$.*

Booth et al. [5] define *LM-entailment* as follows: $\mathcal{K} \hspace{1mm}\approx_{LM} \alpha$ iff $\mathscr{R}_\mathcal{K}^{LM} \Vdash \alpha$. While this satisfies many of the desirable properties of Rational Closure, such as the Single Model, Typical Entailment and Ampliativity properties, it fails to satisfy Strict Entailment. Unfortunately, it turns out that the situation is even worse for BKLM:

Lemma 5. *There is no BKLM entailment relation $\approx_?$ satisfying Ampliativity, Typical Entailment and the Single Model property.*

This is a concrete sense in which BKLM entailment is more constrained than PTL entailment, and raises the additional question of which of these properties we should commit to giving up. Our main result here, which we will prove in the next two sections, is that satisfying the Single Model property for BKLM entailment incurs heavy costs, and hence it is a reasonable candidate for removal.

4.1   Order Entailment

One way of looking at Rational Closure is as a form of *minimal model entailment*; indeed, this is just Definition 3. In other words, given a knowledge base $\mathcal{K}$, we can construct the Rational Closure of $\mathcal{K}$ by placing an appropriate ordering on its set of ranked models (in this case $\leq_G$), and picking out the consequences common to all the minimal models. In this section we provide a formal definition of this kind of entailment, with a view towards understanding the Single Model property for BKLM.

Definition 6. *Let $<$ be a strict partial order on* RI. *Then for all knowledge bases $\mathcal{K} \subseteq \mathcal{L}^b$ and formulas $\alpha \in \mathcal{L}^b$, we say $\mathcal{K}$ $<$-entails α (denoted $\mathcal{K} \mathrel{\mathop{\approx}\limits_{<}} \alpha$) iff $\mathscr{R} \Vdash \alpha$ for all $<$-minimal models $\mathscr{R} \in \mathrm{MOD}(\mathcal{K})$.*

The relation $\mathrel{\mathop{\approx}\limits_{<}}$ will be referred to as an *order entailment relation*. Note that while we have explicitly referred to BKLM knowledge bases here, the construction works identically for KLM and PTL. It is also worth mentioning that the set of models of a consistent knowledge base is always finite, as we have assumed finiteness of $\mathcal{P}$, and hence always has $<$-minimal elements.

Example 5. By Definition 9, the rational closure of any KLM knowledge base $\mathcal{K}$ is the set of formulas satisfied by the (unique) $<_G$-minimal element of $\mathrm{MOD}(\mathcal{K})$. Thus rational closure is the order entailment relation corresponding to $<_G$ for KLM knowledge bases.

In general, order entailment relations satisfy all of the rationality properties except property RM (commonly called *rational monotonicity*). Rational monotonicity holds if $\mathrm{MOD}(\mathcal{K})$ has a unique $<$-minimal model for every knowledge base $\mathcal{K}$, a fact that is closely related to the Single Model property:

Proposition 11. *An order entailment relation $\mathrel{\mathop{\approx}\limits_{<}}$ satisfies the Single Model property iff $\mathrm{MOD}(\mathcal{K})$ has a unique $<$-minimal model for any knowledge base $\mathcal{K}$.*

This is always the case if $<$ is total, for instance, but it is also the case for Rational Closure and LM-entailment. In the next section we will show that, perhaps surprisingly, total order entailment relations are nevertheless (modulo some minor conditions) the *only* entailment relations for BKLM satisfying the Single Model property.

4.2   The Single Model Property

This section is devoted to a proof of the following theorem, mentioned in the preceding discussion:

Theorem 1. *Suppose $\mathrel{\mathop{\approx}\limits_{?}}$ is a BKLM entailment relation satisfying Cumulativity, Ampliativity and the Single Model property. Then $\mathrel{\mathop{\approx}\limits_{?}} = \mathrel{\mathop{\approx}\limits_{<}}$, where $<$ is a total ordering of* RI.

For the remainder of the proof, we consider a fixed BKLM entailment relation $\mathrel{\mathop{\approx}\limits_{?}}$ satisfying the Cumulativity, Ampliativity and Single Model properties. Corresponding to $\mathrel{\mathop{\approx}\limits_{?}}$ is an associated *consequence operator* $\mathrm{Cn}_?$, defined as follows:

Definition 7. *For any knowledge base $\mathcal{K} \subseteq \mathcal{L}^b$, we define $\mathrm{Cn}_?(\mathcal{K}) = \{\alpha \in \mathcal{L}^b : \mathcal{K} \mathrel{\mathop{\approx}\limits_{?}} \alpha\}$.*

In what follows, we will move between the entailment relation and consequence operator notations freely as convenient. To begin with, the following lemma follows easily from our assumptions:

Lemma 6. *For any knowledge base* $\mathcal{K} \subseteq \mathcal{L}^b$, $Cn_?(\mathcal{K}) = Cn_R(Cn_?(\mathcal{K}))$ *and* $Cn_?(\mathcal{K}) = Cn_?(Cn_R(\mathcal{K}))$.

Our approach to proving Theorem 1 is to assign a unique index $\mathrm{ind}(\mathscr{R}) \in \mathbb{N}$ to each ranked interpretation $\mathscr{R} \in \mathrm{RI}$, and then show that $Cn_?(\mathcal{K})$ corresponds to minimisation of index in $\mathrm{MOD}(\mathcal{K})$. To construct this indexing scheme, consider the following algorithm:

1. Set $M_0 := \mathrm{RI}$, $i := 0$.
2. If $M_i = \emptyset$, terminate.
3. By Corollary 1, there is some $\mathcal{K}_i \subseteq \mathcal{L}^b$ s.t. $\mathrm{MOD}(\mathcal{K}_i) = M_i$.
4. By the Single Model property, there is some $\mathscr{R}_i \in M_i$ s.t. $Cn_?(\mathcal{K}_i) = \mathrm{sat}(\mathscr{R}_i)$.
5. Set $M_{i+1} := M_i \setminus \{\mathscr{R}_i\}$, $i := i + 1$.
6. Go to step 2, and iterate until termination.

This algorithm is guaranteed to terminate, since M_0 is finite and $0 \leq |M_{i+1}| < |M_i|$. Note that once the algorithm terminates, for each $\mathscr{R} \in \mathrm{RI}$ there will have been a unique $i \in \mathbb{N}$ such that $\mathscr{R} = \mathscr{R}_i$. We will call this i the *index* of $\mathscr{R}$, and denote it by $\mathrm{ind}(\mathscr{R})$. Given a knowledge base $\mathcal{K}$, we define $\mathrm{ind}(\mathcal{K})$ to be the minimum of the indices of each of the models of $\mathcal{K}$.

When we write $\mathscr{R}_n$, $\mathcal{K}_n$ and M_n in the following lemmas, we mean the ranked interpretations, knowledge bases and sets of models constructed in steps 3 to 5 of the algorithm when $i = n$:

Lemma 7. *Given any knowledge base* $\mathcal{K} \subseteq \mathcal{L}^b$, $\mathrm{MOD}(\mathcal{K}) \subseteq M_n$, *where* $n = \mathrm{ind}(\mathcal{K})$.

The following lemma proves that entailment under $\approx_?$ corresponds to minimisation of index:

Lemma 8. *Given any knowledge base* $\mathcal{K} \subseteq \mathcal{L}^b$, $Cn_?(\mathcal{K}) = \mathrm{sat}(\mathscr{R}_n)$, *where* $n = \mathrm{ind}(\mathcal{K})$.

Consider the strict partial order on RI defined by $\mathscr{R}_1 < \mathscr{R}_2$ iff $\mathrm{ind}(\mathscr{R}_1) < \mathrm{ind}(\mathscr{R}_2)$. By construction, the index of a ranked interpretation is unique, and hence $<$ is total. It follows from Lemma 8 that $\approx_? = \approx_<$, and hence $\approx_?$ is equivalent to a total order entailment relation. This completes the proof of Theorem 1.

5 Related Work

The most relevant work w.r.t. the present paper is that of Booth and Paris [4] in which they define rational closure for the extended version of KLM for which negated conditionals are allowed, and the work on PTL [2,5]. The relation this work has with BKLM was investigated in detail throughout the paper.

Delgrande [10] proposes a logic that is as expressive as BKLM. The entailment relation he proposes is different from the minimal entailment relations we consider here and, given the strong links between our constructions and the KLM approach, the remarks in the comparison made by Lehmann and Magidor [16, Sect. 3.7] are also applicable here.

Boutilier [6] defines a family of conditional logics using preferential and ranked interpretations. His logic is closer to ours and even more expressive, since nesting of conditionals is allowed, but he too does not consider minimal constructions. That is, both Delgrande and Boutilier's approaches adopt a Tarskian-style notion of consequence, in line with rank entailment. The move towards a non-monotonic notion of defeasible entailment was precisely our motivation in the present work.

Giordano et al. [13] propose the system P_{min} which is based on a language that is as expressive as PTL. However, they end up using a constrained form of such a language that goes only slightly beyond the expressivity of the language of KLM-style conditionals (their *well-behaved knowledge bases*). Also, the system P_{min} relies on preferential models and a notion of minimality that is closer to circumscription [17].

In the context of description logics, Giordano et al. [11,12] propose to extend the conditional language with an explicit typicality operator $T(\cdot)$, with a meaning that is closely related to the PTL operator •. It is worth pointing out, though, that most of the analysis in the work of Giordano et al. is dedicated to a constrained use of the typicality operator $T(\cdot)$ that does not go beyond the expressivity of a KLM-style conditional language, but revised, of course, for the expressivity of description logics.

In the context of adaptive logics, Straßer [18] defines the logic R^+ as an extension of KLM in which arbitrary boolean combinations of defeasible implications are allowed, and the set of propositional atoms has been extended to include the symbols $\{l_i : i \in \mathbb{N}\}$. Semantically, these symbols encode rank in the object language, in the sense that $u \Vdash l_i$ in a ranked interpretation $\mathscr{R}$ iff $\mathscr{R}(u) \geq i$. Straßer's interest in R^+ is to define an adaptive logic ALC^S that provides a dynamic proof theory for rational closure, whereas our interest in BKLM is to generalise rational closure to more expressive extensions of KLM. Nevertheless, the Minimal Abnormality Strategy (see the work of Batens [1], for instance) for ALC^S is closely related to LM-entailment as defined in this paper.

6   Conclusion

The main focus of this paper is exploring the connection between expressiveness and entailment for extensions of the core logic KLM. Accordingly, we introduce the logic BKLM, an extension of KLM that allows for arbitrary boolean combinations of defeasible implications. We take an abstract approach to the analysis of BKLM, and show that it is strictly more expressive than existing extensions of KLM such as PTL [3] and KLM with negation [4]. Our primary conclusion is that a logic as expressive as BKLM has to give up several desirable properties for defeasible entailment, most notably the Single Model property, and thus appealing forms of entailment for PTL such as LM-entailment [2] cannot be lifted to the BKLM case.

For future work, an obvious question is what forms of defeasible entailment *are* appropriate for BKLM. For instance, is it possible to skirt the impossibility results proven in this paper while still retaining the KLM rationality properties? Other forms of entailment for PTL, such as PT-entailment, have also yet to be analysed in the context of BKLM and may be better suited to such an expressive logic. Another line of research to be explored is whether there is a more natural translation of PTL formulas into BKLM than that defined in this paper. Our translation is based on a direct encoding of PTL semantics, and consequently results in an exponential blow-up in the size of the formulas being translated. It is clear that there are much more efficient ways to translate *specific* PTL formulas, but we leave it as an open problem whether this can be done in general. In a similar vein, it is interesting to ask how PTL could be extended in order to make it equiexpressive with BKLM. Finally, it may be interesting to compare BKLM with an extension of KLM that allows for nested defeasible implications, i.e. formulas such as $\alpha \mathrel{|\!\sim} (\beta \mathrel{|\!\sim} \gamma)$. While such an extension cannot be more expressive than BKLM, at least for a semantics given by ranked interpretations, it may provide more natural encodings of various kinds of typicality, and thus be easier to work with from a pragmatic point of view.

Acknowlegements. This research was partially supported by TAILOR, a project funded by EU Horizon 2020 research and innovation programme under GA No. 952215.

A   Appendix

A.1   Proofs of Lemmas in Sect. 3

Lemma 2. *Let $\mathscr{R}$ be any ranked interpretation. Then there exists a formula $ch(\mathscr{R}) \in \mathcal{L}^b$ with $\mathscr{R}$ as its unique model.*

Proof. Consider the following knowledge bases.

1. $\mathcal{K}_{\prec} = \{\hat{u} < \hat{v} : u \prec_{\mathscr{R}} v\} \cup \{\hat{u} \not< \hat{v} : u \not\prec_{\mathscr{R}} v\}$
2. $\mathcal{K}_{\infty} = \{\hat{u} \mathrel{|\!\sim} \bot : \mathscr{R}(u) = \infty\} \cup \{\hat{u} \mathrel{|\!\not\sim} \bot : \mathscr{R}(u) < \infty\}$

By Lemma 1, $\mathscr{R}$ satisfies $\mathcal{K} = \mathcal{K}_{\prec} \cup \mathcal{K}_{\infty}$. To show that it is the unique model of $\mathcal{K}$, consider any $\mathscr{R}^* \in \mathrm{Mod}(\mathcal{K})$. Since $\mathscr{R}^*$ satisfies $\mathcal{K}_{\infty}$, $\mathscr{R}^*(u) = \infty$ iff $\mathscr{R}(u) = \infty$ for any $u \in \mathcal{U}$. Now consider any $u, v \in \mathcal{U}$, and suppose that $\mathscr{R}(u) < \infty$. Then $u \prec_{\mathscr{R}} v$ iff $\mathcal{K}_{\prec}$ contains $\hat{u} < \hat{v}$. But $\mathscr{R}^*$ satisfies $\mathcal{K}_{\prec}$, so this is true iff $u \prec_{\mathscr{R}^*} v$ as $\mathscr{R}^*(u) < \infty$. On the other hand, if $\mathscr{R}(u) = \infty$, then $u \not\prec_{\mathscr{R}} v$ and $u \not\prec_{\mathscr{R}^*} v$. Hence $\prec_{\mathscr{R}} = \prec_{\mathscr{R}^*}$, which implies that $\mathscr{R} = \mathscr{R}^*$ by Proposition 2. We conclude the proof by letting $ch(\mathscr{R}) = \bigwedge_{\alpha \in \mathcal{K}} \alpha$. $\qquad\square$

Lemma 3. *Let $\mathscr{R}$ be a ranked interpretation, and $u \in \mathcal{U}^{\mathscr{R}}$ a valuation with $\mathscr{R}(u) < \infty$. Then for all $\alpha \in \mathcal{L}^{\bullet}$ we have $\mathscr{R} \Vdash tr_u(\alpha)$ if and only if $u \Vdash_{\mathscr{R}} \alpha$.*

Proof. We will prove the result by structural induction on the cases in Definition 4:

1. Suppose that $\mathscr{R} \Vdash \mathrm{tr}_u(p)$, i.e. $\mathscr{R} \Vdash \hat{u} \mathrel{\vert\!\sim} p$. This is true iff $u \models p$, which is equivalent by definition to $u \Vdash_{\mathscr{R}} p$. Cases 2 and 3 are similar.
4. Suppose that $\mathscr{R} \Vdash \mathrm{tr}_u(\neg\alpha)$, i.e. $\mathscr{R} \Vdash \neg\mathrm{tr}_u(\alpha)$. This is true iff $\mathscr{R} \not\Vdash \mathrm{tr}_u(\alpha)$, which by the induction hypothesis is equivalent to $u \not\Vdash_{\mathscr{R}} \alpha$. But this is equivalent to $u \Vdash_{\mathscr{R}} \neg\alpha$ by definition. Case 5 is similar.
6. Suppose there exists an $\alpha \in \mathcal{L}^{\bullet}$ such that $\mathscr{R} \Vdash \mathrm{tr}_u(\bullet\alpha)$ but $u \not\Vdash_{\mathscr{R}} \bullet\alpha$. Then either $u \not\Vdash_{\mathscr{R}} \alpha$, which by the induction hypothesis is a contradiction since $\mathscr{R} \Vdash \mathrm{tr}_u(\alpha)$, or there is some $v \in \mathcal{U}$ with $v \prec_{\mathscr{R}} u$ such that $v \Vdash_{\mathscr{R}} \alpha$. But by Lemma 1, $v \prec_{\mathscr{R}} u$ is true only if $\mathscr{R} \Vdash \hat{v} < \hat{u}$. We also have, by the induction hypothesis, that $\mathscr{R} \Vdash \mathrm{tr}_v(\alpha)$ since $v \Vdash_{\mathscr{R}} \alpha$. Hence $\mathscr{R} \Vdash (\hat{v} < \hat{u}) \wedge \mathrm{tr}_v(\alpha)$, which implies that one of the clauses in $\mathrm{tr}_u(\bullet\alpha)$ is false. This is a contradiction, so we conclude that $\mathscr{R} \Vdash \mathrm{tr}_u(\bullet\alpha)$ implies $u \Vdash_{\mathscr{R}} \bullet\alpha$.

Conversely, suppose that $u \Vdash_{\mathscr{R}} \bullet\alpha$. Then $u \Vdash_{\mathscr{R}} \alpha$, and hence $\mathscr{R} \Vdash \mathrm{tr}_u(\alpha)$ by the induction hypothesis. We also have that if $v \prec_{\mathscr{R}} u$ then $v \not\Vdash_{\mathscr{R}} \alpha$, which is equivalent to $\mathscr{R} \Vdash \neg\mathrm{tr}_v(\alpha)$ by the induction hypothesis. But by Lemma 1, $v \prec_{\mathscr{R}} u$ iff $\mathscr{R} \Vdash \hat{v} < \hat{u}$. We conclude that $\mathscr{R} \Vdash (\hat{v} < \hat{u}) \to \neg\mathrm{tr}_v(\alpha)$ for all $v \in \mathcal{U}$, and hence $\mathscr{R} \Vdash \mathrm{tr}_u(\bullet\alpha)$.   □

Lemma 4. *For all $\alpha \in \mathcal{L}^{\bullet}$ and any ranked interpretation $\mathscr{R}$, $\mathscr{R}$ satisfies α iff $\mathscr{R}$ satisfies $tr(\alpha)$.*

Proof. Suppose $\mathscr{R} \Vdash \alpha$. Then for all $u \in \mathcal{U}$, either $\mathscr{R}(u) = \infty$ or $u \Vdash_{\mathscr{R}} \alpha$. The former implies $\mathscr{R} \Vdash \hat{u} \mathrel{\vert\!\sim} \bot$ by Lemma 1, and the latter implies $\mathscr{R} \Vdash \mathrm{tr}_u(\alpha)$ by Lemma 3. Thus $\mathscr{R} \Vdash (\hat{u} \mathrel{\not\vert\!\sim} \bot) \to \mathrm{tr}_u(\alpha)$ for all $u \in \mathcal{U}$, which proves $\mathscr{R} \Vdash \mathrm{tr}(\alpha)$ as required. Conversely, suppose $\mathscr{R} \Vdash \mathrm{tr}(\alpha)$. Then for any $u \in \mathcal{U}$, either $\mathscr{R} \Vdash \hat{u} \mathrel{\vert\!\sim} \bot$ and hence $\mathscr{R}(u) = \infty$ by Lemma 1, or $\mathscr{R} \Vdash \hat{u} \mathrel{\not\vert\!\sim} \bot$ and hence $\mathscr{R} \Vdash \mathrm{tr}_u(\alpha)$ by hypothesis. But then $\mathscr{R} \Vdash \alpha$ by Lemma 3.   □

A.2   Proofs of Lemmas in Sect. 4

Lemma 5. *There is no BKLM entailment relation $\mathrel{\approx_?}$ satisfying Ampliativity, Typical Entailment and the Single Model property.*

Proof. Suppose that $\mathrel{\approx_?}$ is such an entailment relation, and consider the knowledge base $\mathcal{K} = \{(\top \mathrel{\vert\!\sim} \mathsf{p}) \vee (\top \mathrel{\vert\!\sim} \neg\mathsf{p})\}$. Both interpretations in Fig. 1, $\mathscr{R}_1$ and $\mathscr{R}_2$, are models of $\mathcal{K}$. $\mathscr{R}_1$ satisfies $\top \mathrel{\vert\!\sim} \mathsf{p}$ and not $\top \mathrel{\vert\!\sim} \neg\mathsf{p}$, whereas $\mathscr{R}_2$ satisfies $\top \mathrel{\vert\!\sim} \neg\mathsf{p}$ and not $\top \mathrel{\vert\!\sim} \mathsf{p}$. Thus, by the Typical Entailment property, $\mathcal{K} \mathrel{\not\approx_?} \top \mathrel{\vert\!\sim} \mathsf{p}$ and $\mathcal{K} \mathrel{\not\approx_?} \top \mathrel{\vert\!\sim} \neg\mathsf{p}$. On the other hand, by Ampliativity we get

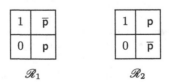

Fig. 1. Ranked models of $\mathcal{K} = \{(\top \mathrel{\vert\!\sim} \mathsf{p}) \vee (\top \mathrel{\vert\!\sim} \neg\mathsf{p})\}$.

$\mathcal{K} \not\approx_? (\top \mathrel{|\!\!\sim} \mathsf{p}) \vee (\top \mathrel{|\!\!\sim} \neg\mathsf{p})$. A single ranked interpretation cannot satisfy all three of these assertions, however, and hence no such entailment relation can exist. $\square$

Lemma 7. *Given any knowledge base* $\mathcal{K} \subseteq \mathcal{L}^b$, $\mathrm{MOD}(\mathcal{K}) \subseteq M_n$, *where* $n = ind(\mathcal{K})$.

Proof. An easy induction on step 5 of the algorithm proves that $M_n = \{\mathscr{R} \in \mathrm{RI} : ind(\mathscr{R}) \geq n\}$. By hypothesis, $ind(\mathscr{R}) \geq n$ for all $\mathscr{R} \in \mathrm{MOD}(\mathcal{K})$, and hence $\mathrm{MOD}(\mathcal{K}) \subseteq M_n$. $\square$

Lemma 8. *Given any knowledge base* $\mathcal{K} \subseteq \mathcal{L}^b$, $Cn_?(\mathcal{K}) = sat(\mathscr{R}_n)$, *where* $n = ind(\mathcal{K})$.

Proof. For all A, $\mathcal{K}_n \not\approx_R A$ iff $\mathscr{R} \Vdash A$ for all $\mathscr{R} \in \mathrm{MOD}(\mathcal{K}_n) = M_n$. But by Lemma 7, $\mathrm{MOD}(\mathcal{K}) \subseteq M_n$ and hence $\mathrm{Cn}_R(\mathcal{K}_n) \subseteq \mathrm{Cn}_R(\mathcal{K})$. On the other hand, $\mathscr{R}_n \in \mathrm{MOD}(\mathcal{K})$ by hypothesis and hence $\mathscr{R}_n \Vdash A$ for all $A \in \mathcal{K}$. By the definition of step 4 of the algorithm we have $sat(\mathscr{R}_n) = \mathrm{Cn}_?(\mathcal{K}_n)$, and thus $\mathcal{K} \subseteq \mathrm{Cn}_?(\mathcal{K}_n)$. Applying Cn_R to each side of this inclusion (using the monotonicity of rank entailment), we get $\mathrm{Cn}_R(\mathcal{K}) \subseteq \mathrm{Cn}_R(\mathrm{Cn}_?(\mathcal{K}_n)) = \mathrm{Cn}_?(\mathcal{K}_n)$, with the last equality following from Lemma 6. Putting it all together, we have $\mathrm{Cn}_R(\mathcal{K}_n) \subseteq \mathrm{Cn}_R(\mathcal{K}) \subseteq \mathrm{Cn}_?(\mathcal{K}_n)$, and hence by Cumulativity we conclude $\mathrm{Cn}_?(\mathcal{K}) = \mathrm{Cn}_?(\mathcal{K}_n) = sat(\mathscr{R}_n)$. $\square$

References

1. Batens, D.: A universal logic approach to adaptive logics. Log. Univers. **1**, 221–242 (2007). https://doi.org/10.1007/s11787-006-0012-5
2. Booth, R., Casini, G., Meyer, T., Varzinczak, I.: On the entailment problem for a logic of typicality. IJCAI **2015**, 2805–2811 (2015)
3. Booth, R., Meyer, T., Varzinczak, I.: A propositional typicality logic for extending rational consequence. In: Fermé, E., Gabbay, D., Simari, G. (eds.) Trends in Belief Revision and Argumentation Dynamics, Studies in Logic - Logic and Cognitive Systems, vol. 48, pp. 123–154. King's College Publications (2013)
4. Booth, R., Paris, J.: A note on the rational closure of knowledge bases with both positive and negative knowledge. J. Logic Lang. Inform. **7**(2), 165–190 (1998)
5. Booth, R., Casini, G., Meyer, T., Varzinczak, I.: On rational entailment for propositional typicality logic. Artif. Intell. **277**, 103178 (2019)
6. Boutilier, C.: Conditional logics of normality: a modal approach. Artif. Intell. **68**(1), 87–154 (1994)
7. Casini, G., Straccia, U.: Defeasible inheritance-based description logics. JAIR **48**, 415–473 (2013)
8. Casini, G., Meyer, T., Moodley, K., Nortjé, R.: Relevant closure: a new form of defeasible reasoning for description logics. In: Fermé, E., Leite, J. (eds.) JELIA 2014. LNCS (LNAI), vol. 8761, pp. 92–106. Springer, Cham (2014). https://doi.org/10.1007/978-3-319-11558-0_7
9. Casini, G., Meyer, T., Varzinczak, I.: Taking defeasible entailment beyond rational closure. In: Calimeri, F., Leone, N., Manna, M. (eds.) JELIA 2019. LNCS (LNAI), vol. 11468, pp. 182–197. Springer, Cham (2019). https://doi.org/10.1007/978-3-030-19570-0_12

10. Delgrande, J.: A first-order logic for prototypical properties. Artif. Intell. **33**, 105–130 (1987)
11. Giordano, L., Gliozzi, V., Olivetti, N., Pozzato, G.L.: Preferential description logics. In: Dershowitz, N., Voronkov, A. (eds.) LPAR 2007. LNCS (LNAI), vol. 4790, pp. 257–272. Springer, Heidelberg (2007). https://doi.org/10.1007/978-3-540-75560-9_20
12. Giordano, L., Gliozzi, V., Olivetti, N., Pozzato, G.: Semantic characterization of rational closure: from propositional logic to description logics. Art. Int. **226**, 1–33 (2015)
13. Giordano, L., Gliozzi, V., Olivetti, N., Pozzato, G.L.: A nonmonotonic extension of KLM preferential logic **P**. In: Fermüller, C.G., Voronkov, A. (eds.) LPAR 2010. LNCS, vol. 6397, pp. 317–332. Springer, Heidelberg (2010). https://doi.org/10.1007/978-3-642-16242-8_23
14. Kraus, S., Lehmann, D., Magidor, M.: Nonmonotonic reasoning, preferential models and cumulative logics. Artif. Intell. **44**, 167–207 (1990)
15. Lehmann, D.: Another perspective on default reasoning. Ann. Math. Art. Int. **15**(1), 61–82 (1995)
16. Lehmann, D., Magidor, M.: What does a conditional knowledge base entail? Art. Int. **55**, 1–60 (1992)
17. McCarthy, J.: Circumscription, a form of nonmonotonic reasoning. Art. Int. **13**(1–2), 27–39 (1980)
18. Straßer, C.: An adaptive logic for rational closure. Adaptive Logics for Defeasible Reasoning. Trends in Logic (Studia Logica Library), vol. 38, pp. 181–206. Springer, Cham (2014). https://doi.org/10.1007/978-3-319-00792-2_7

An Exercise in a Non-classical Semantics for Reasoning with Incompleteness and Inconsistencies

Ivan Varzinczak[1,2]([✉])

[1] CRIL, Université d'Artois & CNRS, Lens, France
varzinczak@cril.fr
[2] CAIR, Computer Science Division, Stellenbosch University,
Stellenbosch, South Africa

Abstract. Reasoning in the presence of inconsistencies and in the absence of complete knowledge has long been a major challenge in artificial intelligence. In this paper, we revisit the classical semantics of propositional logic by generalising the notion of world (valuation) so that it allows for propositions to be both true and false, and also for their truth values not to be defined. We do so by adopting neither a many-valued stance nor the philosophical view that there are 'real' contradictions. Moreover, we show that satisfaction of complex sentences can still be defined in a compositional way. Armed with our semantic framework, we define some basic notions of semantic entailment generalising the classical one and analyse their logical properties. We believe our definitions can serve as a springboard to investigate more refined forms of non-classical entailment that can meet a variety of applications in knowledge representation and reasoning.

Keywords: Logic · Knowledge representation · Non-classical semantics

1 Introduction

The problem of dealing with information that is either contradictory or incomplete (or even both) has long been a major challenge in human reasoning. With the advent of artificial intelligence (AI), such a problem has transferred to AI-based applications and has become one of the main topics of investigation of many areas at the intersection of AI and others.

Classical logic (and its many variants) is at the heart of knowledge representation and the formalisation of reasoning in AI. Alas, the classical semantics is naturally hostile to inconsistencies and does not cope well with lack of information. This has often forced applications of classical logic into resorting to 'workarounds' or limiting its scope.

In this paper, we make the first steps in the study of a generalised semantics for propositional logic in which contradictions and incompleteness are admitted

© Springer Nature Switzerland AG 2020
A. Gerber (Ed.): SACAIR 2020, CCIS 1342, pp. 253–264, 2020.
https://doi.org/10.1007/978-3-030-66151-9_16

at the very basics of the semantic framework. We do so by extending the notion of world (valuation) so that it allows for propositions to be both true and false, and also for their truth values not to be defined. With that as the basis, we define a truth-functional interpretation of complex sentences and show that it is possible to reason in the presence of inconsistencies or in the absence of truth values without resorting to a dialetheist [15,16] or a many-valued stance [2,9].

Of particular interest to us is the notion of entailment under the proposed semantics. In that respect, we also put forward some basic notions of semantic entailment generalising the classical one and analyse their logical properties. We point out which properties and reasoning patterns usually considered in classical logic are preserved and which ones are violated by the new definitions.

We believe that our constructions and preliminary results can serve as a springboard with which to investigate further the role of inconsistencies and incompleteness as basic logical notions and their applications in knowledge representation. The paper concludes by mentioning the next steps in this direction.

2   Basic Semantic Framework

Let $\mathcal{P}$ be a finite set of propositional *atoms*. We use $p, q, \ldots$ as meta-variables for atoms. Propositional sentences are denoted by $\alpha, \beta, \ldots$, and are recursively defined in the usual way:

$$\alpha ::= \top \mid \bot \mid \mathcal{P} \mid \neg\alpha \mid \alpha \wedge \alpha \mid \alpha \vee \alpha \mid \alpha \rightarrow \alpha$$

(As usually done, we see the bi-conditional $\alpha \leftrightarrow \beta$ as an abbreviation for the sentence $(\alpha \rightarrow \beta) \wedge (\beta \rightarrow \alpha)$.) We use $\mathcal{L}$ to denote the set of all propositional sentences built up according to the above grammar.

When it comes to the semantics, our point of departure is the thesis, endorsed by some in the past [17], that *functionality* and *totality* in the assignment of truth values is at the source of many of the criticisms voiced against classical reasoning. Therefore, here we shall forego both properties in the definitions of valuation (or world) and satisfaction below.

A (propositional) *world* is a relation on $\mathcal{P} \times \{0, 1\}$, where 1 represents truth and 0 falsity. $\mathcal{U} \stackrel{\text{def}}{=} 2^{\mathcal{P} \times \{0,1\}}$ is the *universe* (set of all worlds). We use $w, v, u, \ldots$, possibly with primes, to denote worlds. Whenever it eases the presentation, we shall represent valuations as sequences of atoms (e.g., p) and barred atoms (e.g., $\bar{p}$), with the understanding that the presence of p in w abbreviates $(p, 1) \in w$, while the presence of a barred atom $\bar{p}$ in w abbreviates $(p, 0) \in w$. Given $\mathcal{P}$, it is easy to verify that $|\mathcal{U}| = 2^{2 \times |\mathcal{P}|}$.

A *classical* world is a world that is a total function. A *partial* world is a world that is a partial function. An *absurd* world is a world w for which there is $p \in \mathcal{P}$ s.t. $w(p) = \{0, 1\}$. (Notice that there are some absurd worlds not assigning any truth value to at least one atom, i.e., there are absurd worlds that are extensions of partial ones.) A *possible* world is a world that is not absurd. A *non-classical* world is a world that is not classical. We can partition $\mathcal{U}$ into a set of classical worlds, denoted $\mathcal{U}_{\text{cl}}$, a set of partial worlds $\mathcal{U}_{\text{pa}}$, and a set of absurd worlds $\mathcal{U}_{\text{ab}}$, and such that $\mathcal{U} = \mathcal{U}_{\mathrm{cl}} \cup \mathcal{U}_{\mathrm{pa}} \cup \mathcal{U}_{\mathrm{ab}}$. Moreover, with $\mathcal{U}_{\mathrm{p}} \overset{\mathrm{def}}{=} \mathcal{U}_{\mathrm{cl}} \cup \mathcal{U}_{\mathrm{pa}}$ we denote the set of possible worlds, and with $\mathcal{U}_{\mathrm{nc}} \overset{\mathrm{def}}{=} \mathcal{U}_{\mathrm{pa}} \cup \mathcal{U}_{\mathrm{ab}}$ the non-classical ones.

The idea behind our notions of absurd and partial worlds is certainly not new. For instance, they have been explored by Rescher and Brandom [17], even though their technical construction and proposed semantics for the propositional connectives is different from ours (see below).

The definition of satisfaction of a sentence $\alpha \in \mathcal{L}$ by a given world must be redefined w.r.t. the classical tradition because the standard, classical, notion of satisfaction is an 'all-or-nothing' notion. By that we mean $\Vdash$, although called satisfaction *relation*, is usually defined as a (recursive) *function*, which does not allow for a sentence $\alpha \in \mathcal{L}$ to be true and false at w at the same time, or to be just unknown at a given world. Therefore, just as valuations (worlds) in our setting are no longer total functions, which allows for propositions to be true and false simultaneously, or even completely unknown, so will the satisfaction relation be. The crux of the matter become then how to define $\Vdash$ in such a way as to allow α and $\neg\alpha$ to be true at a given w and how to express this in terms of the subsentences and propositions therein. Of course, if we want to give an intuitionistic flavour to our logic, $\Vdash$ should also be such that the values of both α and $\neg\alpha$, for some $\alpha \in \mathcal{L}$, are unknown.

Previous attempts to redefine satisfaction in order to allow for sentences and their negations to be true at the same time have stumbled upon the *exportation principle* [5,6]: the notion of satisfaction, which sits at the meta-level, gets 'contaminated' by inconsistencies at the object level, resulting in a contradictory sentence being satisfied if and only if it is not satisfied (a contradiction 'exported' to the meta-level). Here we aim at avoiding precisely that by ensuring the meta-language we work with remains as much as possible consistent. (We shall come back to this matter at the end of the present section.)

The *satisfaction relation* is a binary relation $\Vdash \subseteq (\mathcal{U} \times \mathcal{L}) \times \{\mathbf{0}, \mathbf{1}\}$, where $\mathbf{1}$ and $\mathbf{0}$ are 'meta-truth' values standing for, respectively, 'is true' and 'is false' at world w. The intuition is that α is *true* at w if $\mathbf{1} \in \Vdash (w, \alpha)$, and *false* at w if $\mathbf{0} \in \Vdash (w, \alpha)$. Of course, to be false does not mean not to be true, and the other way round. (Notice that $\{0,1\}$ and $\{\mathbf{0},\mathbf{1}\}$ are not to be conflated, in the same vein as 'valuation' and 'satisfaction' are not synonyms.[1]) In that respect, a given $\alpha \in \mathcal{L}$ can have a truth value at a given world $w \in \mathcal{U}$ (**0**, **1**, or both, which, importantly, is *not* an extra truth value) or *none* at all (when $\Vdash (w, \alpha) = \emptyset$, which is not an extra truth value either). Before we provide the definition of satisfaction of a sentence in terms of its subsentences, we discuss its expected behaviour w.r.t. the sentence's main connective. For the sake of readability, in Tables 1, 2, 3, and 4, we represent $\{\mathbf{0}\}$, $\{\mathbf{1}\}$ and $\{\mathbf{0},\mathbf{1}\}$ as, respectively, **0**, **1** and **01**, and the lack of truth value as $\emptyset$—which, again, is not an extra truth value. So, in the referred tables, **0** and **1** are read as usual, $\emptyset$ is read as 'has no

---

[1] We could, in principle, also have used $\{0,1\}$ in the definition of satisfaction, but here we shall adopt the (possibly superfluous) stance that truth of a fact within the 'actual' world and truth of a sentence at given worlds are notions sitting at different levels, or, at the very least, are notions of subtly different kinds.

value', and **01** reads 'is true and false', i.e., both truth values apply. (The reader not convinced by some of the entries in Tables 1, 2, 3, and 4 is invited to hold on until we state some of the validities holding under the notion of satisfaction we are about to define.)

Satisfaction of ¬α *at* w: If α is just true or false at a given world, then its negation should behave as usual, i.e., as a 'toggle' function. By the same principle (applied twice), if α happens to be true and false, then its negation should be false and true. For the odd case, namely when α has no (known) value, a legitimate question to ask is 'can we know more about the negation of a fact than we know about the fact itself?' A cautious answer would be 'no'. Table 1 summarises these considerations.

Table 1. Semantics of ¬.

α	¬α
∅	∅
1	0
0	1
01	01

Satisfaction of α ∧ β *at* w: As usual, a conjunction is true if both conjuncts are true, and false if at least one of them is false. A sentence being allowed more than one truth value means this rule can be triggered twice, with the conjunction being true and false at the same time. Not knowing the truth value of a conjunct may cast doubt on that of the conjunction; but if one of the conjuncts is surely false, so should their conjunction be. Table 2 captures all the possibilities.

Table 2. Semantics of ∧.

α	β	α ∧ β
∅	∅	∅
∅	0	0
∅	1	∅
∅	01	0
0	∅	0
0	0	0
0	1	0
0	01	0
1	∅	∅
1	0	0
1	1	1
1	01	01
01	∅	0
01	0	0
01	1	01
01	01	01

Satisfaction of $\alpha \vee \beta$ *at w:* For $\vee$, the truth of at least one of the disjuncts is enough to enforce that of their disjunction, and that even if one does not know the truth value of all disjuncts. If both disjuncts are false, so should be their disjunction. And, once more, the last two rules may apply simultaneously. Table 3 summarises the behaviour of disjunction within our framework.

Table 3. Semantics of $\vee$.

α	β	$\alpha \vee \beta$
$\emptyset$	$\emptyset$	$\emptyset$
$\emptyset$	0	$\emptyset$
$\emptyset$	1	1
$\emptyset$	01	1
0	$\emptyset$	$\emptyset$
0	0	0
0	1	1
0	01	01
1	$\emptyset$	1
1	0	1
1	1	1
1	01	1
01	$\emptyset$	1
01	0	01
01	1	1
01	01	01

Satisfaction of $\alpha \rightarrow \beta$ *at w:* Traditionally, a conditional is deemed true if its antecedent is false or its consequent is true, and is false if the antecedent is true while the consequent is false. Allowing for a sentence to be true and false at the same time carries along a double application of this principle. Nevertheless, not knowing the value of the antecedent or that of the consequent may cast doubt on the application of the above principle: it should only be applied when a *sufficient* condition is met. For instance, if α is unknown and β is true and false, all we know is that β is true, and therefore the conditional is true. Similarly, if α is true and false, and β is unknown, all we know is that α is false, which is enough for the conditional to be verified. This discussion is summarised by Table 4.

In the light of the above considerations, satisfaction of sentences from $\mathcal{L}$ at worlds from $\mathcal{U}$ can be defined recursively as specified below.

Definition 1 (Satisfaction). *The* **satisfaction relation** *on sentences of* $\mathcal{L}$ *is defined in a compositional way as follows:*

Table 4. Semantics of $\rightarrow$.

α	β	$\alpha \rightarrow \beta$
$\emptyset$	$\emptyset$	$\emptyset$
$\emptyset$	**0**	$\emptyset$
$\emptyset$	**1**	**1**
$\emptyset$	**01**	**1**
0	$\emptyset$	**1**
0	**0**	**1**
0	**1**	**1**
0	**01**	**1**
1	$\emptyset$	$\emptyset$
1	**0**	**0**
1	**1**	**1**
1	**01**	**01**
01	$\emptyset$	**1**
01	**0**	**01**
01	**1**	**1**
01	**01**	**01**

- $\Vdash (w, \top) = \{\mathbf{1}\}$;
- $\Vdash (w, \bot) = \{\mathbf{0}\}$;
- $((w, p), \mathbf{1}) \in \Vdash$ *iff* $(p, \mathbf{1}) \in w$;
- $((w, p), \mathbf{0}) \in \Vdash$ *iff* $(p, \mathbf{0}) \in w$;
- $((w, \neg\alpha), \mathbf{1}) \in \Vdash$ *iff* $((w, \alpha), \mathbf{0}) \in \Vdash$;
- $((w, \neg\alpha), \mathbf{0}) \in \Vdash$ *iff* $((w, \alpha), \mathbf{1}) \in \Vdash$;
- $((w, \alpha \wedge \beta), \mathbf{1}) \in \Vdash$ *iff both* $((w, \alpha), \mathbf{1}) \in \Vdash$ *and* $((w, \beta), \mathbf{1}) \in \Vdash$;
- $((w, \alpha \wedge \beta), \mathbf{0}) \in \Vdash$ *iff either* $((w, \alpha), \mathbf{0}) \in \Vdash$ *or* $((w, \beta), \mathbf{0}) \in \Vdash$;
- $((w, \alpha \vee \beta), \mathbf{1}) \in \Vdash$ *iff either* $((w, \alpha), \mathbf{1}) \in \Vdash$ *or* $((w, \beta), \mathbf{1}) \in \Vdash$;
- $((w, \alpha \vee \beta), \mathbf{0}) \in \Vdash$ *iff both* $((w, \alpha), \mathbf{0}) \in \Vdash$ *and* $((w, \beta), \mathbf{0}) \in \Vdash$;
- $((w, \alpha \rightarrow \beta), \mathbf{1}) \in \Vdash$ *iff* $((w, \alpha), \mathbf{0}) \in \Vdash$ *or* $((w, \beta), \mathbf{1}) \in \Vdash$;
- $((w, \alpha \rightarrow \beta), \mathbf{0}) \in \Vdash$ *iff* $((w, \alpha), \mathbf{1}) \in \Vdash$ *and* $((w, \beta), \mathbf{0}) \in \Vdash$.

Henceforth, we shall sometimes use $w \Vdash \alpha$ as an abbreviation for $((w, \alpha), \mathbf{1}) \in \Vdash$, and $w \nVdash \alpha$ otherwise, i.e., when either $\Vdash (w, \alpha) = \emptyset$ or $\Vdash (w, \alpha) = \{\mathbf{0}\}$.

It is easy to see that the *satisfiability problem* for $\mathcal{L}$, i.e., the problem of determining whether for a given $\alpha \in \mathcal{L}$ there is $w \in \mathcal{U}$ s.t. $w \Vdash \alpha$, is at least as hard as the satisfiability problem for classical propositional logic. As for the upper bound, we already know there are $2^{2 \times |\mathcal{P}|}$ valuations to be checked. Furthermore, notice that the size of a world in $\mathcal{U}$ is, in the worst case, double the size of a classical propositional valuation and therefore verifying that a world does indeed satisfy a sentence α can be done in polynomial time. This establishes satisfiability of $\mathcal{L}$-sentences as an NP-COMPLETE problem [4,14].

One of the difficulties brought about by some approaches allowing for the notion of contradiction-bearing worlds is the 'contamination' of the meta-language with inconsistencies via the exportation principle [5]. In such frameworks, when assessing the truth of a sentence of the form $\alpha \wedge \neg\alpha$, the corresponding definition of satisfaction leads to the fact α is true *and* is not true (in the meta-language). Let us see how things go in the light of our definitions above. Assume that $w \Vdash \alpha \wedge \neg\alpha$, i.e., $((w, \alpha \wedge \neg\alpha), \mathbf{1}) \in \Vdash$. By the semantics for conjunction, we have both $((w, \alpha), \mathbf{1}) \in \Vdash$ and $((w, \neg\alpha), \mathbf{1}) \in \Vdash$, which, according to Table 2, happens only if $\Vdash (w, \alpha) = \Vdash (w, \neg\alpha) = \{\mathbf{0}, \mathbf{1}\}$. As far as one can tell, the latter is not an antinomy in the meta-language.

It is worth noting that, for every $\alpha, \beta \in \mathcal{L}$, the truth conditions for both $\neg(\alpha \wedge \beta)$ and $\neg\alpha \vee \neg\beta$ are the same, and so are those for $\neg(\alpha \vee \beta)$ and $\neg\alpha \wedge \neg\beta$. In that respect, the De Morgan laws are preserved under our non-standard semantics. It turns out the truth conditions for $\alpha \rightarrow \beta$ and $\neg\alpha \vee \beta$ also coincide, and therefore the connective for material implication is superfluous. If we admit material implication and the constant $\bot$, then it is negation that becomes superfluous, as the semantics for $\neg\alpha$ and $\alpha \rightarrow \bot$ coincide. Moreover, both $\top$ and $\bot$ can be expressed in terms of each other with the help of negation.

As it is usually done, we can talk of *validity*, i.e., truth at all worlds under consideration. Let $\alpha \in \mathcal{L}$; we say that α is a *classical validity* (alias, α is *classically valid*), denoted $\models \alpha$, if $w \Vdash \alpha$ for every $w \in \mathcal{U}_{\text{cl}}$. (Obviously, our notion of classical validity and that of tautology in classical propositional logic coincide.) We say α is a *partial validity* (alias, α is *partially valid*), denoted $\models_{\text{pa}} \alpha$, if $w \Vdash \alpha$ for every $w \in \mathcal{U}_{\text{pa}}$. As it turns out, partial validity is quite a stingy notion of validity: the only valid sentences in $\mathcal{U}_{\text{pa}}$ are $\top$ and those of the form $\alpha \vee \top$ (or $\alpha \rightarrow \top$). Lest this be seen as a drawback of allowing partial valuations in our framework, here we claim this is rather a reminder that partiality may have as consequence that even the principles of the underlying logic do not hold at worlds where the truth of some or all the propositions is unknown. Moreover, the presence of partial worlds automatically rules out some validities from classical logic that are usually seen as unjustifiable in non-classical circles. Among those are the law of *excluded middle* ($\alpha \vee \neg\alpha$ is a validity), the law of *non-contradiction* ($\neg(\alpha \wedge \neg\alpha)$), the principle of *double negation* ($\neg\neg\alpha \leftrightarrow \alpha$), and the *principle of explosion* ($(\alpha \wedge \neg\alpha) \rightarrow \beta$, for every $\beta \in \mathcal{L}$). Neither of these is a partial validity, as it can easily be checked. (We shall come back to these principles later on.) Finally, we can also define the notion of *absurd validity* (denoted $\models_{\text{ab}}$), which amounts to satisfaction by all absurd worlds. Some examples of absurd validities within our framework are $\top$ and $(p_1 \wedge \neg p_1) \vee \ldots \vee (p_n \wedge \neg p_n)$, for $p_i \in \mathcal{P}$, $i = 1, \ldots, n$, with $n = |\mathcal{P}|$.

Before we carry on, let us consider the so-called 'paradoxes' of material implication [18], namely the sentences $\alpha \rightarrow (\beta \rightarrow \alpha)$, $(\alpha \rightarrow \beta) \vee (\beta \rightarrow \alpha)$, and $\alpha \rightarrow (\beta \vee \neg\beta)$, which are all classical validities. We already know that none of them is a partial validity, and it should not take too much effort to verify that they are not absurd validities either. Furthermore, according to our semantics, the three sentences above do not have the same meaning, i.e., their truth tables are pairwise different from each other. This means that our semantics can distinguish between these syntactically different sentences, which the classical semantics cannot do.

From the discussion above, one can see that not all classical tautologies are preserved in our semantic framework, which is just as intended. In that respect, our framework provides the semantic foundation for an *infra-classical* logic curtailing certain classical conclusions that are often perceived as problematic. In the next section, once we have defined a few forms of entailment, we shall also assess the validity and failure of some commonly considered rules of inference or reasoning patterns from classical logic.

3   Basic Forms of Entailment and Their Properties

Let $\alpha \in \mathcal{L}$. With $[\![\alpha]\!]_{\mathrm{cl}} \stackrel{\text{def}}{=} \{w \in \mathcal{U}_{\mathrm{cl}} \mid w \Vdash \alpha\}$ we denote the *classical models* of α; with $[\![\alpha]\!]_{\mathrm{pa}} \stackrel{\text{def}}{=} \{w \in \mathcal{U}_{\mathrm{pa}} \mid w \Vdash \alpha\}$ we denote the *partial models* of α, and with $[\![\alpha]\!]_{\mathrm{ab}} \stackrel{\text{def}}{=} \{w \in \mathcal{U}_{\mathrm{ab}} \mid w \Vdash \alpha\}$ we denote the *absurd models* of α. The *possible models* of α is the set $[\![\alpha]\!]_{\mathrm{p}} \stackrel{\text{def}}{=} [\![\alpha]\!]_{\mathrm{cl}} \cup [\![\alpha]\!]_{\mathrm{pa}}$, whereas the *non-classical models* of α is the set $[\![\alpha]\!]_{\mathrm{nc}} \stackrel{\text{def}}{=} [\![\alpha]\!]_{\mathrm{pa}} \cup [\![\alpha]\!]_{\mathrm{ab}}$. Finally, the *models* of α *tout court* is the set $[\![\alpha]\!] \stackrel{\text{def}}{=} [\![\alpha]\!]_{\mathrm{cl}} \cup [\![\alpha]\!]_{\mathrm{nc}}$.

The choice of which family of models one wants to work with gives rise to different notions of entailment or logical consequence. Below are those to which we shall give consideration in the present paper.[2]

Definition 2 (Classical entailment). α *classically entails* β, *denoted* $\alpha \models \beta$, *if* $[\![\alpha]\!]_{\mathrm{cl}} \subseteq [\![\beta]\!]$.

Clearly, $\models$ here coincides with standard classical entailment. We shall use $\alpha \equiv \beta$ as an abbreviation for both $\alpha \models \beta$ and $\beta \models \alpha$.

Definition 3 (Possible entailment). α *possibly entails* β, *denoted* $\alpha \models_{\mathrm{p}} \beta$, *if* $[\![\alpha]\!]_{\mathrm{p}} \subseteq [\![\beta]\!]$.

Definition 4 (General entailment). α *generally entails* β, *denoted* $\alpha \models_{\mathrm{g}} \beta$, *if* $[\![\alpha]\!] \subseteq [\![\beta]\!]$.

We use $\equiv_{\mathrm{p}}$ and $\equiv_{\mathrm{g}}$ to denote logical equivalence in the above class of models.

From the definitions at the beginning of the present section, one expects $\models_{\mathrm{g}} \subseteq \models_{\mathrm{p}} \subseteq \models$. This is indeed the case. In the remaining of the section, we look at specific properties of each form of non-classical entailment. Below, $\models_*$ denotes either of $\models_{\mathrm{p}}$ or $\models_{\mathrm{g}}$.

Possible entailment satisfies the following rule of Generalised Modus Ponens:

$$(\text{MP}) \quad \frac{\alpha \models_{\mathrm{p}} \beta, \ \ \alpha \models_{\mathrm{p}} \beta \to \gamma}{\alpha \models_{\mathrm{p}} \gamma}$$

---

[2] We do not rule out the remaining combinations; space and time constraints prevent us from assessing them here.

To see why, let $w \in [\![\alpha]\!]_p$; then, by definition of $\models_p$, we have both $w \in [\![\beta]\!]_p$ and $w \in [\![\beta \to \gamma]\!]_p$, i.e., $w \Vdash \beta$ and $w \Vdash \beta \to \gamma$. Then we have $((w, \beta), 1) \in \Vdash$ and $((w, \beta \to \gamma), 1) \in \Vdash$. Since $w \in \mathcal{U}_p$, this only holds if $((w, \gamma), 1) \in \Vdash$ (cf. Table 4), i.e., $w \Vdash \gamma$, and therefore $w \in [\![\gamma]\!]$.

General entailment, on the other hand, fails (MP). Let $\alpha = \beta = p \wedge \neg p$, and let $\gamma = \bot$. It can easily be verified that $p \wedge \neg p \models_g p \wedge \neg p$, $p \wedge \neg p \models_g (p \wedge \neg p) \to \bot$, and $p \wedge \neg p \not\models_g \bot$.

Neither possible nor general entailment satisfies the rule of Contraposition:

$$(CP) \quad \frac{\alpha \models_* \beta}{\neg \beta \models_* \neg \alpha}$$

For a counter-example, let $\alpha = p \wedge \neg p$ and $\beta = q$. We do have $p \wedge \neg p \models_p q$, because $[\![p \wedge \neg p]\!]_p = \emptyset$, but $\neg q \not\models_p \neg(p \wedge \neg p)$, as there are partial worlds satisfying $\neg q$ which assign no value to p. The same counter-example applies to general entailment.

That both possible and general entailment satisfy the following Monotonicity and Cut rules can easily be verified and we omit the proofs here:

$$(Mon) \quad \frac{\alpha \models_* \beta, \ \alpha' \models_* \alpha}{\alpha' \models_* \beta} \qquad (Cut) \quad \frac{\alpha \wedge \beta \models_* \gamma, \ \alpha \models_* \beta}{\alpha \models_* \gamma}$$

Possible entailment also satisfies the so-called 'easy' half of the deduction theorem:

$$(EHD) \quad \frac{\alpha \models_p \beta \to \gamma}{\alpha \wedge \beta \models_p \gamma}$$

To witness, assume $\alpha \models_p \beta \to \gamma$. By Mon, we have $\alpha \wedge \beta \models_p \beta \to \gamma$. We also have $\alpha \wedge \beta \models_p \beta$. By MP, we conclude $\alpha \wedge \beta \models_p \gamma$.

To see that general entailment fails EHD, let again $\alpha = \beta = p \wedge \neg p$, and let $\gamma = \bot$. We have $p \wedge \neg p \models_g (p \wedge \neg p) \to \bot$, but $p \wedge \neg p \wedge p \wedge \neg p \not\models_g \bot$.

Both possible and general entailment fail the 'hard' half of the deduction theorem:

$$(HHD) \quad \frac{\alpha \wedge \beta \models_* \gamma}{\alpha \models_* \beta \to \gamma}$$

Indeed, we have $p \wedge q \models_p q$, but for some w such that $w(p) = \{1\}$ and $w(q) = \emptyset$, we have $\Vdash (w, q \to q) = \emptyset$, and therefore $p \not\models_p q \to q$. The case for $\models_g$ is analogous.

The following Transitivity rule is a consequence of Monotonicity and is satisfied by both possible and general entailment:

$$(Tran) \quad \frac{\alpha \models_* \beta, \ \beta \models_* \gamma}{\alpha \models_* \gamma}$$

Not surprisingly, possible and general entailment fail the First Disjunctive rule below, just as classical entailment does:

$$(Disj1) \quad \frac{\alpha \models_* \beta \vee \gamma}{\alpha \models_* \beta \ \text{or} \ \alpha \models_* \gamma}$$

To witness, we have $p \rightarrow q \models_* \neg p \vee q$, but neither $p \rightarrow q \models_* \neg p$ nor $p \rightarrow q \models_* q$ holds.

The Second Disjunctive rule below is satisfied by both possible and general entailment, courtesy to the fact that, for every α, β, $[\![\alpha]\!] \subseteq [\![\alpha \vee \beta]\!]$.

$$\text{(Disj2)} \quad \frac{\alpha \vee \beta \models_* \gamma}{\alpha \models \gamma \ \text{ or } \ \beta \models_* \gamma}$$

Possible and general entailment satisfy the rule of Generalised Disjunction below:

$$\text{(GD)} \quad \frac{\alpha \models_* \beta, \ \gamma \models_* \delta}{\alpha \vee \gamma \models_* \beta \vee \delta}$$

To see why, let $w \in [\![\alpha \vee \gamma]\!]_p$, i.e., $w \Vdash \alpha \vee \gamma$, and then either $w \Vdash \alpha$ or $w \Vdash \gamma$, or both. If $w \Vdash \alpha$, then $w \Vdash \beta$, and therefore $w \Vdash \beta \vee \delta$ (cf. Table 3). If $w \Vdash \gamma$, then $w \Vdash \delta$, and hence $w \Vdash \beta \vee \delta$. The proof for $\models_g$ is analogous.

Both possible and general entailment fail the rule of Proof by Contradiction below:

$$\text{(PC)} \quad \frac{\alpha \wedge \neg \beta \models_* \gamma \wedge \neg \gamma}{\alpha \models_* \beta}$$

Indeed, we have $p \wedge \neg (q \vee \neg q) \models_p q \wedge \neg q$. Nevertheless, there is $w \in \mathcal{U}_p$ such that $w(p) = \{1\}$ and $w(q) = \emptyset$, from which follows $\Vdash (w, q \vee \neg q) = \emptyset$, and therefore $p \not\models_p q \vee \neg q$. (For the case of $\models_g$, just let $w \in \mathcal{U}_{ab}$.)

The following rule of Proof by Cases is violated by both possible and general entailment:

$$\text{(D)} \quad \frac{\alpha \wedge \neg \beta \models \gamma, \ \alpha \wedge \beta \models \gamma}{\alpha \models \gamma}$$

Indeed, we have $p \wedge \neg q \models_p q \vee \neg q$ and $p \wedge q \models_p q \vee \neg q$, but $p \not\models_p q \vee \neg q$. The same can be shown for $\models_g$.

We conclude the present section with an assessment of a few more properties of classical reasoning. The first one is Disjunctive Syllogism: $(\neg \alpha \vee \beta) \wedge \alpha \models \beta$ (equivalently, $\beta \wedge \alpha \models \beta$). It is easy to verify that possible entailment satisfies both forms. General entailment, on the other hand, fails the first form and satisfies the second. For the latter, a quick check via Table 2 suffices. For the former, consider $w \in \mathcal{U}_{ab}$ such that $w(p) = \{0, 1\}$ and $w(q) = \emptyset$. Then we have $w \Vdash (\neg p \vee q) \wedge p$, but $w \not\Vdash q$. So, once more, our absurd worlds allow for distinguishing two classically equivalent sentences.

We have seen that the semantics for both $\alpha \rightarrow \beta$ and $\neg \alpha \vee \beta$ coincide, which has as consequence that both possible and general entailment satisfy the Duns Scott law: $\neg \alpha \models_* \alpha \rightarrow \beta$. On the other hand, Reductio ad Absurdum, i.e., $\neg \alpha \rightarrow (\beta \wedge \neg \beta) \models \alpha$, is only satisfied by possible entailment: $\neg \alpha \rightarrow (\beta \wedge \neg \beta)$ is just $\alpha \vee (\beta \wedge \neg \beta)$, which possibly entails α. As a counter-example for general entailment, it suffices to verify that $\neg p \rightarrow (q \wedge \neg q) \not\models_g p$.

It is not hard to see that $\bot \models_* \alpha$, for every $\alpha \in \mathcal{L}$, but notice that we do *not* have $p \wedge \neg p \models_g \alpha$, for every $\alpha \in \mathcal{L}$. Indeed, $\bot \leftrightarrow (p \wedge \neg p)$ is not a validity in our framework, just as $\top \leftrightarrow (p \vee \neg p)$ is not one either. One of the consequences of the latter is that in our framework not all validities are omnigenerated. Nevertheless, it does hold that $\alpha \models_* \top$, for any $\alpha \in \mathcal{L}$, since $[\![\top]\!] = \mathcal{U}$.

4   Concluding Remarks

In this paper, we have revisited the semantics of classical propositional logic. We started by generalising the notion of propositional valuation to that of a world that may also admit inconsistencies, or lack of information, or both. We have seen that our definition of valuation remains suitable for a compositional interpretation of the truth value of a complex sentence, and that without appealing to either a dialetheist stance or the use of more than two truth values. In particular, we have seen that assuming a compositional semantics does not lead to difficulties brought about by the exportation principle, which is one of the limitations of previous approaches sharing our motivations. We have also seen that the adoption of a more general semantics, which brings in a higher number of possible states of affairs to consider, does not increase the computational complexity of the satisfiability problem for the underlying language. We have then explored some basic notions of entailment within our semantic framework and compared them against many of the properties or reasoning patterns that are usually considered in formal logic. Some of these are lost, as expected, while some are preserved.

Immediate next steps for further investigation include (i) an exploration of other definitions of semantic entailment, their properties and respective suitability (or not) for effective non-classical reasoning; (ii) a comparison with standard systems of paraconsistent logic and other existing non-classical logics; (iii) the identification of scenarios for potential applications of the framework here introduced, and (iv) the definition of a basic proof method, probably based on semantic tableaux [8], that can serve as the backbone of more elaborate proof systems for extensions of our semantic framework.

Further future work stemming from the basic definitions and results here put forward can branch in several fruitful directions. A non-exhaustive list includes: (i) investigating a generalisation of the satisfiability problem [4] and the adaption of existing approaches and optimised techniques for its solution; (ii) extending the Kripkean semantics of modal logics [7] to also allow for 'impossible' or 'incomplete' worlds, or the set-theoretic semantics of description logics [3] to capture 'incoherent' or 'partially-known' objects or individuals in formal ontologies, before considering a move to full first-order logic, and (iii) revisiting the areas of belief change [1,10] and non-monotonic reasoning [13] in artificial intelligence, also benefitting from their semantic constructions in order to define more refined forms of entailment in our setting.

With regard to the last point above, extra structure may be added to $\mathcal{U}$, e.g. in the form of a *preference relation* or a *ranking function* [11,12], in order to distinguish worlds according to their level of *logical plausibility*. For instance, absurd worlds can be deemed as the least plausible ones, and possible worlds can be further ranked given extra information (e.g. a knowledge base and its signature of relevant atomic propositions). The associated entailment relation becomes then parameterised by such levels and should give rise to a consequence relation with more interesting properties than those of the basic entailments we have seen.

Acknowledgements. I would like to thank the anonymous referees for their comments and helpful suggestions. This work was partially supported by the National Research Foundation (NRF) of South Africa.

References

1. Alchourrón, C., Gärdenfors, P., Makinson, D.: On the logic of theory change: partial meet contraction and revision functions. J. Symbolic Logic **50**, 510–530 (1985)
2. Arieli, O., Avron, A.: The value of the four values. Artif. Intell. **102**, 97–141 (1998)
3. Baader, F., Calvanese, D., McGuinness, D., Nardi, D., Patel-Schneider, P. (eds.): The Description Logic Handbook: Theory, Implementation and Applications, 2nd edn. Cambridge University Press, Cambridge (2007)
4. Ben-Ari, M.: Mathematical Logic for Computer Science, 3rd edn. Springer, London (2012)
5. Berto, F., Jago, M.: Impossible Worlds. Oxford University Press, Oxford (2019)
6. Berto, F., Jago, M.: Impossible worlds. In: Zalta, E.N. (ed.) The Stanford Encyclopedia of Philosophy. Metaphysics Research Lab, Stanford University, fall 2018 edn. (2018)
7. Chellas, B.: Modal Logic: An Introduction. Cambridge University Press, Cambridge (1980)
8. D'Agostino, M., Gabbay, D., Hähnle, R., Posegga, J. (eds.): Handbook of Tableau Methods. Kluwer Academic Publishers, Dordrecht (1999)
9. Fitting, M.: Kleene's three valued logics and their children. Fundamenta Informaticae **20**(1), 113–131 (1994)
10. Hansson, S.: A Textbook of Belief Dynamics: Theory Change and Database Updating. Kluwer Academic Publishers, Dordrecht (1999)
11. Kraus, S., Lehmann, D., Magidor, M.: Nonmonotonic reasoning, preferential models and cumulative logics. Artif. Intell. **44**, 167–207 (1990)
12. Lehmann, D., Magidor, M.: What does a conditional knowledge base entail? Artif. Intell. **55**, 1–60 (1992)
13. Makinson, D.: Bridges from Classical to Nonmonotonic Logic, Texts in Computing. Texts in Computing, vol. 5. King's College Publications, London (2005)
14. Papadimitriou, C.: Computational Complexity. Addison-Wesley, Boston (1994)
15. Priest, G.: An Introduction to Non-Classical Logic: From If to Is. Cambridge Introductions to Philosophy, 2nd edn. Cambridge University Press, Cambridge (2001)
16. Priest, G., Berto, F., Weber, Z.: Dialetheism. In: Zalta, E.N. (ed.) The Stanford Encyclopedia of Philosophy. Metaphysics Research Lab, Stanford University, fall 2018 edn. (2018)
17. Rescher, N., Brandom, R.: The Logic of Inconsistency. A Study in Non-Standard Possible-Worlds Semantics and Ontology. Basil Blackwell, Oxford; APQ Library of Philosophy (1979)
18. Swart, H.: Logic: Mathematics, Language, Computer Science and Philosophy, vol. 1. Peter Lang (1993)

Machine Learning Theory

Stride and Translation Invariance in CNNs

Coenraad Mouton[1,2](✉) [iD], Johannes C. Myburgh[1,2] [iD],
and Marelie H. Davel[1,2] [iD]

[1] Multilingual Speech Technologies, North-West University,
Potchefstroom, South Africa
moutoncoenraad@gmail.com, christiaanmyburgh01@gmail.com
[2] CAIR, Cape Town, South Africa
http://engineering.nwu.ac.za/must

Abstract. Convolutional Neural Networks have become the standard
for image classification tasks, however, these architectures are not invariant to translations of the input image. This lack of invariance is
attributed to the use of stride which subsamples the input, resulting
in a loss of information, and fully connected layers which lack spatial
reasoning. We show that stride can greatly benefit translation invariance
given that it is combined with sufficient similarity between neighbouring
pixels, a characteristic which we refer to as *local homogeneity*. We also
observe that this characteristic is dataset-specific and dictates the relationship between pooling kernel size and stride required for translation
invariance. Furthermore we find that a trade-off exists between generalization and translation invariance in the case of pooling kernel size,
as larger kernel sizes lead to better invariance but poorer generalization.
Finally we explore the efficacy of other solutions proposed, namely global
average pooling, anti-aliasing, and data augmentation, both empirically
and through the lens of local homogeneity.

Keywords: Translation invariance · Subsampling · Convolutional
Neural Network · Local homogeneity

1 Introduction

Traditional computer vision tasks such as image classification and object detection have been revolutionized by the use of Convolutional Neural networks
(CNNs) [10]. CNNs are often assumed to be translation invariant, that is, classification ability is not influenced by shifts of the input image. This is a desirable
characteristic for image recognition, as a specific object or image must be correctly identified regardless of its location within the canvas area. The assumption
that CNNs exhibit translation invariance, however, has been shown to be erroneous by multiple authors [1,5,14], who all show that shifts of the input image
can drastically alter network classification accuracy. This is especially troubling,
as practical applications of CNNs require that an object be recognizable from

© Springer Nature Switzerland AG 2020
A. Gerber (Ed.): SACAIR 2020, CCIS 1342, pp. 267–281, 2020.
https://doi.org/10.1007/978-3-030-66151-9_17

different viewpoints, camera angles, and at different spatial locations within an image. Therefore, correcting for image translation within CNNs is an active area of study which has been partially addressed by methods such as Spatial Transformer Networks [4], Anti-Aliasing [14], and Global Average Pooling [1].

In this work, we provide an overview of the properties that are required for translation invariance and show why they generally do *not* hold in the case of CNNs. Furthermore we show that subsampling, commonly referred to as "stride" [2], can greatly benefit translation invariance. However, we find that subsampling is only beneficial given that it is combined with sufficient similarity between neighbouring pixels, a characteristic that we refer to as *local homogeneity*.

We empirically explore the relation between local homogeneity and subsampling by measuring the effects of varying pooling kernel size and stride on both invariance and generalization, repeated across several different architectures and datasets. We show that the inter-pixel variance of a given dataset dictates the necessary kernel size to ensure a degree of translation invariance. In addition we examine the efficacy of solutions proposed by other authors, namely global average pooling, anti-aliasing, and data augmentation in terms of local homogeneity, translation invariance, and generalization.

Taken together, we clarify the various aspects that influence translation invariance in CNNs in order to better understand how certain architectural choices affect both invariance and generalization, and we further measure these effects to see if our hypotheses hold true.

2 Background

In order to understand translation invariance, we must first define the terms that play a role and their relation to one another.

2.1 Translation Invariance and Equivariance

Convolutional neural networks make use of convolution and pooling operators which are inherently translational, as filter kernels are shifted over an image to provide an output, commonly referred to as a feature map [2]. The translational nature of CNNs leads to the erroneous assumption that these systems are invariant to translations of the input image, or that the spatial location of internal features are irrelevant for classification. However, Azulay and Weiss [1] show that even for state of the art CNN architectures (VGG16, ResNet50, Inception-ResNetV2), a single pixel shift of the input image can cause a severe change in the prediction confidence of the network. Surprisingly the shift of the input is imperceptible to the human eye, but drastically impedes the network's ability to classify.

Translation invariance can be described as follows (as adapted from [12]):

Definition 1. *A function f can be said to be invariant to a group of translations G if for any g element of G:*

$$f(g(I)) = f(I) \tag{1}$$

This implies that g has no effect on the output of function f, and the result remains equal whether g is applied or not.

A second misconception is that whilst modern CNNs are not translation *invariant*, they are translation *equivariant*. Translation equivariance (also referred to as covariance by some authors) is the property by which internal feature maps are shifted in a one-to-one ratio along with shifts of the input. We define translation equivariance as follows (as adapted from [12]):

Definition 2. *A function f is equivariant to the translations of group G if for any g element of G:*

$$f(g(I)) = g(f(I)) \tag{2}$$

This implies that the output is shifted in accordance with the shift of the input, or in other terms that the output of the function f can be translated to produce the same result as translating the input I before f is applied would.

Intuitively it would be expected that translation equivariance holds for both convolution and pooling layers, and this intuition proves correct for dense convolution and pooling, if edge effects are ignored. To illustrate this property, an arbitrary one-dimensional filter is applied to a one-dimensional input, as well as to shifted values of this input. Consider an input signal $I[n] = [0, 0, 0, 0, 1, 2, 0, 0, 0, 0]$ and a kernel $K[n] = [1, 0, 1]$: the result of the convolution $I[n] \circledast K[n]$ is shown in the second column of Table 1.

Table 1. Dense and strided convolution of a one-dimensional input with a kernel [1,0,1], and shifted variants

Input	Dense convolution	Strided convolution
[0,0,0,0,1,2,0,0,0,0]	[0,0,1,2,1,2,0,0]	[0,1,1,0]
[0,0,0,0,0,1,2,0,0,0]	[0,0,0,1,2,1,2,0]	[0,0,2,2]
[0,0,0,0,0,0,1,2,0,0]	[0,0,0,0,1,2,1,2]	[0,0,1,1]

As per this example, the equivariance property holds, as a shift of the input results in an equal shift of the output, meaning $f(g(I)) = g(f(I))$. However, this intuition fails when considering subsampling.

2.2 Subsampling

In CNNs, subsampling occurs when a convolution or pooling layer is used with a kernel stride greater than one. Using strided filters results in intermediary samples present in the input being skipped over and disregarded. Strided filters are widely used in state-of-the-art architectures, which has both benefits and drawbacks.

We first consider the disadvantages of subsampling. Azulay and Weiss [1] correctly show that subsampling breaks translation equivariance, as subsampling causes a loss of information. In the case of CNNs, an input is sampled at a rate dictated by the kernel stride, implying that information is disregarded if a stride greater than 1 is used. If information is lost, shifts of the input are not guaranteed to result in equivalent responses.

This effect can be shown by using the previous example and a stride of 2 when calculating the convolution (thus a subsampling factor of 2) as the third column of Table 1 illustrates.

Two important characteristics of stride are illustrated by this example:

1. **Signal information is lost.** Compared to the output of dense convolution, it is clear that subsampling disregards intermediary values. It is logical that this property can have an adverse effect on a CNN's ability to detect features in an image, as translating the input signal can cause features present in the input not to line up with the stride of the kernel.
2. **Translation Equivariance is lost.** The output of the convolution operation is no longer shifted in a one-to-one ratio with the input, meaning $f(g(I)) \neq g(f(I))$, as can be seen by comparing the output of $I[n] \circledast K[n]$ to that of $I[n-1] \circledast K[n]$. This implies that shifts of the input signal result in outputs that are not equivalent. The result of the strided filtering of a translated input is not guaranteed to be sufficiently similar to that of its untranslated counterpart if equivariance does not hold; this partly explains why CNNs are so susceptible to small shifts.

The main benefit of subsampling is that it can **greatly reduce the training time** of CNNs. As He and Sun [3] show, the time complexity of convolution layers in a CNN is given by:

$$O(\sum_{l=1}^{d} n_{l-1} \cdot s_l^2 \cdot n_l \cdot m_l^2) \tag{3}$$

where l is the index of the convolutional layer, d is the number of convolutional layers, and for any layer l, n_l is the number of output channels, s_l the spatial size of the filter, and m_l the size of the output feature map. The subsequent output size of any given layer has a large effect, given that m_l is squared. It can also be shown that the output width of a layer W_l given the previous layer width W_{l-1} is specified by:

$$W_l = \frac{W_{l-1} - k_w + 2p}{s} + 1 \tag{4}$$

where k_w is the kernel width, p is padding, and s is stride (the same equation holds for height). Given that stride acts as a divisor, we conclude that subsampling drastically reduces the size of the output, and in doing so substantially reduces the time complexity. Furthermore, through spatial reduction, the size of the input layer to the fully connected layers is greatly reduced, implying there are less learn-able parameters which further reduces training time and memory consumption [3].

Whilst subsampling reduces spatial dimensions, it is worth noting that this can also be achieved by downsampling in CNNs. We define downsampling as the reduction in spatial size caused by the size of a kernel during a convolution/pooling operation, where information along the edges of an input is disregarded (commonly referred to as "edge effects"). Conversely, subsampling causes spatial reduction by explicitly disregarding intermediary samples. Whilst downsampling does have an effect on translation invariance [6], we attempt to mitigate this effect through the use of adequate padding.

3   Signal Movement, Signal Similarity, and Local Homogeneity

In this section we show how subsampling plays a role in achieving translation equivariance, and identify the characteristics required for it to be present.

3.1   Shiftability

Whilst subsampling breaks the equivariance property, we propose that it can greatly benefit translation invariance under certain circumstances due to a third property we define as shiftability. Shiftability holds for systems that make use of subsampling and is defined as follows (note: this definition differs from that provided in [1] for shiftability):

Definition 3. *A function f with subsampling factor s is shiftable for a given translation if*

$$f(g(I)) = g'(f(I)) \tag{5}$$

where g is a translation function with translation vector $\vec{u}$ and input X

$$g(X) = t(\vec{u}, X) \tag{6}$$

and

$$g'(X) = t(\frac{\vec{u}}{s}, X) \tag{7}$$

Put otherwise, shiftability holds for translations that are factors of the subsampling factor s of f. When subsampling shifted inputs, equivalence will hold if a given translation is in accordance with the stride. To illustrate this property, consider an arbitrary input signal that is subsampled by a factor of four and various shifts of the signal, as shown in Table 2.

In this example, shiftability holds for translations that are factors of the subsampling factor (shifts of 4 and 8), and so a scaled form of equivariance is kept. It is further evident that subsampling scales shifts of the input signal: in this example, a shift of four in the input results in only a shift of one in the output.

The subsampling factor dictates how many versions of the output signal can potentially exist after translation (again ignoring edge effects): In this example four discrete outputs are present, where all other outputs are merely shifted variants. In the case of two-dimensional filtering, inputs are subsampled both

Table 2. Subsampling factor of four for an arbitrary input

Input	0 0 0 0 0 0 0 0 0 3 2 5 2 4 1 6 3 4 6 5 5 0 0 0 0 0 0 0 0 0
Shift	Subsampled output
0	**0 0 0 2 3 5 0 0**
1	0 0 0 5 6 5 0 0
2	0 0 0 2 1 6 0 0
3	0 0 0 3 4 4 0 0
4	**0 0 0 0 2 3 5 0**
5	0 0 0 0 5 6 5 0
6	0 0 0 0 2 1 6 0
7	0 0 0 0 3 4 4 0
8	**0 0 0 0 0 2 3 5**

vertically and horizontally, meaning s^2 output signals can exist given a single input and a bounded translation. This further implies that a given input will only be shiftable for $\frac{1}{s^2}$ of possible translations [1].

To explain how shiftability benefits translation invariance, we must first define two distinct characteristics that must be accounted for when comparing outputs of translated inputs to that of untranslated inputs.

3.2   Signal Similarity and Signal Movement

We propose two characteristics that influence translation invariance when subsampling is present:

- **Signal Similarity:** How much of the untranslated signal's output information is preserved after translation.
- **Signal Movement:** How far the translated output has been moved from the original position of the untranslated output.

As an example, consider an output signal of [0,0,1,2,0,0] and another of [0,0,0,1,2,0]. These signals are similar except that the second is shifted by one to the right. Conversely, an input of [0,0,1,2,0,0] and [0,0,2,3,0,0] are not exactly similar, but do not exhibit any shift (signal movement).

As subsampling scales shifts in accordance with the property of shiftability, it is evident that subsampling reduces signal movement, but leads to the loss of signal similarity, conversely using no subsampling leads to perfect signal similarity but allows the output to shift in a one-to-one ratio with the input. For translation invariance in CNNs signal similarity must be kept but signal movement must also be reduced to the extent possible. Whilst the reduction of signal movement during translation is fully dependent upon the subsampling factor, we propose that the degree of signal similarity that is preserved during subsampling is dependent upon *local homogeneity*.

3.3 Local Homogeneity

As subsampling disregards intermediary pixels in a given feature map, translated versions will results in more equivalent outputs if neighbouring pixels are more similar to each other in a given region. Put otherwise, preserving signal similarity requires that the variance between intermediary elements in a given window are sufficiently low enough, the size of which is dictated by the subsampling factor. We refer to this property as "local homogeneity".

To illustrate the effect of local homogeneity, consider an input that is fully locally homogeneous in accordance with the subsampling factor and the resulting output when shifting the signal. This is shown in Table 3 where a subsampling factor of 2 is used. Given that successive elements are similar in accordance with the subsampling factor, subsampling results in equivalent responses, yet the initial shift of the input is also scaled; implying that signal similarity is preserved and signal movement is negated. Our hypothesis surrounding local homogeneity brings about two logical conclusions:

Table 3. Subsampling of a locally homogeneous signal

Input	0 0 0 0 0 0 2 2 3 3 1 1 2 2 0 0 0 0 0 0
Shift	Subsampled output
0	0 0 0 2 3 1 2 0 0
1	0 0 0 2 3 1 2 0 0
2	0 0 0 0 2 3 1 2 0
3	0 0 0 0 2 3 1 2 0
4	0 0 0 0 0 2 3 1 2

- **Pooling improves local homogeneity:** Dense pooling (max and average pooling alike) reduces the variance of any given input, therefore providing more similarity between neighbouring pixels.
- **Strided pooling can benefit translation invariance:** Combining a pooling window of sufficient size (and therefore sufficient local homogeneity) with subsampling leads to the reduction of signal movement. This implies that translated samples will result in outputs that are more equivalent to untranslated samples.

In the following section we empirically explore our hypothesis surrounding local homogeneity by observing the effects of stride and pooling on translation invariance, as well as the role of local homogeneity in solutions proposed by other authors.

4 Analysis

In this section we empirically measure the translation invariance of different architectures and explore how these results relate to local homogeneity.

4.1   Experimental Setup

Training: Two datasets are used for analysis, namely MNIST [11] and CIFAR10 [8]. For prepossessing, MNIST networks are zero padded by 6 (meaning 6 rows of zeros are added to every edge of the image) and 10 for CIFAR10, resulting in 40×40 and 52×52 sized images respectively. This allows space on the image canvas for translation.

We use cross-entropy loss and ReLU activation functions, along with the Adam optimizer [7]. Batch size is kept constant at 128 for MNIST networks, and a smaller batch size of 64 is used for CIFAR10 due to a lack of video memory to train exceptionally large networks. Validation set size is constant at 5 000 for both MNIST and CIFAR10.

All MNIST networks are trained for a minimum of 100 epochs and 200 epochs for CIFAR10; furthermore, if a network has shown improvement in validation accuracy within the last 10 epochs an additional 15 epochs are added to training. Step-wise learning rate decay is also used and the starting learning rate for a group of networks is chosen empirically, within the range of 0.001 to 0.0001. It is confirmed that all networks are trained to 100% train accuracy.

Post-training, the epoch exhibiting the highest validation accuracy is chosen to ensure the best generalization possible for the specific architecture. Apart from early stopping, we do not make use of use any explicit regularization methods such as dropout or batch-norm.

In terms of architectural choices, all convolution/pooling layers use padding to adjust for the downsampling caused by the size of the kernel, but not to mitigate the effects of subsampling, according to the following equation:

$$p = \lfloor \frac{k_w - 1}{2} \rfloor \tag{8}$$

We use a standard three-layer architecture for both datasets, with 128 channels on the final layer and 3×3 dense convolution kernels, whilst pooling size and stride is varied for each experiment. This architecture is useful as it performs relatively well on both datasets, given that no explicit regularization is used, but is still simple enough to interpret any subsequent results.

Metrics: We measure translation invariance across different architectures by comparing the activation value vectors at the network output layer of an original and translated sample. Two measurements are used:

1. Mean Cosine Similarity (MCS): As defined in Eq. 9, MCS uses the angle between any two vectors a and b as a similarity measure. Since only the angle is used, differences in vector magnitudes are ignored.

$$cos(\theta) = \frac{a \cdot b}{\|a\| \|b\|} \tag{9}$$

2. Probability of top 1 change (PTop1): The probability of the top class prediction of a given network changing after an image is translated, as originally

proposed by Azulay and Weiss [1]. This allows us to determine an exact probability of a sample being incorrectly classified given a range of translation. This is useful as it purely measures a change in prediction accuracy and does not concern itself with other secondary effects.

Method of Comparison: For each measurement, we report on the average value of the metric, across all test samples that are translated according to randomly sampling from a specified range, for both vertical and horizontal translation. This results in a single scalar value specifying the network's translation invariance for a given maximum range of translation. Furthermore, when comparing several networks, only the samples that are correctly classified (before translation) by all networks present in the comparison are used. Finally, all results are averaged over three training seeds. For results displayed with graphs, we include error bars indicating the standard error.

4.2 Strided Pooling and Translation Invariance

We explore the effects of strided pooling on translation invariance, using an architecture without subsampling as baseline. Three other networks are trained with subsampling factors of 2, 4, and 8 respectively for the MNIST dataset. The subsampling factor is varied by consecutively setting the stride of the 2×2 max pooling filters in the network to 2, starting at the first layer. The comparative MCS is shown in Fig. 1.

This result shows that subsampling improves translation invariance for MNIST, where networks using subsampling show a substantially higher MCS. This further implies that 2×2 max pooling is sufficient to provide local homogeneity given a stride of 2 for each layer, however samples in the MNIST dataset are generally inherently highly homogeneous.

CIFAR10 is a more complex and detailed dataset, and is therefore generally less homogeneous and would require a larger degree of filtering to ensure translation invariance. To ascertain the required max pooling size for this dataset, the previous experiment is repeated for kernel sizes ranging from 2×2 to 5×5 for each layer. This is shown in Table 4, which shows the mean cosine similarity

Table 4. MCS for CIFAR10 networks with varying subsampling and max pooling kernel sizes (10 Pixel Range)

Subsampling factor	Kernel size			
	2×2	3×3	4×4	5×5
1	0.630	0.598	0.595	0.618
2	0.554	0.635	0.683	0.731
4	0.622	0.674	0.759	0.789
8	0.610	0.660	0.762	0.791

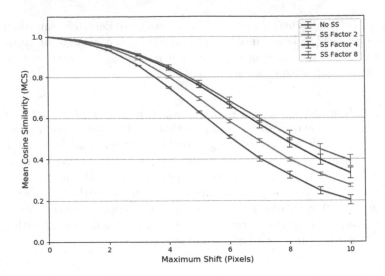

Fig. 1. MCS comparison for MNIST architectures with varying subsampling

for a maximum shift of 10 pixels for each network. We observe that in the case of CIFAR10 2×2 max pooling is not sufficient, and a substantial increase in translation invariance following subsampling is only observed at 3×3 pooling and larger.

For networks that make use of subsampling, we observe that larger kernel sizes always result in greater invariance. Conversely, for networks that do not make use of subsampling (the first row of Table 4) we observe a significant decrease in translation invariance as kernel size is increased. Intuitively one would expect larger kernels to always provide greater translation invariance, but this intuition fails since these networks are fully translation equivariant. Finally, we observe that greater subsampling always results in greater invariance when adequately sized kernels are used (as in the case of 4×4 and 5×5 pooling) which are aligned with our findings on MNIST.

These results support our proposal that stride can significantly increase the translation invariance of a network, given that is combined with sufficient local homogeneity. Furthermore we also find that the inherent homogeneity of a given dataset dictates the required filtering for subsampling to be effective.

4.3   Anti-aliasing

In terms of ensuring local homogeneity, average pooling outperforms that of max pooling, as an averaging kernel acts as an anti-aliasing (blurring) filter which greatly benefits translation invariance during subsampling. However, Scherer et al. [13] show that max pooling results in better generalization than that of average pooling when used in CNNs.

Zhang [14] proposes a solution to this problem which allows the generalization benefits of max pooling without compromising translation invariance. The author alters strided max pooling by separating it into two distinct layers: (1) Dense Max Pooling, and (2) Strided Anti-Aliasing. By applying an anti-aliasing filter, local homogeneity is ensured and the subsequent subsampling operation's affect on signal similarity is strongly mitigated, which results in a more translation invariant network.

The efficacy of this method is explored for both the MNIST and CIFAR10 datasets using the three layer 2×2 pooling networks from the previous section. Each pooling layer present in the network is replaced with a dense max pooling layer and a bin-5 anti-aliasing filter. These networks are then compared to their baseline counterparts that do not make use of anti-aliasing. The comparative MCS for a maximum shift of 10 pixels is shown in Table 5.

Table 5. Mean Cosine Similarity for MNIST and CIFAR10 networks with and without anti-aliasing for a maximum shift of 10 pixels

Subsampling factor	AA	MNIST	CIFAR
1	No	0.248	**0.630**
	Yes	**0.329**	0.518
4	No	0.383	0.620
	Yes	**0.654**	**0.710**
8	No	0.447	0.611
	Yes	**0.638**	**0.690**

For MNIST, anti-aliasing seems to always provide better translation invariance regardless of whether subsampling is used or not. However, the greatest increase in translation invariance occurs when subsampling is applied, as it is not solely anti-aliasing that provides invariance, but its combination with stride. For CIFAR10 the results are slightly different, anti-aliasing greatly reduces the invariance of the architecture without subsampling. However, as is the case with MNIST, a large increase is evident when it is combined with subsampling.

In conclusion, these results confirm that both signal similarity must be preserved and signal movement must be reduced to increase the network's invariance to translation, and that anti-aliasing is an effective solution for ensuring local homogeneity.

4.4   No Subsampling and Global Average Pooling

Whilst we have shown that the use of subsampling can greatly benefit translation invariance, Azulay and Weiss [1] propose a different approach that makes use of Global Average Pooling (GAP) and avoiding any subsampling throughout the network. Global pooling is not influenced by signal movement, and with no subsampling, equivariance is kept, resulting in a perfectly translation invariant system.

We verify this by adding a final global average pooling layer to our baseline model without subsampling for CIFAR10, and we find that it has a 0% Ptop1 change for shifts within the canvas area. Put otherwise, the system is completely translation invariant.

Although this might seem to be a complete solution, GAP is not without its drawbacks. Ignoring the benefits of subsampling, the GAP operation disregards a tremendous amount of information and could lower the classification ability of a given architecture, and is therefore not necessarily a suitable solution for every dataset. However, Fully Convolutional Neural Networks (FCNNs) do make use of GAP, and withholding the use of subsampling in these architectures could be a suitable solution for ensuring translation invariance.

4.5 Learned Invariance

We explore the effects of learned invariance by training our previous MNIST architectures of Fig. 1 on a translated data set. We keep the size of the train set constant and randomly translate each sample up to a maximum of 8 pixels, furthermore we apply the same translation to the validation set (the test set remains untranslated). In this way we explicitly optimize our models for translation invariance, and then examine whether our previous findings still hold true. The comparative MCS of these networks is shown in Fig. 2.

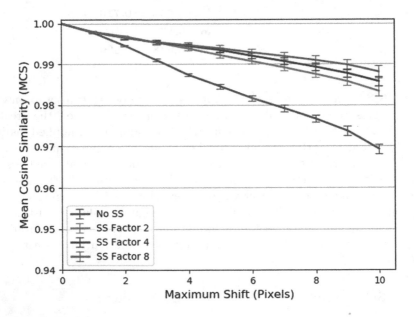

Fig. 2. MCS comparison for MNIST architectures with data translation

Observing this result, we find that the same pattern emerges as that of Fig. 1, where greater subsampling leads to greater translation invariance.

However, these networks are much more translation invariant than those not trained on translated data, with the lowest MCS at a staggering 0.97.

Whilst learned invariance is certainly a powerful tool, Azulay and Weiss point out that this method can potentially result in models that are overly biased to translations of the train set and it can not be expected to generalize well to translations of unseen data in all cases. We also point out that MNIST is a particularly easy problem compared to more complex datasets such as CIFAR100 or ImageNet [9], and usually data augmentation would be required for these networks to achieve good performance. This implies that the training set must be explicitly augmented with translated data, which leads to a substantial increase in training time.

4.6   Translation Invariance and Generalization

We explore the relationship between translation invariance and generalization by comparing the test accuracy of our architectures to their MCS. The test accuracy of our CIFAR10 networks of varying kernel size and subsampling from Table 4 is shown in Table 6.

Table 6. Test accuracy for CIFAR10 networks with varying subsampling and kernel size

Subsampling factor	Kernel size			
	2×2	3×3	4×4	5×5
1	72.33	75.00	76.10	76.00
2	74.43	77.00	77.57	76.69
4	73.94	76.72	77.25	76.76
8	72.53	75.31	76.69	75.95

We observe that larger kernel sizes generally generalize better, but also that kernels that are too large (such as 5×5 in this case) lead to a reduction in test set accuracy. This is an expected result - larger kernels lower the variance of a given sample and result in more locally homogeneous regions, but also implies that more information is disregarded which negatively impacts the model's ability to generalize to samples not seen during training. Similarly, some subsampling seems to always provide better generalization regardless of kernel size, but too much subsampling leads to a reduction in model performance. These differences suggest that there is a slight trade-off between a model's inherent invariance to translation and its generalization ability.

For the anti-aliased models of Sect. 4.3 we observe a very small overall effect on generalization: Table 7 shows the test accuracy of these models with and without the use of anti-aliasing filters.

The combination of subsampling with anti-aliasing actually improves generalization for the CIFAR10 dataset, and only slightly hampers accuracy for that

Table 7. MNIST and CIFAR10 test accuracy with and without anti-aliasing (AA)

Subsampling factor	AA	MNIST	CIFAR10
1	No	**99.36**	72.33
	Yes	99.18	**73.62**
4	No	**99.38**	73.94
	Yes	99.35	**74.71**
8	No	**99.3**	72.53
	Yes	99.21	**73.40**

of MNIST. These results are aligned with that of Zhang [14] which show a slight improvement in generalization for state-of-the-art ImageNet networks using anti-aliasing. These results, along with those of Sect. 4.3, show that for these data sets anti-aliasing is effective at improving translation invariance without reducing generalization ability.

5 Conclusion

We investigated the effect of stride and filtering on translation invariance and generalization in CNNs. Our main findings are summarised below:

- Subsampling can greatly benefit translation invariance, given that it is combined with local homogeneity. If sufficient filtering is used, greater subsampling leads to greater translation invariance.
- The amount of filtering required depends on the inherent homogeneity of a given data set.
- Too much filtering or subsampling negatively affects generalization, as such, a trade-off exists between translation invariance and generalization.
- Anti-Aliasing performs well in ensuring local homogeneity and therefore greatly increases an architecture's invariance to translation; it also performs better than large max pooling kernels in terms of generalization.
- We find that data translation, or learned invariance, is very effective, but can not be expected to perform well in all cases.

In terms of practical implications, we highlight the advantages and disadvantages of different methods for translation invariance. We hope that these findings can guide others in designing better models for specific tasks, depending on the translation invariance, accuracy, and computational requirements.

For further research, we do not yet measure the effects of strided convolution, which could also be beneficial to translation invariance, nor do we quantify the effects of downsampling. Along with this, we believe that our results can further be verified by using synthetic data with specific signal properties, which would allow us to measure the effects of filtering and subsampling in a more controlled manner.

References

1. Azulay, A., Weiss, Y.: Why do deep convolutional networks generalize so poorly to small image transformations? CoRR abs/1805.12177 (2018). http://arxiv.org/abs/1805.12177
2. Goodfellow, I., Bengio, Y., Courville, A.: Deep Learning. MIT Press, Cambridge (2016). http://www.deeplearningbook.org
3. He, K., Sun, J.: Convolutional neural networks at constrained time cost. CoRR abs/1412.1710 (2014). http://arxiv.org/abs/1412.1710
4. Jaderberg, M., Simonyan, K., Zisserman, A., Kavukcuoglu, K.: Spatial transformer networks. CoRR abs/1506.02025 (2015). http://arxiv.org/abs/1506.02025
5. Kauderer-Abrams, E.: Quantifying translation-invariance in convolutional neural networks. CoRR abs/1801.01450 (2018). http://arxiv.org/abs/1801.01450
6. Kayhan, O.S., van Gemert, J.C.: On translation invariance in CNNs: convolutional layers can exploit absolute spatial location (2020)
7. Kingma, D., Ba, J.: Adam: a method for stochastic optimization. In: International Conference on Learning Representations (December 2014)
8. Krizhevsky, A.: Learning multiple layers of features from tiny images. University of Toronto (May 2012)
9. Krizhevsky, A., Sutskever, I., Hinton, G.E.: ImageNet classification with deep convolutional neural networks, pp. 1097–1105 (2012). http://papers.nips.cc/paper/4824-imagenet-classification-with-deep-convolutional-neural-networks.pdf
10. LeCun, Y., et al.: Backpropagation applied to handwritten zip code recognition. Neural Comput. 1(4), 541–551 (1989)
11. LeCun, Y., Cortes, C., Burges, C.: MNIST database of handwritten digits. http://yann.lecun.com/exdb/mnist/
12. Lenc, K., Vedaldi, A.: Understanding image representations by measuring their equivariance and equivalence. CoRR abs/1411.5908 (2014). http://arxiv.org/abs/1411.5908
13. Scherer, D., Müller, A.C., Behnke, S.: Evaluation of pooling operations in convolutional architectures for object recognition. In: ICANN (2010)
14. Zhang, R.: Making convolutional networks shift-invariant again. CoRR abs/1904.11486 (2019). http://arxiv.org/abs/1904.11486

Tracking Translation Invariance in CNNs

Johannes C. Myburgh[1,2](✉) ⓘ, Coenraad Mouton[1,2] ⓘ, and Marelie H. Davel[1] ⓘ

[1] Multilingual Speech Technologies, North-West University,
Potchefstroom, South Africa
christiaanmyburgh01@gmail.com, marelie.davel@gmail.com
[2] CAIR, Pretoria, South Africa
moutoncoenraad@gmail.com
http://engineering.nwu.ac.za/must

Abstract. Although Convolutional Neural Networks (CNNs) are widely used, their translation invariance (ability to deal with translated inputs) is still subject to some controversy. We explore this question using translation-sensitivity maps to quantify how sensitive a standard CNN is to a translated input. We propose the use of cosine similarity as sensitivity metric over Euclidean distance, and discuss the importance of restricting the dimensionality of either of these metrics when comparing architectures. Our main focus is to investigate the effect of different architectural components of a standard CNN on that network's sensitivity to translation. By varying convolutional kernel sizes and amounts of zero padding, we control the size of the feature maps produced, allowing us to quantify the extent to which these elements influence translation invariance. We also measure translation invariance at different locations within the CNN to determine the extent to which convolutional and fully connected layers, respectively, contribute to the translation invariance of a CNN as a whole. Our analysis indicates that both convolutional kernel size and feature map size have a systematic influence on translation invariance. We also see that convolutional layers contribute less than expected to translation invariance, when not specifically forced to do so.

Keywords: Convolutional Neural Networks · Translation invariance · Deep learning

1 Introduction

With the impressive performance of Convolutional Neural Networks (CNNs) in object classification [8,9], they have become the go-to option for many modern computer vision tasks. Due to their popularity, many different architectural variations of CNNs [2,4,14] have arisen in the past few years that excel at specific tasks. One of the reasons for their rise in popularity is their capability to deal with translated input features. It is widely believed that CNNs are capable of learning translation-invariant representations, since convolutional kernels themselves are shifted across the input during execution. In this study we omit complex variations of the CNN architecture and aim to explore translation invariance

ⓒ Springer Nature Switzerland AG 2020
A. Gerber (Ed.): SACAIR 2020, CCIS 1342, pp. 282–295, 2020.
https://doi.org/10.1007/978-3-030-66151-9_18

in standard CNNs. We study specific standard components of CNNs, as nearly all CNN variations contain convolutional layers, pooling layer and fully connected layers.

Our goal is to investigate how the various components of a CNN influence and contribute to translation invariance, with a focus on convolutional kernel size, feature map size, convolutional layers and fully connected layers. We achieve this goal by using a translation-sensitivity metric introduced by [5] to quantify translation invariance. By investigating CNNs with different convolutional kernel sizes, while implementing zero-padding to control feature map size, we are able to see how convolutional kernel size influences translation invariance. Removing the zero-padding allows us to see how feature map size influences the translation sensitive of a CNN.

We propose a slight change to the translation sensitivity metric that allows us to measure translation invariance within a CNN, allowing us to determine the extent to which convolutional and fully connected layers, respectively, contribute to the translation invariance of a CNN as a whole. We do our analysis on CNNs trained to fit the MNIST dataset and repeat all experiments on the CIFAR10 dataset.

In our work we focus on convolutional kernel size and find that smaller kernels tend to produce feature maps that are less sensitive to translated inputs. We also study how convolutional and fully connected layers combine efforts to achieve translation invariance. We find that – unless forced to – convolutional layers do not automatically extract shift-invariant features, but rather leaves a large part of this task to the fully connected layers.

2   Related Work

When investigating translation invariance, we require a performance metric that measures the magnitude of the effect when a sample is translated in a given direction: both direction and magnitude are important. To address this, Kauderer-Abrams [5] developed translation-sensitivity maps that can be used to visualize and quantify exactly how sensitive a network is to shifted inputs. They then use these translation-sensitivity maps to explore the effects of the number of pooling layers and convolutional kernel size on translation invariance. They find that these architectural choices only have a secondary effect, and identify augmented training data as the biggest influence on translation invariance.

Due to CNNs containing moving kernels, many believe that CNNs are fully translation invariant. Kayman et al. [6] challenge this assumption by showing that CNNs have the capability to learn filters that abuse absolute spatial location. Due to the large receptive fields of CNNs, they are able to exploit boundary effects quite far from the image border. In their work they use different forms of padding to remove spatial location encoding which then improves translation invariance.

In work by Zhang [15], it is shown that introducing anti-aliasing before subsampling, and implementing it correctly, results in higher classification accuracy and better generalization over many architectures on ImageNet [1]. Taking a more theoretical approach, Lenc and Vedaldi [11] explore equivariance, invariance and equivalence in detail. They propose a number of methods to empirically establish these properties and later apply them to a CNN. Their work shows how earlier layers learn to identify general geometrical patterns while deeper layers learn to be more task-specific.

The current study is different from earlier studies in that we investigate how the different components of a CNN contribute to translation invariance.

3   Optimization and Architecture

In this section we discuss the CNN architectures and optimization protocol used in our experiments.

3.1   General CNN Architectural Choices

We investigate the translation invariance of standard CNN architectures, defining such architectures as consisting of multiple sets of convolutional layers and pooling layers, followed by a set of fully connected layers. As stated in Sect. 1, we study these specific components as they are ubiquitous within CNN architectures. We do not investigate the effects of dilation, regularization, dropout or skip connections. All networks use Max-Pooling [12] with kernel size and stride of 2, as is commonly used in many popular CNN architectures [13], and as it works well with the size of our input data. Most popular CNNs contain multiple convolutional layers [2,4,13], thus our CNNs all contain 3 convolutional layers, each followed by a Max-Pool layer, connected to a 500 node hidden layer that connects to the output. All architecture-specific details can be found in the Appendix.

3.2   Datasets

In our analysis we use the MNIST dataset [10] containing 28×28 pixel samples of handwritten digits, and the CIFAR10 dataset [7] containing 32×32 pixel samples of different class colour images. We decide on the use of these two datasets as our translation-sensitivity quantification metric is quite computationally expensive. We thus want to perform our analysis on a somewhat simple task (MNIST) and a more complex task (CIFAR10) without being forced to use massive CNN architectures to fit the datasets. The MNIST dataset is split into a training set containing 55 000 samples, a validation set containing 5 000 samples and a test set containing 10 000 samples. The CIFAR10 dataset is split into a training set containing 45 000 samples, a validation set containing 5 000 samples and a test set containing 10 000 samples. To be able to generate translation-sensitivity maps without loss of features, all samples are zero-padded with a 6-pixel border.

3.3   Network Optimization

All networks are initialized with He initialization [3] using 3 different seeds. Adam is used to optimize Cross-Entropy Loss with a batch size of 128. Four initial learning rates are used: when the best performing learning rate is found at the edge of the learning rate sweep, the learning rate is varied by 0.001 outside the sweep range to ensure that only fully optimized networks are used to generate results. All networks are trained to near-perfect train accuracy ($> 99\%$) and are optimized on validation accuracy. All results shown are averaged over 3 seeds.

4   Translation Sensitivity Quantification

In this section we define translation invariance and discuss the sensitivity metric we use to quantify translation invariance.

4.1   Translation Invariance

For a system to be completely translation invariant, its output must not be influenced by any translation of the input. The output of a translation-invariant system must thus remain identical for translated and untranslated inputs. Although translation-invariance is a desirable quality for many image classification systems, it is seldom achieved in practice. Knowing that complete translation-invariance is near impossible for standard CNN architectures, we redefine the term "translation-invariance" to refer to a system's sensitivity to translated inputs. This means that a system can be more or less translation-invariant based on the values received from our translation sensitivity quantification metric.

4.2   Translation-Sensitivity Maps

To quantify and measure translation sensitivity, we use translation-sensitivity maps and radial translation-sensitivity functions, as introduced by [5], with a slight change to the sensitivity metric.

Translation-sensitivity maps are 2D graphs that consist of multiple pixels. Each pixel has a value that represents the network's sensitivity to a specific shift in the input. To calculate the values of these pixels, we determine the similarity between two vectors, namely the base output vector and the translated output vector. These vectors are generated by passing an input sample through a network with the output of the final fully connected layer being referred to as either the base output vector or the translated output vector. The base output vector is generated by passing a non-translated input to the network. The translated output vector is generated by passing a translated input image to the network, with the x-axis and y-axis shifts corresponding to the pixel's location in the translation-sensitivity map. The similarity between these two vectors is then used as the translation-sensitivity metric. If there is a high similarity between the base output vector and the translated output vector, the network is less sensitive to that specific translation. This high similarity is then represented by a brighter pixel in the translation-sensitivity map. To generate a translation-sensitivity map, we calculate this similarity for each sample with 441 different translations (-10 to 10 pixel shift in the x-axis and -10 to 10 pixel shift in the y-axis) and calculate the average translation-sensitivity map over all samples in a class of the test set.

4.3   Cosine Similarity

In the introductory paper [5], the Euclidean Distance between the two vectors is used as similarity metric. The outputs from the Euclidean Distance calculation are non-normalized, restricting comparisons at different locations within a network. (Even if two layers have the same dimensions, the activation values at different layers may have different size distributions.) To address this normalization issue, we propose the use of Cosine Similarity (Eq. 1) to calculate the similarity between the two vectors. Cosine Similarity measures the cosine of the angle between two vectors a and b in a multi-dimensional space, producing a similarity value between 1 (high similarity) and -1 (high dissimilarity).

$$\cos(\theta) = \frac{a \cdot b}{\|a\|\|b\|} \tag{1}$$

To ensure that the Cosine Similarity measurement produces comparable results to the Euclidean Distance measurement, we use the classification accuracy of a network as a baseline sensitivity measurement to compare the two metrics. We generate translation-sensitivity maps, for each MNIST class, using the three metrics and calculate Pearson Correlation Coefficients to see how correlated Cosine Similarity and Euclidean distance is with classification accuracy.

Both sensitivity metrics show a very strong positive correlation with classification accuracy (and with each other). From the results in Fig. 1, it seems that Cosine Similarity does provide similar information to Euclidean Distance with the added benefit of the results being normalized, allowing for comparisons across network architecture layers. We thus decide to use Cosine Similarity as the similarity metric in our work.

Dimensionality

Although Cosine Similarity has the advantage of producing normalized results, it does not allow for the direct comparison of vectors with different dimensions. When using either Euclidean Distance or Cosine Similarity the dimensions of the datasets greatly influence the calculated metric. As dimension increases, the average Euclidean Distance value tends to increase while the average Cosine Similarity value decreases. This effect produces warped results when comparing either Euclidean Distance or Cosine similarity values. As we use different output vectors to generate our results, we ensure to never directly compare results generated from vectors with different lengths.

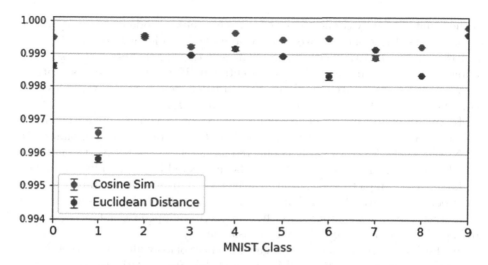

Fig. 1. Pearson Correlation Coefficients. The Cosine Similarity and Euclidean Distance correlation coefficients with classification accuracy are calculated for each class of the MNIST dataset. These results are generated with the first CNN architecture in Table 1 in the Appendix. Results are averaged over three seeds.

4.4   Radial Translation-Sensitivity Functions

Radial translation-sensitivity functions are used to compare translation-sensitivity maps [5]. These functions are generated by calculating the radial mean of a translation-sensitivity map at different radii. The output is a set of radial mean values that illustrate how sensitive a network is to the average translation that occurs at a specific radius. To generate these radial translation-sensitivity functions, all samples of the corresponding test set are used to generate an average translation-sensitivity map per class. These translation-sensitivity maps are used to generate radial translation-sensitivity functions for each class. The final radial translations-sensitivity functions shown in our results are the average sensitivity functions for all classes of a network.

In Fig. 2, 4, 5 and 6 the lines show the average sensitivity of a CNN to a shift at a specific radius. The y-axis values show translation invariance with the value of 1 indicating perfect translation invariance and 0 indicating poor translation invariance.

5   Tracking Invariance

As previously stated, standard convolutional neural networks consist mainly of convolutional layers, separated by pooling layers, followed by a final set of fully connected layers. The convolutional layers can be seen as encoders that morph and highlight important features within the input. This is achieved by applying convolutional kernels, with weights that are finetuned to identify certain features in the input. The fully connected layers then use these encoded inputs to perform certain tasks. In essence, convolutional layers learn to identify certain features and their characteristics within the input and then pass these features to the following layers in a more efficient representation. These efficient representations are referred to as "feature maps" and their size depends on several variables such as kernel size, stride, pooling, padding and input size.

In this section, we aim to determine the extent to which convolutional and fully connected layers, respectively, contribute to the translation invariance of a CNN as a whole. Since the fully connected layers of a CNN act as the classifier, it is desired that the inputs they receive be unaffected by input shifts. Although we know that complete translation invariance is unlikely with a standard CNN architecture, it is still desired that the convolutional layers compensate for most of the translation in the input since they are more equipped (with moving kernels and spatial awareness) to deal with translation.

In the first experiment, we investigate the effect of convolutional kernel size on translation invariance on the MNIST dataset. We also investigate how sensitive a standard CNN is to translation at two locations within the network: before and after the fully connected layers. To test translation-sensitivity at the first location, we use the output of the last convolution layer to generate sensitivity maps. This is done to investigate the effect that convolutional layers have on the network's sensitivity to translation. For the second location, the output of the final fully connected layer is used to generate translation-sensitivity maps allowing us to see for how much translation invariance the fully connected layers are responsible for.

All convolutional kernel sizes are kept constant throughout each convolutional layer of each network, but varied over the three different networks. Zero-padding is used to ensure that all feature maps have the same size regardless of the change in convolutional kernel size. This is done to allow us to compare convolutional layer outputs across the three CNNs. By keeping the size of the feature maps produced by the final convolutional layer the same across the different CNNs (5×5 pixels), we can be assured that changes in dimensionality do not affect the results. The number of channels per convolutional layer is kept constant across all three networks. The output from the final fully connected layers all have a length of 10 and require no modifications to be comparable with one another. All networks are optimized as described in Sect. 3, and achieve comparable performance on the held-out test set.

In Fig. 2(a) we see the radial translation-sensitivity functions generated from the outputs of the final convolutional layers of the CNNs. It seems that smaller convolutional kernels produce a feature map that is slightly less sensitive to translated inputs. Although it is expected that the convolutional layers would be responsible for most translation invariance of the network, the fully connected layers drastically change the results. The results in Fig. 2(b) are generated from the final fully connected layers of the CNNs and show that networks with larger convolutional kernel sizes tend to be more translation-invariant after the fully connected layer.

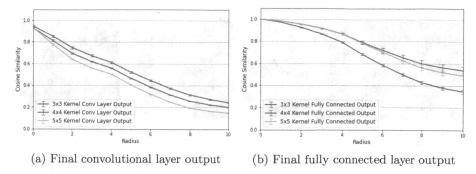

(a) Final convolutional layer output   (b) Final fully connected layer output

Fig. 2. Radial translation-sensitivity functions generated from (a) the final convolutional layer output and (b) the fully connected layer output on MNIST. Detailed CNN architectures can be found in Table 1 in the Appendix.

It is interesting to see that although the convolutional layers reduce the network's sensitivity to translation, it clear that the fully connected layers reduce the network's translation-sensitivity even further. On the one hand, as the final layer is specifically trained to classify correctly, it is expected that a good model would have low translation sensitivity (high cosine similarity) at the output layer. On the other hand, the fact that the last layer is responsible for much of the low translation sensitivity is somewhat counter-intuitive, as it is expected that the convolutional layers would be able to compensate for the translated inputs far better than the fully connected layers.

To further investigate this effect, we examine the first three output feature maps of the final convolutional layer of the 5×5 kernel size CNN (used in the first experiment) given a normal and shifted input. The results in Fig. 3 show a normal and shifted input sample and the feature maps produced by the final convolutional layer. One can see that the convolutional layers have highlighted and morphed the input features, but the input shift is still somewhat present in the convolutional layer output feature maps, now forcing the fully connected layers to compensate for the shift.

One hypothesis is that, since these experiments were performed on a very simple task (MNIST), the convolutional layers were never forced to learn a better encoding scheme, since the fully connected layers were easily able to memorise all of the transformed samples. This would explain the results in Fig. 2, and why it seems that the fully connected layers contribute more to translation invariance than the convolutional layers. One way to test this hypothesis would be to limit the size of the convolutional layer output feature maps, limiting the number of output pixels available to the convolutional layers, and forcing them to learn a more effective encoding scheme. We explore this further in Sect. 6.

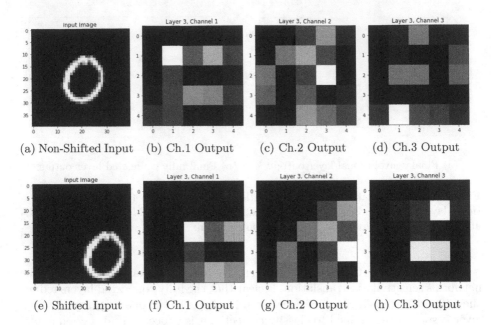

Fig. 3. Feature maps from the final convolutional layer of a CNN given a normal and shifted input sample. These feature maps were randomly selected to show the presence of translation after three convolutional layers. Similar translation effects are present in all 150 feature maps.

Another way to shed light on this observation, is to repeat the experiment on a more complex dataset such as CIFAR10. We increase the number of channels per layer to allow the models to fit the CIFAR10 dataset. In Fig. 4(a) we see the radial translation-sensitivity functions generated from the final convolutional layer outputs that show a similar trend as in Fig. 2(a) where smaller convolutional kernels produce less sensitive feature maps. Interestingly, in Fig. 4(b), the radial translation-sensitivity functions generated from the final fully connected layers, all the outputs seem to have the same level of translation invariance regardless of convolutional kernel size. Although all three networks seem to have the same sensitivity to translation, it is surprising to see how much of an influence the fully connected layers have on the total translation invariance of the CNNs. The inter-class samples in CIFAR10 are less homogeneous than the samples in MNIST, explaining the high translation invariance observed in Fig. 4(b).

6   Feature Map Size and Translation Invariance

Having explored the effects of convolutional kernel size on translation invariance when using zero-padding to control feature map output size, we now omit zero-padding to analyse how varying feature map size in conjunction with convolutional kernel size affects translation invariance.

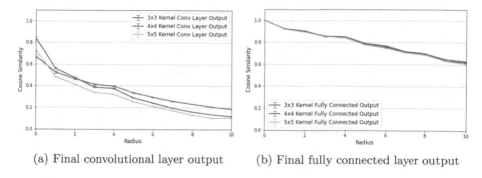

(a) Final convolutional layer output   (b) Final fully connected layer output

Fig. 4. Radial translation-sensitivity functions generated from (a) the final convolutional layer output and (b) the fully connected layer output on CIFAR10. Detailed CNN architectures can be found in Table 2 in the Appendix.

In this experiment we investigate how changes in feature map size due to convolutional kernel size influence translation invariance on MNIST. All convolutional kernel sizes are kept constant throughout each convolutional layer of each network, but varied over the different networks. No zero-padding is used, allowing for reduced feature map sizes. Over all three networks, varying amounts of channels are added to keep the number of effective nodes (kernel size × number of channels) per layer comparable.

Results are shown in Fig. 5. These results show the translation-sensitivity functions calculated from the final fully connected layer outputs of the CNNs. It is clear that there is a large increase in translation invariance when the feature map reaches a size of 1×1 pixel. Since there is no room for movement in a 1-pixel feature map, it seems that the convolutional layers are forced to better deal with input translations. Although it is clear that fully connected layers still add translation invariance, it does seem that reducing the feature map output size does not have significant effect on translation invariance.

With the benefit of less translation sensitive networks, why not reduce all convolutional layer output feature maps to 1×1 pixel? This is indeed possible, as is the case with fully convolutional networks. However, these networks limit capacity in a way that additional fully connected layers do not. Neural networks trained for a classification task require adequate capacity to be able to learn the characteristics and features of the different classes. Small map sizes are possible, but reducing feature map size can become a bottleneck in large networks trained for demanding classification tasks.

We repeat this experiment on the CIFAR10 dataset to see how feature map size would affect a CNN trained on a more complex dataset with less homogeneous samples. The architectures we use are very similar to the architectures used on MNIST, except we add more channels to give the CNNs sufficient capacity to fit the more complex CIFAR10 dataset.

The results in Fig. 6, the radial translation-sensitivity functions generated from the fully connected layer outputs, show a similar pattern as the results

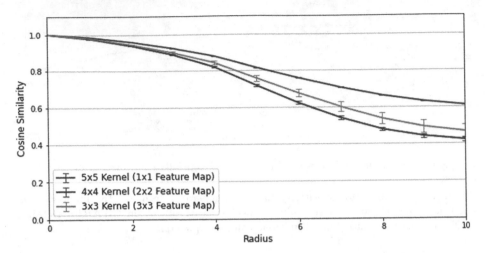

Fig. 5. Radial translation-sensitivity functions of CNNs with different feature map sizes on MNIST. These results are generated from the fully connected layer outputs of the CNNs since varying feature map sizes do not allow for direct comparisons of feature maps generated by final convolutional layers. Detailed CNN architectures can be found in Table 3 in the Appendix.

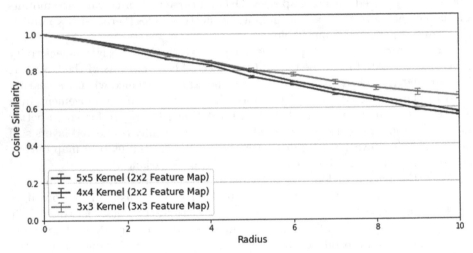

Fig. 6. Radial translation-sensitivity functions of CNNs with different feature map sizes on CIFAR10. These results are generated from the fully connected layer outputs of the CNNs since varying feature map sizes do not allow for direct comparisons of feature maps generated by final convolutional layers. Detailed CNN architectures can be found in Table 4 in the Appendix.

in Fig. 5. It seems that reducing feature map size has little to no influence on translation invariance, especially in a CNN trained on a more complex dataset that forces the network to be more translation invariant during training.

7   Conclusion

In this paper we use translation-sensitivity maps to analyse how different components of a standard CNN affect the network's translation invariance. We train several standard CNNs on the MNIST and CIFAR10 datasets. We propose a slight change to the similarity metric and demonstrates that it produces comparable results to the prior metric, with the added benefit of normalizing results across layers. Specifically, we focus on convolutional kernel size and find that smaller kernels tend to produce feature maps that are less sensitive to translated inputs. We also study how convolutional and fully connected layers affect translation invariance and find that although convolutional layers contribute, it seems that fully connected layers are responsible for the majority of translation invariance in a standard CNN. In our study we also vary feature map size and find that it has little effect on translation sensitivity.

In our study we focus on standard CNN architectures that can fit the MNIST and CIFAR10 datasets. Although these datasets have varying levels of complexity, the samples they contain are relatively small in size. We believe that an indepth study on the effects of convolutional kernel size on translation invariance in larger CNNs able to fit a complex dataset such as ImageNet may produce interesting insights. We would expect to see a similar pattern as in out work (smaller convolutional kernels result in more translation invariance) but to a much larger extent as larger inputs tend to contain more location information.

A   Appendix: Network Architectures

Here we show the network architectures and accuracies of the CNNs used in our experiments.

Table 1. MNIST architectures used in Sect. 4 and Sect. 5

Layer	Kernel size	Stride	Padding	Output size	Channels	Activation
CNN1	5,4,3	1	2,2,1	40	10	ReLU
Max-Pool1	2	2	0	20	–	
CNN2	5,4,3	1	2,2,1	20	20	ReLU
Max-Pool2	2	2	0	10	–	
CNN3	5,4,3	1	2,1,1	10	30	ReLU
Max-Pool3	2	2	0	5	–	
FC	–	–	–	500	–	ReLU
Out	–	–	–	10	–	Softmax

All networks in Table 1 achieve a minimum training accuracy of 100%, validation accuracy of 99.16% and test accuracy of 99.19%.

Table 2. CIFAR10 architectures used in Sect. 5.

Layer	Kernel size	Stride	Padding	Output size	Channels	Activation
CNN1	5,4,3	1	2,2,1	44	50	ReLU
Max-Pool1	2	2	0	22	–	
CNN2	5,4,3	1	2,2,1	22	100	ReLU
Max-Pool2	2	2	0	11	–	
CNN3	5,4,3	1	2,1,1	11	150	ReLU
Max-Pool3	2	2	0	5	–	
FC	–	–	–	500	–	ReLU
Out	–	–	–	10	–	Softmax

All networks in Table 2 achieve a minimum training accuracy of 99.89%, validation accuracy of 74.45% and test accuracy of 74.67%.

Table 3. MNIST architectures used in Sect. 6

Layer	Kernel size	Stride	Padding	Output size	Channels	Activation
CNN1	5,4,3	1	0	36,37,38	10,16,28	ReLU
Max-Pool1	2	2	0	18,18,19	–	
CNN2	5,4,3	1	0	14,15,17	20,31,56	ReLU
Max-Pool2	2	2	0	7,7,8	–	
CNN3	5,4,3	1	0	3,4,6	30,47,83	ReLU
Max-Pool3	2	2	0	1,2,3	–	
FC	–	–	–	500	–	ReLU
Out	–	–	–	10	–	Softmax

All networks in Table 3 achieve a minimum training accuracy of 99.99%, validation accuracy of 99.18% and test accuracy of 99.30%.

Table 4. CIFAR10 architectures used in Sect. 6.

Layer	Kernel size	Stride	Padding	Output size	Channels	Activation
CNN1	5,4,3	1	0	40,41,42	50,78,139	ReLU
Max-Pool1	2	2	0	20,20,21	–	
CNN2	5,4,3	1	0	16,17,19	100,156,278	ReLU
Max-Pool2	2	2	0	8,8,9	–	
CNN3	5,4,3	1	0	4,5,7	150,234,416	ReLU
Max-Pool3	2	2	0	2,2,3	–	
FC	–	–	–	500	–	ReLU
Out	–	–	–	10	–	Softmax

All networks in Table 4 achieve a minimum training accuracy of 99.93%, validation accuracy of 74.31% and test accuracy of 74.40%.

References

1. Deng, J., et al.: ImageNet: a large-scale hierarchical image database. In: CVPR 2009 (2009)
2. He, K., Zhang, X., Ren, S., Sun, J.: Deep residual learning for image recognition. CoRR abs/1512.03385 (2015). http://arxiv.org/abs/1512.03385
3. He, K., Zhang, X., Ren, S., Sun, J.: Delving deep into rectifiers: surpassing human-level performance on imagenet classification. CoRR abs/1502.01852 (2015). http://arxiv.org/abs/1502.01852
4. Huang, G., Liu, Z., Weinberger, K.Q.: Densely connected convolutional networks. CoRR abs/1608.06993 (2016). http://arxiv.org/abs/1608.06993
5. Kauderer-Abrams, E.: Quantifying translation-invariance in convolutional neural networks. CoRR abs/1801.01450 (2018). http://arxiv.org/abs/1801.01450
6. Kayhan, O.S., Gemert, J.C.: On translation invariance in CNNs: convolutional layers can exploit absolute spatial location. In: Proceedings of the IEEE/CVF Conference on Computer Vision and Pattern Recognition (CVPR), June 2020
7. Krizhevsky, A., Nair, V., Hinton, G.: CIFAR-10 (Canadian Institute for Advanced Research). http://www.cs.toronto.edu/~kriz/cifar.html
8. Krizhevsky, A., Sutskever, I., Hinton, G.: Imagenet classification with deep convolutional neural networks. Neural Inf. Process. Syst. **25** (2012). https://doi.org/10.1145/3005386
9. Lecun, Y., Bottou, L., Bengio, Y., Haffner, P.: Gradient-based learning applied to document recognition. Proc. IEEE **86**(11), 2278–2324 (1998)
10. LeCun, Y., Cortes, C.: MNIST handwritten digit database (2010). http://yann.lecun.com/exdb/mnist/
11. Lenc, K., Vedaldi, A.: Understanding image representations by measuring their equivariance and equivalence. CoRR abs/1411.5908 (2014). http://arxiv.org/abs/1411.5908
12. Scherer, D., Müller, A., Behnke, S.: Evaluation of pooling operations in convolutional architectures for object recognition. In: Diamantaras, K., Duch, W., Iliadis, L.S. (eds.) ICANN 2010. LNCS, vol. 6354, pp. 92–101. Springer, Heidelberg (2010). https://doi.org/10.1007/978-3-642-15825-4_10
13. Simonyan, K., Zisserman, A.: Very deep convolutional networks for large-scale image recognition. CoRR abs/1409.1556 (2014). http://arxiv.org/abs/1409.1556
14. Szegedy, C., et al.: Going deeper with convolutions. CoRR abs/1409.4842 (2014). http://arxiv.org/abs/1409.4842
15. Zhang, R.: Making convolutional networks shift-invariant again. CoRR abs/1904.11486 (2019). http://arxiv.org/abs/1904.11486

Pre-interpolation Loss Behavior
in Neural Networks

Arthur E. W. Venter[1,2]([⊠]) (iD), Marthinus W. Theunissen[1,2] (iD),
and Marelie H. Davel[1,2] (iD)

[1] Multilingual Speech Technologies (MuST), North-West University,
Potchefstroom, South Africa
aew.venter@gmail.com, tiantheunissen@gmail.com, marelie.davel@nwu.ac.za
[2] CAIR, Pretoria, South Africa

Abstract. When training neural networks as classifiers, it is common to
observe an increase in average test loss while still maintaining or improving the overall classification accuracy on the same dataset. In spite of the
ubiquity of this phenomenon, it has not been well studied and is often
dismissively attributed to an increase in borderline correct classifications.
We present an empirical investigation that shows how this phenomenon
is actually a result of the differential manner by which test samples are
processed. In essence: test loss does not increase overall, but only for a
small minority of samples. Large representational capacities allow losses
to decrease for the vast majority of test samples at the cost of extreme
increases for others. This effect seems to be mainly caused by increased
parameter values relating to the correctly processed sample features. Our
findings contribute to the practical understanding of a common behavior
of deep neural networks. We also discuss the implications of this work
for network optimization and generalization.

Keywords: Overfitting · Generalization · Deep learning

1 Introduction

According to the principal of *empirical risk minimization*, it is possible to optimize the performance on machine learning tasks (e.g. classification or regression)
by reducing the empirical risk on a surrogate loss function as measured on a training dataset [5]. The success of this depends on several assumptions regarding the
sampling methods used to obtain the training data and the consistency of the
risk estimators [14]. Assuming such criteria are met, we expect the training loss
to decrease throughout training and that the loss on samples not belonging to
the training samples (henceforth referred to as validation or evaluation loss) will
initially decrease but eventually increase as a result of overfitting on spurious
features in the training set.

Actual performance is usually not directly measured with the loss function
but rather with a secondary measurement, such as classification accuracy in a

© Springer Nature Switzerland AG 2020
A. Gerber (Ed.): SACAIR 2020, CCIS 1342, pp. 296–309, 2020.
https://doi.org/10.1007/978-3-030-66151-9_19

classification task. It is implicitly expected that the classification accuracy will be inversely proportional to the average loss value. However, in practice we often observe that the validation loss increases while the validation accuracy is stable or still improving, as illustrated by the example in Fig. 1.

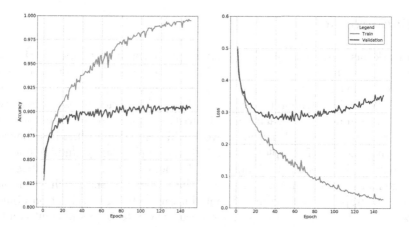

Fig. 1. Learning curves of an example $1 \times 1\,000$ MLP trained on $5\,000$ FMNIST samples using SGD with a mini-batch size of 64. The network clearly shows an increasing validation loss with a slightly increasing validation accuracy.

The cause of this behavior can easily be thought to be shallow local optima or borderline cases of correct classification. While this explanation is consistent with classical ideas of overfitting, it does not fully explain observed behavior. Specifically, if this is the extent of the phenomenon, there is no reason for improvement in validation accuracy if a local optimum is found, and an obvious quantitative limit to the amount that the validation loss can increase.

By investigating the distribution of per-sample validation loss values and not just a point estimation (typically averaged over all samples) we show that the increase in average validation loss can be attributed to a minority of validation samples. This means that the discrepancy between the validation loss and accuracy is due to a form of *overfitting* that only affects the predictions of some validation samples, thereby allowing the model to still generalize well to most of the validation set.

The following is a summary of the main contributions of this paper:

- We present empirical evidence of a characteristic of empirical risk minimization in MLPs performing classification tasks, that sheds light on an apparently paradoxical relationship between validation loss and classification accuracy.
- We explain how this phenomenon is largely a result of quantitative increases in related parameter values and the limits of using a point estimator to measure overfitting.
- We discuss the practical and theoretical implications of this phenomenon with regards to generalization in related machine learning models.

In the following section we discuss related work. In Sect. 3 we explain our experimental setup and methodology. Section 4 presents our empirical results and their interpretation. The final section discusses and summarizes our findings with a focus on their implications for generalization.

2   Background

Much work has been done to characterize how a neural network's performance changes over training iterations [7,10,17,20]. Such work has lead to some powerful machine learning techniques, including drop-out [8] and batch normalization [11]. While both theoretically principled and practically useful generalization bounds remain out of reach, many heuristics have been found that appear to indicate whether a trained neural network will generalize well. These heuristics have varying degrees of complexity, generality, and popularity, and include: small weight norms, flatness of loss landscapes [9], heavy-tailed weight matrices [13], and large margin distributions [19]. All of these proposed metrics have empirical evidence to support their claims of contributing to the generalization ability of a network, however, none of them have been proven to be a sufficient condition to ensure generalization in general circumstances.

A popular experimental framework used to investigate generalization in deep learning is to explore the optimization process of so-called "toy problems". Such experiments are typically characterized by varying different design choices or training conditions, in an often simplified machine learning model, and then interpreting the performance of resulting models on test data [6,18]. The performance can be investigated post-training but it is often informative to observe how the generalization changes *during* training.

A good example of why it is important to consider performance during training is the *double descent phenomenon* [2,15]. This phenomenon has enjoyed much attention recently [1,3,16], due to its apparent bridging of classical and modern regimes of representational complexity. In its most basic form it is characterized by poor generalization within a "critically parameterized" regime of representational capacities near the minimum that is necessary to interpolate the entire training set. Slightly smaller or larger models produce improved generalization. However, if early stopping is used the phenomenon has been found to be almost non-existent [15].

Having an accurate estimate of test loss and how it changes during training is clearly beneficial in investigating generalization. In the current work we show that averaging over all test samples can result in a misrepresentation of generalization ability and that this can account for the sometimes paradoxical relationship between test accuracy and test loss.

3   Approach

We use a simple experimental setup to explore the validation loss behavior of various fully-connected feedforward networks. All models use a multilayer perceptron (MLP) architecture where hidden layers have an equal number of ReLU-activated nodes. This architecture, while simple, still uses the fundamental principles common to many deep learning models, that is, a set of hidden layers optimized by gradient descent, using backpropagation to calculate the gradient of a given loss function with regard to the parameters being optimized.

We first determine whether the studied phenomenon (both validation accuracy and loss displaying an increase during training) occurs in general circumstances, and then select a few models where this phenomenon is clearly visible. We then probe these models to better understand the mechanism causing this effect.

The experiments are performed on the well-known MNIST [12] and FMNIST [21] classification datasets. These datasets consist of 60 000 training samples and 10 000 test samples of 28×28 grayscale images with an associated label $\in [0, 9]$. FMNIST can be regarded as a slightly more complex drop-in replacement for MNIST. Recently these datasets have become less useful as benchmarks, but they are still popular resources for investigating theoretical principles of DNNs.

All models are optimized to reduce a cross-entropy loss function measured on mini-batches of training samples. Techniques that could have a regularizing effect on the optimization process (such as batch normalization, drop-out, early-stopping or weight decay) were omitted as far as possible. Networks are trained till convergence, with the exact stopping criteria different for the separate experiments, as described per set of results.

A selection of hyperparameters were investigated to ensure a variety of validation loss behaviors during training. These hyperparameters are:

- Training and validation set sizes;
- The number of hidden layers;
- The number of nodes in each hidden layer;
- Mini-batch sizes;
- Datasets (MNIST or FMNIST); and
- Optimizers (Adam or SGD).

Parameter settings differed per experiment, as detailed below. Take note that the validation sets are held out from the train set, so a larger train set will result in a smaller validation set and vice versa.

4   Results

Our initial experiments show that the average validation loss can indeed increase with a stable or increasing validation accuracy for a wide variety of hyperparameters (Sect. 4.1). Based on this result, we select a few models where the phenomenon is clearly visible, and investigate the per-sample loss distributions throughout training, as well as weight distributions, to probe the reason for this behavior (Sects. 4.2 and 4.3).

4.1 Increasing Risk During Training

We begin our investigation by training 95 two-layer MLPs, varying the width of the hidden layer and the optimization algorithm over multiple random initializations. Networks are trained on 5 000 MNIST training samples using a mini-batch size of 64. All models were trained until interpolation (training accuracy of 100%), which occurred at around 3 000 epochs for the smaller models. Out of the 95 models trained, 57 (3 initializations of 19 widths) were optimized with Adam and the remaining 38 (2 initializations of 19 widths) with SGD.

The results are presented in the scatter plots in Fig. 2. The measurement for the horizontal axis is made at the epoch where the model achieved the lowest validation loss. The measurement for the vertical axis is made at the epoch where the model first interpolated the entire training set. Using the linear curve as reference, all models falling above the line increased the relevant metric after the point of minimum validation loss. The models marked by a triangle saw increases in both validation loss and accuracy.

Notice that the models with limited representational capacity, in this case referring to the number of nodes in the hidden layer, had increasing validation loss and decreasing validation accuracy as one would expect. This is in contrast with the larger models that tend to display an increase in both validation accuracy and loss even before interpolation. An additional observation we can make is that a higher minimum validation loss seems to be indicative of very large increases in validation loss later in training.

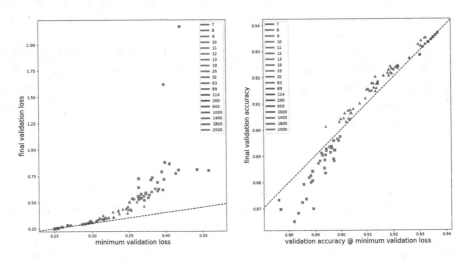

Fig. 2. Final validation loss (left) and validation accuracy (right) vs the same metric at the epoch with *minimum* validation loss. 95 MLPs are trained on 5 000 MNIST samples with the number of nodes in the hidden layer ranging from only 7 (red) to 2 000 (blue). Models marked with a triangle had increasing validation loss and accuracy between the epoch of minimum validation loss and the epoch of first interpolation. (Color figure online)

We repeated this experiment in a more general setting to produce the results presented in Fig. 3. These models have hyperparameters that vary beyond just the hidden layer width and optimizer. Specifically:

- The data is either MNIST or FMNIST with a train set size as defined in the legend;
- The number of hidden layers is either 1, 3, or 10;
- The number of nodes in each hidden layer is either 100 or 1000;
- Mini-batch sizes are either 16, 64 or 256; and
- The optimizers are again either Adam or SGD.

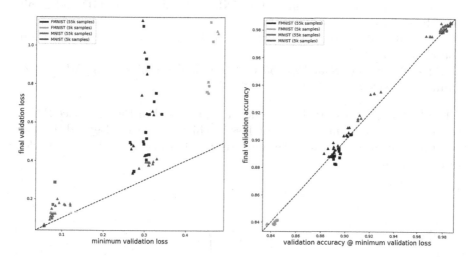

Fig. 3. Final validation loss (left) and validation accuracy (right) vs the same metric at the epoch with *minimum* validation loss. 80 MLPs are trained with varying hyperparameters; colors refer to different training sets. Models marked with a triangle had increasing validation loss and accuracy between the epoch of minimum validation loss and the epoch of first interpolation. (Color figure online)

These networks are trained for 150 epochs. In order to ensure that each model's performance is good enough to be considered typical for these architectures and datasets, we use optimized learning rates. The learning rate for each set of hyperparameters is chosen by a grid search over a wide range of values. The selection is made in accordance with the best validation error achieved by the end of training. In some cases this resulted in final training accuracies slightly below 100%. In these cases we selected the "final" epoch at the epoch where maximum training accuracy was achieved.

As expected, the models trained on MNIST or on larger training sets had lower validation losses and higher validation accuracies in general. However, we also note that models trained on FMNIST tend to have much higher increases in validation loss while the validation accuracy is still improving when compared to models trained on MNIST. In the next section we investigate how the loss distributions change for selected models from this section.

4.2 Loss Distributions

In order to take a closer look at how both loss and accuracy can increase during training, we present a case study of four selected models from the previous section. From the dataset-optimizer combinations, models are handpicked that showed a clear increase in validation loss without detrimental effects on the validation accuracy. They are defined below.

- A: 3×100 model trained on 5 000 MNIST samples using Adam and a mini-batch size of 64.
- B: 3×100 model trained on 5 000 MNIST samples using SGD and a mini-batch size of 64.
- C: 3×100 model trained on 5 000 FMNIST samples using SGD and a mini-batch size of 64.
- D: 3×100 model trained on 55 000 FMNIST samples using Adam and a mini-batch size of 16.

The learning curves for these models are presented in Fig. 4. Notice that for all four models a minimum validation loss is achieved early on. Beyond this point the validation loss increases while the corresponding accuracy is either stable or improving slightly.

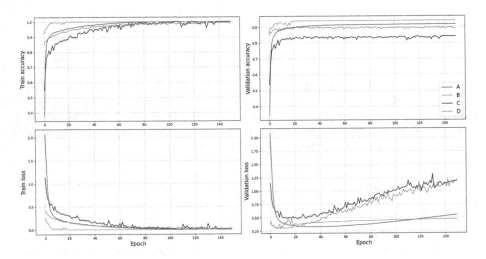

Fig. 4. Learning curves for four selected models (A-D, see text) showing increasing validation loss, despite an increasing or stable validation accuracy.

The validation loss curve, as seen in Fig. 4, is often used as an estimate of the level of overfitting that is occurring as the model is optimized on the training set. However, by averaging over the entire validation set we are producing a point estimate that implicitly assumes that the loss of all validation samples are close to the mean value. This assumption is reasonable with regards to the training set because most loss functions (e.g. cross entropy) work with the principle of maximum likelihood estimation [5,14]. This means that by minimizing the dissimilarity between the entire distribution of the training data and the model the estimate of loss is all but guaranteed to be indicative of performance on the entire training set.

There is no such guarantee with regards to any set other than the training set. This makes the average loss value a poor estimate of performance on the validation set. The results presented in Fig. 5 motivate this point for model A. See Appendix A for the same results for models B, C, and D. The plots show heatmaps of loss distributions for the four selected models at several training iterations for three datasets (training, validation and evaluation). The validation set is the held-out set that is used to estimate performance during training and model selection, and the evaluation set is the set that is used post-training to ensure no indirect optimization is performed on the test data. The iterations refer to parameter updates, not epochs. We show the distributions at log-sampled iterations because many changes occur early on (even before the end of the first epoch) and few occur towards the end of training. A final note with regards to these heatmaps is that the colors, which define the number of samples that have the corresponding loss value, are also log-scaled. This visually highlights the occurrence of samples with extreme loss values.

The loss distributions in Fig. 5 show that while the loss value for a vast majority (indicated by the red and orange colors) of samples reduces with training iterations there is a small minority of samples for which the loss values increase. For the training set, this increase is relatively low and eventually reduces as the entire set is interpolated. For the validation and evaluation sets the loss values of these "outliers" seem to only increase. This is why it is possible for the average validation loss to increase while the classification accuracy remains stable or improves.

Figure 6 shows the weight distributions for the same model in the same format as Fig. 5. See Appendix A for models B, C, and D. It can be observed that there is a clear increase in the magnitude of some weights (their absolute weight values) at the same iterations where we observe a corresponding increase in validation and evaluation loss values in Fig. 5. This appears to occur even more after most of the training sample losses have been minimized. This is consistent with the notion of limiting weight norms to improve generalization and it suggests that the reason for the increase in validation losses is because particular weights are being increased to fit idiosyncratic training samples.

While these heatmaps show that there are *outlier* per-sample loss values in the validation set, they do not guarantee that these extreme loss values are due to specific samples. It is possible that the extreme values are measured on completely different samples at every measured iteration, in which case there is nothing extreme about them and the phenomenon has something to do with the optimization process and not training and validation distributions. We address this question in the next section.

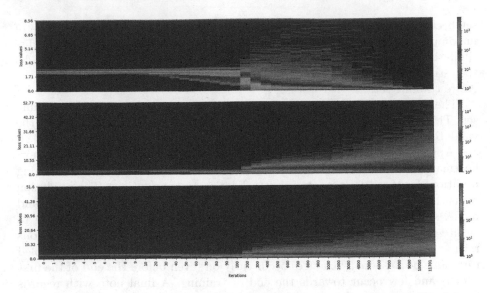

Fig. 5. Change in loss distributions during training for model A (5k MNIST, Adam, mini-batch size of 64). The three heatmaps refer to the train (top), validation (center), and evaluation (bottom) loss distributions.

Fig. 6. Change in weight distributions during training for model A (MNIST, Adam, mini-batch size of 64). Each heatmap refers to a layer in the network, including the output layer, from top to bottom.

4.3   Validation Set Outliers

In this section we investigate whether the validation set samples with extreme loss values are individual samples that are consistently modeled poorly, or whether these outliers change from iteration to iteration due to the stochastic nature of the optimization process. Towards this end, we analyze the number of epochs for which a sample can be regarded as an outlier and compare it with its final loss value.

We classify a sample as an outlier when its loss value is above the upper Tukey fence, that is, larger than $Q_3 + 1.5 \times (Q_3 - Q_1)$, where Q_1 and Q_3 are the first and third quartile of all loss values in the validation set, respectively [4]. This indicator is simple and adequate to illustrate whether some specific samples consistently have much larger loss values than the majority.

In Fig. 7 we show that the validation samples with extreme loss values at the end of training are usually classified as outliers for most of the training process. This means that the extreme validation loss values are due to specific samples that are not well modeled. In addition to this, it is worth observing that a large majority of validation samples are never classified as an outlier and these samples always have small loss values at the end of training.

5   Discussion

We have shown that validation classification accuracy can increase while the corresponding average loss value also increases. Empirically, we have noted that this phenomenon is most influenced by the interplay between the training dataset and model capacity. Specifically, it occurs more for larger models, smaller training datasets, and more difficult datasets (FMNIST in our investigation). We can, however, combine the first and second factors because capacity is directly related to the size and complexity of the training set.

By taking a closer look at per-sample loss distributions and weight distributions we have noted that the phenomenon is largely due to specific samples in the validation set that have extremely large loss values and obtain progressively larger loss values as training continues. These loss values then become large enough to distort the average loss value in such a way that it appears that the model is overfitting the training set, when most of the validation set sample losses are still being minimized. From a theoretical viewpoint this is unsurprising because the average validation loss is only a good measure of risk with regards to the train set, where it is directly being minimized by the principle of maximum likelihood estimation. From a practical viewpoint it appears that increased weight values are sacrificing the generality of the distributed representation used by DNNs in order to minimize training loss as much as possible.

Practically, these findings serve as a clear cautionary tale for (1) assuming an inverse correlation between loss and accuracy, and for (2) measuring overfitting with point estimators such as average validation loss. Rather, we show that loss distribution heatmaps (Fig. 5) provide additional, useful information.

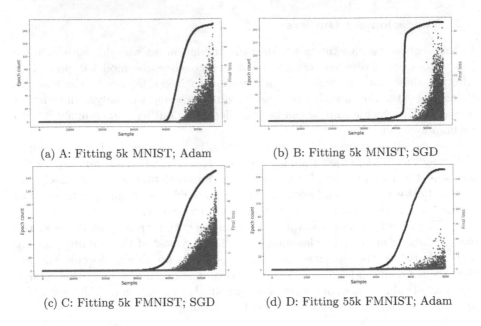

(a) A: Fitting 5k MNIST; Adam   (b) B: Fitting 5k MNIST; SGD

(c) C: Fitting 5k FMNIST; SGD   (d) D: Fitting 55k FMNIST; Adam

Fig. 7. Outliers in the validation set. The blue datapoints show the number of epochs for which each sample is considered an outlier. The red datapoints show the loss value of each sample at the end of training. Samples are ordered in ascending order of epoch counts.

The findings also highlight a more general aspect of generalization and deep learning: DNNs optimize parameters with regards to training data in a heterogeneous manner. With sufficient parametric flexibility, these types of models can fit generalizable features and memorize non-generalizable features concurrently during training. Formally defining how this is achieved, and subsequently, how generalization should be characterized in this context, remains an open problem.

6   Conclusion

By means of a small but focused empirical investigation we have contributed the following findings, in the context of using fully-connected feedforward networks as classifiers:

- If the representational capacity is large enough, validation classification accuracy and loss can both increase simultaneously during training.
- Under common conditions, average validation loss is a poor estimate of generality because validation samples are not guaranteed to obtain loss values near the mean value.
- We show that sample-specific heatmaps provide a far more nuanced view of the training process, and can be a useful tool during model optimization.
- We propose that investigations of generalization should consider the fact that DNN optimization is distributed and heterogeneous, which is why simple measures of overfitting can be misleading.

These findings imply that a validation loss that starts increasing prior to interpolation of the training set is not necessarily an implication of overfitting; and also that it is dangerous to assume a negative correlation between validation accuracy and loss (which is often done when selecting hyperparameters).

We note that this study focused on a narrow set of architectures and datasets. Testing our findings for different scenarios – more complex architectures and more challenging datasets, such as imbalanced and sparse datasets – remains future work. While this study aimed to answer a very specific question, we hope it will contribute to the general discourse on factors that influence the optimization process and generalization ability of neural networks.

A   Appendix

We include the results when models B, C and D are analyzed, using the same process as described in Sect. 4.2.

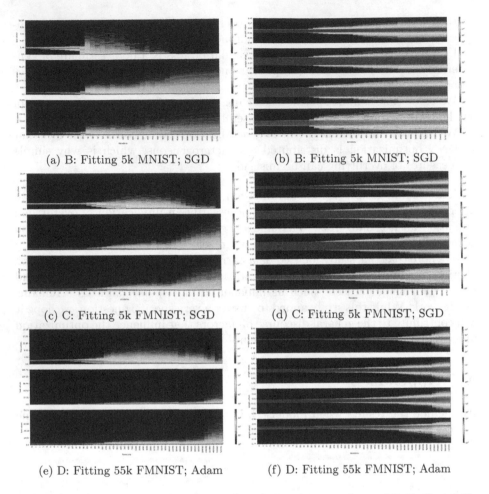

(a) B: Fitting 5k MNIST; SGD (b) B: Fitting 5k MNIST; SGD

(c) C: Fitting 5k FMNIST; SGD (d) C: Fitting 5k FMNIST; SGD

(e) D: Fitting 55k FMNIST; Adam (f) D: Fitting 55k FMNIST; Adam

Fig. 8. Change in loss (left) and weight (right) distributions, for models B, C, and D, during training. See Fig. 5 and 6 for plot ordering. (Color figure online)

References

1. Ba, J., Erdogdu, M., Suzuki, T., Wu, D., Zhang, T.: Generalization of two-layer neural networks: an asymptotic viewpoint. In: International Conference on Learning Representations (2020)
2. Belkin, M., Hsu, D., Ma, S., Mandal, S.: Reconciling modern machine-learning practice and the classical bias-variance trade-off. Proc. Natl. Acad. Sci. **116**, 15849–15854 (2019)
3. d'Ascoli, S., Refinetti, M., Biroli, G., Krzakala, F.: Double trouble in double descent: bias and variance(s) in the lazy regime. In: Thirty-seventh International Conference on Machine Learning, pp. 2676–2686 (2020)
4. Devore, J., Farnum, N.R.: Applied Statistics for Engineers and Scientists. Thomson Brooks/Cole, Belmont (2005)

5. Goodfellow, I., Bengio, Y., Courville, A.: Deep Learning. MIT Press, Cambridge (2016). http://www.deeplearningbook.org
6. Goodfellow, I.J., Vinyals, O.: Qualitatively characterizing neural network optimization problems. CoRR abs/1412.6544 (2015)
7. Hardt, M., Recht, B., Singer, Y.: Train faster, generalize better: stability of stochastic gradient descent. In: International Conference on Machine Learning, pp. 1225–1234. PMLR (2016)
8. Hinton, G.E., Srivastava, N., Krizhevsky, A., Sutskever, I., Salakhutdinov, R.: Improving neural networks by preventing co-adaptation of feature detectors. CoRR abs/1207.0580 (2012). http://arxiv.org/abs/1207.0580
9. Hochreiter, S., Schmidhuber, J.: Flat minima. Neural Comput. **9**, 1–42 (1997)
10. Hoffer, E., Hubara, I., Soudry, D.: Train longer, generalize better: closing the generalization gap in large batch training of neural networks. In: Advances in Neural Information Processing Systems, pp. 1731–1741 (2017)
11. Ioffe, S., Szegedy, C.: Batch normalization: accelerating deep network training by reducing internal covariate shift. In: Proceedings of the 32nd International Conference on Machine Learning, 2015, Lille, France, 6–11 July 2015. JMLR Workshop and Conference Proceedings, vol. 37, pp. 448–456. JMLR.org (2015)
12. Lecun, Y., Bottou, L., Bengio, Y., Haffner, P.: Gradient-based learning applied to document recognition. Proc. IEEE **86**, 2278–2324 (1998). https://doi.org/10.1109/5.726791
13. Martin, C., Mahoney, M.: Implicit self-regularization in deep neural networks: evidence from random matrix theory and implications for learning. ArXiv abs/1810.01075 (2018)
14. Murphy, K.P.: Machine Learning: A Probabilistic Perspective. The MIT Press, Cambridge (2012)
15. Nakkiran, P., Kaplun, G., Bansal, Y., Yang, T., Barak, B., Sutskever, I.: Deep double descent: where bigger models and more data hurt. In: International Conference on Learning Representations (2020)
16. Nakkiran, P., Venkat, P., Kakade, S.M., Ma, T.: Optimal regularization can mitigate double descent. ArXiv abs/2003.01897 (2020)
17. Neyshabur, B., Tomioka, R., Srebro, N.: In search of the real inductive bias: on the role of implicit regularization in deep learning. CoRR abs/1412.6614 (2015)
18. Novak, R., Bahri, Y., Abolafia, D.A., Pennington, J., Sohl-Dickstein, J.: Sensitivity and generalization in neural networks: an empirical study. In: International Conference on Learning Representations (2018)
19. Sokolic, J., Giryes, R., Sapiro, G., Rodrigues, M.: Robust large margin deep neural networks. IEEE Trans. Signal Process. **65**, 4265–4280 (2017)
20. Wilson, D.R., Martinez, T.: The general inefficiency of batch training for gradient descent learning. Neural Netw. Off. J. Int. Neural Netw. Soc. **16**(10), 1429–51 (2003)
21. Xiao, H., Rasul, K., Vollgraf, R.: Fashion-MNIST: a novel image dataset for benchmarking machine learning algorithms. CoRR abs/1708.07747 (2017). http://arxiv.org/abs/1708.07747

Author Index

Printed in the United States
By Bookmasters